Protestantism and State Formation in Postrevolutionary Oaxaca

Protestantism & State Formation *in* Postrevolutionary Oaxaca

KATHLEEN M. MCINTYRE

University of New Mexico Press • Albuquerque

© 2019 by the University of New Mexico Press
All rights reserved. Published 2019
Printed in the United States of America

First Paperback Edition, 2022
Paperback ISBN: 978-0-8263-6391-6

Library of Congress Cataloging-in-Publication Data
Names: McIntyre, Kathleen M., 1978– author.
Title: Protestantism and state formation in postrevolutionary Oaxaca / Kathleen M. McIntyre.
Description: Albuquerque: University of New Mexico Press, 2019. | Includes bibliographical references and index. |
Identifiers: LCCN 2018034572 (print) | LCCN 2018054336 (e-book) | ISBN 9780826360250 (e-book) | ISBN 9780826360243 (printed case : alk. paper)
Subjects: LCSH: Oaxaca (Mexico: State)—History—20th century. | Protestant churches—Missions—Mexico—Oaxaca (State)—History. | Conversion—Christianity—Social aspects—Mexico—Oaxaca (State) | Conversion—Christianity—Political aspects—Mexico—Oaxaca (State) | Evangelicalism—Mexico—Oaxaca (State)
Classification: LCC F1321 (e-book) | LCC F1321 .M396 2019 (print) | DDC 972/.74—dc23
LC record available at https://lccn.loc.gov/2018034572

Cover illustration courtesy of Flaticon
Cover designed by Catherine Leonardo
Interior designed by Felicia Cedillos
Composed in Minion Pro 10.25/14.25

For Erik

Contents

Acknowledgments ix

Abbreviations xv

INTRODUCTION 1

CHAPTER ONE
"As Fast as Men and Means Are Furnished"
Protestant Missions during the Porfiriato 17

CHAPTER TWO
"La sangre está clamando justicia"
Constructing Martyrdom in Postrevolutionary Oaxaca 37

CHAPTER THREE
Contested Spaces
Local Conflicts, CONEDEF, and the Mexican State 67

CHAPTER FOUR
The Summer Institute of Linguistics in Oaxaca 89

CHAPTER FIVE
Liberation Theology, Indigenous Rights, and Nationalism 131

CHAPTER SIX
"Here the People Rule"
Customary Law and State Formation 159

CONCLUSION
Reimagining Communities 183

Notes 191

Bibliography 241

Index 263

Acknowledgments

I am indebted to a long list of individuals and institutions in the United States and Mexico for sponsoring me throughout this investigation of religious conflict in Oaxaca. Research grants from Clarion University's College of Arts, Education, and Sciences Faculty Professional Development Fund allowed me to return to Mexico for additional research. My colleagues in history, Bob Frakes, Mike LaRue, and Martha Robinson supported my book manuscript from day one. Special thanks to Bob for guiding me through the book proposal process and to Martha for reading and commenting on several chapter drafts. Other colleagues and friends at Clarion University were also supportive of this study. Susan Prezzano encouraged me to present early selections of this book at CU's Brown Bag Research Series. Discussing the anthropology of religion with Laurie Occhipinti resulted in fruitful methodological considerations. Tom Rourke strengthened my analysis of liberation theology. Miguel Olivas gave important input on Mexican political cartoons. Barry Sweet, Mike Di Giacomo, and Jeffrey Diamond also offered helpful feedback on the final manuscript. Kay Fineran Luthin proofread multiple chapter drafts. Librarians Ginger McGiffen and Melissa Pierce assisted with numerous interlibrary loan requests. Social Sciences administrative assistant Lana McClune organized my complex web of travel paperwork. Kevan Yenerall, Julia Aaron, Kathleen Welsch, Jamie Phillips, Jane Walsh, Cathie Petrissans, Todd Lavin, Phil Terman, and Herb Luthin made interdisciplinary collaboration enjoyable and rewarding at CU. At the University of Rhode

Island, I thank my new colleagues, Rosaria Pisa, Donna Hughes, Jody Lisberger, and Lynne Derbyshire, for their support of my work. I also thank URI's Center for the Humanities for supporting my book.

The University of New Mexico's Latin American and Iberian Institute funded my dissertation research. I also received short-term grants from UNM's History Graduate Student Association, the Feminist Research Institute, and the Graduate Professional Student Association. I studied the Mixtec language in Oaxaca through the Foreign Language and Area Studies Fellowships Program. A 2010 dissertation completion fellowship from the American Association of University Women allowed me to dedicate a year to solely finishing the final draft. I also owe a great deal of gratitude to my dissertation chair at the University of New Mexico, Linda B. Hall, and committee members Cynthia Radding, Elizabeth Hutchison, Manuel García y Griego, and Les W. Field. Despite her retirement, Linda offered superb advice as I transitioned from dissertation to book. Cynthia has been a friend and generous colleague during research trips to Mexico City.

The Centro de Investigaciones y Estudios Superiores en Antropología Social (CIESAS-Pacífico Sur) sponsored me as a visiting researcher while I completed the dissertation. Participating in the *seminario interno* gave me the opportunity to share my early work with an incredible cohort of scholars including Margarita Dalton, Sergio Navarrette, Salvador Sigüenza, Daniela Traffano, and Jutta Blauert, who all strengthened my approach to indigenous identity, the state, and religious conflict in important ways. In particular, I thank former CIESAS director Dr. Salomón Nahmad Sittón, who permitted me to explore his personal papers from his years as the director of Indigenous Education and as the director of the National Indigenist Institute. CIESAS librarian Ramiro Pablo Velasco helped make my research in Oaxaca go smoothly. Also at CIESAS, Raúl G. Alvarez Chávez accompanied me on several interviews and provided background on Mixtec Pentecostalism. Juan Julián Caballero helped me set up my initial research trips to the Summer Institute of Linguistics library in Mitla. Xicohténcatl Luna Ruiz was a loyal research partner during long days at the Centro Coordinador Indígenista in Tlaxiaco.

In Mexico City, archivists at the Archivo General de la Nación and Universidad Nacional Autónoma de México's (UNAM) Hemeroteca were incredibly patient and helpful. I met Rubi Barocio through UNAM's Coloquio

Internacional "Historia, Protestantismo e Identidad en las Américas" in 2011. Rubi shared her family's collection of *La Luz Bautista* with me and was my guide to historic Protestant churches in Mexico City. Many thanks to Fabiola Salguero at *El Universal* for assisting me in using images for this book. I am also very appreciative of Deyssy Jael de la Luz García and Abdías Pérez, who both gave me insight into the early role of the Comité Nacional Evangélico de Defensa in defending religious freedom in Mexico. Organizing a panel paper with Oswaldo Ramírez González afforded me new opportunities to expand my research of Methodist missionaries. In addition, long conversations with Father Enrique Marroquín in Guadalajara also helped me define this project and forge connections with scholars of religious conflict.

In Oaxaca City, Sergio Osorio Carrizosa assisted me with transcriptions and invited me to patron saint day fiestas in the Mixteca. Laura Olachea Magriñá edited transcription drafts. Catechist Nacho Franco helped set up my research at the archdiocesan archive and was a great hiking partner. Guadalupe García Hernández took me out for truchas and long talks in the Sierra Norte. Edmundo López López tracked down missing newspaper articles, accompanied me around the Panteón General, and introduced me to historians Francisco José Ruiz Cervantes and Javier Sánchez Pereyra. It was through Edmundo's suggestions that I delved into the history of Protestantism and education in Oaxaca.

The staff at Biblioteca Francisco de Burgoa, Fundación Bustamante, the Archivo General del Poder Ejecutivo del Estado de Oaxaca, Hemeroteca Pública de Oaxaca, and the Archivo del Poder Judicial de Oaxaca provided expert archival services and a pleasant atmosphere for research. I particularly thank Penélope Orozco Sánchez and David Karminski Katz at Burgoa for helping me utilize rare books in their collection. I am also indebted to Grupo Noticias for permission to use images. Edgar López at the Departamento de Asuntos Religiosos took an early interest in this project and helped me figure out the logistics of my research. At the Welte Institute for Oaxacan Studies, the late librarian Gudrun Dohrmann located sources for me and set up meetings with local scholars. I also thank Ramona Pérez for her enthusiasm for my work while I was a student in her San Diego State University Mixtec summer language program. Summer Institute of Linguistics administrator Stephen Butler offered a welcoming environment and full use of the organization's library in Mitla. Pastor Saúl Velazco Cervantes of the Iglesia

Nacional Presbiteriana de San Pablo helped me locate countless documents on his congregation's early history.

I am greatly appreciative of the municipal officials in Santiago Yosondúa and San Jerónimo Tlacochahuaya who hosted me and to the families there who invited me to church services. The late Elvira Cruz García represents the heart of this book. Elvira opened up her Tlacochahuayan home to me many times to learn about her family's Baptist history. Her daughter, Abigail García Hernández, also shared family photographs with me. I wish I could sit down for another *atole* with Elvira.

Growing up in New York's mid-Hudson Valley gave me an early interest in transnational Oaxacan history. In many ways, the roots of this book stem from visiting Poughkeepsie migrant friends in San Agustín Yatareni and La Ciénega de Zimatlán and observing firsthand the new questions Protestant growth brings to *fiestas patronales* or local civic events. This book also owes its foundation to the mentoring I received at Vassar College from Leslie S. Offutt. She continues to champion my research ideas with good questions and thoughtful suggestions.

In the broader historical profession, colleagues have profoundly shaped this book. Participating on panels with Jason Dormady and David Burden led to new ways to conceptualize my work. Bill Beezley helped me come up with the book's organization over a Oaxacan *desayuno*. Benjamin Smith offered tips on researching in Oaxaca City. Todd Hartch's early aid opened doors for me in Oaxaca. I also appreciate Deborah Baldwin's and Christy Thornton's helpful comments on recent conference papers. I'm also very appreciative of *Gender and History* for allowing me to use parts of an earlier article in Chapter Two of this manuscript.

I would like to thank staff at the Presbyterian Historical Society and the University of Texas's Benson Latin American Collection Library. I also owe a great deal of thanks to Clark Whitehorn, executive editor of the University of New Mexico Press, whose enthusiasm guided this project from the beginning. UNM Press acquisitions coordinator Sonia Dickey did an amazing job in preparing the manuscript for copyediting and keeping me on schedule. I also thank the anonymous reviewers who strengthened this book in significant ways.

Friends from my Albuquerque graduate student days continue to root for me during the ups and downs of historical research. Thank you to Joe Lenti,

Brandon Morgan, Colin Snider, Sue Taylor, Meg Frisbee, Erin Cole, Blair Woodard, Brandi Townsend, Lucy Grinnell, Leah Sneider, Hilda Gutiérrez, Siobhán McLoughlin, Marcial Martínez, Wendy Cervantes, Julian Dodson, Will Veeder, Yann Kerevel, María José Bosanko García, Brian Stauffer, Chad Black, Nydia Martínez, and Bill Convery. Additional thanks to Joe, Brandon, and Colin for reading chapter drafts and to MJ for checking my translations. Finally, I am grateful for Andy Albertson's editing advice.

My family provided incredible support throughout this project. I especially thank my parents, Bill and Cassie McIntyre, for nurturing my academic career even as they probably wondered why I didn't write about Ireland. My siblings and their families bring me joy and happiness: William J. McIntyre, OFM; Kevin, Clare, Ryan, Griffin, Declan, and Maeve McIntyre; Siobhán, Mike, Patrick, Anne, Maggie, Luke and Nora Bubel; and Sean, Megan, Ciara and Aine McIntyre. Queens cousins Maura Ryan and Siobhán Murphy provided me with places to stay and fun nights between research trips and conferences. In-laws Ray and Linda Loomis, Daryl Loomis, and Kris and Carlie DiOrio, continuously encourage my work.

Most of all, I thank my husband Erik Loomis for his support along each stage of this project. I could not have finished this manuscript without his constant encouragement and patience. Sharing with him my love for Oaxaca has been truly amazing. *Te amo siempre.*

Abbreviations

APPO	Popular Assembly of the Peoples of Oaxaca/Asamblea Popular de los Pueblos de Oaxaca
CCI	Centro Coordinador Indigenista/Indigenist Coordinating Center
CEAS	Colegio de Etnólogos y Antropólogos Sociales/National College of Ethnologists and Social Anthropologists
CELAM	Consejo Episcopal Latinoamericano/Conference of Latin American Bishops
CIA	Central Intelligence Agency
CIESAS	Centro de Investigaciones y Estudios Superiores en Antropología Social/Center for Social Anthropology Research
CNBM	Convención Nacional Bautista de México/National Baptist Convention of Mexico
COCEI	Coalición Obrera, Campesina, Estudiantil del Istmo/ Coalition of Workers, Peasants, and Students of the Isthmus
CONEDEF	Comité Nacional Evangélico de Defensa/National Evangelical Defense Committee
COPACEO	Confraternidad de Pastores Cristianos Evangélicos del Estado de Oaxaca/Confraternity of Evangelical Christian Pastors of Oaxaca

DAAI	Departamento Autónomo de Asuntos Indígenas/ Department of Indigenous Affairs
DAR	Departamento de Asuntos Religiosos/Department of Religious Affairs
EZLN	Ejército Zapatista de Liberación Nacional/Zapatista National Liberation Army
ILV	Instituto Lingüístico de Verano/Summer Institute of Linguistics
INAH	Instituto Nacional de Antropología e Historia/National Institute of Anthropology and History
INI	Instituto Nacional Indigenista/National Indigenist Institute
JAARS	Jungle Aviation and Radio Services
MIEPI	Movimiento Iglesia Evangélica Pentecostés Independiente/ Independent Evangelical Pentecostal Church Movement
PRD	Partido de la Revolución Democrática/Party of the Democratic Revolution
PRI	Partido Revolucionario Institucional/Institutional Revolutionary Party
SEP	Secretaría de Educación Pública/Ministry of Public Education
SIL	Summer Institute of Linguistics/Instituto Lingüístico de Verano
WBT	Wycliffe Bible Translators

INTRODUCTION

ON AUGUST 16, 1923, Presbyterian Lawrence Van Slyke wrote to his mission board outlining his desire to evangelize indigenous peoples in the southern Mexican state of Oaxaca. Originally from western New York, Van Slyke intended to set up a missionary base in San Baltasar Yatzachi, a Zapotec community high in the Sierra Norte Mountains and a three-day mule ride from the Presbyterian church in Oaxaca City. Making the case for the new mission, he drew connections between indigenous evangelization and contemporary modernization projects in Mexico.

> The Indian is worth the best we have. . . . There is a special interest in an effort to win to the Protestant religion the same race that produced Benito Juárez, the great Liberal of Mexico. . . . [Indians] will hold back the entire state until they are evangelized and educated, so that in reality, work among the Indians is the foundation work in this state.[1]

Some sixty years later, on January 29, 1982, Zapotec mayor Efraín Cruz Orozco submitted a petition to state officials explaining why he refused approval of the construction of a Protestant church. Cruz Orozco represented Santiago Choápam, a municipality in the Papaloapan region of Oaxaca, just above the Sierra Norte. The leader's argument hinged on the authority of collective rights over individual rights. The Protestant sects, he noted, brought divisions and conflicts; converts did not contribute to cooperative work assignments or serve positions in the civil-religious governance hierarchy. Fearful of divisions and the weakening of Zapotec communalism, he concluded: "We have a careful agreement in this town that there is no other religion than the one that's already here."[2]

Although separated by several decades, these examples touch upon a deep historical ambiguity shaping the Mexican government's relationship with Native communities in modern Mexico: collective versus individual rights. In the 1860s, president and Oaxaca native Benito Juárez broke up indigenous collective landholdings, expecting that the policy would integrate Native peoples into a market economy. In contrast, 1990s indigenous rights proponents made the case that ejidal (communally owned) lands were cultural rights. As Mayor Cruz Orozco's objection to Protestantism implies, religious diversity contributed to the ongoing debate over rights and tested the relationship between Native communities and the Mexican government. His case highlights some of the complexities surrounding Protestant conversion in Oaxaca.

Indigenous municipal leaders framed their opposition to Protestantism around the premise that it violated the social norms at the heart of their communities' identity, leading to violence and divisions. The relationship between identity and tradition profoundly influenced how Catholics viewed Protestant expansion. Protestantism did not just challenge Catholic theologies; it also rejected traditional rituals and social organization embedded in the *usos y costumbres* (ways and customs) governance system. Individuals converting to Protestant faiths often challenged customary law that privileges the collective rights of the community.[3] Rule by customary governance intersects with rights of indigenous communities to control community resources and political organization.

This book contributes new insights into the complex relationship between popular worship, ethnic identity, and the state in Mexico. In particular, it examines the terms and processes by which indigenous identity is constructed vis-à-vis religious conflict.[4] My work conceptualizes indigenous identity as constantly changing in response to historical processes rather than as a fixed category. Protestant conversion in Native communities ultimately fueled broad discussions of indigenous rights and autonomy. By "autonomy," I mean authority over ejidal landholdings, the opportunity to make political decisions via customary law, and a degree of control over natural resources in their communities. As Deborah Yashar puts it, indigenous rights movements often argue that their communities represent an "autonomous sphere of political rights, jurisdiction, and autonomy."[5] Thus, a Zapotec community like Choápam could argue that their practice of customary governance trumped federal law.

The impact of Protestant conversion challenged notions of indigenous identity, leading to contentious debates at the local and national levels. This book presents case studies of regional religious conflicts and oral histories uncovering patterns of community self-defense through appeal to a form of traditional indigenous identity that included syncretic Catholicism. Protestantism questioned collective identity in indigenous villages, leading to competing conceptualizations of tradition, identity, and political power.

This book is also a study about state formation in modern Mexico. A central concern is the examination of how indigenous communities, Protestant organizations, and the state negotiated religious conflicts. Framed by the 1910 Mexican Revolution and the 1994 Zapatista Revolution—uprisings with differing conceptualizations of indigenous peoples' role in modern Mexico—an examination of Protestantism yields important findings on the impact conversion had on social organization and identities in indigenous communities. Focusing on Native communities of Oaxaca offers a case study that enhances the larger picture of Protestant growth in Latin America. Given Oaxaca's peripheral status and geographic distance from the center of power in Mexico City, local indigenous communities had a long history of setting their own parameters for legal, spiritual, and cultural practices. The cases examined herein test whether political power resided locally in Native communities or with the state.

The Mexican Revolution called for the incorporation of Mexico's indigenous peoples into the fabric of the nation. The postrevolutionary government's cabinet members, often educated at Protestant schools, believed that strict adherence to Catholicism was holding Mexico back. To that end, the Mexican state enforced the anticlerical components of the 1917 Constitution: regulations of public worship, restrictions on church land ownership and building inventories, quotas on domestic and especially foreign priests, and the removal of the church and its clergy from the political scene.[6]

While many of these provisions affected ministers from diverse denominations, Protestant missionary organizations were adept at dovetailing state agendas with their religious outreach programs.[7] Protestant missionary work could support Spanish language training and market competition into traditionally isolated communities that identified more with their village than the nation. With its large monolingual indigenous population and high poverty rate, Oaxaca became a priority for the newly formed Ministry of Public Education as well as for Protestant missionary movements anxious to work in Mexico following the Revolution.[8]

This book traces the historical interactions between North American missionaries, indigenous communities, government officials, Protestant churches, and the Catholic Church hierarchy from the postrevolutionary period to the 1994 Zapatista uprising. My study focuses mainly on municipal (county) conflicts in Oaxaca's Central Valleys, the Mixteca Alta, the Sierra Norte, and the Cañada.[9] These regions possess substantial Protestant populations, exhibit high rates of both internal migration within Mexico and external migration to the United States, and are home to large concentrations of monolingual indigenous language speakers. These are also regions with sustained periods of conflict between Catholics and Protestants, some lasting over fifty years. How converts negotiated their new religious practices with syncretic customs and communal obligations is key to this story.

Home to over ninety-six million Catholics, Mexico has the second-largest Catholic population in the world. Yet, as in much of Latin America, Protestantism has been growing in the last few decades. Prior to the Mexican Revolution (1910–1920), only 1 percent of Mexicans identified as Protestant. Currently, Mexico is about 10 percent Protestant—less than Guatemala or Honduras (both 41 percent), Nicaragua (40 percent), or Brazil (26 percent)—but the rate has expanded rapidly in recent decades.[10] In Mexico, Protestant growth is most visible in the heavily indigenous southern states. Campeche, Chiapas, Oaxaca, Quintana Roo, Tabasco, and Veracruz all have Protestant populations ranging from 12 to 20 percent.[11] While Oaxaca is at the lower end of this spectrum (about 13 percent), it has the fastest growth rate: between 1970 and 2000, Protestantism increased by 531 percent.[12] The 2010 census documented 502,013 Oaxacan Protestants (comprising individuals over the age of five) out of a total state population of about 3.8 million.[13]

Protestantism is a complex and contested term in Latin America.[14] In fact, it is more common to hear *evangélico* (evangelical) used to refer to all Christian, non-Catholic denominations. Furthermore, believers often use the

Figure 1. Map of the Eight Regions of Oaxaca. Source: Wikimedia Commons, https://commons.wikimedia.org/wiki/File:Oaxaca_regions_and_districts.svg.

terms *cristiano* (Christian), *evangélico*, and *hermano* (brother) interchangeably, emphasizing their shared Christ-centered identities and close relationship to each other.[15] Early religious conflict cases in this study generally involve mainline (historic) denominations that arrived in indigenous Mexico in the late nineteenth and early twentieth century. Historic/mainline Protestantism includes those churches emerging from the Protestant Reformation in Europe—Lutherans, Presbyterians, Baptists, Methodists, and Anglicans. Neo-Protestant groups are denominations formed primarily in the twentieth century, such as Pentecostalism.

The Mexican census—conducted each decade—often changes the parameters of what constitutes *Protestant.* Prior to 2000, for example, the Mexican census lumped Mormons, Adventists, and Jehovah's Witnesses into the category of Protestantism. Yet by the 2010 census, Adventists, Jehovah's Witnesses, and Mormons represented nonevangelical, Bible-based religions. Opponents of these newer Protestant and alternative Christian denominations pejoratively call them *sectas*: minority religious groups that are divisive and removed from the community.[16] At present, Pentecostals and alternative Christians (Jehovah's Witnesses and Mormons) are the fastest growing denominations in Mexico.[17] This rapid growth has created tension in insular communities.

The impact of Protestant growth on traditional governance is at the core of religious conflicts in Oaxaca. Usos y costumbres is a critical component of village communal identity. At the basic level, usos y costumbres is a set of collective norms that Oaxacan indigenous communities rely on for self-government. For example, communities that follow usos y costumbres may elect local leaders by raising hands at an *asamblea* (open meeting), not through a private ballot process. They may also assign residents (usually men) to a series of positions that increase with responsibility based on age. These *cargos* (obligations) make up the cargo system, a civil-religious hierarchy organizing Native communities. Participation in the cargo system also means volunteering for *tequio* (collective work) projects.[18]

Protestant converts increasingly abstained from tequio and the cargo system altogether. These abstentions occurred because of Protestant discomfort with extrabiblical or pre-Christian religious traditions, the *quema de dinero* (waste of money) resulting from the fiesta system, and the general desire to distance themselves from Catholicism. The loss of labor and monetary donations toward patron saint day fiestas concerned Catholics who saw the new faiths as challenging not only religious practices but also the central function of community identity. Participation in a patron saint's day mass and celebration, and working one's way up the cargo ladder through service to the community, were no longer central to Protestant converts' daily lives. Thus, the mechanism for earning prestige as a *ciudadano de bien* (good citizen) with rights to communal resources (lumber, ejidal land, water, etc.) changed dramatically. As this book will illustrate, conflicts between Protestants and local government often started over a convert's refusal to fund fiestas or contribute labor to a community project.

State Formation and Religion

Cases of religious conflict offer important insights into the role of the Mexican state in Native communities.[19] Religion can be a tool of the state when supporting its interests, but it can also work against the centralization of state power. The trajectory of twentieth-century Mexican state formation started with the 1917 Constitution. The state redefined itself as highly nationalistic, prolabor and anticlerical. Although most of those provisions were not fully implemented until the presidencies of Plutarco Elías Calles (1924–1928) and Lázaro Cárdenas (1934–1940), this document profoundly affected labor laws, land tenure regulations, foreign interests in the mining and petroleum industries, and church-state relations.[20] Postrevolutionary goals for Native communities included fluency in the Spanish language, the construction of public schools, limiting patron saint day fiesta celebrations, and integrating new agricultural practices and job training. Driven by the tenets of *indigenismo* (a political, intellectual, and social movement emphasizing outreach to indigenous peoples), postrevolutionary administrations celebrated Mexico's rich indigenous heritage through an emphasis on cultural folklore but ultimately pushed modernization and assimilation.[21] Protestants anxious to evangelize indigenous Mexico shared all of these goals. Missionary Lawrence Van Slyke's fear that Native Oaxacans would "hold back the entire state" was not too far off the mark from the state's goal of "defanaticization" (reduction of Catholicism's influence) of the indigenous population through literacy and apprenticeship training that would bring economic progress.[22]

To that end, the Mexican state, at various times, carefully cultivated its partnership with Protestant organizations. At first glance, an anticlerical state's openness to Protestant missionary work might seem counterintuitive; however, Protestantism and state postrevolutionary goals went hand in hand. Missionaries went into indigenous communities and collaborated with state institutions including the Ministry of Public Education (Secretaría de Educación Pública, SEP), the National Indigenous Institute, and the Department of Health's ongoing hygiene campaigns. As educational, agrarian, and health reform all made up the ongoing Revolutionary project, it is not surprising that President Cárdenas approved contracts with the Summer Institute of Linguistics (SIL) starting in the 1930s.[23] When not translating the New Testament into every indigenous language in Mexico, SIL missionary-linguists assisted with literacy and public health programs in isolated zones.

However, this partnership between the state and Protestant missionary organizations faded in the late 1970s; aligning itself with North American churches contradicted the government's newer emphasis on more participatory indigenismo trajectories.[24] While the 1920s through the 1950s were the heyday of official indigenismo, the 1960s and 1970s brought a shift in government policy: indigenous people should set the parameters of their relationship with the nation; there was no need to drop Native language, religious customs, or traditional governance practices to be a part of modern (read: mestizo) Mexico. Yet religious competition challenged this new type of indigenismo. By the 1990s, the Mexican state still vacillated between respecting indigenous religious practices while concomitantly protecting individual rights to religious freedom as laid out in Article 24 of the Mexican Constitution.

For their part, local municipal governments from the 1970s through the 1990s framed their resistance to Protestant incursion by asserting that Protestantism attacked indigenous cultural traditions. In response, the state government sent mediators out to rural communities or ordered both sides to report to government offices in Oaxaca City, where feuding parties signed an agreement to respect one another's religious beliefs. However, an official paper from Oaxaca City or Mexico City had limited authority in their home communities because, as Mixe leaders in San Juan Juquila told a state mediator in 1983, "Aquí manda el pueblo [Here the people rule]."[25] This common refrain hurled at government officials represented local customary governance decisions that the state could not understand and in which the state had no business getting involved. By taking advantage of the absence of the state or using the reach of the state to their advantage, local leaders asserted that Protestantism was an attack on tradition and, furthermore, Protestantism was inherently antipatriotic. Protestant converts fought hard to gain permits for new churches and made some strides. Ultimately, however, when local communities made a collective decision to deny basic services to or expel converts, it was difficult for the state to provide adequate recourse to Protestants. In the end, rights to local autonomy won out over federal law, giving important insight into the negotiated authority of the state in religious conflicts.

Mexicanists have recently debated what historian Alan Knight refers to as the "weight of the state" in modern Mexico.[26] Captivated by the Institutional Revolutionary Party's (Partido Revolucionario Institucional, PRI) populist roots of the 1930s and 1940s, scholars puzzled over how the party that was supposed to be the embodiment of the Mexican Revolution could evolve into one capable of brutal state violence against university student protesters in the Tlatelolco plaza in 1968.[27] In analyzing post-Tlatelolco Mexico, historians argued that the one-party state from its inception was incredibly powerful, unable or unwilling to concede to civil society's demands. However, in the last two decades, historians have called for a re-examination of this narrow conceptualization of state formation.[28] The PRI was not monolithic or beyond reproach; the PRI constantly negotiated relationships with key constituent groups in modern Mexico. As the national government sought to exert control over Oaxaca, Native communities adeptly repackaged state mandates to meet local needs, hence creating "alternate narratives" and alternate political structures to support but often challenge PRI government policies.[29] For instance, state directives on constitutional rights filtered through local traditions in customary governance, thus blending state mandates with indigenous autonomy. This negotiation between national and local government exemplifies the contested nature of state policy in religious conflicts. The PRI was powerful, but it picked its battles carefully and understood that its top-down administrative policies might be integrated into local practices, especially in Oaxaca with its sixteen distinct indigenous groupings spread out over eight geographically isolating regions and a long history of resistance to state incursion.

Recent assessment of the midcentury PRI suggests that it acted as a "dictablanda," or soft dictatorship. Historians Paul Gillingham and Benjamin Smith call for a closer look at the "soft authoritarian" nature of PRI rule between Cárdenas's bold 1938 oil expropriation and the eve of the 1968 crackdown on university students. The party clearly operated with more public buy-in rather than just "hard authoritarian" style rule characterizing the overt state violence in 1968.[30] Studies of state formation in an ethnically and geographically diverse region such as Oaxaca offer a new perspective on Mexico's political history; past studies on postrevolutionary Mexico focus on central and northern Mexico.[31] By focusing on religious conflict cases in southern Mexico, my study contributes a new way to examine postrevolutionary state formation, spanning policies of indigenism to participatory indigenismo to neoliberalism.

Despite its massive expansion in Latin America, scholarship on Latin American Protestantism has only just begun to explore the cultural complexities of the evangelical movement.[32] Lamenting the gap, anthropologist

David Stoll once rationalized, "Few of us go all the way to Oaxaca to listen to Gospel hymns reverberating inside cement-block chapels."[33] Within the context of the Cold War, scholarship of the 1970s and 1980s framed Protestant growth as another example of North American cultural imperialism in Latin America. Similarly, a generation of scholars influenced by liberation theology's "preferential option for the poor" and its ideological underpinnings for socialist revolutions in Latin America, focused on church-state relations in Latin America.[34] Historians of modern Mexico analyzed the 1926 Cristiada movement or 1930s Cardenista corporatism to get at the state's new postrevolutionary relationship with the Catholic Church.[35] Yet as recent scholarship on Luz del Mundo's foundational history in Guadalajara suggests, by analyzing state interactions with non-Catholic denominations, one better understands how the PRI carved out its agenda—and alliances—in poor, urban intentional religious communities.[36]

The fieldwork in my study is a response to the historiographical gap in rural Oaxaca.[37] Oral histories offer insight into how Protestant growth affected local social organization. Thus, in addition to consulting Oaxaca's state and local archives, I also draw on field interviews.[38] I interviewed Protestant converts in their churches and homes. Sometimes the space indeed was a Pentecostal congregation in an unfinished cement building; other times it was a mainline Presbyterian church with almost a century of roots in the region. By exploring Protestant growth firsthand, my fieldwork offers a closer examination of this shift. I conducted these interviews in Spanish, lasting between thirty minutes and two hours, and sometimes continuing across multiple visits. They usually occurred after a Sunday service gathering, wedding, or Bible study meeting. To augment and contextualize these oral histories, I used missionary literature and the personal accounts of missionary teams returning to the United States. Conceptualizing individual and collective narratives of local conflicts in Oaxacan villages sheds light on the impact of Protestantism on identity.

Indigenous identity is never static or homogenous. Rather, identity recreates and negotiates through interactions with state, religious, and foreign entities.[39] As such, defense of traditional identities surfaces during situations of conflict or competition. Anthropologist Lynn Stephen argues that "past identities and meanings" play an important role in how contemporary Zapotecs and Mixtecs construct ethnic identity.[40] Religious conflict in Oaxaca demonstrates how identities can be reimagined and, at times, reinvented altogether in response to change or to shifting relations of power. Communities opposed to Protestantism cite tradition as a buffer against its growth. As Eric Hobsbawm puts it, "the past, real or invented . . . gives any desired change (or resistance to innovation) the sanction of precedent, social continuity and natural law as expressed in history."[41] For indigenous Catholics, the incursion of Protestantism into their communities drastically altered social organization and communal rituals. Evangelical and alternative Christians challenged a core element of indigenous communal identity: syncretic Catholicism.[42] Thus, how converts negotiated indigenous identity with new religious beliefs is also key to this story.

Latin American Protestantism is also an act of social and political nonconformity.[43] Protestants, especially Pentecostals or Seventh-day Adventists, may disrupt social norms; they usually do not drink, smoke, or dance, nor do they participate in obligations such as tequio.[44] Evangélicos might invest more in their own businesses or education instead of the collective cofradía system.[45] In its place, they create new networks—often with Protestants from external communities.[46] Thus, Protestantism provides dissatisfied villagers with connections to the outside while at the same time breaking down local power monopolies. These new Protestant communities differ from majority Catholic communities who support rule through customary governance, testing the parameters of local versus national articulations of power.

The social spaces that Protestantism ruptures, negotiates, or creates reflect Benedict Anderson's much-cited but still applicable paradigm of "imagined communities."[47] The Mexican state originally envisioned assimilation as the only option for indigenous Mexicans to become national citizens; ethnic and cultural identities were not compatible with modernization projects. However, Catholic indigenous leaders embraced usos y costumbres' practice of rule through public asamblea (meeting) as a traditional aspect of customary governance that kept the *ciudadanos* (citizens/people) united and protected from outside threats.

Protestant converts broke from reciprocal societal ties and forged a community not limited to a local village identity but to a larger Christian one that united Protestants with indigenous peoples from other areas of Mexico and the United States, hence forging a transnational identity. Protestantism is an "imagined community," straddling transnational spaces.[48] Indigenous

Oaxacans might convert after meeting Protestant organizations providing social services' type of outreach, while working in Mexico City, or in a border town, or while living in the United States. Returning migrants might still watch, read, or listen to their former ministers' sermons and church activities via social media, or perhaps host US-based Protestant groups doing short-term missions to Oaxaca.[49] By opting out of Catholicism, converts were redefining their social status in their home villages.

Local religious conflicts reflected national concerns. As the book's opening vignette suggests, it was North American missionaries who made the first permanent Protestant inroads in Mexico. Consequently, indigenous leaders argued that Protestantism resulted from North American cultural imperialism.[50] While it is true that well-funded and often pro-US missionary organizations dominated the Protestant landscape for most of the twentieth century, Mexican Protestants are not mere pawns of "Yankee imperialism."[51] Instead, Protestant conversion includes its own internal factors that make indigenous Latin Americans active agents in their own religious choices.[52]

Finally, outmigration also influenced how and where communities organized social and political space, including how ethnic identities are (re)constructed through migration.[53] Many Catholic migrants managed to strengthen indigenous identity, and hence Catholic rituals, through migration.[54] In fact, contemporary examinations often concentrate on the impact of migration on patron saint day *mayordomías* (sponsorships).[55] Studies on rural indigenous Mexico tend to focus on the vibrant Catholic fiesta systems with little acknowledgment of Protestant growth throughout southern Mexico.[56] Few scholarly studies on Protestant growth have focused on Oaxaca and virtually none have examined shifting interpretations of indigenous identities. While anthropologists and sociologists have long researched the impact of Mexican migration on community customs and rituals, the history of Protestant conflicts remains underexplored. Bridging state formation, religious studies, and identity historiographies, my book is the first major historical study to focus primarily on Protestantism in Oaxaca and its impact on indigenous identities.

Throughout this study, I will employ the term *Protestant* generally to mean non-Catholic Christians. I recognize that the majority of Protestants in present-day Oaxaca are more likely to be Pentecostal or Adventist than from a mainline denomination such as Methodism. However, given the fluidity of the term in Latin America and the fact that archival sources often listed any non-Catholics as evangélicos, regardless of denomination, I use *Protestant* in this study, albeit an imprecise term. On occasion, I use the term *alternative Christians* to describe Adventists, Mormons, and Jehovah's Witnesses.[57] I want to acknowledge that while they identify as Christians, their beliefs and practices differ in some important respects from those of mainline faiths and Pentecostals. When available, I use the name of the particular denomination.

This book is divided into six chapters. Chapter One offers background to late nineteenth-century North American Protestant missionary work in Oaxaca's indigenous communities in rural zones. These missionaries benefited from policies implemented by Benito Juárez following Mexico's War of La Reforma in the 1860s. At the same time, Oaxaca became a hub for North American Protestant mining magnates. North American Episcopal pastors attended to the wealthy Anglo-American Protestant community living in Oaxaca City. The Presbyterian Church's pastors (mostly Mexican) ministered to Oaxaca City's educated and growing middle-class population. Mexican-born missionaries ultimately laid the groundwork for themes of revolutionary nationalism, economic development projects, and indigenous education and assimilation. By the 1920s, many key cabinet members identified as Protestants and once again helped open up Mexico to non-Catholic evangelization.

Chapter Two examines the themes of postrevolutionary religious violence in the Central Valley. Baptists constructed a new type of martyr—one who is indigenous, Protestant, and patriotic. Such martyrs project an image that differs from the Catholic conception of a martyr who was tied (usually) to ancient Rome. Through oral histories, I use Protestant memories in the Zapotec community of Tlacochahuaya to trace the formation of a collective memory and a shared identity that looks with pride on Protestant success in the region, despite periods of persecution.[58] Chapter Two also probes the role of Mexican Protestant women in bringing the Revolution to the countryside by focusing on the ways women negotiated revolutionary citizenship in an era when women could not vote or assume public office. Northern Mexican Baptist women raised funds for the Oaxaca mission and hoped to improve the health of women and children through modern medicine. Furthermore, the chapter examines the reactions of northern Mexican missionaries venturing down to the southern region for the first time.

Oaxacan Protestants sought and received legal support from national Mexican Protestant organizations and support networks, including from the 1948 founded Comité Nacional Evangélico de Defensa (CONEDEF/National Evangelical Defense Committee).[59] Chapter Three highlights the early effectiveness of such movements in enforcing constitutional law over local customary law. This coalition of Protestant pastors and attorneys argued that Protestantism should promote itself as an important extension of Mexican nationalism. CONEDEF frequently stressed that Catholicism was a vestige of Spanish colonialism that held Mexico back, while Protestantism supported the goals of the 1910 Revolution and, hence, Mexico's future.

Chapter Four analyzes the controversial role of the Summer Institute of Linguistics in indigenous communities of Oaxaca. A nondenominational North American Protestant missionary organization, the SIL (Instituto Lingüístico de Verano, ILV, in Spanish) arrived in Oaxaca in the late 1930s. This organization worked closely with state institutions in producing bilingual textbooks for indigenous children. During its five decades of work in Mexico, the SIL dominated the Protestant landscape in Mexico, easily the most visible missionary organization. By the 1970s, however, a growing intellectual and indigenous rights movement argued that Protestantism—especially its North American missionaries—represented a new type of cultural imperialism in Mexico. Paternalistic observations, like Lawrence Van Slyke's comment that indigenous Oaxacans needed Christian missionaries, were rejected by indigenous Catholics in the 1970s and 1980s when some indigenous communities fought to expel foreign missionaries from their villages and, in many cases, banned Protestantism outright. Expelling the SIL from Native communities became a rallying point for rights to autonomy and contributed to the ongoing construction of indigenous identity in Oaxaca.

Chapter Five examines liberation theology's take on "la invasión de las sectas" in southern Mexico. Throughout the 1980s, the Obispos de la Región Pacífico Sur (Southern Pacific Regional Episcopacy) advocated for collective rights of indigenous peoples in Oaxaca and Chiapas, even as the national episcopacy and the Vatican clamped down on the progressive church in Latin America.[60] The southern episcopacy argued that sectas (sects) weakened Native communities and left them vulnerable to state violence. Pope John Paul II's 1979 visit to Oaxaca is a key touchstone in this chapter; the Pope promised to be the voice of Native peoples, not fully recognizing the ongoing *lucha* (struggle) for indigenous rights in the Cold War context. This chapter highlights the complications arising when Mexican nationalism, indigenous rights, liberation theology, and foreign relations all intersect.

Conflicts between converts and local leadership often began over refusal to participate in tequio, especially if it involved supporting the Catholic Church. This conflict is illustrated in Chapter Six's focus on a religious conflict between Pentecostal families and Catholic municipal authorities in the Mixe community of San Juan Tabaá. The Pentecostal families filed complaints with state and federal offices when threatened with expulsion from the community for not contributing funds or labor toward the renovation of a colonial-era church located in the community. Municipal governments maintained that the structural viability of colonial-era Catholic churches as both local and national cultural patrimony was a central symbol of indigenous identity and, as such, should be protected by all ciudadanos, regardless of faith. Local authorities reminded the Pentecostal petitioners, "Here the people rule."[61] By sometimes threatening to shut down their municipal offices if the government sided with the Protestants, indigenous leaders affirmed that they had the authority to rule the way that they believed worked for local social and political dynamics. This dynamic between indigenous communities and the Mexican government throughout the twentieth century was a complex one, involving a negotiated relationship over the reach of the state.

The book's conclusion looks at the Mexican government's recent attempts to address multicultural rights. In 1998, looking to avoid a Chiapas type of uprising, the Oaxacan state government legalized customary law. While many of its villages had operated under customary law since either before or shortly after the Spanish Conquest, the fact that the Oaxacan state government—the only state in Mexico to do so—officially recognized this system dramatically altered the trajectory of Protestantism in indigenous communities.[62] In a sense, by legalizing usos y costumbres, the state was allowing local communities to set the collective social pulse at the expense of minority rights. Indigenous autonomy and the parameters of local versus federal citizenship continues to be a pressing issue in Latin American state-indigenous relations today; conceptualizations of Christian citizenship add to the complexity.[63]

CHAPTER ONE

"As Fast as Men and Means Are Furnished"

Protestant Missions during the Porfiriato

OAXACAN PROTESTANTISM TRACES its roots to the state's most famous native son, Benito Juárez. Originally from the Zapotec village of Guelatao in the Sierra Norte, and illiterate and monolingual until he moved to Oaxaca City, Juárez advanced from attorney to state governor to president of the nation. The Liberal leader's sweeping 1857 Ley de la Reforma drastically reduced the power of the Catholic Church and resulted in the Religious Freedom Act of 1860, officially separating Church and State and thus paving the way for North American Protestants to evangelize Mexico.[1] By diminishing the power and privileges of the Church, Juárez intended to modernize Mexico through secular education and a free-market system. Protestantism, he thought, would offer competition for the Catholic Church and "force Indians to read rather than wasting savings on prayer candles for the Saints."[2] Protestant missionaries readily linked themselves to his legacy of religious reform.

North American Baptist, Methodist, and Presbyterian missionaries established small private schools and Bible study classes along the Mexican border beginning in the late 1860s.[3] This was not Protestantism's first foray into Mexico; various British and American Bible Societies entered Mexico for short periods beginning in 1824 but never maintained permanent missions.[4] British colporteur (Bible distributor) James Thompson, for example, managed to work in Oaxaca for three weeks in 1828, handing out Spanish-language New Testaments. Furthermore, the American Bible Society distributed Bibles to Mexicans at the port of Veracruz as US marines arrived during the Mexican-American War (1846–1848). The Catholic Church would later use this as a point of contention when arguing that Protestant denominations represented American imperialism. Conflicts between the Conservatives (allies of the Catholic Church) and the Liberals (Juárez's party) over the Reform Laws led to civil war.

The Liberal party ultimately triumphed, but not until after a Conservative-backed French occupation from 1862 to 1867. After Juárez's death in 1872, Mexico transitioned into the Porfiriato (1876–1911), a thirty-five-year dictatorship in which a handful of elite families and foreign investors enjoyed social, political, and economic progress as the rest of Mexico grew poorer. Although a Liberal, President Porfirio Díaz gingerly dealt with the Catholic Church. Vowing "Order and Progress" for Mexico, he viewed the Church as an ally in placating the masses left out of Mexico's new era of prosperity.[5] While he certainly did not capitulate to all Church demands, he did not strictly enforce Juárez's Lerdo Law, a reform limiting collective ownership by the Church as well as in indigenous communities. In fact, Catholic Church property ownership increased during his reign.[6] However, Díaz's appetite for foreign investment and quest for modernization meant he was also accommodating to Protestant interests.

During the Porfiriato-era railroad boom and expansion of lines to southern Mexico, missionaries set their sights on the indigenous populations of Chiapas and Oaxaca. The Methodists established the first permanent Protestant church building in Oaxaca in the early 1890s.[7] San Pablo Methodist Church primarily targeted middle-class Mexican professionals living in the capital. Concurrently, the Methodists sent their missionaries all over the state to set up rural missions. In addition, the Episcopalians established the Holy Trinity Episcopal Church in 1906 with the goal of serving Oaxaca City's English-speaking community—primarily mining managers and coffee plantation owners. Living in Oaxaca exposed US Protestants to Mexican Catholic traditions celebrating the Virgin Mary.

This chapter examines the beginnings of Oaxacan Protestantism during the Porfiriato era. Protestant growth dovetailed with modernization, capitalism, and US economic interests. Visiting Protestant pastors ministered to American and British citizens who took advantage of Porfirian incentives for foreign companies and investors. In contrast, career missionaries focused more on indigenous zones, albeit overwhelmed with language diversity and vast geographic territorial assignments. By exploring the role of transnational Protestant organizations in shaping the beginning of Protestantism in Oaxaca, it is apparent that as much as the Catholic Church tried to associate the religion with US imperialism and economic exploitation, Protestantism made important strides in Porfirian Oaxaca. Ultimately, Protestant missionaries laid the groundwork for postrevolutionary themes of nationalism, economic development projects, and indigenous education and assimilation. In a sense, the growth of Protestantism in Oaxaca galvanized antiforeign sentiment against the wealthy Anglo mining community while, at the same time, empowering many Oaxacan converts to join in the revolutionary cause as a way to limit the power of the Catholic Church.

Protestant Beginnings in Oaxaca

The Congregationalist missionary couple Francis and Harriet Clark toured Latin America in the early 1900s. In their guidebook for missionaries, they cautioned that sixty-five missionaries had died in Mexico in the first fifty years of Protestant evangelization. "Protestant missions have been baptized in the blood of the martyrs."[8] The Clarks were not alone in documenting religious violence. Protestant martyrdom narratives are a recurring theme throughout the late nineteenth and early twentieth centuries as missionaries perceived themselves as introducing Christianity for the first time to indigenous peoples.

Missionaries frequently complained that Catholics treated converts just as harshly as they had Reformation-era Protestants in Europe. Thomas Westrup of the American Bible Society established the Primera Iglesia Bautista de Monterrey (First Baptist Church of Monterrey) in Nuevo León in 1864. Westrup's brother, John Westrup, died in 1880 while organizing a congregation in the neighboring state of Coahuila. Convención Bautista de México (Mexican Baptist Convention) leader Alejandro Treviño Osuna accused "fanáticos romanistas" of murdering the missionary. Treviño vowed that Westrup's killing was the blood that formed the first Baptist Church in Mexico.[9] Missionaries heading into Mexico readily integrated genres of martyrdom into their recruitment narratives and fund-raising drives.

In her 1878 memoir, Presbyterian missionary Melinda Rankin affirms that "Martyrdom oftentimes bears precious fruit" and that the Christian Church only grew stronger with each wave of persecution.[10] Originally from New England, Rankin taught at a Mexican American girls' school in Brownsville, Texas. By the 1860s, she had moved across the border to Monterrey, Nuevo León, to build a Presbyterian school and set up the first permanent Protestant mission site in Mexico.[11] No easy task, Rankin notes, since male missionaries underestimated her. She also worked in "the very heart of Popery," her description of Monterrey's abundance of Catholic churches. She challenged young Protestants "to take up the fallen banner of the lamented Stephen" and bring the Gospel to Mexico as "Christ is bidding us to take that land for Him."[12]

Rankin praised peer-led Bible study "societies" springing up throughout Mexico.[13] In support of Oaxaca's first "Evangelical Society," she advises converts to be "firm, consistent, and self-denying" while seeking liberty of worship.[14] Rankin never made it to Oaxaca, but other missionaries did. They canvassed the Oaxacan countryside in the late nineteenth century, making connections with colporteurs and locals already familiar with Protestantism.

Oaxaca City resident Manuel Martinez Peña led weekly Gospel readings with his family and friends.[15] Seeking a larger space and more members, Peña founded the Oaxacan Evangelical Society in the summer of 1871. In an official announcement in the state government newspaper, *La Victoria*, Peña described how his new organization adhered to the Religious Freedom Act of 1860 by publicly listing the group's officers and sending a copy of the group's charter to the governor's office, as well as to his society's counterparts in New York and London.[16] After its recognition by state authorities, the Oaxacan Evangelical Society moved to a larger, public space in the fall of 1871.

Building upon the interest of the Oaxacan Evangelical Society, the Methodist Episcopal Church arrived to Oaxaca City in 1872.[17] The Evangelical Society transitioned into a Methodist congregation, offering Sunday services and Thursday night Bible study. The Methodists met in a former Jesuit Church turned Conceptionist convent. The convent closed following Juárez's War of La Reforma, and the Methodists rented out a subdivided space. It was a common practice for early Protestant groups to utilize spaces originally built for Catholic clergy. While the Protestant missionaries often complained of the "large and ugly crucifixes" adorning their secondhand churches, these

Figure 2. La Compañía Church and Convent served as a Methodist church in the 1890s.

spaces were logical choices.[18] The Templo de la Compañía (Jesuit Church) was located just a block from Oaxaca City's zocalo (main plaza); it was a prominent place to start a new denomination as its busy location received lots of pedestrian and mule-trolley traffic, along with vendors and professionals renting subdivisions within the old convent.[19] It was also symbolic; la Compañía dated back to 1579, one of the oldest and most well-known Catholic churches in Oaxaca City. Catholic organizations, however, expressed outrage over their sacred sites morphing into Protestant ones.

One prominent Oaxacan Catholic newspaper, *La Hoja del Pueblo*, repeatedly published a column with "Important Warnings to Catholics," admonishing those who attended Protestant services, even those held in former Catholic sites. As an example, it warned Catholics about the former Jesuit church, La Compañía. "It is illicit to attend Protestant services that take place on Sundays and each Thursday at the *templo evangélico*."[20] The reprimand suggested that some Catholics still worshiped there, not realizing or perhaps not caring that it was Methodist.

Catholic newspapers constantly tied Protestantism to antipatriotism as part of their strategy to combat Protestantism. Catholic papers pointed out the bitter territorial losses Mexico suffered during the Mexican-American War as a way to link Protestantism to earlier North American imperialism. *La Voz de la Verdad* reminded its readers that US Army chaplains and colporteurs "spread the bad seed of Protestantism with the bibles they left in Mexico."[21] *La Hoja del Pueblo* similarly posited that becoming Protestant was tantamount to siding with the United States during the invasion. Protestant proselytizers, *La Hoja del Pueblo* warned, divided the Mexican people. "That's why the North American Protestants that come here preaching their errors are truly pernicious foreigners; they come to weaken national unity."[22] Not only was Protestantism spreading bad information and false religious teachings to Oaxacans, it was also a threat to the nation.[23]

Catholic papers emphasized how Protestant publications originated from "Los Estados Unidos del Norte." *La Hoja del Pueblo* particularly criticized a Methodist newsletter for not listing its affiliation on its masthead. The paper implied that *La Bandera del Evangelio* purposely disguised its "protestante-semi-yankee" origins as it handed out free Bibles.[24] Any Catholic possessing Protestant Bibles or pamphlets, *La Hoja* advised, should hand them over to the Diocese.[25]

In 1887, *La Hoja del Pueblo* criticized "yankee" publisher David W. Carter's presence in Oaxaca. *La Hoja* was reacting to a recent article in *La Bandera del Evangelio* in which Carter described Methodism's growth in Oaxaca despite opposition from "fanatical Catholics." Carter also mentioned meeting with Governor Mariano Jiménez, who assured him Mexicans could practice the religion of their choice. Outraged that this American would call Oaxacan Catholics intolerant fanatics, *La Hoja del Pueblo* demanded evidence. The editorial sneered, "Are we intolerant of Mr. Carter just because we don't treat him as if he were sent as a messenger from heaven?"[26] As this example attests, using connections to political officials was also a strategy for Protestant expansionism in Oaxaca. Ultimately, Methodism expanded.

Members of the original Oaxacan Evangelical Society helped found the Methodist Church of San Pablo, numbering eighty congregants by 1890.[27] Missionary Lucius Smith purchased the Ex-Convento de San Pablo (Former Saint Paul's Convent) a few blocks from La Compañía. This colonial-era convent was on the free market because of Juárez's Lerdo Law.[28] With the Oaxaca City church established, Methodists could now focus on indigenous Oaxaca.

In the early 1890s, the Methodists built a church in the Central Valley

Zapotec village of Zaachila, just eight miles south of Oaxaca City. Methodist literature frequently wrote about Pérez, a descendant of the last Zapotec ruler in Zaachila. The Zapotec prince declared it "his happiest day" when the church came to the town.[29] Methodist missionaries shared Pérez's conversion story of receiving a Bible in 1860 from a Protestant colporteur. Eventually Pérez's entire family converted to Methodism.[30] Pérez represented indigenous converts when he attended national Methodist conferences.[31] He was also instrumental in starting a Methodist girls' school in 1901, declaring, "I want my daughters educated."[32] Methodist superiors wrote that on his deathbed, Pérez renewed his subscription to the Methodist newsletter, hoping that Zaachilans would continue learning the Gospel.[33] Clearly, the Methodist missionaries used Pérez's testimonial to reach out to indigenous families, especially girls.

Taking advantage of a complete railroad line between Mexico City and Oaxaca City by 1892, the Methodist Church became the leading missionary organization in Oaxaca. Instead of mission personnel taking more than a week via a train from Mexico City to Puebla and then horseback to Oaxaca City, they could now travel between the two cities in a few days; the Southern Mexican Railway also connected the state's capital to dozens of other Oaxacan destinations, including the Sierra Norte, the Isthmus, and the Cañada region. Protestant churches generally sprang up right near railroad stations.[34] Although missionaries complained about public drunkenness near the stations, it was an effective location to hand out thousands of religious pamphlets.[35] The Methodist Church followed such patterns in Mexico and South American zones. The early circuit missionary field included not just Oaxaca but also parts of Chiapas and Veracruz, making the region cumbersome for missionaries.[36]

The "John Wesley of Oaxaca"

Missionary Lucius Smith toured remote areas of Oaxaca on horseback in the spring of 1892. The minister gushed: "As fast as men and means are furnished we intend, with God's blessing, to spread the Gospel to the thousand villages that nestle among the glorious mountains of Oaxaca. The people there greatly need the Gospel we have. Should we not give it to them?"[37]

A graduate of Boston Theological Seminary, Smith had been serving as a missionary in Latin America since his first assignment to Chile in 1878. Smith described the state as "practically virgin soil" for evangelization.[38] To that end, he often rode on a horse for fourteen hours a day when traveling to isolated villages, switching to mules while traversing mountainous gorges in the Sierra Madre de Oaxaca. Smith eventually evangelized throughout much of southern Mexico, visiting regions comprising over twenty indigenous languages. His bishop nicknamed him the John Wesley of Oaxaca for his frequent circuit riding.[39]

In addition to publishing religious tracts in Mexico, he developed a successful Spanish grammar guide (used by native Spanish speakers and Anglo-American students alike). He also gave instrumental and vocal lessons, making the case that liturgical music helped attract indigenous converts. "Curious people," wrote his superiors, "would remain through the preaching simply to hear another song."[40] Smith divided his missionary assignment into four zones, starting with Oaxaca City and surrounding villages. Through conversations with converts, he compiled an alphabet for some of the native languages of Oaxaca.[41] His interest in native languages foreshadows the Summer Institute of Linguistics's work decades later.

Narratives of Smith's missionary work—albeit patronizing—often come across as anthropological descriptions of Oaxaca's diverse cultures. In 1894, he provided an ethnography of the daily life of tortilla vendors in Oaxaca City's main market. He described how the Zapotec women ground the corn on their metates (stone slab) to roll out the masa (dough), then toasting it on comal (griddle) pans over a smoky fire, to sell to customers. He wagered that they walked rapidly at five miles an hour, carrying the tortilla baskets over their backs. With the meager profit, the women shopped for necessities before returning home.[42] Smith targeted such communities surrounding the capital city and then ventured further into the interior of the state. As is evident in later chapters, missionaries made the case that saving money was more important than participating in the Catholic fiesta system.

Smith's first permanent rural mission was in the district of Cuicatlán.[43] Located along the railroad line in the Cañada region of northern Oaxaca, Cuicatlán was a logical base for Smith to begin his evangelization of Mazatecan Indians. While Cuicatlán was primarily indigenous, there was also a small pocket of mestizos as well as US and British agricultural executives—often

Protestants themselves—residing in the district seat of four thousand.[44] Smith reported in 1892 that he sold five subscriptions to the Methodist *El Abogado Cristiano Ilustrado* weekly bulletin and arranged to preach there biweekly. Smith also established schools for indigenous children in the region.

Some new converts viewed Methodism as a way to get an education and enter the modern workforce. Building schools complemented modern, capitalistic industries springing up in Porfirian Oaxaca.[45] Missionary Smith noted it was a telegraph operator in Ojitlan, Tuxtepec District, who volunteered his office for a Methodist service targeted at Chinanteco Natives laboring in the region's tobacco fields.[46] Similarly, historian Rubén Ruiz Guerra notes that in many rural communities, Methodist schools were the only ones around.[47] Missionaries served rural zones still lacking the state's reach. Pastor-teachers brought literacy to poor regions and included girls and women in their programs, hoping "women would carry books instead of rosary beads" since education would "remove them from fanaticism."[48] This example fits Zapotec Pérez's testimonial asking for girls' education. Reaching out to women was key to missionary work in Mexico.

For its part, Methodist schools consistently celebrated Mexican civic and patriotic holidays. Attesting to Methodism's prominence in the region, the governor of Oaxaca even visited the Methodist Jayacatlán (district of Etla) church for Christmas in the late 1880s. The Methodists had a least a dozen schools in Oaxaca by 1910, including in Cuicatlán, Tuxtepec, and Oaxaca City. Oaxacan native Reverend Euroza recalled entire Mixtec towns donating five dollars per month to fund schools.[49] But it was not just a lack of schools that concerned missionaries; they also commented on the seeming absence of priests in many rural parts.

Protestant missionaries frequently remarked on the ubiquitous Catholic churches and shrines in stark contrast to the relatively few priests serving the people. Missionaries expressed horror upon observing Oaxacans praying to the saints or the Virgin Mary to intercede in times of distress. In his first visit to San Juan Quiotepec, a Chinantec-speaking town in the district of Ixtlán de Juárez, Smith observed that, despite being Catholic, the Chinantecs appeared to have little exposure to the Gospel. The community lacked a priest, Smith noted, but there was a large chapel with what locals revered as "a very miraculous image of Saint James." Smith lamented that the villagers prayed "to that lifeless image" instead of God.[50]

Protestant criticisms often centered on indigenous syncretic religious rituals. In his 1893 report for the Methodist Mission Society, Smith observed:

> But really the religion of the Indians of this state is a crude mixture of the semi pagan superstitions of Rome and the wholly pagan superstitions of their ancestors of pre-Spanish times, and it is difficult to tell which predominates.... [This] seems to us sufficient to prove that the Indians of Oaxaca are generally in bondage to Satan, and need the labors of the Christian missionary as much as any people on the face of the globe.[51]

Twentieth-century missionaries would later share Smith's criticism of religious syncretism.

Of course, this concern over religious syncretism did not stop Smith from collecting some of the ancient relics. In 1894, Smith purchased a Zapotec urn (AD 600–800) found in a Zaachilan grave. The piece ended up at the Smithsonian in 1899.[52] Academics and tourists commissioned Smith to accompany them to indigenous sites; famed US anthropologist Fredrick Starr described Smith not as a missionary but as a language interpreter and guide in Oaxaca.[53]

Although Smith was in charge of the Methodists' burgeoning mission in Oaxaca, his work afforded him the chance to travel widely among the state's diverse regions. While establishing missionary zones, he also toured the state as an amateur botanist.[54] Smith teamed up with scholars in Oaxaca and the United States to collect species of plants to share with North American herbariums, helping round out the southern Mexican collections at these institutions.[55] This practice later came under scrutiny in the postrevolutionary period when Mexico started to promote its own museums and institutes. By the 1970s, indigenous communities frequently expelled missionaries who collected artifacts or flora that were national patrimony.

It was on one of those plant collection/evangelization excursions to Tuxtepec that Smith developed an infection from an insect bite. After having his left foot amputated and suffering from blood poisoning, he passed away in March of 1896 in Oaxaca City.[56] His death was a huge blow to the Methodist mission zone in Oaxaca and to regional botanical studies. The Italian educator Cassiano Conzatti published a Mexican botany volume with long dedications in memorial to Smith, his former coauthor (fig. 3).

Figure 3. Lucius C. Smith. In *Flora Sinóptica Mexicana*, 1896. Courtesy of Francisco de Burgoa Library, Santo Domingo Cultural Center, Oaxaca City.

Smith's experience provides important insight into the conflicts Protestant missionaries encountered in Mexico. His superiors recognized him as a martyr for the Methodist faith, suggesting he died from Catholics stoning him while he preached. As Bishop C. C. McCabe recalled, "He washed off the blood and went on with his sermon. He never got over that blow, and three years afterward, it cost him his life."[57] While the Methodist church hierarchy preferred to remember his illness as remnants from injuries sustained while preaching to intolerant Catholics, his death certificate and his friends' memorials about his death suggest he died from an insect bite infection that led to a severe case of septicemia.[58]

Smith was the only Methodist missionary at the time buried in Mexico. Bishop McCabe complained that the Methodist Church had to pay one hundred dollars to have Smith's headstone inscribed with *perpetuidad* (perpetual ownership) in Oaxaca City's cemetery (fig. 4). McCabe stated drily, "Love and reverence for the dead bring large revenues to the Roman Church."[59] Smith's legacy as a martyr fit in with the Methodist Mission's narrative that

Figure 4. Lucius C. Smith tombstone, Panteón General, Oaxaca City. Photograph by author, 2014.

Protestant evangelization in Mexico rivaled Reformation-era violence. It also illustrates the building tension between Protestants and Catholics over cultural traditions.

After Smith's death, the Methodist Mission encouraged Mexican-born missionaries to work in indigenous communities. Oaxacan men, educated in Methodist schools, took up this task. For example, Severo I. López ran the Methodist Mission in 1896. Methodist Bishop Butler posited that the Catholic Church had almost abandoned the communities in López's district. Butler remarked that the priest came once a year, not for mass but to collect tithes. However, despite the poverty in Oaxaca, devout Mixtec Protestants used their meager railroad salaries to help purchase a musical organ for the new church.[60] López in particular hoped for a Women's Foreign Missionary Society in Oaxaca. In his assessment, "The Blessed Gospel" stopped drunk fathers from beating their children and elevated family life. López gave the example of a Oaxacan bullfighter who, upon conversion, renounced his profession and stopped using profanities.[61] Indeed, many Protestant faiths encouraged Mexican men to reject "blood sports" altogether.[62] To that end, surely women could play an important role in backing conversion. As explored in the next chapter, women's organizations provided much of the key groundwork in converting indigenous peoples to the Protestant faith. Methodists even encouraged women to become politically active.

Victoriano D. Báez, another native Oaxacan missionary educated in Methodist schools, headed the Oaxaca mission assignment from 1906 to 1911.[63] Báez integrated his religious beliefs with political movements opposing Oaxacan governor Emilio Pimentel and President Porfirio Díaz. In office since 1877, Díaz was running for re-election in 1910. In his original Methodist congregation, Báez started an "Anti-Reeleccionista" Madero Club. Furthermore, Báez encouraged State Normal School students (including women) to form Madero Clubs.[64] Madero Clubs supported presidential candidate Francisco I. Madero's movement by distributing pro-Madero literature and writing political newsletters. Much to the dismay of the state's científicos, Báez openly cheered for Madero during his 1909 campaign stop in Oaxaca.[65] In contrast to the científico governor's close relationship with the Catholic archdiocese, Báez criticized the Church's role in indigenous communities in his 1909 *History of Oaxaca* volume.[66]

The Methodist Church celebrated Native ministers like Báez as they became involved in leadership roles. For example, Báez served as a delegate to the Methodist conference in Baltimore, Maryland, in 1909. He also traveled to New York City in 1909 and then Spain to lead the American Bible Society's translation commission.[67] Báez produced a smoother translation of the New Testament for native Spanish speakers.[68] While Báez's Methodist Church of San Pablo made inroads with professional Mexicans living in Oaxaca City, the Episcopalian mission focused on English-speaking residents of the capital. Unlike the middle-class Mexican Methodists, the Anglo community favored strong ties with Porfirian government officials as US business interests and investments expanded deeper into Oaxaca.

Foreign mining companies that had operated in Oaxaca since 1902 as state-financed expeditions discovered new quantities of silver, coal, copper, lead, iron, and marble.[69] Labor was cheap in southern Mexico and the type of unrest exemplified by the 1906 Cananea mining strike along the Sonora-Arizona border did not seem possible in remote and highly indigenous

Oaxaca.[70] Seizing on the opportunity, newly founded American mining companies arrived in droves to the Central Valley of Oaxaca and the Sierra Juárez for mining; coffee, sugar, and tobacco crops proliferated in the state's Cañada and coastal regions. In fact, Pittsburgh's *Index* reported "failure has no place" for investors in Oaxaca.[71] Political cartoons in Oaxaca's English-language newspaper depicted American businessmen as the first wave of an imminent mad rush of investors.[72]

The mining industry also drove the English-speaking Protestant community in Oaxaca City. Mainline Protestant denominations knew the importance of ministering to the American and British engineers, mining magnates, and plantation owners who sought services in English. Those who became prosperous in the mining industry usually brought their families and built homes in Oaxaca City, creating what they frequently referred to as the "American colony." For example, Holy Trinity Episcopal Church's social events brought colonists together for American holiday cuisine, games, and public lectures.

The Episcopalian church started with two small rented rooms on the corner of Independencía and Díaz Ordaz, just on the corner edge of the zocalo plaza. Visiting reverend William Watson arrived in Oaxaca in March of 1907 and immediately began his outreach to the Anglo community. Each week he used the *Oaxaca Herald* newspaper to invite Protestants of any denomination—and eventually even Catholics—to attend his services. He stated, "I am most desirous of meeting all foreigners in the city."[73] Watson predicted that American Catholics would choose English services over Spanish masses. By the end of 1907, Watson added a Wednesday prayer meeting, in addition to the two Sunday services and Sunday school. There was also a full-time Episcopalian school for the expat children.[74]

Watson initially encountered challenges in doing an Episcopal mission in a Catholic region. He also was competing with an established Methodist congregation in Oaxaca City that already had a permanent church. Despite difficulty renting space, Watson nonetheless commissioned a five-hundred-dollar "exquisitely artistic" altar. Even his Catholic neighbors who did not like Protestant services in their building started putting vases of flowers in the room after seeing the handmade altar that looked like it could "grace a cathedral."[75] In early 1909, Watson promised visiting bishop Henry D. Aves "a home roof over that altar someday."[76] The bishop praised Watson's "pluck and perseverance."[77]

The Episcopal Church's growth was dependent on the wealth of the local expat community. Throughout 1907, Reverend Watson solicited donations to build a permanent church in Oaxaca. Typically, expat families hosted church socials in their homes. For example, Magdalena Smelting and mining manager Lloyd Hamer and his wife, W. R. Hamer, offered their backyard for a fund-raising dinner.[78] But the *Oaxaca Herald* was quick to note that it was not just the Episcopal Women's Committee who planned it but rather "most of the Ladies of the American colony."[79] Organizing events or serving on committees was a socially acceptable way for women to exert a small degree of power in public.[80] For example, Constantine Rickards Jr. served as Holy Trinity Episcopal Church's warden while his wife, Adela Durán Rickards, headed the fund-raising committee.[81] Similarly, for Mexican Catholic women, participation in lay organizations, such as the Ladies of Charity of St. Vincent de Paul, was a gender appropriate way to minister and stem the tide of Protestantism during the Porfiriato.[82]

Each week, the *Oaxaca Herald* published lists of confirmed donors to Holy Trinity's construction fund.[83] Soon enough, Watson purchased an organ and furniture made in the United States, delivered free by an American executive of the Mexican Southern Railroad.[84] By early 1908, Holy Trinity Episcopal Church leased a few rooms at the Masonic Lodge centrally located on Murgía Street. Given the overlapping memberships between Masonry societies and Protestantism, the Lodge welcomed the Episcopalians.[85] *Oaxaca Herald* described the space as having "a very pretty and cozy appearance."[86] Of course, its services certainly differed from Catholic churches whose holiday celebrations spread into the streets.

Living in Oaxaca exposed American expats to different religious practices, and this was a frequent topic in the *Oaxaca Herald*. Around Christmas, it reminded the Americans about the Mexican "Posada" customs. During the Easter season, the paper included background references to how Oaxacan Catholics traditionally celebrated *semana santa* (Holy Week). The paper informed Americans of street processions and business closings.[87] Indeed, in 1909, all work ceased at Tapiche mine because of semana santa processions and celebrations. Overall, however, the *Oaxaca Herald* concluded that while American managers were "perplexed" over the closings, it was better to accept the tradition than to make labor compulsory during Holy Week.[88]

While some Anglo businesses may have complained of work slowdowns, the son of one mining magnate embraced these traditions. After his staunchly Episcopalian father's death in 1905, twenty-six-year-old Edward Rickards entered Catholic seminary—using his mining inheritance to support his study. Rickards became pastor of Nuestra Señora de La Merced (Our Lady of Mercy), just off the llano (park), close to his Episcopalian older brother Constantine Rickards's home. Unlike his Episcopalian family, Father Edward Rickards reveled in the Catholic traditions favored by his working-class indigenous and mestizo parishioners in the neighborhood. In particular, his parish had a special devotion to Mercedarian Saint Raymond Nonnatus, the patron saint of midwives, the imprisoned, and caretakers of livestock.[89] On August 31 each year, Oaxacans brought mules, bulls, and donkeys to the patio of La Merced church to be blessed with holy water.[90] Father Rickards also blessed the elaborately costumed pet dogs of American children.[91] Catholic devotion to Saints' Day feasts such as Saint Raymond surely surprised the Protestant Anglo-American expat community. Festivities for the Virgin Mary were no exception.

For the celebration of La Virgen de la Soledad, Oaxaca's patron saint, devotees come from all over the state and even the nation.[92] Train lines offered extended schedules, including extra runs from mining centers to Oaxaca City on the December 18 feast day. It was the biggest church holiday in the state and "thousands and thousands" of visitors arrived to attend the mass, processions, and fireworks commemorating her sixteenth-century apparition to a humble mule-driver.[93] Archbishop Eulogio Gillow tried to link Oaxaca's Catholicism with the rest of the nation; the elaborate fiestas surrounding La Soledad illustrated this goal.[94]

For the subsequent special coronation of the Virgin of Soledad in January 1909, Pope Pius IX sent a delegation from Rome. While covering the ceremony, the *Oaxaca Herald* noted dryly that the coronation of "the richest Virgin in the Americas" offered "the pomp and splendor that only the Catholic Church could give to the occasion." The article wagered that the Virgin's fifteen-inch diamond-jeweled crown valued at least twenty-five thousand dollars.[95] The archbishop's office displayed the crown and robe briefly for the public to admire in the week following the ceremony.

Given the differences between Protestant and Catholic interpretations of the Virgin Mary's place in Christianity, it is not surprising that there was tension surrounding the veneration of La Virgen de la Soledad.[96] In fact, there was a rumor that an American colonist planted dynamite inside a candle in front of the Virgin of Soledad. When the prayer candle did not light, a Oaxacan Catholic inspected the candle and found the dynamite. The *Oaxaca Herald* reported that the police concluded it was an unfounded rumor designed to provoke a riot during the Soledad festivities.[97] Whether or not it was a rumor, tensions between the Anglo-American colony and Mexicans broke down along Protestant competition with Catholicism. Special devotions to the Virgin Mary continued to spur controversies in Oaxaca.

In the spring of 1909, a new "Juan Diego" arrived in Oaxaca. This time an indigenous man in the mining village of Etla claimed to see the Virgin of Guadalupe, just as peasant Juan Diego had outside of Mexico City in 1531. Juan Diego II intended to build a church dedicated to Guadalupe in Etla. Mestizo authorities called him a false prophet, but Zapotecs in the district believed in him. Juan Diego II ended up in prison, charged with illegally taking money from believers.[98] Such examples gave Protestant missionaries ample material to criticize the role of Catholicism in Native villages as one of wasting money on saints and candles, just as President Júarez had lamented in the 1870s.

Much like Protestant missionaries criticized the ubiquitous Catholic holidays and expenses surrounding worship of the saints, the local pro-Madero newspaper *La Unión* also complained about the traditions. *La Unión* argued that frequent observance of religious holidays was bad for business. It could also hurt workers because mangers ended up requiring employees to work longer hours on regular days, potentially paving the way for sickness or injury. *La Unión*'s article served as a foreshadowing of some of the labor grievances Revolutionaries had against American companies. Mexicans received less pay than American employees, lacked benefits, and lived hand-to-mouth, often in debt to the company store. For its part, the Catholic Church would blame Protestantism and its link to foreign capitalism as the root of indigenous peoples' exploitation.

Conflicts between the Catholic Church and new Protestant missionary work were apparent in spats between the Anglo-American community's *Oaxaca Herald* and the local Catholic paper, *La Voz de la Verdad*. In a 1909 article, the *Oaxaca Herald* complained about the Catholic paper's accusation that North Americans living in Mexico engaged in séances and other rituals of spiritism. The *Oaxaca Herald* argued that these papers tried to "stir up all of the animosity possible between [Mexicans] and foreigners," when it was American investments driving Oaxaca's economy.[99] Although the Anglo business community largely pulled out of Oaxaca during the revolutionary era, such debates foreshadow how Protestantism tied in to later discourses on US neocolonialism in Latin America.

With the onset of the Mexican Revolution in 1910, Episcopalian Holy Trinity Church, serving mainly the wealthy English-speaking residents of Oaxaca City, closed. The Methodist church, San Pablo, in contrast, continued to thrive with growing interest in their schools. It served middle-class Mexican professionals, many of whom supported—even joined—the revolutionary forces. In fact, many early Protestant converts also became military generals.[100] Methodist pastors Victoriano D. Báez and Leopoldo A. García, who both ministered in Oaxaca City and in large-scale agricultural zones in Cuicatlán, had short stints in the Revolution.[101]

Conclusion

Lucius Smith's missionary work clearly played a huge role in the Methodist Church's early success in the region. His experience also foreshadows some of the criticisms of North American missionaries living in Oaxaca. As Chapter Four will illustrate, missionaries who collected artifacts or plants tested communities sensitive to North American exploitation.

Reflecting on the Mexican Revolution, Methodist bishop John Wesley Butler wrote that "Romanist Missionaries" tried to stir things up, hoping to reclaim the Catholic Church's position prior to President Juárez's Reforma laws.[102] By the close of the revolutionary stage, with the religious limitations in the 1917 Constitution that clamped down on the power of the Catholic Church—and also limited the foreign presence in Mexico—the Methodist Mission encouraged Mexican nationals to perform missionary work. Butler reported that there were over thirty-eight Methodist congregations in Mexico by the end of the Revolution, with over five hundred Mexican children enrolled in Methodist schools. Yet Butler lamented that many places still "were begging" the Methodists for more schools, especially in indigenous zones.[103] Butler ended his 1918 memoir vowing that Oaxacan-born teachers and preachers would evangelize the state in place of the North Americans. However, North American Protestant organizations introduced a major territorial change.

Planning for missionary work in the postrevolutionary period, US Presbyterians, Methodists, Baptists, Disciples of Christ, Congregationalists, Episcopalians, the American Bible Society, and the Young Men's Christian Association (YMCA) convened in Cincinnati, Ohio, in July 1914. They carved out spheres of influence in Mexico, finalizing the territorial details in Mexico City in 1919. Methodists and Presbyterians swapped geographic regions through that "Plan de Cincinnati." Consequently, the Presbyterian Church gained missionary jurisdiction over Oaxaca and the Methodists moved to northern Mexico.

Of course, all religious personnel faced changing government regulations in postrevolutionary Mexico. During the Cristiada era (1926–1929), the Calles Law enforced the anticlerical articles of the 1917 Constitution, including limits on foreign clergy. Catholic priests struggled to comply with these restrictions. The story of the Rickards brothers is particularly illustrative of these changes. In 1926, government officials arrested Father Edward Rickards in Oaxaca City and threatened to deport him. Officials accused him of publicly celebrating sacraments and processions without permits at La Merced Church.[104] The Rickardses, born in Oaxaca into a wealthy mining family, were technically British citizens. Using diplomatic channels, Episcopalian Constantine Rickards Jr. convinced the Calles regime to release his Catholic brother. Tension over postrevolutionary religious legislation led to serious conflicts between Protestants and Catholics.

The postrevolutionary period offered an important but still challenging opportunity for Protestant evangelization. While late nineteenth-century and early twentieth-century missionaries spoke of Protestant duties to conquer Mexico spiritually, postrevolutionary North American missionaries took a more nuanced approach. Missionary organizations perceptively understood the strength of Revolutionary nationalism by Mexican Protestants as the face of evangelization.

Thus, just as US miners and agriculturalists rushed into Oaxaca in the early 1900s, believing opportunities were limitless, so too did Mexican-born Protestant missionaries stream into Native villages in the 1920s, seeing indigenous Oaxaca as ripe again for religious evangelization. It was within the postrevolutionary period that the Protestant evangelization of indigenous communities become a permanent fixture in Benito Juárez's home state of Oaxaca.

CHAPTER TWO

"La sangre está clamando justicia"

Constructing Martyrdom in Postrevolutionary Oaxaca

THE STORIES OF early Christian- and Reformation-era martyrs influenced twentieth-century Protestant missionaries as they evangelized Oaxaca. Missionaries used terms like "fanatical" and "Romanish" to describe what they interpreted as overly zealous Catholic parishioners or regions. Presbyterian W. Reginald Wheeler remarked in 1922 that despite physical and verbal threats, his missionary team endured. "Our workers have not ceased to visit the Mixteca. The blood of martyrs has bought it for Christ. Probably Rome will take more lives before religious toleration and an open Bible becomes the rules in these mountains; but we go forward."[1] In the same report on missionary sites in Oaxaca, Wheeler included a picture of a Zapotec man driving an oxen team fastened to the cart by "Roman Yoke." The photograph's caption stated that the cart's crosspiece resembled those "employed in Palestine in the time of Christ," further exemplifying his observation that indigenous Oaxacans were literally and figuratively repressed by the Roman Catholic Church.[2] Protestant missionaries sought to spread the Gospel and modernize indigenous communities, which they believed were trapped in the ancient past.

These references to Protestant persecution became more common with increased evangelization efforts in the region following the triumph of the 1910 Revolution. Though the Mexican Revolution officially ended in 1920, the postrevolutionary period ushered in sustained religious violence in much of Mexico. Working as a missionary for the Convención Nacional Bautista de México (CNBM/National Baptist Convention of Mexico), Samuel Juárez García established the Baptists' earliest congregation in Oaxaca.[3] Echoing the grievances of early Christians, Juárez García claimed that villagers irrationally blamed the drought on the Baptists.[4] In a June 1923 letter to his superiors in the CNBM, Juárez García complained that superstition and intolerance from Catholics jeopardized his missionary program in his hometown of Tlacochahuaya, Oaxaca. "The scarcity of rains was blamed on us, and it is up to three times now that fanatics have tried to expel us. If they have not done it yet, it is because now we have a good number of believers. They all fear there will be friction between Evangelicals and Romans here."[5] His comments in this Baptist newsletter are eerily prescient as Catholics murdered Juárez García in 1935. His followers today celebrate him as the first indigenous Baptist martyr in Mexico.

This chapter examines Protestantism's impact on conceptualizations of indigenous identities, nationalism, and the construction of Protestant martyrdom in postrevolutionary Mexico. My analysis of this contentious Baptist project in the Central Valley of Oaxaca illustrates the intersection of missionary and revolutionary agendas with contrasting notions of ethnic, regional, and gender identities. Although the mestizo men and women of the National Baptist Convention felt a Christian obligation to support indigenous converts, they saw Zapotec culture as a frustrating obstacle in attaining a dual (and at times competing) Mexican/Christian identity. Local conflicts in the Central Valley community of Tlacochahuaya led to alternate martyrdom narratives that speak to the larger religious conflicts in Mexico. This martyrdom connects Protestants to Mexican nationalism and patriotism. By examining an oral history of martyrdom, I trace a community's construction of as well as its contestation of collective memory.[6] Primarily a local history of one Baptist congregation, these events and experiences are representative of a larger pattern of religious conflict in Oaxaca. However, what makes Tlacochahuaya particularly important is that, unlike many of the first Protestant missionaries in Oaxaca, Juárez García was Zapotec himself, providing an intimate look at the interworking of a new belief system in a centuries-old village.

Convención Nacional Bautista de México in Oaxaca

Radical postrevolutionary legislation gave Protestant missionaries the opening for which they had long awaited. Missionaries adeptly couched their religious agendas in revolutionary language. To their advantage, several of the most prominent leaders of the Revolution and some cabinet members identified as Protestant or had been educated at Protestant schools.[7] By sharing the postrevolutionary government's desire to bring literacy, improved healthcare, and sobriety to indigenous communities, missionaries had much in common with civil servants and schoolteachers, the vanguards of the state's "Cultural Missions" program.[8] Much of their missionary literature also called for the "defanaticization" (reduction of Catholicism's influence) of the indigenous population through literacy and apprenticeship training.[9] For Protestant missionaries, the tightening of Catholic privileges in Mexico meant that they were given opportunities to penetrate previously Catholic zones of indigenous Mexico if they paired their religious agendas with state educational and modernization goals. If indigenous people could read the Bible for themselves, they might reduce their dependence on local priests and rituals and, hence, more quickly assimilate into the fabric of the mestizo nation.

Postrevolutionary Baptist missionaries were sensitive to issues of Mexican nationalism.[10] The Baptist Church General Missionary to Mexico, A. B. Rudd, worried that missionaries could lose their influence if they were seen as Yankee imperialists. Rudd stated in 1917 that "Mexicans, rather than North Americans, must evangelize this country. Our work is to prepare the men for this work. God help me to do this and keep the way open for us!"[11] He founded a seminary in Saltillo in 1917 specifically for training Mexican citizens to proselytize in their home communities. Rudd adamantly warned that foreign missionaries should not preach from the pulpit; when invited, he gave sermons from his seated pew as a regular member, not as a leader.[12] The missionaries understood their vulnerable status as foreigners during a time of heightened nationalism; choosing Mexican citizens as missionaries strengthened their credibility. Evangelization in indigenous communities soon became the CNBM's primary focus. This missionary organization entered Oaxaca vowing to bring Christianity and the tenets of the Mexican Revolution to southern Mexico.

During the autumn of 1920, the CNBM gathered in Torreón, Coahuila. "What can we do to evangelize the Indians?" was the principal theme of the national meeting. CNBM president Alejandro Treviño Osuna wrote in his memoir that the challenge created "a spirit of generosity among the attendees." Sara Hale, a US Baptist missionary working in northern Mexico, offered to contribute three hundred dollars annually for evangelization in indigenous communities.[13] Encouraged by Hale's offer, the CNBM pledged one thousand dollars more and developed a comprehensive plan for the Baptist Church's penetration into Mexico's interior.[14] To that end, Missionary Rudd discussed the potential fruitfulness of Baptist evangelization of the Tarasca in Michoacán and the Zapotec in Oaxaca and persuaded the convention to nominate Samuel Juárez García as a missionary for the Zapotec region.[15]

Juárez García convinced the convention that his native San Jerónimo Tlacochahuaya, a town of about two thousand mostly monolingual Zapotec residents located twenty-one kilometers east of Oaxaca City, had a commercial market that brought residents of neighboring villages into the town each weekend and was a logical center for evangelization that would soon stretch across the state. Born in 1895 in Tlacochahuaya, Juárez García converted to Protestantism at age twelve when he accompanied his mother to Oaxaca City to sell her homemade tortillas door to door. Through his mentor and tortilla client Josué Valdez, who was a visiting Baptist pastor in Oaxaca, he earned a scholarship to study at a northern Mexican Baptist seminary and graduated in 1919.[16] A talented musician, he choreographed a Spanish-language hymnal for Mexican Baptists—instead of relying on the heretofore nondenominational Spanish Evangelical Hymnal—before being trained as a missionary. The Baptist Convention's Unión Nacional Femenil Bautista (Women's National Baptist Union) gushed that Juárez García was "a pure blooded Indian" who would make great strides in his natal village.[17]

Arriving at the neighboring town of Abasolo's train station, twenty-five-year-old Juárez García marveled at the potential for his evangelization in the extensive Zapotec region.[18] In early correspondence with the Baptist Convention, Juárez García described his Zapotec village in the tone of a superior outsider. After all, he was educated in northern Mexico, was a fluent Spanish-speaker, and was Protestant. But he also identified as an intimate member.

He closed his letters warmly as "el misionero entre los Zapotecos" (the missionary among the Zapotecs). He frequently dedicated full columns of his newsletter extolling pre-Hispanic Zapotec architectural achievements such as Monte Albán and Mitla.[19] Juárez García's vacillation between paternalism toward and pride in Tlacochahuayans speaks to national but also regional interpretations of indigenismo and especially *Oaxaqueñismo*—celebration of Oaxaca's indigenous archaeological sites, regional cuisines, and colorful dress and dance.[20] Throughout the 1920s and 1930s, Oaxacan government officials, schoolteachers, and civic organizations praised past indigenous accomplishments while concomitantly trying to bring the Revolution to the countryside. While the government sought to modernize and assimilate Native peoples, "the Indian was lauded as the vessel of important and often sophisticated folk traditions."[21] But when it came to religion, Juárez García concluded that it was the Evangelical's duty "to awaken this race" by sharing the Gospel, which would ultimately "illuminate this dark region where Satan and Romanism has prevailed. The religion of the Zapotecs is the one that the conquerors brought: the Catholic religion with all of its gross idolatry."[22]

Juárez García argued that it was the Catholic Church's hegemonic hold on his community that was responsible for the serious challenges he faced. In an early *El Atalaya Bautista* column, Juárez García complained that as soon as he initiated regular worship services, "the local priest began his slanderous attacks on the Baptists in this town."[23] Juárez García responded by challenging Father Ignacio Morales to a theological debate, a common Protestant missionary technique to show off their competence in biblical scripture. Juárez García claimed the priest backed down and left Juárez García alone since "the truth of [Scripture] prevailed."[24]

Juárez García repeatedly asserted that Zapotec cultural identity coupled with Catholicism made his neighbors painstakingly difficult to convert. He wrote in a 1921 missionary report: "It is not easy to convert Indians. Their ideas are so deeply ingrained that despite Reason and Scripture they offer no argument other than this is the custom of our people."[25] For Juárez García, as for many Protestant missionaries and national political leaders during the Cristiada period and the nascent stage of indigenismo, Roman Catholicism was a dangerous religion for indigenous Mexico. Juárez García further remarked: "Since Romanism offers its followers a wide door and a spacious path, immorality invaded this town."[26] By "immorality," he meant profanity, idolatry, and alcoholism. He sarcastically remarked that curse words were used so frequently in households that children did not know the difference between proper and obscene language.²⁷

Despite being a Native Zapotec, Juárez García disparaged many "traditional" Zapotec customs as well as Catholicism. He argued that these customs were actually vestiges of colonialism. Juárez García referred to indigenous religious traditions as a form of paganism that mixed easily with Catholic saint worship and traditional healing practices. "The idolatry practiced by the Indian is double because he has received two forms of it: that of his race and that of Catholicism."²⁸ In early correspondence, he criticized Zapotec syncretic rituals that he believed misrepresented the tenets of Christianity. As an example, he described how Zapotecs in Tlacochahuaya worshiped a statue in the Church depicting Christ triumphantly riding into Jerusalem on Palm Sunday. "There are Indians who kiss, not our savior . . . but the donkey."²⁹ Horrified by Indians venerating any type of image, let alone a donkey, he also condemned their practice of worshiping Saints. "When they lose an animal or whatever little thing, they lock up Saint Anthony in a 'chiquihuite' (palm woven basket) in the middle of the patio, in the sun, or with a candle lit, and that is how they wait to find their lost item."³⁰ Missionaries regarded such examples of folk Catholicism as superstitious and a misunderstanding of Christian scripture.

Like his Baptist missionary colleagues in other regions, Juárez García had little time for traditional healing or worship. Reverence for the mountains, local rivers and streams, and the cornfields plays an important role in indigenous Oaxacan spiritual life since they "represented the main symbol of a people and its territory; of identity and customs."³¹ However, Juárez García viewed Mexico's indigenous population like contemporary politicians and intellectuals who pitied them as trapped in the colonial past.³² Only when they could jettison their folk Catholicism could they become truly free Mexican citizens.

Finding examples of paganism consumed Juárez García. He often pondered which traditional practices were vestiges of Catholicism and which ones were of pre-Hispanic derivation. For example, the missionary described Zapotec worship of the pre-Hispanic gods as a form of paganism. He described how, when they prayed to Catholic saints, they were simultaneously worshipping the God of the Sun, of the mountain, of the river, and idols from the past. He lamented that these gods occupied a place on the

Roman Catholic altar where Zapotecs mixed Christian and pre-Hispanic deities. In particular, Juárez García railed against worship of images of the Virgin Mary. In Oaxaca, the devotion to the Virgin of Juquila, La Soledad, and Guadalupe, among other Virgin invocations, is perhaps the most noticeable component of folk Catholicism. It was also the part that Protestant missionaries hoped most to extinguish. Juárez García's mentor and teacher from the seminary, A. B. Rudd, perhaps best summed up Protestant aversion toward the Virgin of Guadalupe. On December 12, 1921, the feast day of the Virgin, Rudd bitterly complained in his journal about what he observed in the hilltop village outside of Mexico City.

> La virgen de Guadalupe holds sway—and such sway! I went to La Villa and was thoroughly disgusted. . . . Dirty, filthy *pulquerías*, drinking, gambling, poverty, and this right at the doors of the great temple of '*Nuestra Señora de Guadalupe*'—all in the name of religion!! An eloquent though unintentional confession of the absolute moral insufficiency of Catholicism.[33]

Rudd viewed Catholicism as a complete anathema to "real" Christianity. Missionaries in Oaxaca spent considerable time disputing the story of the Virgin of Guadalupe's apparition on the cloak of indigenous peasant Juan Diego in 1531 at Tepeyac.[34] By undermining the credibility of the Virgin Mary's apparition in colonial Mexico, Protestants sought to sever the Virgin's prime spot in indigenous religious rituals and bring their worship back to a Christ-centered one.

Juárez García singled out mescal as another significant obstacle to conversion. His letters and missionary updates reveal a clear impatience with the presence of alcohol in holiday celebrations. Juárez García criticized the evils of the traditional Oaxacan liquor in a Baptist newsletter in 1921.

> There is never a party without numerous bottles of *mescal*. If it's a Catholic holiday, the mescal is the stimulant for religiosity, and if it's a patriotic holiday, it's the stimulant for patriotism. Mescal appears everywhere. There are some individuals who go on binges for two weeks straight or even whole months. And it's not just the men who practice this vice, but also the women.[35]

His primary strategy to combat this vice was to hand out pamphlets produced by the Convención Bautista condemning alcohol. Before visiting the neighboring town of San Juan del Río, renowned for its mescal factories, Juárez García and his assistants went "bien equipados" (well prepared) with copies of the popular prohibition pamphlet "Oye."[36] Yet, only one or two families in each of the six villages surrounding Tlacochahuaya accepted his literature. He remarked that the telegraph employees or the postmasters of these neighboring villages seemed most receptive to his new religious ideas.[37] For Juárez García, these individuals had accepted the progress brought by the Revolution, whereas Catholics remained tied to the past.

In particular, the Zapotec missionary condemned the patron saint's day fiesta customs in most indigenous communities. He viewed it as a money drain, an excuse to get drunk, and a misrepresentation of Christianity. During the feast day of San Jerónimo, patron saint of Tlacochahuaya, all town members brought flowers to the altar before the mass started (figs. 5 and 6). Afterward, a mayordomo (appointed fiesta sponsor) led a procession with the saint statue, tenderly washed and dressed by women related to or appointed by the mayordomo, around the town square. In the late afternoon, the mayordomo invited residents to his home for a meal.

Like his mestizo superiors in northern Mexico, instead of dwelling on Catholic fiestas, Juárez García put great effort into supporting civic holidays. However, the much-anticipated centennial celebration of Mexico's independence from Spain on September 15, 1921, was a dilemma for Protestant Mexicans. Some Protestant organizations chose not to participate in the festivities because of the traditionally celebrated narrative of the Catholic Church and its clergy as liberators. Looking to change some of the iconic symbols of the movement—such as the Virgin of Guadalupe—and put a Revolutionary spin on the Independence Movement, Baptist senator Jonás García asked A. B. Rudd to form an interdenominational committee of Protestants in Mexico City to participate in the holiday.[38] Juárez García reported proudly that he and his newly converted Zapotec night school students attended the Independence Day celebrations in the nation's capital.[39] After the 1921 celebrations, which highlighted civic rather than Catholic symbols in the parades and aerial shows, Rudd wrote approvingly: "Rome's hold on the masses was never weaker. They are tired of papal domination, of Catholic miracles, ancient and modern, and are feeling their way to better and higher things."[40]

Figure 5. Mayordomos outside of the Catholic church on the Feast Day of St. Jerome, Tlacochahuaya, September 30, 2010. Photograph by author.

Figure 6. Interior of the Catholic church on the Feast Day of St. Jerome, Tlacochahuaya, September 30, 2010. Photograph by author.

Juárez García received substantial Baptist support for the CNBM pioneer mission in Oaxaca.[41] The CNBM awarded Juárez García a stipend to rent a home, which also served as a classroom for Sunday school and night classes, as well as a horse to travel to the six neighboring villages in his missionary jurisdiction. By fall of 1921, Juárez García listed approximately fifty converts who attended Bible study in his crowded home. One month he sold twenty Bibles, four times as many as his lone Baptist missionary colleague in Michoacán.[42] Ensured of his base, Juárez García's next step was to establish a permanent chapel for his members. His rental home only had a small spare room in which to conduct ceremonies. Visitors from neighboring villages had to sleep outdoors in the town plaza if they stayed for an evening service. Town authorities fined or incarcerated these followers for violating public curfew laws.[43] He also complained that his "drunken" Catholic landlady interrupted his services and that the local priest threatened not to marry the landlady's son unless she evicted him.[44] Juárez García argued that without his own church building, his mission would never succeed. His proposed Capilla Bautista de Tlacochahuaya represented an opportunity to reinforce the Convención's network in southern indigenous Mexico, a project taken up by northern mestiza Baptist women.

Figure 7. Pastor Samuel Juárez García, 1920. Courtesy of Elvira Cruz García.

La Unión Femenil and the New Chapel

As in other missionary regions, Protestant women made up a large proportion of volunteers and permanent staff.[45] Protestant women could concomitantly support the goals of the revolutionary state and curb the influence of the Roman Catholic Church by funding churches in indigenous communities. Though lacking formal electoral rights, Mexican women played a central role in bringing the tenets of the 1910 revolution to the countryside. Founded in 1919, the Unión Nacional Femenil Bautista (Women's National Baptist Union) had over twenty-five chapters, mostly in northern and central Mexico. The Unión Femenil perceived Catholicism in Oaxaca, "that far off region of our Republic," as a central obstacle to modernization and progress for postrevolutionary Mexico.[46]

In 1922, the Unión Femenil launched a national campaign to raise funds for Juárez García's proposed church. The Unión Femenil particularly was concerned with indigenous Mexico, "where our brothers and sisters are lacking some of the blessings we enjoy." Northern Protestant Esther Gutiérrez de Montes expressed such sentiments in her January 1922 Unión Femenil newsletter. "Aren't we ready as Christian women to contribute, even if we are sacrificing, to help our brothers and sisters who are subjugated by idolatry and ignorance? Many Catholic societies are increasingly publishing false propaganda against us. Why don't we make an effort, Christian women, so that the truth may triumph?"[47]

Unión Femenil leadership pitied indigenous Mexicans as vulnerable victims of Roman Catholic traditions. Esther G. de Montes reminded her readers of their duties as Christian women to rescue the Zapotecs, even if she had never been to Oaxaca. "Oh, how the heart saddens when it sees our indigenous class so full of absolute fanaticism. By working for our brothers and sisters less favored and less wealthy, we honor our Lord who we serve."[48] The Unión Femenil viewed Mexico's indigenous population as trapped in Catholic fanaticism and idolatry from the conquest period. In her subsequent fund-raising columns, de Montes described Zapotecs as unfortunate souls in need of guidance from their "wiser" (mestiza) sisters. She described witnessing indigenous women and children exhaustedly dancing the *son de tamboriles* for hours in honor of pre-Hispanic deities who they fused with Catholic saints. She challenged her readers:

Doesn't it seem to you sisters that the time has come, that we stop this fanaticism and help our brothers and sisters who have been misled for so many years? How many sisters will take advantage of this opportunity, remembering the words of our blessed Teacher who said in Mathew 25:40—"I tell you the truth, whatever you did for one of the least of these brothers of mine, you did for me."?[49]

Her pleas for contributions were successful. Originally, her organization had planned to pay for half of the Oaxacan chapel construction costs. Early into her campaign, she notified her members that they could pay for the total estimated cost of five hundred dollars and asked the National Baptist Convention to fund-raise for the furnishings and the new organ.[50] National Baptist Convention president Donato Ramírez Ruiz praised the Unión Femenil for their "heroic" fund-raising labors in 1922. Ramírez Ruiz enthusiastically concluded that their work would lead to literacy and introduce the Gospel to the five million indigenous Mexicans who were monolingual.[51]

Throughout the process of building the chapel, the Unión Femenil leadership expressed irritation over the slow pace of progress and threatened to freeze funds until Juárez García and his Oaxacan staff could give evidence of progress. In November 1925, Unión Femenil president Amada T. de García informed her readers "with much embarrassment" that the chapel was still not ready because of what Juárez García claimed were frequent rains and scheduling conflicts with the contractor.[52] A year earlier, de García had written an exasperated letter to CNBM president Andrés R. Cavazos asking why the Oaxacan missionary did not consider the potential delays with the rainy season beforehand and why did he not find a different contractor. Cavazos and national missionary director Ernesto Uriegas traveled to Tlacochahuaya to oversee the last stage of construction. Juárez García explained to the northern mestizo men that within the traditional cargo system—a civil-religious hierarchy in the indigenous communities of Oaxaca—the contractor had been obligated by the community to fulfill a municipal position, and hence there was a delay. Cavazos and Uriegas knew little about this tradition and saw it as an obstacle to efficiency and progress.[53] Mestizo frustration with indigenous customs is evident in their insinuations that the Zapotec chapel would have dragged on for years if it had not been for their supervision. The debate over whether Protestantism jeopardizes the functioning of tequio and cargo—two essential components of usos y costumbres—remains a contentious issue in Oaxacan communities today.

After substantial delays, the chapel finally opened on May 30, 1926, and its photograph graced the cover of *El Atalaya Bautista*. The total cost of the chapel was $2,300 (4.6 times the original budget), which the Unión Femenil of Mexico had raised in full. When explaining the construction delays, Juárez García informed the Unión Femenil and Convención missionary board that from the master bricklayer down to the last laborer, everyone involved in the construction of the Church was of Zapotec ethnicity. "We acknowledge our ignorance because, well, we're not engineers," a response that seemed to affirm the minister's exaltation of past Zapotec architectural achievements, but scant confidence in contemporary culture.[54] He also reported that Catholics unsuccessfully tried to burn down the door of the chapel the night before the dedication. It was "a true miracle from Christ," the minister proclaimed, that no damage was done to the church that day.[55]

Meanwhile, the Unión Nacional Femenil Bautista sent a delegation down to Oaxaca to attend the church dedication. Eva Borocio, treasurer of the Unión, wrote: "Despite all of the intrigues of the devil to obstruct the dedication ceremony, the temple has enjoyed larger than usual attendance, and it was filled up entirely the day we dedicated it to the TRUE God. It is a beautiful building, as you can see, and represents with dignity the Baptist cause in that far off region of our Republic."[56] Although the Unión Femenil members were pleased with the completion of the chapel, they soon articulated serious concerns about Zapotec religious practices.

Based on the Unión Femenil's trip to Tlacochahuaya for the church inauguration, their editorial page in *El Atalaya Bautista* on June 17, 1926, featured an article entitled "Costumbres Típicas de los Zapotecas." The ethnographic-style piece was overflowing with criticism of women's subordination in folk Catholicism, the fiesta system, and traditional healing methods. The Unión Femenil described Zapotecs as "a very strong and clean race but their ignorance has brought them to ruins. All of their customs are daughters of their religion; from this religion, mixed with the primitive adoration of idols, has come to form a disgusting cult."[57] The Baptist women hoped to eradicate what they deemed vestiges of paganism: the syncretic fusion of saints with Native deities and pre-Hispanic rituals that they believed fueled expensive, alcohol-driven fiestas. In their efforts, they also highlighted gender inequalities.

The Unión Femenil's account described the condition of the Zapotec woman as "sadder than you can imagine," citing illiteracy and unbalanced gender roles in marriage and civic life, in which a woman lives in a "virtual state of slavery, subject to all of the desires of the man practically treating her like a cargo animal; she has no rights to anything." In particular, the account lamented how Zapotec women sat on the ground during civic ceremonies while men sat on benches.[58] Although Mexican women could not vote, the Baptist women interpreted their role as Revolutionary Mexican citizens to integrate indigenous peoples into the fabric of the nation. Unión Femenil members instructed Oaxacan women to be "dignified" Christian women, emulating the middle-class mestiza Baptist women. Part of this integration meant learning Spanish, breaking from the grips of Catholicism, and ending their dependency on *curanderas*, or healers.[59]

Like many missionary organizations, the Unión Femenil representatives disapproved of traditional healing methods and favored Western-style clinics to operate in indigenous communities.[60] The representatives were particularly horrified by the Zapotec practice of searching for a child's *alma* (soul) if she became ill, the "peculiar" practice of feeding a hard-boiled egg to an infant stricken by *mal de ojo* (evil eye), and preserving umbilical cords in healing ceremonies.[61] The Unión Femenil newsletter described the practice:

> When a child gets sick and naturally is weak and sad, they say: the soul has already left the child, and then they start thinking and investigating about how the soul might have gotten kicked out by a bang or maybe frightened away by a startle. Once they have found the site, they clear it out and clean it, decorating it with flowers and put in the center of it a pot with water and flowers. Once all of this has been arranged, they bring the child there and sing to him until he falls asleep in the arms of his mother. Later they lay the child down on the ground, placing the pot with water and the flowers near the child's head. A new pitcher, this one is broken on top of a large rock prepared for the effect, producing a strong noise that makes the child wake up, very frightened. Then the mother in a loud voice in Zapotec says: "Let's go, let's go child, to the house," and saying this, she hits the ground with the palm of her right hand and, taking the child by his feet, hangs him over the pot that has the water and

flowers. After this strange ceremony, she takes the child in her arms and gives him a boiled egg to eat without letting a piece of egg fall.[62]

The newsletter concluded that Zapotec mothers "almost always prefer their remedies or visit witches or healers, than accept the services of a doctor."[63] In other words, the northern Mexican Baptist women, like the nascent Mexican government's health outreach programs, did not trust traditional health remedies in Zapotec communities. The closing line of the article perhaps best exemplifies the Unión Femenil's aspirations for indigenous Mexico: "We wish that Christ blesses work with the Indians, so that, illuminated by the Gospel, the Indians can raise themselves up, dignified by better luck, free of the fanaticism and ignorance that drowns them in misery."[64] Like their male counterparts, the Unión Femenil viewed the residents of Tlacochahuaya as dual victims of Catholicism and their indigenous heritage. For the mestiza women, indigenous Mexicans needed their spiritual and educational guidance to progress. Revitalizing or preserving their present culture(s) was not an option.

The mestizo/indígena binary was not only a geographic northern/southern one but also a gendered one: Mestizos played the dominant, sanctioned male role and indigenous peoples played the subordinate, unsanctioned female role. Mestiza women from northern and central Mexico viewed indigenous Mexico as weak and childlike, much like the original Spanish colonizers saw indigenous peoples. Spanish colonizers viewed Native religious traditions as weak, feminine, and sacrilegious and the Catholic religion as the powerful, masculine, and sacred opposite.[65] In the case of the construction of the Tlacochahuaya Baptist chapel, it was the northern mestizo men, A. R. Cavazos and Ernesto Urigas, who assured CNBM members that they had intervened and made sure the construction work was carried out efficiently.

His first church built with the help of the Unión Femenil, Juárez García cast his eye to the Zapotec coastal region of Oaxaca and even Mayan Chiapas. The missionary asked for more funding to expand his missionary territory and to purchase a horse. He mentioned that, in addition to the bicycles and ox teams that he and his assistants utilized, another horse would allow them to reach more remote areas. His request was granted, but his superiors in the Baptist Convention reflected over how unrealistic the convention's original timeline was for evangelical conversion in Oaxaca. Missionary president Moisés Arévalo concluded in October 1926: "The general perspective of the work in the Zapotec region is good. But it demands patience and steadiness so that it may work actively, although the results achieved will be very slow. But remember it is promised in the Holy Word that these works of the faithful are not done in vain."[66] The northern Baptists, mostly mestizos visiting "Indian country" for the first time, underestimated the strongly woven cultural norms and social organization in Oaxacan communities.

Relations with the Presbyterian Church

Juárez García turned his focus to the Isthmus of Tehuantepec and Juchitán, coastal Zapotec regions hundreds of miles away where he longed to proselytize.[67] However, the missionary's goals competed with nascent Presbyterian evangelization projects in neighboring Chiapas. Presbyterians had been in Oaxaca since the Plan de Cincinnati granted them jurisdiction in Chiapas and Oaxaca in 1914, replacing the Methodists.[68] On August 16, 1923, Presbyterian missionary Lawrence Van Slyke remarked that his own mission site in the Zapotec community Yatzachi in the Sierra Norte was making considerable progress. However, he lamented that, as much as he tried to learn Zapotec, he was unable to carry on a conversation in the language, making it difficult to connect with villagers: "No well-trained Indian has as yet, in our own field, gone back to his people with the Gospel."[69]

Presbyterians were keenly aware that they lacked a seminary-trained native Zapotec speaker in the Central Valleys. Van Slyke was, however, quick to report that Juárez García had not accomplished as much as he should have because of a lack of guidance from his Baptist superiors. Van Slyke concluded: "At the same time, his work has been far better than nothing.... We feel that the training of young Indian men to be the teachers of their people is a vital part of the program of evangelization, but we do not feel that it alone, with occasional visitations from the missionary, would be at all adequate."[70] The Presbyterian minister recognized the importance of having a Native missionary similar in skill to the Baptist Juárez García. However, Van Slyke did not want to repeat the practice of Catholic Dominican friars in the sixteenth century who brought the Gospel to remote Zapotec communities like Yatzachi and then could not serve them.

A competition over Chiapas in the late 1920s soon led to conflicts between the Presbyterians and Baptists. In spring of 1927, Juárez García headed to Chiapas to establish a Baptist network in Mayan communities. He had the backing of the General Missionary Board and expressed excitement about reaching a new region. During a weeklong journey by horse to the isthmus—the much-anticipated train line never materialized—García distributed Bibles and met with Zapotec *creyentes* (believers) in San Bartolo Coyotepec, Ocotlán, Tehuantepec, and Juchitán. He distributed over fifty thousand pages of Protestant pamphlets and sold eleven Bibles and five New Testaments.[71] Upon hearing about Baptists in Chiapas, he visited Tapachula, a city near the border of Guatemala. However, Juárez García described difficulties with the already established Presbyterian Church.[72] The Presbyterian authorities accused him of poaching their congregants and of not seeking permission to visit their jurisdiction. The Presbyterian publication in Mexico, *El Nuevo Faro*, wrote a scathing denunciation of Juárez García's visit to Chiapas. Juárez García responded by accusing the Presbyterian missionaries of not honoring the Lord's command to "Go into all the World and Preach his Gospel, (Mark 16.15)."[73] Juárez García further lamented that, instead of working together as Evangelicals, the Presbyterians treated his Baptist team as the enemy.[74] Juárez García returned to the Central Valleys of Oaxaca, eventually becoming a postmaster in Tlacochahuaya.

The Presbyterian/Baptist rivalry fits into the transnational struggle over Protestantism. Competition was not always between Catholics and Protestants but also between different Protestant denominations. Despite the allegedly firm Plan de Cincinnati that divided Mexico between the different Protestant missionary organizations, Baptists wanted to penetrate into Chiapas, historically Presbyterian territory. In an increasingly competitive religious marketplace, Protestant denominations had to work hard to protect their territories much like Franciscans, Dominicans, and Augustinians competing for prime mission zones in sixteenth-century Mexico.[75]

Protestantism and Political Violence

Agrarianism, nationalism, and anticlericalism were at the heart of the 1917 Mexican Constitution. The document laid out the nation's bold new relationship with the Catholic Church, hacendados (large landholders), and foreign companies. The revolutionary government sought to unite Mexico through an emphasis on civic education and allegiance to the state, not to the Roman Catholic Church. Although President Álvaro Obregón (1920–1924) only superficially challenged the Catholic Church, President Plutarco Elías Calles (1924–1928) sought to create a new revolutionary civil religion.[76] In July 1926, he issued a decree, the "Calles Law," that strengthened the Constitution's anticlerical provisions by enforcing financial and legal penalties against clergy who wore religious garb in public or criticized the government. Calles asserted that Mexico's only option for the future was to be secular and progressive, not reactionary and fanatical. Calles declared: "Drought must be countered by prudent public works, not parading saints around parched fields."[77]

In reaction to the Calles Law, the Mexican national episcopate voted to go on strike and suspend all masses and sacraments beginning on July 31, 1926.[78] In defense of the Church, Catholic peasants shouted "¡Viva Cristo Rey!" (Long live Christ the King!) and fought the federal army in a three-year civil war. Ninety thousand Mexican soldiers, cristeros, and civilians lost their lives during the Cristiada rebellion.[79] US ambassador Dwight Morrow mediated a compromise between the Church and the State in 1929, but religious violence stemming from the anticlerical Constitution continued well into the 1930s. In 2000, Pope John Paul II canonized as martyrs twenty-five Catholic priests who were executed during the Cristiada for their commitment to religious freedom in Mexico.[80]

While religious conflicts during the 1920s in Oaxaca paled in comparison to the Cristero violence in central Mexico, the 1930s were especially volatile in Oaxaca.[81] As was the trend at the federal level, the Oaxacan government welcomed Protestant organizations as a means of modernizing and incorporating Oaxaca's sixteen distinct indigenous groupings.[82] However, such governmental involvement led to Protestants and Catholics engaging in often violent interactions in their claim to indigenous souls. Violence also led to constructions of martyrdom, particularly in the case of Juárez García.

Oaxacan governor Anastasio García Toledo (1932–1936) closely followed Calles's model for limiting the Catholic Church's authority.[83] For its part, the Oaxacan archdiocese was careful to encourage nonviolent resistance in Oaxaca. The archdiocese, led by Archbishop José Othón Núñez y Zárate, was adamant that Catholics use legal channels and nonviolence to protest the Calles Law. This resistance did not stop government inventories of everything from how many pews the building had to whether the chalices were made of real gold. Priests had to hand over the keys to the church to the local authorities because these structures and land were now property of the nation.[84]

The Confederación Oaxaqueña de Campesinos (COC) was an agrarian group particularly concerned with making sure the Catholic Church followed such anticlerical provisions of the Constitution. In October 1934, the COC fined San Agustín Etla priest Ramón Ramírez de Aguilar five hundred pesos for allowing additional priests to operate in his parish, violating the strict clergy quota in the state of Oaxaca.[85] During the late 1920s and the early 1930s, Archbishop Núñez y Zárate was expelled from Oaxaca several times because of his nonconformity with state restrictions on clergy ratios and church closings.[86]

The Catholic archdiocese was also concerned with the growth of Protestantism in Oaxaca. Throughout the 1920s and 1930s, the archdiocese's monthly *Boletín Oficial* warned its readers to be cautious of the "amistoso" (friendly) Protestant missionaries, especially since their churches could have links to socialist-influenced schools in Oaxaca. Archbishop Núñez y Zárate closed his pastoral letter by warning all parents not to let their children accept gifts such as Bibles, pencils, or candies from Protestant missionaries.[87]

Tlacochahuayan Protestants were active supporters of agrarian and educational reform policies. Protestants there participated in the burning of images of saints and demanding an audit of the Catholic Church's inventory. But on September 19, 1923, Archbishop Núñez y Zárate visited Tlacochahuaya, declaring: "Despite the farcical attempts by the Protestants to convert the town, they've failed to do so, because the residents still strongly practice the faith bestowed upon them by their elders."[88] Sometimes this faith led to violence.

A series of violent conflicts between Catholics and Protestants impeded Baptist growth just after the Tlacochahuayan chapel was completed.[89] One of Juárez García's earliest converts, Eliseo Manzano argued that Juárez García infuriated local Catholics in the late 1920s by inviting Protestants from neighboring towns and cities to visit his home and admire the new church. Manzano added that, while Father Ignacio Morales had good-naturedly engaged Juárez García in theological discussion during the early 1920s, by 1928, a new priest with less tolerance for Protestantism and certainly opposed to the anticlericalism of the Cristiada period arrived. Father Enrique López was suspicious of Juárez García's activities and complained to the Archdiocese of Oaxaca about the spread of Protestantism in his town.[90] Elvira Cruz García, one of the eldest surviving Baptists in Tlacochahuaya, recalled the local religious roots of the conflict. "Everything was fine until, I'm not sure exactly what year, a priest arrived, and this priest began to provoke disturbances here. He began to fill people's heads with ideas like they shouldn't be friends with Samuel García."[91]

The conflict between Catholics and Protestants was the frequent subject of local newspaper accounts and petitions sent to local, state, and federal authorities. In Tlacochahuaya, this religious conflict also broke down along political lines. The Protestants identified themselves as *agraristas*, supporters of President Lázaro Cárdenas's bold land-distribution program, while Catholics opposed such legislation, arguing that it resembled socialism. This conflict is readily apparent in Tlacochahuaya. According to Catholics, Tlacochahuaya's evangelical preacher, Samuel Juárez García, "provoked prejudice and attracted adversaries."[92] Manzano's simple explanation that Father López felt threatened by the competition from the charismatic Protestant minister's presence in the town and, therefore, asked Catholics to murder him is insufficient. There was more than a decade-long buildup of tensions between Catholics and Protestants, the latter of whom often supported the implementation of revolutionary education in Cardenista Oaxaca.[93]

By 1934, Juárez García was a prominent missionary in the state known throughout the Sierra Juárez and beyond, making him a potential target for violence between religious groups. He was also the local postmaster and a card-carrying Mason in Oaxaca City. Given the Masons' general criticism of Catholicism, it is not surprising that Protestant conversion would sometimes concomitantly include joining a Mason temple.[94] Above all, he was a staunch supporter of Cardenista land reform projects. While his religion was certainly an important factor, his death also points to the connection between Protestantism and prorevolutionary ideologies that were an anathema to traditionally Catholic communities.

In the fall of 1934, Damián Ángeles, leader of the town's Catholic Association, was shot six times in the back as he worked in his garlic field.[95] With assistance from Acción Católica (Catholic Action, a lay advocacy group) in Oaxaca, Catholics in Tlacochahuaya wrote letters to the district court, to Governor García Toledo, and eventually to President Lázaro Cárdenas (1934–1940) demanding an investigation of Ángeles's murder.[96] The agrarista Protestant assailants were not charged despite the Catholic pressure. Ángeles's murder was their rallying call for justice.[97]

Memory and Martyrdom

Exactly one year from the date of his murder, Catholics attended an all-night vigil mass honoring Damián Ángeles on October 4, 1935. The memorial mass concluded the weeklong celebration honoring Saint Jerome, the town's patron saint. The morning of the fourth, before dawn, a group of Catholics murdered Pastor Samuel Juárez García in his home along with five other evangélicos active in the agrarian society.[98] The murder ensured Juárez García's martyrdom for Baptists in the village. For Baptists, Juárez García's murder was religiously motivated. Catholics disagree, arguing that Juárez García's death was just another example of agrarista violence that had plagued Mexico throughout the 1920s and 1930s, thus disconnecting religion from politics. Furthermore, Catholics in Tlacochahuaya maintain that Protestant deaths in Oaxaca received more attention from authorities than Catholic ones, since the Protestants were more likely to support agrarianism. Indeed, Juárez García was a supporter of President Cárdenas's land reform policies.

Many community elders remember the deep divisions in Tlacochahuaya over agrarianism. Salomón Hernández Juárez, a Protestant and a teacher in Tlacochahuaya, was eight years old in 1935, but he remembers the divisions in the town through the stories his father and uncles told him.

> Back then, the municipal authorities were influenced by the *ejidatarios*, the *agraristas*, let's call them, that's what they were called back then, no? The town divided into two sectors. Starting in 1928, the division started and it lasted until 1935 when the popular sector killed Samuel. The town was already divided, and there was already a popular and an agrarian sector; that's how they identified. That's why I believe that Samuel was killed unjustly.[99]

Similarly, Elvira Cruz García was only two years old at the time of the minister's murder, but she remembers her mother telling her about the morning of October 5, 1935: "What happened there, I know about it because of my mother; my mother went to the molino de nixtamal [corn mill] that morning."[100] Cruz García said her mother waited at dawn to use Juárez García's mechanized corn mill, but no one answered the door. Seconds later, a group of men and women rushed out of the house, slamming the door. Cruz García alleges that one of the Catholic women smashed Samuel Juárez García's head with a metate (flat grinding stone) after he was already wounded from shots to his chest, leaving a stain of blood on the wall behind him. "The woman grabbed the metate . . . and she goes over and she hits him, she hit him on the head with the metate, resulting in the late Samuel's brains gushing out all over the wall."[101] She said the stain on the wall is still there today.

> What happened the year they killed Samuel is very, how shall I put it, well remembered. So, there where he fell against the piles of corn, they beat him in the head and then his brain stained the wall behind him. And it doesn't matter how many times they tried to remove the stain, it has never disappeared. My father-in-law was doing some maintenance on that house. And in that room, said my father-in-law, he's said it several times, it's been painted and repainted but the stain never was removed. That's why I say that the blood is still demanding justice.[102]

In Cruz García's interview, memory is social and shared. She knows what happened because of oral tradition passed down from her mother and her father-in-law.

Additionally, Cruz García's emphasis that Catholic women were involved in Juárez García's murder provides insight into the intersection of gender, religion, and tradition. Cruz García's narrative suggests that the Catholic women transgressed proper gender roles by taking part in the murder. The fact that the assailant used a traditional and laborious domestic tool to engage in violence contrasts sharply with Cruz García's mother, who was waiting patiently outside to grind her corn into tortilla masa (dough) using Juárez García's more efficient, mechanized appliance. Indeed, the Agrarian Department under President Cárdenas promoted the *molino de nixtamal* as a means to eradicate the "shameful slavery" rural women endured each day grinding kernels.[103] In a sense, the Catholic women were smashing modernization introduced by town native Juárez García, who as a Protestant, educated, Spanish-speaker and local postmaster epitomized the accomplishments of the Revolution. Elvira Cruz García's professional training as a nurse in northern Mexico is also significant. "Well, back then there wasn't anyone around [in Tlacochahuaya] who knew how to inject medication, so I would do all the injections. I would go all over town attending to people." Cruz García recalled that ironically she was the one who decades later cared for the Catholic woman assailant when she was dying.

The state government intervened and initiated an investigation into Juárez García's murder; seven suspects were arraigned in the district seat at Tlacolula. Federal soldiers occupied Tlacochahuaya for several months and collected all firearms. Acknowledging Juárez García's dedication as postmaster, Oaxacan governor García Toledo approved Juárez García for a government-funded burial with honor in Oaxaca City's civic cemetery.[104] As a result of Juárez García's death and continued tensions in the community between Catholics and Protestants, the National Baptist Convention abandoned its missionary work in Tlacochahuaya for several decades.[105]

Historical Memory

Elvira Cruz García has been at the forefront of the Baptist Church's efforts to depict Samuel Juárez García as a crucial indigenous Protestant martyr for Mexico, thus doubly inscribed as a martyr by religion and national identity given his political stance on agrarianism.[106] When she describes his death, she always associates Juárez García with images of corn, collapsing in his home with stalks of corn surrounding him as if he blended into the corn and returned to the earth. It is significant that he falls onto corn stalks, back into the earth, which has ties to Christianity and pre-Hispanic sacredness. As the Baptists in town struggle to rebuild his church, Cruz García's belief that the minister's blood is still clamoring for justice suggests that she interprets his death as martyrdom for religious freedom in her town.[107] It also suggests a blending of indigenous and Baptist beliefs.

Such imagery is similar to the symbolism surrounding the 1919 murder of Revolutionary leader Emiliano Zapata, whose push for agrarian reform became the embodiment of Article 27 of the Constitution. Discussing the 1910 Zapatista Revolution in the context of the recent 1994 Zapatista uprising in neighboring Chiapas, one Oaxacan Zapotec woman stated in 1995: "Zapata saw the suffering of the peasants.... That is why he died."[108] During the 1930s agrarian movement that Juárez García supported, President Cárdenas and the Ministry of Education had appropriated Zapata as a symbol of the national government. As historian Mary Kay Vaughan explains: "When the SEP constructed Zapata as a hero, they sanitized him. He did not drink, womanize, or gamble, nor did he carry the banner of the Virgin of Guadalupe."[109] Such imagery and symbolism creates martyrs out of both Zapata and Juárez García on national, indigenous, and religious levels. Zapata's "sanitized" values and Christlike sacrifices mirror those that Protestants were trying to emulate. Such values are examples of respectable masculinity used to encourage men to abstain from Catholic traditions and convert to Protestantism.[110] Thus, Cruz García's description of the former minister's death straddles Protestant, indigenous, and patriotic identities.

Was Cruz García's description of Pastor Samuel Juárez García's the dominant narrative or was it contested? Catholics in Tlacochahuaya insist that the focus on Juárez García's religion obfuscates agrarian violence in which they also lost family members. In fact, Catholics contest the suggestion of religious persecution as a reason for Juárez García's death and its impact on the community. For example, Catholic Carlos Martínez has a very different perspective on religious conflict in Tlacochahuaya and offers insight into current problems with Protestants not contributing to community fiestas. Martínez, who was thirteen years old in 1935, recalled that many Tlacochahuayans (Catholic and Protestant) fled the town and sought refuge in Oaxaca City or relocated to Mexico City during this time. His family left for six months out of fear there would be more violence in retribution for Juárez García's murder. Martínez recalled:

> The Protestants used to call us owls because we'd go to mass very early, before dawn. In the 1930s, they began to burn images of the saints....
> I remember when the Catholics did their religious processions, the Protestants tried to offend the Catholics on the day of San Jerónimo

[town patron saint], September 30th. They began to march and collect images of the saints to burn. They would shout, "Here goes another one!" I ask you if this is evidence of progress and intelligence for our town? We [the Catholics] were not agraristas because we didn't want to be such loudmouths. However, the funny thing is that although they [Protestants] say that Catholics are friends of the devil because we drink, they have no problem accepting mescal in a party if it's free. But, they won't give any money [toward a festivity] because they hide behind their religion.[111]

Martínez, like many Catholics in his town, interprets Protestant opposition to traditional rituals or customs as politically and financially, not religiously, motivated. By asserting that Catholics did not want to be such loudmouths [*tan habladores*], Martínez is also implying that the Protestants were all talk and no action. Finally, he also elucidates the conflict at the core of religious conflicts in Oaxacan Native communities today. Protestants tend to promote individualism instead of collective identity by abstaining from the town's patron saint day fiesta.[112]

Martínez's interview raises important questions about the relationship between traditional notions of respectable masculinity and Protestantism in indigenous communities. Religious conversion created a different set of problems for closely knit communities.[113] For example, what is the impact of Protestantism on the annual patron saint fiesta, participation in nonremunerated tequio (communal work) projects, and fulfillment of a cargo (civil-religious hierarchy) position, all concepts that Zapotec Catholics argue are key components of communal identity? New converts, as Martínez's interview suggests, chose not to participate consistently or at all in the fiesta system. In contrast, Protestants argue that many of the community rituals involved alcohol and dancing and that the collective labor projects served the Catholic churches where they no longer worshiped. Religious conflicts continued to invoke these same focal points—especially collective labor projects and participation in fiestas—that were closely associated with indigenous identity.

After Juárez García's death, his church remained empty for almost eighty years. His followers worshiped in their homes or traveled to Oaxaca City to attend services at other churches. Today, Baptist men and women in Tlacochahuaya are working to revitalize Juárez García's legacy by rebuilding his church and presenting his murder as a central example of Protestant martyrdom in Oaxaca. School curriculums only recently started teaching about the Cristiada rebellion and the execution of Catholic clergy who refused to abide by the federal restrictions on public displays of religion in the late 1920s.[114] Protestants want to be a part of this history of struggle for religious freedom but not in opposition to the state; rather, they feel that they helped advance the cultural benefits of the 1910 Revolution by bringing literacy, health care, and freedom from the "yoke" of Catholicism. This narrative breaks from the official Catholic story of twentieth-century martyrdom in Mexico that tends to focus on the Jesuits and other priests killed in Central Western Mexico between 1926 and 1929. Protestant narrative also competes with colonial-era indigenous martyrs from the Sierra Norte who died defending Catholic missionaries.[115]

It is also significant that Cruz García focuses on the concept of martyrdom—often thought of as an intimately Catholic saints' theme—in her memories of the deceased pastor. Like late nineteenth-century missionary Melinda Rankin who reminded Protestants to "take up the banner of the fallen Stephen," Cruz García is advancing the story of Samuel Juárez García's murder and restoring his church as a means to integrate Baptist history in the historical narrative. In a region like Oaxaca with a rich colonial history, the Catholic sacred sites stand out: the shrine to the Virgin Mary in Juquila, the Dominican convent where Independence leader José María Morelos was executed, or, more important, Tlacochahuaya's sixteenth-century Dominican church, which still maintains its original murals made from the Oaxacan cochineal dye.

To begin revitalizing Baptists' century-long history in Oaxaca, Tlacochahuayan Baptists are trying to have the church recognized as a historic site through the Instituto Nacional de Antropología e Historia (INAH). Elvira Cruz García and her extended family are actively working with the Convención Nacional Bautista to renovate the church—now overgrown with weeds and on the verge of collapsing—and celebrate services on the original site (figs. 8 and 9). Yet as of 2018 they remain embroiled in a lawsuit over the boundaries of the property. As they rebuild the church and defend the original property lines, the Tlacochahuayan Baptists have received visits from US- and Mexico City–based missionary organizations.

Figure 8. Remains of the original Baptist church of Tlacochahuaya, 2010. Photograph by author.

Conclusion

Zapotec Baptists are forming a history that asserts their claims to martyrdom and patriotism. The abandoned 1926 church is a testament to Protestants' contested history in the community. The mantels in their homes showcase old photographs from Juárez García's ministry in Tlacochahuaya arranged carefully between vases of flowers, similar to a Catholic home altar but missing the Virgin of Guadalupe and patron saints. As Lynn Abrams elucidates, "Historical memory is a memory (or a representation) of a past that is lost, whereas collective memory is anchored in the social group that actively preserves and reinterprets that past via the consciousness of those who are still alive."[116] Cruz García was not present when the Baptist minister was murdered, yet the shared collective memory of his church's history lived on so strongly in her family that she felt an intimate connection. Abrams suggests that shared collective memory can have "such a powerful impact on those growing up within it that they have adopted the memories as their own and seek to ensure that these memories (and the victims) are not forgotten."[117] In Tlacochahuaya, Baptist Protestant memory is straddling both the collective and historical realms. Yet this memory is also gendered; Cruz García focuses her narrative on a description of how women participated in the murder of the Baptist minister. She also affirms that she knows what happened because her mother shared this story with her. Cruz García acts as a protector of the Baptist church's intimate but contested memory in the community, yet she also enters the legal realm of the Oaxaca City court system to regain the original territory owned by the Baptist Church in 1926.

Northern Mexican Baptist missionary women interpreted Zapotec culture and gender norms as frustrating obstacles in attaining dual (and at times competing) Mexican/Christian identities. The women uniformly viewed Zapotecs as "subjugated by idolatry and ignorance." Similar to the goals of public school teachers, social workers, and activists in postrevolutionary Mexico, Protestant women sought to bring the tenets of the Mexican Revolution to Native communities. The Unión Femenil members saw it as their duty as more "fortunate sisters" to introduce Protestantism to indigenous Mexico. Baptist women sought to "dignify" the lives of their Zapotec "sisters" by emphasizing the moral autonomy and basic civil rights Zapotec women lacked in Tlacochahuaya.

Eighty years later, Zapotec Baptist Elvira Cruz García argues that Protestantism brought progress to her town; however, she maintains that her family has been able to negotiate Protestant values with Zapotec traditions. Practicing "respectable masculinity" by not drinking, gambling, or engaging in domestic violence was an important set of values Protestant missionaries and postrevolutionary administrations promoted. Her husband, as a regidor (town delegate) and later municipal president, took part in local festivities, but he offered atole (a traditional corn-based beverage) and tamales at his house during the town's feast day, never alcohol. Cruz García contends that Baptist congregants still participate in tequio and have maintained fluency in the Zapotec language.[118] Her family, in a sense, generated their own space for and their own conceptualization of Protestant indigenous identity.

In southern Mexico where Catholic images are ubiquitous in colorful public murals, in sixteenth-century Dominican cathedrals, and on plastic

Figure 9. Elvira Cruz García sitting behind the original Tlacochahuaya Baptist Church, 2010. Photograph by author.

Figure 10. Aurora and Salomón Hernández Juárez holding framed picture of Samuel Juárez García. Photograph by author.

market bags, *lucha libre* (wrestling) masks, belt buckles, and home altars, the religious battle lines in Oaxaca are symbolically drawn over worship of the Virgin and the patron saint celebrations. For Protestants, the Virgin of Guadalupe (or the Virgin of Juquila or La Soledad) is not their brown mother but merely a tool of conquest whose entrenched presence in Oaxacan homes and worship sites is dangerous and blasphemous, a product of colonialism and fanaticism. Instead, in Protestant homes, businesses, and churches, President Benito Juárez is presented as a spiritual father, while missionaries, especially Native ones like Samuel Juárez García, are revered as the fruition of his liberal Reform-period legislation further strengthened by the 1917 constitutional limits on the Catholic Church's authority.

While the 1926–1929 Catholic Cristero rebellion against the federal government is the central narrative of twentieth-century Mexican martyrdom, Protestant Mexicans want to insert their stories into the historical record. Postrevolutionary Zapotec Baptists attempted to create their own sacred space and sense of community, which in turn affected new social organization and identity in Tlacochahuaya. The imagery surrounding Samuel Juárez García's death links Baptists in the community to an indigenous, Christian, and Mexican narrative that transcends their community and connects them with a larger narrative of martyrdom and patriotism. Juárez García's missionary work demonstrates the intersection of nationalism, gender, ethnic identities, tradition, and memory.

CHAPTER THREE

Contested Spaces

Local Conflicts, CONEDEF, and the Mexican State

IN A MAY 1958 telegram to Oaxacan governor Alfonso Pérez Gasca, Cuicatlán Catholics expressed their disapproval of the state's inquiry into a local dispute. Catholic leader Arturo Rivera proclaimed: "The entirely Catholic population of Cuicatlán categorically objects to the new Protestant Church being constructed here."[1] The highly charged language in this message provides insight into the religious attitudes among Cuicatlán residents. From the Catholics' point of view, Cuicatlán had one religion. Protestantism was an unwelcome addition. The letter also implies that indigenous communities such as Cuicatlán had a history and familiarity with negotiating with the state government. That is to say, Mazatecan communities still maintained some political autonomy and often negotiated with the state regarding local rule. Additionally, the use of the telegram suggested decent communication between the peripheral district of Cuicatlán and the state capital.[2]

Cuicatlán was not a new site for Protestant evangelization. Methodist missionary Lucius C. Smith had started a school in the community and had visited various villages in the district back in the 1890s. Methodist and Presbyterian missionaries swapped geographic regions in 1914 in an agreement called the Plan de Cincinnati. By the final years of the Revolution, it was the Presbyterian Church who had missionary jurisdiction over Oaxaca, while the Methodists moved to northern Mexico.[3] Protestants in the district would use this history to anchor their faith's historical presence in the region.

This chapter examines the extent of legal leverage local communities had had over the state. Throughout the 1950s and 1960s, Oaxacan communities like Cuicatlán challenged state and federal laws on religious freedom by arguing that "en el pueblo, la costumbre es ley [in the town, custom is law]." Indigenous Catholics framed their objection to a new Protestant church building by arguing that tradition trumped individual rights. Article 24 of the 1917 Mexican Constitution guaranteed freedom of religion, but local authorities argued that community cohesion and ancient tradition trumped ephemeral laws.

The friction between customary and constitutional laws is apparent in many of these conflicts; tradition and communal cohesion outweighed minority religious rights. This chapter describes the different strategies Catholic majorities used to oppose Protestant incursion in the districts of Cuicatlán, Tlaxiaco, and Pochutla that emphasize the strength of local traditions over religious choice. This chapter also focuses on the networking movements Protestant converts utilized to publicize their lack of religious freedom in Oaxaca. Despite the intervention of national pro-Protestant organizations, decisions involving religious conflicts were still made at the local level.

Mirroring the trend at the federal level, the Oaxacan government tolerated Protestant organizations as a means of modernizing and incorporating Oaxaca's sixteen distinct indigenous groupings. Despite these openings at the state and national levels, religious conflicts remained a problem in Oaxaca. Many conflicts echoed the local criticism of Protestantism in Oaxaca that these new religions would divide and weaken indigenous communities. Although articulated in contrasting ways, the following case studies demonstrate that opponents to Protestantism used collective rights to prohibit the penetration of Protestant missionaries, churches, and influence in predominantly Catholic communities. Local custom and regional identity were central to Catholic prioritization of collective rights in indigenous communities over the individual rights of Oaxacan Protestants. Despite the intervention of national Protestant organizations and the federal government, religious conflict was still very much a local issue that reflected community power dynamics. At times, this collective rights defense engaged Catholic and Protestant Oaxacans in complex and competing webs of articulations of indigenous and Mexican identities.

CONEDEF

Protestant Oaxacans sought and received legal support from national organizations. Many Oaxacan Protestants benefited from the legal support of a powerfully connected evangelical movement. Founded in 1948, the Comité Nacional Evangélico de Defensa's (National Evangelical Defense Committee, CONEDEF) foundational statement called on its members to publicly demand justice and freedom of conscience for Protestants. The Mexico City-based organization modeled itself in the spirit of Oaxaca native Benito Juárez's 1857 religious reforms.[4] This coalition of Protestant pastors and attorneys strategically marketed Protestantism as an extension of Mexican nationalism. The committee frequently argued that Catholicism was a vestige of Spanish colonialism that held Mexico back, while Protestantism supported the goals of the 1910 Revolution and, hence, Mexico's future. CONEDEF was particularly effective in advancing Protestants' rights in indigenous communities.[5]

The 1950s were an important decade for Protestant religious freedom in Mexico.[6] During the presidency of Adolfo Ruiz Cortines (1952–1958), the Mexican government publicly intervened in cases of religious intolerance, most notably the 1953 Protestant-Catholic conflict over a new Iglesia de Dios (Church of God) building in Tepeji del Río, Hidalgo. In Tepeji, about nine hundred employees at a local textile factory destroyed the new Protestant church in the town and went on strike with the demand that the five Protestant employees at the factory be fired.[7] This intervention was a watershed moment for Mexico's minority Protestant population. The government responded immediately with federal troops to protect Protestants, a marked contrast to the delayed reactions of Presidents Manuel Ávila Camacho (1940–1946) and Miguel Alemán Valdés (1946–1952).[8] Ruiz Cortines's intervention meant that "the free hand that anti-Protestants had enjoyed . . . was finally being checked."[9] This action encouraged Protestant congregations to apply for more church permits, since Ruiz Cortines's Ministry of the Interior more efficiently approved applications for new Protestant churches.[10] President Adolfo López Mateos (1958–1964) continued Cortines's protection of Protestantism by also intervening in cases of religious intolerance. Notably, López Mateos's wife, Eva Sámano de López Mateos, a Methodist, took the lead in intervening in several religious intolerance cases around Mexico, including in Oaxaca.[11] Toleration of Protestantism dovetailed with López Mateos's agenda for modernizing rural Mexico through new social and educational programs.

Between 1957 and 1960, CONEDEF intervened in twelve conflicts in Oaxaca.[12] CONEDEF's process in highlighting a case of intolerance started with a direct letter written to the local municipal president reminding him of the religious freedom guaranteed in Article 24. In fact, the organization's very own letterhead included in its margin the full text of Article 24. The notice was usually copied to a local Protestant leader and the state governor's office. In each letter addressed to the municipal authorities, CONEDEF reminded the mayor that it was, for example, illegal to threaten to cut off Protestants' water or electricity if the Protestants chose not to pay toward a fiesta or contribute labor to a tequio assignment. If a particular case did not get addressed right away, CONEDEF used Mexico City government officials to pressure the Oaxacan governor's office.

In one prolonged conflict in the Juchitán municipality along the Zapotec isthmus, CONEDEF president Agapito Ramos Ramírez followed up on a case in the village of Santa María del Mar in which an evangelical minority group refused to donate funds toward the annual fiesta. As a result, the evangelicals were fined and their animals were denied access to communal grazing land, causing one bull to die. In response to hermano Narciso Toledo's incarceration for not supporting Catholic rituals, Ramos Ramírez stated in a March 27, 1957, letter to town mayor Cándido Ramírez, "In a respectful but urgent manner I ask you, Mr. Mayor, to address these anomalies and suggest that you use your influence in this serious situation in a village of our beloved Homeland. If this does not happen, we will regretfully have to resort to higher powers to make sure you rectify the situation."[13]

Frustrated with the local government's failure to act, CONEDEF sought the intervention of the state government. On June 8, 1957, Agapito Ramos Ramírez wrote to Oaxacan Governor Pérez Gasca that the municipal government of Santa María del Mar "persisted in its hostile attitude toward evangelicals."[14] Ramos Ramírez reported that his attempts at mediation with Santa María del Mar municipal authorities was futile since the mayor "has declared that no one else but he is in charge, and so accordingly he has continued his abuse of individuals' Constitutional rights."[15] Ramos Ramírez went on to protest to Governor Pérez Gasca the flagrant violations of religious freedom in Mexico that Cándido Ramírez and his coauthorities were guilty of in Santa María del Mar. Later that month, the subsecretary of state government, Guillermo Martínez León, sent a copy of the governor's office memo ordering the Public Ministry of Justice to investigate the allegations against the Santa María del Mar municipal president.[16] By subordinating the Church to the state, Article 24 of the Mexican Constitution insured the authority of secular, not Catholic, authority in government. CONEDEF advocated for a stronger secular state.

CONEDEF effectively used the press to draw national awareness to abuses committed against Protestant Mexicans. Beginning in 1950, it requested and often received meetings with Mexican presidents to discuss cases of religious persecution.[17] CONEDEF also authored a column in the newsweekly *Tiempo*, a magazine founded by Mexican novelist and *El Universal* correspondent Martín Luis Guzmán in 1942. The column reported on Protestant news throughout Mexico including gruesome photographs of religious violence victims and direct passages from CONEDEF's public speeches and organizational literature. Guzmán himself often wrote editorials on Catholic "fanaticism" in Mexico including his criticism of the Church's opposition to some public-school curricula.[18]

CONEDEF framed itself as a Mexican civic organization: patriotic, well-versed in constitutional law, and in contact with key political figures in its defense of Mexican evangelicals in the press. From 1948 to this day, the organization remains in its same Mexico City location, ironically on the historic downtown avenue Isabel la Católica, named for the Spanish queen who sought to claim the "New World" for Catholicism. CONEDEF's biggest event is its annual Benito Juárez holiday rally against religious persecution of Protestants, again tying its civic and religious identity to the famous Mexican president who, while chief justice of the Mexican Supreme Court, precipitated the War of La Reforma (1858–1861) over his determination to curb the Catholic Church's privileges (fig. 11).

El Divino Pastor, Cuicatlán

A religious conflict in Cuicatlán provides a compelling example of the contested nature of religious spaces in Oaxacan indigenous communities.

Figure 11. Online poster advertising CONEDEF's Benito Juárez Day Rally in Mexico City on March 21, 2011. Source: Noticiero Milamex, March 18, 2011. Courtesy of the National Evangelical Defense Committee.

Located in the Cañada region of northern Oaxaca, Cuicatlán has a long history of Protestantism stretching back to the 1890s. Yet the process of obtaining the construction permit for a new church, El Divino Pastor National Presbyterian Church, lasted for over a decade. In this conflict, CONEDEF, Presbyterian ministers in Oaxaca City, and local congregants united to advocate for the church, but not before meeting stiff resistance at the local level.

Beginning in 1946, residents of San José del Chilar, Cuicatlán District, first started petitioning the state governor for permission to offer public services for the Presbyterian faith. In a July 25, 1946, letter, Minister Manuel Donato Valencia Arriaga asked the local municipal mayor, Waldo Altamirano, to pass on his official petition to the state governor's office. Valencia used a Mexico City attorney to help him frame his demands, a practice common with Protestants in Oaxaca—seeking out Mexico City professionals to carry out the official paperwork.[19] Presbyterians had been celebrating services in a private home and now sought permission to officially open to the public. Valencia mentioned the property dimensions and exact location of the new church structure. In return, officials in Mexico City asked the municipal president of San José del Chilar how he felt about the prospect of a Protestant church opening in his town. There did not appear to be a conflict then; Mayor Altamirano forwarded Valencia's petition to the governor's office. However, the church permit process dragged on, with members carrying out religious worship at home instead of in the new church.

The major conflict began on May 12, 1958, when a group of 150 Catholics crowded into the municipal president's office and stated that they would not permit Cuicatlán to open itself to other religions.[20] Catholic Arturo Rivera asked the municipal authorities to conduct an asamblea (public meeting) to determine if a Protestant church should be built. The municipal president forwarded the Catholics' statement to the governor's office, along with a photograph of the Catholics gathered in the main plaza of Villa de Cuicatlán, ostensibly to demonstrate the large crowd of Catholics complaining.

In this example, Catholic resistance to Protestantism revolved around regional norms superseding guarantees for individuals' constitutional rights. The Cuicatlán Catholics stated in their letter to Governor Alfonso Pérez Gasca (1956–1962): "While it is certain that in Mexico there is freedom of religion of one's choosing, but in places like here where passions ignite and degenerate into violent acts, you should consider the importance of public peace."[21] The Catholic petitioners recognized that their disapproval of the church's construction might violate the individual rights of their neighbors. However, they argued that the guarantees of the Constitution did not coincide with local realities where Catholics were the majority. To bolster their position, the Catholics also gave examples of Protestant-Catholic clashes in neighboring villages that erupted into serious conflicts the previous year.[22]

Cuicatlán Presbyterians adeptly used their Protestant connections in Oaxaca City and Mexico City to effectively criticize the Oaxacan state government's slow response. On August 27, 1958, CONEDEF wrote a letter to Governor Pérez Gasca demanding that the governor investigate the permit delays for El Divino Pastor Church. Comité president Agapito Ramos Ramírez conveyed that the approval process had gone smoothly in Mexico City, but the comité was concerned about the failed permit approval implementation in Oaxaca. Ramos Ramírez insinuated that he knew that the Ministry of the Interior had already approved the permit application and that it was the Oaxacan state and local government that stood in the way of the Presbyterian church's opening.[23]

In order to follow religious worship laws properly, the Presbyterians needed a stamp of approval from the state government, who in turn relied on local authorities to report on whether the proposed church adhered to the federal religious association property guidelines.

This process seldom went smoothly. The following month, Cuicatlán public justice minister Enrique Sánchez advised the governor's office: "My belief is that the Protestant Church should not be built; the Evangelicals should continue worshiping in a private home, that way any disturbances would be avoided. . . . These conflicts can lead to bloodbaths."[24] Despite the federal approval, local authorities agreed with Catholics in Cuicatlán that the Presbyterian church should not open. Another agent from Cuicatlán's Ministry of Justice, Ricardo Pacheco Armas, worried that animosity between Protestants and Catholics would erupt in violence such as had occurred in the neighboring communities that same year.[25] Instead, Pacheco Armas advised that they hold off on granting the permit until the "passions of the fanatical" subsided.[26]

The Mexican Ministry of the Interior fielded constant complaints and pressure from CONEDEF and Oaxacan Presbyterian ministers to intervene in Cuicatlán. By November 16, 1960, Mexico City's Ministry of the Interior pressured Governor Pérez Gasca to move on the case. General Director of the Ministry of the Interior Tristan Canales Valverde reminded Governor Pérez Gasca that the case had been dragging on for two years. Pérez Gasca's office responded quickly to the Presbyterians' complaints when prodded by federal officials like Canales Valverde. Nevertheless, in 1962, the local Cuicatlán public ministers rejected the permit application. Despite federal and state approvals, local authorities took matters into their own hands to maintain peace and protect local traditions.

Like CONEDEF, the central Oaxaca City Presbyterian Church intervened when their Cuicatlán congregants did not receive the permit to build their church. Presbyterian ministers Epifanio Contreras and Saúl Velasco complained to Oaxacan governor Rodolfo Brena Torres (1962–1968) that the state government was doing little to move forward the approval of the permit for their temple. On August 21, 1964, the ministers wrote to Mexico City and Oaxaca City government officials reminding them that the Presbyterian Church had operated since 1914 (prior to that it had been Methodist) in the district of Cuicatlán without disturbances and in full accordance with

Figure 12. Iglesia Nacional Presbiteriana "San Pablo," Oaxaca City. Photograph by author.

religious conduct regulations as stipulated in the Mexican Constitution.[27] They reminded the governor that the federal government's Ministry of the Interior backed their request but was still waiting to hear back from the state office about the permit application. The ministers also threatened to appeal for assistance to the First Lady, Eva Sámano de López Mateos, who had publicly intervened in cases of Protestant persecution throughout Mexico.[28] The Oaxaca City–based Presbyterian Church ministers used their understanding of constitutional law and experience utilizing federal agencies and powerful individuals to help advance their causes.

The Presbyterians in Cuicatlán mounted evidence in favor of their church by documenting the long history of Protestantism in their community. In a collective letter to Governor Brena Torres, they stated that Protestants (first Methodists, then Presbyterians) had operated in their district since 1890. Their letter described the Protestant primary school in Cuicatlán that operated from 1900 until 1915, a school recognized by the SEP.[29] Several elderly Cuicatecos also sent the governor testimonial statements on the educational benefits they had received from the Presbyterian school.[30] The early Methodist/Presbyterian missionaries had offered literacy classes and published Spanish-Mazatecan language dictionaries. The Evangelical presence in their town, they argued, far from harming the community, had actually brought cultural advantages to Cuicatlán.[31] The Cuicatlán Protestants closed the letter by reminding Governor Pérez Gasca that they had followed the federal protocol for establishing a new church, but it still had not opened because of local opposition.

Whole Cuicatlán families had converted to Protestantism in the late nineteenth century; many were baptized as Protestants and had attended a Presbyterian school while others had organized Bible studies for decades. Now they wanted their own church. In this case, the Cuicatlán Presbyterians framed their argument historically. Protestants had operated in the district since the 1890s. They effectively countered the Catholics' argument that they were outsiders to the region or that their congregations were made up of foreigners.

In contrast, Catholics drew a connection between the growth of Protestant churches and North American influence in Mexico.[32] On June 8, 1964, a group of Catholics presented another petition in protest of the Presbyterians' construction plans. In the petition, they bluntly stated that Protestants made up just a small percentage of the village population: "The density of the population of our *cabecera* (municipal seat) is about four thousand inhabitants and as it is well known, the Evangelicals do not even number twenty individuals."[33] The Catholics argued that the new church would not be financially supported by the handful of Protestants in Cuicatlán but rather by the "Colossus of the North" and "fortified by Yankee gold." Furthermore, the Catholics complained that the Presbyterians were using Cuicatlán as a launching point for "proselytizing their beliefs in this village and in all of the towns of our district."[34] They argued that Protestantism threatened Mexican nationalism and, at the same time, hurt local identity and customs.

Community resistance to Protestantism described a regional and national identity that had no room for the new religion. The petitioners accused North American Protestants of "playing a Machiavellian divide and conquer game with Mexico."[35] The Catholics argued that Protestants were "unraveling our customs... changing our language so that it erases our nationality. The heart of our nationality is based in these three inseparable pillars. LANGUAGE, RELIGION AND OUR CUSTOMS."[36] The petitioners closed by asking the municipal president to inform state government officials about the incompatibility of these divisive "sects" in their district. The Catholic petitioners cited national heroes such as 1810 Independence leader Ignacio Allende as a symbol of Mexican nationality who fought against imperialism. By citing the heroes of Mexican Independence, the petitioners linked opposition to Protestantism with resistance to European colonialism; Protestantism was anathema to Mexican sovereignty. Protestants used the reverse argument to criticize Catholicism in Mexico; Catholics were loyal to Rome, not the nation.[37] The aforementioned Catholic and Presbyterian assertions suggest contrasting conceptualizations of Mexican national and local identity.

On August 24, 1964, the Oaxacan state office finally approved the Presbyterians' new church.[38] The Oaxacan state government informed Tristan Canales Valverde, general director of the Ministry of the Interior, that in agreement with the Governor of Oaxaca, it was appropriate to authorize Contreras and Hernández and the other residents of Cuicatlán to open the new National Presbyterian Church. In his letter authorizing the church to open in Cuicatlán, Oaxacan Secretary General Rubén Pérez Peña reminded Catholic leaders in Cuicatlán that, despite their ongoing protest, the Presbyterian church was approved. Additionally, in the letter, Pérez Peña reminded Catholic protesters that Article 24 of the Mexican Constitution guaranteed all Mexicans the right to worship freely, not just Catholics.[39] Yet, despite state and federal approvals, El Divino Pastor did not open until 1968.[40]

The Cuicatlán case illustrates the intersection of evangelical defense movements and state and federal government with conceptualizations of patriotism and the strength of collective rights. It also shows the deep complexity of Protestantism in insular indigenous villages. Furthermore, it demonstrates the persistence of local law over constitutional law as it took a decade before the church in Cuicatlán could officially open. This case also provides insight into the state and federal bureaucratic red tape that Protestants faced when trying to open a church. Ultimately, with the assistance of organized Protestant organizations, constitutional law prevailed over customary laws, but not before a protracted struggle. Cuicatlán was not a lone case. Protestants petitioning for worship spaces increasingly employed national and transnational networks in fighting for their religious identity and individual rights.

Coyula

As evident in the Cuicatlán case, Mazatecan Protestants challenged Catholic appropriations of religious space and town obligations. The coastal Zapotec town of Coyula also illustrates the role of a united Mexican Evangelical movement intervening in local religious conflicts in Oaxaca. Having key backing from national organizations bolstered Protestants' complaints of religious intolerance. What is different in the Coyula case is that Protestants also sought support from US-based churches.

The Coyula conflict began in early May 1960 when a large contingent from Acción Católica, led by the wives of the municipal officials, showed up at Protestant Fortunata Martínez's home. Martínez claimed the women threatened to physically assault her for hosting a luncheon for out-of-town evangelicals in her home. The Catholic women advised her to pack up her possessions and leave town immediately if she did not want trouble. In response, Martínez filed a complaint at the district office for violation of her constitutional rights. Additionally, Martínez contacted Felipe Sánchez Muñiz, elder director of the Interdenominational Christian Church in Mexico City, who in turn demanded a legal investigation into the matter by Oaxaca City and Mexico City government officials.[41]

Similar to the Presbyterian case in Cuicatlán, Sánchez Muñiz disputed the common Catholic assertion that Protestants were outside agents of American imperialism. He implored Governor Alfonso Pérez Gasca (1956–1962): "I am begging you, Mr. Governor, that you permit our Evangelical Brothers and Sisters to enjoy the guarantees of the Mexican Constitution that they deserve and that you instruct the aforementioned people to respect the Constitutional guarantees of these Brothers. Don't let them expel the Evangelicals from the town, a place they have lived in for many, many years."[42] By grounding his description of the Coyulan Protestants as native-born residents of a community and not foreign residents, Sánchez Muñiz challenged the municipal authorities' argument that Evangelicals were always foreigners. He stressed that Protestantism was a religious choice for indigenous peoples, not a religion imposed and controlled by outsiders.

More important, Sánchez Muñiz's letter came to the attention of CONEDEF and inspired a national campaign to protect evangelical rights and contest Catholic narratives of community space. Throughout the last week of May 1960, evangelical churches and committees all over Mexico and in parts of the US Southwest sent telegrams to Governor Pérez Gasca protesting Fortunata Martínez's expulsion from Coyula. Most telegrams asked the Oaxacan governor to intervene in Coyula and were signed by a specific Evangelical church, suggesting an organized petition that included form letters. A typical letter dated May 25, 1960, from Tampico, Tamaulipas, stated: "The Iglesia Cristiana Interdenominacional respectfully but vehemently protests the lack of rights our Christian brothers in Oaxaca are experiencing. Please guarantee their rights." Not all of the churches conformed to formulaic letters; some made more strident statements in recognizing the global perspective of religious freedom. For example, Timoteo Ortega López representing Protestant churches in Nuevo León in his May 31, 1960, telegram addressed to Governor Pérez Gasca: "The Churches of Monterrey demand justice for the Evangelicals in the town of Coyula, Pochutla. We ask you to remember Article Eighteen of the Universal Declaration of Human Rights."[43] On June 3, 1960, La Iglesia de Tlaltenco in Puebla demanded justice for the Evangelicals of Coyula Pochutla for all the abuses they had suffered."[44] These examples suggest a united Evangelical movement that, with modern technology, was able to quickly uncover and act upon allegations of repression in the nation's remote areas. Through CONEDEF's communicative alerts, they were able to swiftly organize and substantiate their demands with an advanced understanding of constitutional law.

Because of CONEDEF's campaign, Oaxacan subsecretary Martínez León reported to the Oaxacan attorney general that his office was inundated with telegrams from churches in Veracruz, Puebla, Tlaxcala, Nuevo León, and Tamaulipas soliciting guarantees for the Evangelical residents in Coyula. He recommended that the state government rapidly look into the case, as it was attracting much attention in Protestant churches throughout Mexico and in the US Southwest.[45] Martínez León preferred that the attorney general's office handle it directly and find a solution since the local Pochutla Ministry of Justice had not returned his messages.[46] The tone of Martínez León's letter hinted at his frustration with the extra work the Coyula conflict caused his office: In one day they received thirty-two protest telegrams. The state government finally did intervene the following month. On July 8, 1960, Martínez León informed the municipal president José Ortiz that he had received numerous complaints about the "unlawful attitude" of the Coyula local government, which consistently turned a blind eye toward violence against Evangelicals. Martínez León reminded the town president that, as the representative of justice in his community, he should take the time to study the Mexican Constitution.[47] If the conflict persisted and Fortunata Martínez was not allowed back into the community, the governor would send in the state police to protect the rights of Coyulan Protestants. In this case, CONEDEF's press campaign worked; national and state officials threatened to intervene in local communities if they did not uphold federal guarantees of religious freedom.

The extant documents on Coyula end here. We do not know whether Martínez returned to the community, though the firm response of the Oaxacan state administration suggests pressure from the top to respect individual rights and solve the conflict in favor of the Protestants. The Mexican Protestants' organized and widespread response to Martínez's case depicts the vigor with which they challenged Catholic community leaders' portrayal of them as outsiders. Instead, Protestants wrapped themselves in the Mexican Constitution, suggesting its long-term ramifications in local communities unprepared and sometimes unwilling to accept nationally guaranteed rights when these rights interfered with traditional notions of religious and communal space. In this case, as in many of the conflict cases, the Oaxacan state government struggled with supporting federal laws at the local level. Many communities cared little about the stipulations of the 1917 Constitution's Article 24, if they had even read the Constitution. These local authorities knew what legal codes had worked in their communities for centuries and were reluctant to change time-honored practices. They did not refuse to acknowledge their identity or responsibilities as Mexican citizens but rather had a long history of negotiating with the colonial and then Mexican governments and fighting to retain some of their traditions and political organizations.

This case also illustrates the importance of technology, such as telegrams, in organizing Evangelical Oaxacans. Mobilizing through outside networking are key resources for the success of social movements.[48] Once CONEDEF became involved, hundreds of protest telegrams from different Mexican Protestant churches poured into the Oaxacan governor's office as well as the to the Ministry of the Interior in Mexico City. Fortunata Martínez's expulsion became a rallying call for Protestants throughout Mexico and the US Southwest.

Santa María Texcatitlán

The Santa María Texcatitlán case in the Cuicatlán district further illustrates the friction between national and local law. However, this case is somewhat different in nature because it involves a newer, nonmainline Protestant organization not represented by CONEDEF. The following section will discuss one of the earliest Seventh-day Adventist conflicts in Oaxaca.

In the municipality of Santa María Texcatitlán, a group of Seventh-day Adventists formed a congregation in 1960. During their services, they accompanied religious hymns with music blasting from their speakers, often on weekdays. Local authorities declared Adventists' loud music a public nuisance. The exasperated Texcatitlán mayor Feliciano Hernández Jiménez described the Adventists as "worshiping and singing hymns all day and all night."[49] On February 10, 1963, Hernández Jiménez wrote a letter to Governor Brena Torres complaining that Adventist leader Antonio Serrano Rivas had been illegally passing out Protestant "propaganda" since 1960 and now had ten families following his "secta."[50] He said that Serrano Rivas and fellow Evangelical Pablo Castillo were "leading the majority of the town astray so that with time, they're going to dissolve the social organization of the town."[51] Hernández Jiménez asserted that the men did not have official permission to celebrate evangelical services in town, and he intended to indict them if they did not stop their worship sessions.

His letter points to the friction between local customs and constitutional law. Hernández Jiménez complained that the evangelical men did not respect his authority. He said of the Protestant leaders: "No one can stop them, not even myself, the town president, or the state government because they only care about the [federal Mexican] Political Constitution, and for no reason will they stop following their religion."[52] He closed by saying that, in his town, there were over one thousand Catholics, constituting "the absolute majority," in contrast to the handful of Protestants.[53] Again, majority rights outweighed minority religious rights in the mind of the municipal president.

Besides complaining about their proclivity for loud music, town authorities stated that Seventh-day Adventists refused to cooperate with community obligations such as tequio. In a letter to the Oaxacan secretary general's office, Hernández Jiménez described that, in addition to perplexing town residents with attacks on the Catholic Church and by not respecting local authorities, the Adventists refused to fulfill town council's cargos. "They do not show up to give labor for public works that benefit the whole community; they also convince local parents not to send their children to public school; instead their children attend the biblical schools, which they desecrate."[54] Hernández Jiménez closed his letter by pleading with the secretary general's office to deny the Adventists permission to open their church. The mayor argued that the only way that the town could go back to its tranquil disposition would be if the Adventists stopped their services.[55] The Adventist congregations were particularly controversial in Oaxacan towns because Adventists did not work on Saturdays.[56] Most tequio projects took place on Saturdays, their day of worship, which meant the Adventists refused to participate.

For their part, on March 31, 1964, the Adventists wrote a letter to the Oaxacan attorney general that was passed first to Governor Rodolfo Brena Torres and then to the Ministry of the Interior in Mexico City. The Adventist men complained that they were victims of Catholic persecution. Antonio Serrano, the Adventist leader, stated that the residents who opposed them in town utilized "religion as a powerful, invincible weapon to continuously fight us."[57] Serrano further claimed that Adventist children were treated unjustly in the local primary school because of their religion.[58] Finally, he accused leaders of the Catholic group of burning up an Adventist member's haystacks, causing eight hundred pesos' worth of damage.[59] Yet, when they went to file a complaint with the town municipal government, Mayor Hernández Jiménez refused to question the accused men. Serrano closed by asking for the Oaxacan attorney general's office to intervene and protect Adventists' rights and possessions.

It took six months before the federal government responded to the Evangelicals' request for an investigation. On September 2, 1964, Julio Patiño ordered Governor Brena Torres to conduct an investigation of Santa María Texcatitlán municipal authorities' persecution of the Evangelicals, but the conflict continued. On March 15, 1965, Mayor Hernández Jiménez complained to the public minister of justice in Cuicatlán that despite the investigation ordered by the federal government, the Adventists still did not have Oaxacan state or local permission for the new church. Hernández Jiménez hinted that the Cuicatlán public minister of justice could enforce local law: "Since these men do not have the respective permit from the Oaxacan State

Government, order them to cease worshiping and spreading Evangelical sect propaganda inside our town."[60] This was a challenging premise for the Adventists. Their application for an official church permit had been approved at the federal level but was delayed at the state level. If they continued holding services at the church, they would be violating state and local law. If they held services in private homes, they were in violation of Article 24, which prohibited worship outside of church buildings except for occasional preapproved events.

Texcatitlán mayor Hernández Jiménez tried to use the state office to limit the Adventists' actions. He warned that trouble would erupt if he did not receive help from state authorities in keeping peace between the Catholics and the Adventists. The federal and state officials' delay in backing the Adventists' persecution claims resulted in a legal stalemate in which all parties claimed the law was on their side. Mayor Hernández Jiménez won in the short term. The federal government backed the Adventists' application to open their church, but, because the state government sat on the case so long, the Adventists' church building was in disuse throughout the waiting period. Without the backing of a powerful defense movement or connections in Mexico City, it was difficult for Adventists to receive their permit in a timely fashion.

Yolotepec, Yosondúa

Unlike the case in Coyula, the use of the national press did not always bring success. Despite headlines in Mexico City dailies on violence in the Mixteca region, Presbyterian Bartolo Hernández López did not receive permission to hold worship sessions in his home or in a neighborhood church he helped build. The Yolotepec case follows a similar argument used by local authorities as seen with the Adventists in Santa María Texcatitlán that converts used their new religions as an excuse not to participate in collective projects that benefited the whole community. It also follows the same argument as in Cuicatlán that local customs are more important to community solidarity than individual rights to practice a new religion.

Yolotepec is a rancheria, or small hamlet, located in the municipality of Santiago Yosondúa, in the district of Tlaxiaco in the Mixteca Alta. The first

Protestant Mixtec families in Yosondúa converted to Presbyterianism after returning from seasonal labor on a coffee plantation in Nopaltepec, Veracruz, in 1949.[61] During the bracero program between 1942 and 1964, only a small percentage of indigenous Oaxacans took agricultural jobs in the United States.[62] More frequently, they migrated to Veracruz to work on coffee or sugar plantations, to northern Oaxaca to do mining work, or to Mexico City for factory jobs.[63] Unlike Cuicatlán, where the Mazatecans converted after prolonged missionary visits by Methodist and then Presbyterian missionaries, Yolotepec migrants brought the religion back with them after working in Veracruz.

The conflict began in May 1957 when Bartolo Hernández López filed a grievance with district, state, and federal authorities alleging that Catholics had burned down his home on December 14, 1956. Hernández López complained that municipal authorities refused to investigate the purported crime.[64] On July 7, 1957, Hernández López informed the governor of Oaxaca, Pérez Gasca, that the municipal authorities were repressing him and the other Presbyterians: "The Municipal Authorities, guided by five individuals, have dedicated themselves to harming us in the following ways: burning our homes, incarcerating us at times, they've told us to leave town, that we are a bad example, when in fact they are the ones who want to strip us of everything we have."[65] In response, the Catholic Yolotepec authorities also wrote a letter to President Adolfo Ruiz Cortines defending their actions against Hernández López and accusing the Presbyterians of fomenting violence in the community.

Presbyterians and Catholics in Yolotepec vehemently disagreed about the place of religion in social organization. Convert Bartolo Hernández López recalled that, in Yolotepec, local authorities constantly warned him that "everyone is Catholic here; these other religions don't exist."[66] For their part, municipal authorities stated in a 1958 letter to district judicial superiors that Hernández López "hides behind his religion" when he wanted to break local laws.[67]

Aside from being a Presbyterian, Hernández López also shook up local norms by refusing to participate in tequio projects. Yolotepec mayor Francisco Jiménez fined him for not participating in a road construction project. Hernández López took his complaint above Jiménez to Yosondúa municipal president Tadeo García Gatica. Hernández López argued that it was not just his religious beliefs that made him question participating in collective labor projects that often went hand in hand with Catholic rituals but also the sentiment behind it. He stated: "By the grace of Christ we are not living in times of slavery but rather in an era in which we enjoy liberty of choice in many aspects of life, including our labor and our religion, as guaranteed in the Mexican Constitution."⁶⁸ For Hernández López, being compelled to participate in nonremunerated tequio projects constituted a violation of his constitutional rights.

The case attracted national attention when Mexico City's *El Universal* newspaper featured a story about the conflict in Yolotepec on August 16, 1958.⁶⁹ The article mentioned that the Presbyterians' complaints to local and state authorities had reached the federal Ministry of the Interior. The article included excerpts of Hernández López's letter to Governor Pérez Gasca describing the damage done to his home in December of 1956.⁷⁰ Hernández López said Catholic men, with the backing of local authorities, burned down his house because he was holding Bible studies there with two other Presbyterian men in Yolotepec. Almost immediately following the news story, letters of concern from ordinary Protestant citizens and state and national government offices flooded the Yosondúan mayor's office. On August 18, 1958, Miguel García Cruz, secretary general of the Mexican Social Security Institute, sent a letter to Yosondúa municipal president García Gatica warning him that conflicts in Yolotepec could easily escalate into "fatal conflicts" throughout the district.⁷¹ The district minister of justice also sent a letter to García Gatica inquiring about the whereabouts of the Catholic men who Hernández López accused of burning his home. Mayor García Gatica wrote back that while he had attempted to cooperate with the Yolotepec authorities to apprehend the suspected men, the search was futile because the men's families reported they "had gone out to collect corn without specifying their location."⁷² As this feeble attempt at an excuse suggests, authorities never charged the Catholic men.

The correspondence between town, district, and state officials continued until the end of 1958 when all the individuals involved were ordered to appear at Oaxaca City's state government office for a mediation session with representatives from the state attorney general's office. The document trail fades out here, but in 2010 Hernández López mentioned that instances of religious conflict continued in his community.⁷³ He still did not have permission to run public services at the now decrepit church in Yolotepec. However, as discussed in the following chapter, his conflict paled in comparison to the one in 1977 between Yosondúa authorities and the SIL missionary team.

Conclusion

This chapter has described the intersection of constitutional law, local custom, national movements, and religious conflict. These cases demonstrate how the Ministry of the Interior attempted to enforce constitutional law by sending copies of the Mexican Constitution's Article 24 to village leaders and emphasizing the unlawful stance of the locals. These cases further reveal the strength of tradition vis-à-vis constitutional rights and the strong connection between charges of cultural imperialism and Protestantism. Despite the federal government's evident backing of religious freedom in Mexico, actual religious freedom was difficult to implement at the local level. While the Mexican federal and Oaxacan state governments intervened in favor of nascent Protestant congregations, these entities also struggled with how to arbitrate individual versus collective rights in indigenous communities. Protestants argued that they were the true supporters of the tenets of the Mexican Revolution. Opponents of Protestantism stated that collective rights were sacred to indigenous communities and religious ritual outweighed the preferences of minorities. The Mexican state feared bloodshed in the communities but ultimately had to defend individual rights guaranteed in the Constitution. These examples elucidate how conflicts between customary and constitutional law can be seen as attempts by locals to defend their community by strengthening local autonomy and using tradition as a justification against outside influences. Defending traditional customs also meant that these communities would not tolerate prolonged visits by outsiders, nor would they accept new religious beliefs that disrupted daily life. Clearly, conversion caused social disruption to indigenous communities in Oaxaca that had larger political implications.

Most important, this chapter reveals an organized evangelical defense movement that successfully negotiated with national government offices when advising Protestant congregations in Oaxaca. This partnership meant that Oaxacan Protestants started to identify with other converts throughout the state and often throughout Mexico and sometimes the United States. Protestant identity shifted from one based principally locally to one that transcended territorial boundaries. Coupled with new technology that offered missionary radio programs and increased phone lines connecting rural areas of Oaxaca to the state and national capitals, cases of religious conflict generated hundreds of responses directed toward local and federal political offices. Regarding the alleged case of religious intolerance in Coyula, hundreds of protest telegrams from different Mexican Protestant churches poured into the Oaxacan governor's office as well as to the Ministry of the Interior in Mexico City.

Yet not every Protestant group could take advantage of these networks. Groups like the Adventists in Santa María Texcatitlán found their ability to take advantage of the Constitution's religious freedom clauses difficult because they existed in isolation, without the mainline denomination national support networks that could put pressure on the federal and state government. Today, the media of choice to document and disseminate examples of religious persecution in Oaxaca to a national and international audience are YouTube, Facebook, and Twitter, discussed further in Chapter Six.[74]

Protestant conversion for indigenous Oaxacans was both a personal and public decision with immediate social ramifications in their communities. Protestants abstaining from religious rituals threaten and often alter existing social structure in their home communities. Yet, by doing so, they strengthen and share their own identities as cristianos with indigenous peoples across the state as well as with mestizos and foreigners. Consequently, Catholics often associated Oaxacan Protestants with American influences; Oaxacan Catholics, indigenous or mestizo, derisively referred to Protestantism as a form of North American cultural imperialism in Mexico.

The Summer Institute of Linguistics' troubled history in Oaxaca became a prime target for indigenous rights movements and academics concerned with the US organization's role in indigenous communities. By the late 1970s, local leaders, social scientists, the Ministry of Education, and the National Indigenist Institute started to challenge the organization's presence in Native communities. Left-leaning academics in Mexico City, influenced by Cold War US foreign relations, started linking North American organizations to neocolonialism and especially individualistic capitalistic goals a la Weber's Protestant ethic thesis.[75]

CHAPTER FOUR

The Summer Institute of Linguistics in Oaxaca

> Sooner or later, whether we like it or not, civilization is going to come to these tribes. Our concern is that it be Christian civilization.
> —WILLIAM CAMERON TOWNSEND, SIL FOUNDER, 1958

> If our ancestors were capable of creating magnificent civilizations and building Mitla and Monte Alban, indigenous peoples are clearly not inferior citizens. Nor should we permit the intrusion of the ways or idiosyncrasies of those serving North American imperialism.
> —RAÚL TOVAR HERNÁNDEZ, DIRECTOR OF CASA DE LA CULTURA DE OAXACA, 1979

BUILT IN AD 450, Mitla is Oaxaca's most striking Zapotec religious center. The site is a rare example of fifth-century Zapotec mosaics fused with eleventh-century Mixtec motifs. Today, only a few of the original monuments still stand. Spanish settlers destroyed most of the dwellings by building on top of the foundations or carting off the stones for construction projects. Sixteenth-century Dominican friars built the Church of San Pablo on top of Mitla's sacred temple, symbolically demonstrating the Catholic conquest of paganism. Visitors to Mitla seldom venture outside of the tourist zone to notice another architecturally incongruous housing compound a few miles from the ruins.

Besides being Oaxaca's second most visited historic site, Mitla is also the headquarters of the Instituto Lingüístico de Verano (Summer Institute of Linguistics, ILV/SIL) in Mexico. Before they commence evangelization programs in indigenous communities, SIL linguist-missionaries to this day spend weeks at the Mitla center sharpening their language skills and participating in pedagogical workshops. Beginning with SIL founder W. C. Townsend's 1935 recruitment pamphlet, "A Thousand Tribes without the Bible," the SIL set ambitious goals. These included a pledge to translate the New Testament into every unwritten language across the world, a task that would take about a decade per language to complete.[1] By 1969, the SIL was the largest Protestant missionary organization in the world, with a sizable budget and contracts with host country governments in Mexico, Peru, Guatemala, Bolivia, Honduras, Surinam, Ecuador, Colombia, Brazil, and Panama, as well as several Asian and African nations.[2] In Mexico, the SIL had worked with fifty-six indigenous languages and 110 local dialects by 1979.[3]

Mexican federal entities such as the Instituto Nacional Indigenista (National Indigenist Institute, INI) initially worked closely with the SIL, but INI increasingly shifted away from assimilation policies and toward multiculturalism in 1979, along with national political currents.[4] While many of the SIL's early programs complemented national integration goals, by the 1970s, the organization had failed to adapt to intellectual trends and indigenous rights movements: The SIL's continued presence in Mexico was seen as a hegemonic incursion of "el american way of life."[5]

The state also changed its policies toward Native communities in the 1970s. It transitioned from its top-down paternalistic forms of indigenism to a more inclusive governing strategy known as "participatory indigenism." Starting in Luis Echeverría Álvarez's administration (1970–1976), government agencies called for more consultation with and participation from Native communities in forging their own destinies within the nation-state.[6] Once an important ally of Protestant organizations, the state recognized the political cost of siding with North American organizations such as the SIL over indigenous Mexican Catholics.

It is within this context of "participatory indigenism" that the SIL's presence in the Americas, particularly in Oaxaca, became emblematic of neocolonialism with religious evangelization, the relocation of indigenous peoples into central areas, and with working hand in hand with high-ranking political officials on development projects that all seemed reminiscent of Spanish colonization in the sixteenth century.⁷ Eduardo Galeano's widely read 1971 book, *Open Veins of Latin America*, set the stage for a discussion on the legacy of the conquest of the Americas. The Uruguayan journalist argued that, despite abundant mineral resources, the majority of Latin Americans lived in abject poverty, mostly due to five centuries of European and US imperialism.⁸ Marxist-leaning intellectuals in Mexico who also drew connections between the role of the US government and exploitation of natural resources in Latin America shared Galeano's perspective. This wealth disparity was readily apparent in the indigenous regions of Latin America. Within this context, Mexican anthropologists acknowledged the colonial vestiges inherent in their discipline, particularly the influence their research had on national state-building and development goals.

This chapter examines the SIL's history in Oaxaca from 1935 to the early 1980s by focusing on the impact of the SIL's presence in two regions of Oaxaca: the Mixteca and the Sierra Norte.⁹ These regions were particularly targeted by the SIL because of a high poverty index and the largest population of monolingual Oaxacans. Because the SIL gave such prominence to Oaxaca, cases from that state illustrate quite well the organization's activities in Mexico. However, many of the SIL and the Mexican government's decisions were national in scope and also applied to regions outside of Oaxaca. I first trace the SIL's early relationship to the Mexican government and then use Oaxaca as a lens to illustrate the various reactions, successes, and challenges that the SIL faced in Mexico. I then follow the SIL's impact on conceptualizations of indigenous identity through the mixed results of recent language revitalization movements.

The SIL

In 1917, twenty-one-year-old William Cameron Townsend dropped out of Occidental College in Los Angeles to become a missionary. Raised on a perpetually insolvent farm in nearby Downey, California, Townsend aspired to become a Presbyterian minister after graduation.¹⁰ However, after hearing China missionary John R. Mott speak at Occidental, Townsend joined the Student Volunteer Movement and devoured the memoirs of American missionaries abroad.¹¹ In September of what would have been his junior year, he signed a short-term contract to work as a salesman in Guatemala for the Bible House of Los Angeles. Townsend ended up staying fifteen years in an indigenous village outside of Antigua. While struggling to convert Cakchiquel Mayans in San Antonio, Guatemala, under the auspices of the Central American Mission, a North American Protestant organization, Townsend concluded that before Mayans could be interested in reading the Gospel in Spanish, they first needed to be able to read it in their native tongue.[12] Cakchiquel was thus far an unwritten language.

In a November 1917 journal entry, Townsend recorded a provocative conversation with a Cakchiquel Mayan. He challenged Townsend by asking, "Why, if your God is so smart, hasn't He learned our language?"[13] Despite lacking formal linguistics training, Townsend came up with a scientific formula for breaking down the structure of Cakchiquel by its own terms, not by trying to fit it into English grammar norms. He started the project by completing a Cakchiquel grammar, which was reviewed by renowned linguist Edward Sapir in 1926.[14] In 1931, after over a decade of work, Townsend presented the Cakchiquel version to San Antonio residents, as well as to Guatemala's president, Jorge Ubico.[15]

That same year, Townsend met Moisés Sáenz, the undersecretary of Mexico's Ministry of Public Education (Secretaría de Educación Pública, SEP), who was touring Guatemalan schools. A devout Presbyterian like Townsend, Sáenz was interested in exploring new pedagogical techniques to reach Mexico's non-Spanish–speaking students. Sáenz observed Townsend's holistic language approach and invited him to try his methods with indigenous groups in Mexico.[16] With Sáenz's proposal in mind, Townsend organized the Camp Wycliffe linguistics workshop in Sulphur Springs, Arkansas.[17] Townsend began his 1934 summer session with two students training in phonetics, Bible translation, and basic cultural anthropology. With the help of his fellow missionary L. L. Legters, Townsend transformed Camp Wycliffe into the Summer Institute of Linguistics by August of 1935.[18] The institute eventually attracted anthropology students studying Native American languages in North American universities. Consequently, by 1941, institute participants could receive college credit from US universities that attracted nonmissionary secular students.

The SIL's workshops quickly grew into a multicampus institute that registered five hundred doctoral students enrolled in classes at the Universities of

Oklahoma, Washington, and North Dakota by 1969.[19] Encouraged by Sáenz's interest, Townsend chose Mexico as the institute's first fieldwork opportunity for his neophyte linguists. Later, he envisioned sending a legion of gifted evangelical Protestant linguists to translate the New Testament into indigenous languages across the globe. Townsend's proposal to teach indigenous peoples to read in both their native languages and Spanish answered President Lázaro Cárdenas's challenge to "Mexicanize the Indian."[20] Postrevolutionary administrations celebrated Mexico's rich indigenous heritage through "the artistic renaissance, the popular legacy of the revolution, and the development of the social sciences."[21] The establishment of the Departamento Autónomo de Asuntos Indígenas (DAAI) in 1936 and the Instituto Nacional de Antropología e Historia (INAH) in 1939 represented the Cardenista administration's (1934–1940) commitment to indigenismo, or the valorization of indigenous cultures.[22] At the same time, however, indigenistas vowed to modernize indigenous communities through assimilation.[23] In 1936, Cárdenas called for "the fusion of all of the nation's ethnic groups."[24]

Townsend was keenly aware of the niche his organization filled. "Knowing that Mexico is one of the countries where there is a great deal of enthusiasm for the cultural incorporation of the Indian," wrote Townsend in a 1935 letter to President Cárdenas, "we want to form one of the first such societies here."[25] Sensitive to Mexico's strict anticlerical constitution, Townsend emphasized the language goals of his organization.[26]

Beginning in the Cárdenas presidency, the SIL forged close relationships with high-ranking Mexican officials working in indigenous languages and rural education.[27] Arriving in Mexico in August 1935, the SIL introduced itself to prominent Mexican linguists and politicians at the Seventh Inter-American Scientific Conference in Mexico City.[28] Townsend developed a particular partnership with the director of rural education, Rafael Ramírez.[29] Despite his initial discomfort with foreign missionaries living in indigenous communities, Ramírez concluded that the support the SIL would give to rural education outweighed the risk of proselytism.[30] Ramírez assigned Townsend the task of evaluating indigenous education programs in southern Mexico. Perpetually short of teachers in Oaxaca, Ramírez also paid two female SIL linguists the salaries of public school teachers in the Mazatecan town of Huáutla de Jiménez, Oaxaca, beginning in 1936.[31]

Townsend's close relationship with Cárdenas had benefits for both parties. In 1936, Cárdenas recognized Townsend's Nahuatl field site in Tetelcingo, Morelos, as a model program of modernization.[32] As a result, Tetelcingo received abundant seed, fertilizer, and technical support for the crops that the Townsends introduced.[33] In hopes of gaining US support for Cárdenas's controversial oil nationalization, the SIL organized a "Good Neighbor" picnic, held along the US-Mexican border in Tijuana in July 1939. President Cárdenas addressed a crowd of two hundred well-heeled evangelical Protestants from southern California.[34] Knowing that Townsend was an acquaintance of the US ambassador to Mexico, Josephus Daniels, and concerned about US-Mexican relations following the October 1938 petroleum expropriation, Cárdenas asked Townsend to lobby for him among Protestant politicians and businessmen in the United States.[35] In his 1940 booklet, "The Truth about Mexico's Oil," Townsend included a letter he had written to President Franklin Roosevelt proposing a "Good Neighbor" statue on the border between Mexico and the United States as a testament to the special relationship between the two nations.[36] The eighty-six-page booklet was mailed to every single US congressman.[37] In his support of Cárdenas's move against Standard Oil, Townsend proved that he was committed to backing Mexican government initiatives.

Townsend's high-ranking friendships paid off. By 1948, the SIL collaborated with the newly formed Instituto Nacional Indigenista on the "Indian Problem" by promoting literacy campaigns, economic development, and medical attention to indigenous communities. Influenced by the SIL's early success in learning indigenous languages and its experience advising rural teachers, the SEP outsourced the production of bilingual primary textbooks to the SIL from 1951 to 1979.[38] In return for the SIL's educational collaboration with the Mexican government, the organization received office buildings in Mexico City, permission to lease a portion of the Lacandón rain forest in Yaxoquintelá, Chiapas, as a "jungle training camp" for prospective missionaries, access to federal airstrips for the SIL's Jungle Aviation and Radio Services (JAARS) planes, and leases to government property for regional centers in several states.[39]

In order to maintain such vital connections with federal entities in Mexico, the SIL downplayed the Protestant evangelization component of their organization. All SIL public relations literature emphasized the SIL's role as linguists, not missionaries, in Mexico. For example, the SIL's own letterhead sported a seal with the Aztec symbol for speech, thus representing "high Indian culture" and the SIL's role in incorporating "primitive peoples through their own languages."[40]

This is not to say that the SIL deceived the Mexican government—Cárdenas, SEP, and INI officials knew quite well that Townsend's ultimate goal was Bible translation. Rather, it adeptly gave its missionary agenda a low public profile.[41] As journalist N. Pelham Wright described in 1958, "SIL workers are missionaries. But they represent no religious body, they hold no services, they distribute no tracts, they baptize no babies."[42] In instructional literature, Townsend reminded his missionaries: "Our purpose is to translate the Word as soon as possible."[43] The SIL presented its employees as detached from church-building. Townsend advised: "When several Indians have believed, it is well to meet with them regularly in their homes to study the Word. Call it a 'study,' not a 'service.' Singing and praying should be in the Indian language with Indians leading, though the missionary may have to do some unobtrusive steering from his seat in the audience."[44] Once indigenous converts wanted to establish churches, SIL personnel encouraged them but took a supporting, not leading, role; maintaining a church would get in the way of translating and jeopardize the organization's nonsectarian identity, as well as attract unwanted attention from government officials trying to curb religious influences in Mexico.

The SIL rapidly extended its missionary fields to Central and South America. Peru in 1945, Ecuador and Guatemala in 1952, Bolivia in 1955, and Brazil in 1956. In 1958, *Reader's Digest* reporter Clarence Hall noted Townsend's knack for impressing Latin American governments: "He has not had to wrangle permission to enter; they invite him in—fast, with full government cooperation."[45] The SIL solicited funds from US churches and private donors under the auspices of Wycliffe Bible Translators (WBT) to maintain its operations in Latin America. By naming its US counterpart after fourteenth-century New Testament translator John Wycliffe, the SIL strategically marketed itself domestically as an evangelical organization serving disadvantaged populations. As a result, Wycliffe could "present the disguised Jesus to evangelicals in the U.S." while the SIL denied religious evangelization goals to Latin American governments.[46] Ultimately, though, it was the SIL's obfuscated religious agenda that caused the organization's demise in Mexico and most of Latin America by the late 1970s.

The SIL and Indigenous Mexico

The focus on rapid economic modernization by mid-twentieth-century Mexican governments meant that the SIL's work in indigenous communities went hand in hand with federal plans for a literate, industrialized workforce.[47] While Cárdenas had attempted to develop the countryside through his bold distribution of ejido land, his successors, Manuel Ávila Camacho (1940–1946) and especially Miguel Alemán Valdés (1946–1952), focused intensely on development projects that prepared indigenous peoples for their entrance into urbanization and industrialization.[48] The SIL's service to the state in literacy campaigns, irrigation projects, and vaccination crusades set the organization up for powerful alliances in the 1940s and 1950s.

In a 1948 speech, Director of Indian Affairs Héctor Sánchez outlined "the Indian Problem" for INI. Sánchez lamented that indigenous peoples were "living in distant communities, practicing either primitive industries or agriculture, living in huts which cannot furnish adequate protection, exposed to disease and destructive social ills, coming indeed from the negative influences of civilization, isolated from the national civic currents, and with norms of extreme inferiority in some cases."[49] Sánchez posited that indigenous peoples' marginalization was a national crisis that needed to be approached on several fronts. Until then, Mexico as a whole could not progress, since "as long as the conditions of backwardness exist among the Indians, it will not be possible to truly unite the Mexican nation."[50] INI and the SIL approached "backwardness" in different ways but with the same goals in mind.

In the SIL's 1953 report on its operations in Mexico, director John McIntosh discussed the organization's role in helping modernize indigenous communities.[51] He mentioned that the SIL consistently supported INI "in their noble task of bringing the Indian population into the full enjoyment of Mexican national life."[52] The SIL were active members in their host communities. McIntosh stated that SIL employees "quickly find themselves to be a part of the native life" by contributing to projects such as irrigation or basic medical assistance. McIntosh gave as an example an SIL linguist who helped a Zapotec village build a school, describing it as a "privilege" for members to participate in such projects.[53] The Zapotecs had begun the project but did not have the architectural design skills to finish the roof. The jack-of-all-trades

SIL linguist provided his expertise. In other words, the SIL supported educational and structural development in its host villages. The report suggests that if not for the SIL presence, the Zapotec community would have failed in their endeavor.

SIL publications frequently boasted the unassuming linguistic prowess of SIL linguists. An anecdote from Wright's "Gift of Tongues" illustrates this relationship between linguist and community. In the Chinantec village of San Lucas Ojitlán, Oaxaca, Paul and Dorothy Smith published a Chinanteco-Spanish dictionary in 1955 that mestizos used to communicate with monolingual laborers.[54] Wright quoted one "leading Mestizo resident" in San Lucas Ojitlán who effusively praised Paul Smith's linguistic skills. "He's fantastic. He speaks to our Indians as if he was one of them, and they love him. I was born here fifty years ago, and I've never left the place, but I can't understand a word they say. He's not a priest. Who knows what he's doing here, but he's a fine fellow."[55] This account by Wright, a British journalist and admirer of the SIL, reveals several insights into the organization's position in the community. The SIL's top-notch near-native language skills astounded locals in their proficiency. Wright also portrayed SIL employees as so unassuming that an influential mestizo did not know they had come to convert the community to Protestantism. But regardless of such reports, evangelization shaped relationships between indigenous peoples and missionaries.

SIL literature stressed missionaries' responsibility in preparing indigenous populations for the onslaught of modern civilization. By spreading both literacy and the Gospel to indigenous peoples, SIL personnel hoped indigenous Protestants would enter mainstream mestizo life with "Christian" values.[56] In an interview with the *New York Times* in 1969, SIL president Kenneth Pike described the organization's guiding principle: "If we can get the Bible to them in their own language, and get them to try to read it, and take it as a source of hope and courage, they may be able to survive the transition."[57] Yet as the Casa de la Cultura director Raúl Tovar Hernández's quote in the beginning of this chapter asserts, Oaxacan indigenous peoples were the descendants of a highly sophisticated set of civilizations; Zapotecs, Mixtecs, Mixes, and the dozen other distinct indigenous Oaxacan societies already had their own advanced set of religious traditions that had thrived for centuries without the Bible. They did not need help surviving the transition to modernity. They wanted to deal with outsiders on their own terms, and with respect toward the traditions and natural resources they possessed long before the conquest of Mexico. By the 1970s, integrationist indigenism had transitioned into multicultural "participatory indigenism" designed *with*, not *for*, indigenous citizens.[58]

SIL and 1970s Intellectual Climate

From its inception, the social sciences in Mexico closely aligned with postrevolutionary nationalism. The founders of Mexican anthropology—Manuel Gamio, Alfonso Caso, and Gonzalo Aguirre Beltrán—promoted a Mexican national identity that the new revolutionary state endorsed and patronized.[59] In the 1930s and 1940s, that identity homed in on *mestizaje*.[60] Yet, by the 1970s, Mexican anthropologists started to detach themselves from national goals and policies vis-à-vis indigenous communities. Instead, a cohort of anthropologists influenced by the tumultuous 1968 student protests in Mexico criticized Mexico's indigenous policy. The challenges to the hegemonic PRI ruling party created an opening for the reassessment of intellectuals' roles in Mexico.[61] A new generation of anthropologists questioned official nationalism and saw indigenous identity as not exclusively Mexican but as linked to the historic struggles of indigenous communities globally.[62]

By the 1970s, INI's policies of indigenous incorporation collided with anthropological ideologies that backed indigenous peoples in forging their own destinies within the nation-state. This transformation involved several key moments in Mexico. On January 20, 1971, Latin American social anthropologists gathered in Barbados to discuss their roles in the struggle for indigenous rights. Together they produced the Declaration of Barbados, which called for the liberation of indigenous peoples, the commitment of anthropologists to activist scholarship, and the immediate departure of foreign missionaries from indigenous communities.[63] The declaration's authors were primarily a cohort of Mexican anthropologists, including future INAH director Guillermo Bonfil Batalla and future INI director Salomón Nahmad Sittón.[64]

The declaration demanded that social scientists and Latin American governments "contribute significantly to the process of Indian liberation."[65] It referred back to the European conquest of the Americas and the exploitation of Native lands for mining.⁶⁶ Its architects argued that the official Latin American governments' "Indian policies" were a complete failure: "These policies are employed to manipulate and control Indian populations in order to consolidate the status of existing social groups and classes, and only diminish the possibility that Indian society may free itself from colonial domination and settle its own future."⁶⁷ Furthermore, the declaration pronounced religious missionaries, anthropologists, and business entrepreneurs as acting against indigenous peoples' rights to self-determination within a multicultural nation.

The declaration was a bold challenge to social scientists to acknowledge their own ignominious contribution to neocolonialism. It pushed academics to position themselves within the interests of the groups they studied, not with, in Karl Marx's terms, the dominant oppressors.⁶⁸ In perhaps the most well-known passage from the declaration, the authors demanded that governments guarantee "to all the Indian populations, by virtue of their ethnic distinction, the right to be and to remain themselves, living according to their own customs and moral order, free to develop their own culture."⁶⁹ Here precisely is where the Mexican anthropologists parted from national indigenismo, which had called for indigenous peoples' integration into national life. This nueva antropología called for a radical rethinking regarding whom, and for what purposes, the social sciences serve.⁷⁰

As an outcome of the Barbados Declaration and Indigenous Congresses, Mexican anthropologists and activists pressured INI and SEP to stop relying on North American missionaries for their bilingual education curriculum. This criticism of foreigners' primers for indigenous children is readily apparent in Nahmad Sittón's 1979 investigation of SEP and in the writings of anthropologist Margarita Nolasco. SIL opponents such as Nahmad Sittón and Nolasco insisted that the SIL advocated "el american way of life" in indigenous communities in ways that bordered on ethnocide.⁷¹ Sociologist Kurt Bowen notes that, with the growth of the social sciences in Mexico, it became "perhaps inevitable that resentment should grow towards a foreign agency defining itself as a defender of Indigenous culture."⁷² In fact, this very premise, that indigenous cultures needed outsiders to lead them, led to challenges of the SIL's presence in Oaxaca.

The circumstances holding indigenous Mexico in poverty, as Director of Indigenous Affairs Héctor Sánchez spoke of at INI's inauguration, were now turned on its head. The "Indian Problem" that the SIL was so determined to solve in previous decades was now *their* problem. The SIL's anecdotes about indigenous children pulling themselves up by their huaraches and becoming assimilated into national life no longer had an audience.[73] As anthropologists Søren Hvalkof and Peter Aaby stated in their 1981 condemnation of the SIL, *Is God an American?*, the SIL had overstayed its welcome in Latin America not because of its Bible translations but for its emphasis on American ideologies, capitalism, and national development projects in indigenous communities.[74] The following case study of a Mixtec community in the Mixteca Alta of Oaxaca exemplifies a village's resistance to the SIL's overarching ideological underpinnings and the SIL's violation of indigenous rights to sovereignty.

Santiago Yosondúa, Tlaxiaco

The SIL carefully selected and groomed its missionaries. As Pike described in a 1969 *New York Times* article, "We recruit for motive and the first has to be religious motive."[75] After attending two mandatory Summer Institute of Linguistics training sessions at the Universities of Oklahoma, North Dakota, or Washington, starting in 1941, prospective missionaries had to complete a three-month Wycliffe Jungle Camp in Chiapas. If the missionaries could endure the physical and emotional challenges of the Lacandón rain forest, they would be prepared for living abroad in villages with few basic services. In addition to learning survival skills, camp participants took classes on basic anthropological methodology, practiced linguistic techniques with Chiapan Tzeltal Indians, and engaged in long hours of Bible study on their own. Once in their assigned villages, SIL linguists analyzed the sounds and syntax of an unwritten language, assembled a dictionary, and, above all, translated the New Testament into a Native language. Pike acknowledged how daunting this task was: "When we turn our people loose in the jungle on a language, they often get started all right and then run into problems."[76] Such problems could include ambiguity in translation exercises, cultural barriers, and suspicion regarding missionaries' agendas.

Bible translation could be particularly challenging with tonal languages in which one word might have several meanings depending on the pitch. One example occurred in the Shapra language of Peru. An SIL linguist kept mixing up the tone for "sinner" and was saying God loves "the fat person" instead of God loves "the sinner," which confused tribe members who were learning about forgiveness.[77] Ambiguity in translation was also a major issue for missionaries in Oaxaca. Pike began translation work in the Mixteca region in 1936.[78] He explained that in the Mixtec language a sound such as *chaa* could mean "man," "come," or "smoke" depending on whether one used a low, medium, or high pitch. Such variance in pitch could be problematic when translating Matthew 19:14, which states, "Jesus said let the children come to me." If translated incorrectly, the Gospel passage could be confused with "Jesus said let the children smoke with me."[79]

The experiences of Edwin and Kathryn Farris provide insight into the challenges SIL missionaries faced. Both in their early thirties in 1969, the Californians brought their three children to the Mixtec community of Santiago Yosondúa in western Oaxaca. Located in the district of Tlaxiaco, Yosondúa is a southern municipality divided into eight smaller rancheria entities. The Farrises offered Bible study classes, published scholarly articles on Mixtec tones, and recorded local histories and legends. Writing in a 1989 Presbyterian Church in America (PCA) missionary outreach bulletin, Kathryn Farris explained their interest in deciphering an unwritten language in the Mixteca region: "We wanted to make a positive impact on that culture—to leave a permanent work. We also knew the Lord had called us to do Bible translation. That was the real key."[80]

Members of the community found the Farrises' presence quite suspicious.[81] Some community members wondered why they were interested in developing a written form of the Mixtec language in the first place.[82] Some mestizos suspected that the Farrises were collecting their language findings for the Central Intelligence Agency (CIA) as a code language for espionage.[83] Farris also noted that mestizos were surprised that she and her husband viewed Mixtec as a full-fledged language, not a minor dialect. One mestizo familiar with Mixtec labor migration to the United States bluntly asked them: "Aren't there [Mixtec] people in the United States for you to mock? Why did you have to come here?"[84]

The Farrises had multiple goals in translating the Gospels into Mixtec. First, they wanted to spread literacy to the indigenous population. More important, the couple hoped to eradicate what they deemed to be vestiges of paganism: the fusion of saints with Native deities and pre-Hispanic rituals, which they believed fueled expensive alcohol-driven fiestas. Kathryn Farris described the wake of a Yosondúa infant as an example of what motivated her as a missionary:

> Candles and wild flowers stood guard around the lifeless body. A saint's picture, moved from its prominent place, rested on a shelf above the homemade altar. Beside the baby's head a transistor radio blared rock music. . . . The men in the town band stood outside drinking, then entered one by one. Soon undisciplined music filled the room, inaugurating a festive wake. Excitement heightened and laugher soared. The bottle of firewater slipped from one to another. . . . At the funeral, powerful fireworks shatter above us and the church bells clanged. Sweet incense filled the air. The funeral dirge began. The drunken musicians reeled forward.[85]

Prayer candles, a home altar with images of saints, and alcohol are all examples of folk Catholicism that distressed Protestant missionaries. Farris implies that the Mixtec-Catholic rituals surrounding death were irreverent. She insinuates that the child's wake was basically an excuse for men to socialize with loud music and aguardiente. For Farris, this example reaffirmed why she and her husband were translating the New Testament. She reflected: "Suddenly, in the midst of death it became more than a need. It emerged as an urgent mission that must dominate our lives and dictate our future."[86] This missionary team vehemently objected to traditional mourning rituals and planned to change such practices by dedicating themselves to bringing the Gospel to Yosondúans.

Aside from translating Scripture, the Farrises wanted to prepare Mixtecs to enter modern society. Kathryn Farris discussed their goals in the community: "We had faith that God's Word would one day make a difference, but not for a long time. We also wanted to see them with improved farming techniques, a better understanding of hygiene, and the ability to read. The mainstream of Mexican life was impinging upon them and we wanted them equipped to adjust to the changes."[87] For missionaries, farming methods, hygiene, and literacy were the keys to assimilation. Protestant missionaries like the Farrises sought to introduce and protect Mixtecs from modern, mestizo cultural norms.

A significant outcome of the Farris legacy in Yosondúa was their influence on Protestant conversion. First, they led Bible study courses in their assistant Isidoro Santiago Ojeda's home. In addition, Edwin Farris and Santiago Ojeda collaborated to translate the complete New Testament into Yosondúan Mixtec, a nineteen-year project.[88] Perhaps their most important contribution was the formation of a Presbyterian church, the New Bethel Church of Yosondúa. While Edwin Farris did not officially build the church, he paved the way for Santiago Ojeda to attract a congregation and receive backing from established Oaxacan Presbyterian ministers. By 1988, the congregation numbered two hundred members. Santiago Ojeda's family still worships there today, although Santiago Ojeda himself had a falling out with the congregation in the 1990s after he returned from working in Baja, California.[89]

Santiago Ojeda's family was one of the earliest families to convert to Protestantism. Santiago Ojeda himself vehemently argued that Protestantism did not compromise indigenous identity or tradition. He stated that Protestantism had the opposite effect; it revitalized respect for indigenous tradition. As an example, he cited the role his pastor played in building the New Bethel Church. Pastor Sergio Morales was from Coatlán, a Mixe-speaking community in the northeastern highlands of Oaxaca. Morales converted as a teenager when he started visiting SIL missionaries Searle and Hilda Hoogshagen's home to listen to liturgical hymns in Mixe.[90] In the 1980s, Morales formed a Presbyterian presbytery with the clever name "Mizami" since he served Presbyterian congregations in Mixe, Zapotec, and Mixtec zones of Oaxaca. Santiago Ojeda stated that Morales was a perfect example of reaffirming the value of indigenous languages. In Morales's Mixe services, Santiago Ojeda noted that all members spoke and sang in Mixe and socialized according to Mixe customs:

> There are many beautiful customs in indigenous communities representing different cultures and different ideas regarding how people behave, how people eat, how they work, how they respect each other, and how they greet each other. Indigenous culture and customs are very beautiful, and because of this, we can't say that evangelicals are opposed to indigenous culture; it's actually the opposite. When I was here [in Yosondúa], we made lots of books in Mixtec, teaching people how to read and write in Mixtec. After every Sunday service, which lasted an

hour and a half, I'd spend a half an hour teaching Mixtec. We'd have a chalk board and chalk there, and I would teach the parishioners how to read and write in Mixtec. I gave out the Mixtec language books to the hermanos. There are eleven lessons in the book for learning Mixtec, and that's how the hermanos at the church learned to read Mixtec, and that's why since then they've been able to read the New Testament more easily in their language. That's what I did when I was working with the church.[91]

For Isidoro Santiago Ojeda, indigenous identity was strengthened by conversion to Protestantism.

While not as prolific in scholarly publications as their renowned colleague and Mixtec expert Kenneth Pike, the Farrises published important studies on Mixtec tone and syntax.[92] Even today, their Mixtec dictionaries remain some of the most cited references by researchers in the Mixteca.[93] Aside from the dictionaries and New Testament translation, Edwin Farris dedicated substantial time to recording local history and legends. His most popular and widely distributed historical work was the bilingual Spanish-Mixtec "Cuando Cárdenas visitó nuestro pueblo," an account of the 1970 three-day visit by former president Lázaro Cárdenas to Yosondúa.[94] The collection chronicles a number of community members' reflections on Cárdenas's visit to inaugurate a new boarding school for Mixtec children from more isolated zones of the district.

Farris's account of Cárdenas's 1970 visit displayed for the community the importance of the Mixtec language by translating every interview into Mixtec. Yet, while the book showcased the SIL's linguistic prowess, it was careful to emphasize Yosondúan Juventino Martínez Cruz's authority over the publication. Farris was identified as the assistant, not the editor, following the SIL's modus operandi to emphasize its supporting, not central, role in indigenous communities. Just as SIL personnel were supposed to let indigenous converts establish Protestant churches, the SIL encouraged its linguists to emphasize local contributions in language translation projects.

Cárdenas's visit was a moment of great pride for the community. SEP representative Alicia Leal stated that the legacy of the general's visit "left an inerasable footprint for all of the inhabitants of this town."[95] The publication on Cárdenas's visit was a local history but also an important affirmation of the SIL's legitimacy. It represented the organization's commitment to the scientific and cultural study of Native languages; not a biblical tract but rather a community history of a famous president's visit.[96] General Cárdenas's decades-long support had been crucial in the SIL's continued acceptance by Mexico's government. Cárdenas continued working for the Mexican government on development projects such as the Balsas River Dam in the Mixteca until his death in October 1970.[97] SIL missionary-linguists like Farris walked a fine line between religious evangelization and government approval. Having a publication on "tata Lázaro" upped his street credibility. Politicians also recognized the significance of Cárdenas's popularity in rural Mexico.

Throughout his 1970–1976 presidency, Luis Echeverría channeled Cardenista populism.[98] He supported campesino land invasions of ex-haciendas and, more important, encouraged the creation of the 1975 First National Congress of Indigenous Peoples, a large-scale replication of Cárdenas's regional congresses in the late 1930s.[99] The National Congress of Indigenous Peoples was an important step in creating a network of indigenous activists across Mexico.[100] The national congress brought indigenous agency to the forefront of populist Echeverría's rural programs. While the congress was certainly an appendage of the PRI party, it nonetheless served "as a catalyst" for indigenous organizing throughout the nation.[101] Echeverría's emphasis on "participatory indigenism" changed the trajectory of SEP, INI, and PRI interactions with indigenous communities.[102] By the late 1970s, many indigenous communities asserted their rights to autonomy and control over natural resources.[103] One recurring theme in national and local conversations on indigenous autonomy was the presence of foreigners in indigenous communities. This topic is readily apparent in a conflict between the SIL and Yosondúan leadership.

In June of 1977, Yosondúan leaders called an asamblea with all male members of the community. The elders discussed a serious problem. Municipal president Flaviano Nicolás López accused Edwin Farris of exploring nearby archaeological zones without first seeking the community elders' permission.[104] On June 27, 1977, the municipal leaders of Santiago Yosondúa met with a local PRI official, Dr. Juan Alcalá, and SEP's *promotor bilingüe* (bilingual advocate), Cándido Coheto Martínez. The municipal officials announced that they had met in an asamblea and had decided to tell Farris that he had thirty days to leave the town. In particular, Farris had entered the Yucuñu zone, a sacred spot where Mixtec kings were allegedly buried. López insinuated that his community believed there were valuable artifacts possibly made of gold in the zone. López said that Farris's actions particularly offended the community because he explored the areas with other North American missionaries who were strangers to the community. López's municipal regidor, Ismael Osorio, suggested that since Farris's linguistic fieldwork was done, he had no business being in the community. Finally, the Yosondúa authorities complained that Farris built his house without authorization from the town and cut down forest wood without the approval of the town.[105]

PRI official Alcalá backed López and Osorio by affirming that Farris had visited the archaeological sites to collect *tepalcates*, or pottery shards, in the past. He gave as an example an occasion in 1973 when Farris tried to acquire a pottery piece that belonged to a town resident.[106] Authorities intervened and prevented Farris from obtaining the piece. While it is not clear from the documents whether Farris allegedly sold the pieces on the black market or was trying to discourage the pre-Hispanic worship practices that occurred at the site, it is clear that the municipal authorities wanted to expel him immediately. SEP bilingual advocate Coheto Martínez suggested that the town members give Farris more notice before expelling him. In response, the town government decided to give him until the last day of the year, December 31, 1977, to terminate his linguistic responsibilities and to leave the community. The petition also stipulated that in Farris's remaining time he would enjoy the support of the municipal authorities providing that he limit his work to linguistic research, but he was strictly prohibited from entering the community's archaeological zones.[107] Copies of the meeting's minutes were sent to the SIL national office in Mexico City, SEP's Office of Indigenous Education, and INI.

Farris's case provides insight into how some communities were suspicious of missionary intentions in their country. Town authorities used the example of foreigners violating community norms and sacred space as a reason to expel local missionaries. Mexicans also suspected that North Americans with planes could be searching for valuable minerals, resources, or archaeological sites.[108]

Local Protestants maintain that Farris's purportedly suspicious hikes around the archaeological zone were just an excuse to expel SIL personnel and exemplified the new political stance that the Mexican government was taking vis-à-vis the SIL in Mexico. SIL language assistant Isidoro Santiago Ojeda described the archaeological zone and the 1977 conflict:

> The gringo maybe was curious and, since there are beautiful places here and they [gringos] like to see beautiful and exotic sites in nature, probably what happened is that they went to see the site but didn't take anything. What happened is that the people in town who go and gossip to each other, their rumors make their way to town authorities who get mad and start talking and saying, "We're going to take him out of here since he's investigating where there's riches, where there's treasures." So, in time, they threw out the gringo. This didn't just happen here but came from Mexico City, from the Secretaría de Relaciones Exteriores (SRE), I think. They rejected all of the gringos who had expired visas; they sent them back to their country.... He came back later, but in the time he could not be here to work, he invited me to go to the United States. He got me my passport and took me there for a time. That's how the gringos were rejected, and I believe this was at the national level as well; I don't think it was just here. But the gringo who was here didn't get involved with archaeological matters because he was a missionary. He was a good person that taught the Word of God here. That's what he was dedicated to; he wasn't involved in matters other than the Word of God. That's what I can tell you about him.[109]

Santiago Ojeda's interview complicates the dominant intellectual narrative in the 1970s that the SIL missionary presence in Mexico was an example of neocolonialism.

The Farris family moved to a newly formed SIL center in Catalina, Arizona. Like many SIL personnel, they no longer qualified for long-term Mexican work visas. As Santiago Ojeda mentioned, the couple worked on translations in Catalina, sometimes with his assistance. While they never lived permanently in Yosondúa again after 1977, Ed and Kathryn Farris returned to Yosondúa several times in the 1980s to celebrate completed renovations of the Presbyterian church and to distribute copies of Farris and Santiago Ojeda's translation of the New Testament into Mixtec. At the time of Farris's death in 1995 in Oaxaca City, he was an associate president of SIL Mexico. His gravestone in Catalina, Arizona, attests to his proudest accomplishment in life. It reads: "Edwin Riley Farris: Translator of the New Testament into Mixtec of Santiago Yosondúa, Oaxaca."[110] In Yosondúa, his wooden home, the construction of which initially led to tension in the tight-knit community, still stands.

The case against the Farrises was a typical example of how local authorities, SEP, and INI supported the Mexican government's growing recognition of indigenous autonomy. The situation in Yosondúa was a regional example of the national condemnation of the SIL by indigenous rights leaders and anthropologists. Yet, the criticism of the North American organization's work in Oaxaca was not across the board. Santiago Ojeda's statement suggests some indigenous people have positive memories of the organization's impact.

San Baltazar Yatzachi el Bajo

The Zapotec community of San Baltazar Yatzachi in the Villa Alta district of the Sierra Norte provides another example of the SIL's significant impact. Yatzachi has a long history of cooperation with Protestant missionaries. Starting in 1920, Presbyterian Reverend Lawrence P. Van Slyke and his wife ran a hostel for destitute Zapotec boys working in the city out of their Oaxaca City home.[111] In 1923, the couple chose to work as full-time missionaries in Yatzachi, a three-day mule ride from the state capital. As mentioned in the Introduction, Van Slyke pleaded for funding and permission to enter the Sierra Norte by declaring to his mission board: "The Indian is worth the best we have."[112] The Van Slykes worked in Yatzachi for thirteen years before turning the community over to newly arrived SIL missionaries.

Yatzachi hosted three SIL missionaries: Californians Otis and Mary Leal and Oregonian Inez M. Butler. The Leals worked in Yatzachi from 1937 to 1987, translating the New Testament into Zapotec. Otis Leal believed Zapotecs could "never be truly evangelized if they have only heard [the Gospel] in Spanish alone."[113] Leal often wrote about the unique challenges SIL linguists faced in translating the Bible into a tonal language like Zapotec.[114] He also described how linguists could not dedicate long hours to just translation work; simple household chores such as preparing safe drinking water involved a long walk to the well and an hour of fanning the barely boiling water over an open wood fire.[115] Early into his translation work, he described feeling deathly ill 25 percent of the time he resided in Yatzachi. Of the causes for his frequent bouts with dysentery, Leal believed: "It has been our experience that the taking of God's Word to an area where it has never been available in a language which the people can understand will result in a Satanic attack."[116] Despite the Leals' health issues, they managed to support local Protestants in establishing a Baptist church, Cristo el Salvador, in June of 1973.[117] Following his wife's passing in 1989, Otis Leal remained in Los Angeles, where he ministered to Zapotec migrants, many from Yatzachi, until his death in 2005 at age ninety-eight.[118]

Arriving at Yatzachi in 1952, Inez Butler published nine SIL works on the Zapotec language and culture, including her much cited analysis of Zapotec witchcraft fables.[119] Not just writing for a missionary audience, Butler also published her secular linguistics articles, such as "Reflexive Constructions of Yatzachi Zapotec," in peer-reviewed journals, including the *International Journal of American Linguistics*. Her 1980 Zapotec-Spanish compilation remains the most comprehensive Zapotec dictionary in the Sierra Norte region.

Telésforo López Llaguno, Yatzachi's former mayor and the leader of the Pentecostal church in Yatzachi el Bajo, was one of the first residents who converted to Protestantism after the arrival of these SIL missionaries. He praised the Leals and Butler for beginning literacy programs, health care, and missionary work in his community. He asserted that the missionaries translated the New Testament and contributed to improving the community through outreach programs. The Leals and Butler often published for outside audiences but also directed their publications toward the local community. Pastor López Llaguno noted:

> Of course, the initial purpose [for the Leals and Butler to study Zapotec] was that one would read the Word of God in the Zapotec language, so that people could study the Bible and have some religious hymns in Zapotec. It's clear that those who don't speak Spanish appreciate the chance to be read to in Zapotec. [The missionaries] also made bilingual primers to teach literacy, and these primers did not just focus on the New Testament; they were also designed to help Zapotecs learn to read and write.[120]

For López Llaguno, the SIL missionaries helped strengthen Zapotec identity through their affirmation of Zapotec language.

Reminiscing about the positive contributions of missionaries like Butler and the Leals, López Llaguno noted that the missionaries built an airplane landing strip in the community. This landing strip benefited not just the missionaries as they brought in visitors or supplies but also the larger community and region. For example, individuals suffering from life-threatening conditions such as poisonous snakebites were airlifted out to hospitals in Oaxaca City or Puebla.[121] López Llaguno also gave examples of the Leals and Butler transporting community residents to the SIL Oaxaca headquarters in Mitla for medical check-ups by SIL physicians. He stated:

> They were very friendly, and I can say that through [the missionaries] many lives were saved.... Their services helped the community quite a bit.... Their health-care work benefited many who lived around the community; in fact, people would look for these linguists to obtain preventative medicine and treatments for adults as well as children. At the time there wasn't a way for us to get help; we were a remote town. There were no highways to the outside, and air service was the only way to get quickly out of the region. The missionaries put in a radio network that kept them in touch with the [JAARS] pilot and that's how so many people benefited from the services.[122]

Thus, unlike Flaviano López's suspicion over aerial activity in Yosondúa, Telésforo López Llaguno suggests that the JAARS service benefited the whole community, not just SIL personnel or converts.

López Llaguno also noted that Butler spent more time in Yatzachi than in the United States. He was particularly impressed to learn after her death that she was a well-respected college professor in Oregon, since she had always been humble about her background.[123] He further recalled how Butler supported women in opening small businesses such as bakeries.[124] The fact that some residents of his community traveled to SIL headquarters in Catalina, Arizona, for her 2000 funeral also suggests the connection community members felt with the North American missionary, as well as demonstrates transnational connections between the community and the SIL Arizona office near the US-Mexican border. Most important, López Llaguno asserted that Butler truly identified with the Zapotecs and privileged their culture over American culture.[125]

López Llaguno provides key insight into the conflict between Protestant beliefs and traditional costumbres of the town. As discussed in Chapter Three, indigenous Catholics argued that Protestantism was incompatible with ancient customs and rituals. These practices included financial cooperation for the annual patron saint fiesta, regular participation in voluntary tequio (collective work) projects, and fulfillment of a cargo (public service) position. Protestants, in turn, argued that many of the community rituals involved alcohol and dancing and that the collective labor projects served the Catholic churches where they no longer worshiped. This type of conflict in Yatzachi provides an example of adapting traditional obligations to religious values.

López Llaguno insists that he was able to complete his cargo assignments as municipal president and director of the elementary school board without any incidents; he marched in patriotic parades with the Mexican flag and he led his community in the Grito de Dolores on Independence Day. "So, that is why people here never complain about us, because we always fulfilled our obligation."[126] He claims that he was able to negotiate religious differences quite easily. He said some in the community were nervous about doing the feast day with him as president because they doubted he would participate in the traditional dance that opens the festival. When asked how he adapted his religious beliefs with community customs, he said he never had any major difficulties balancing the two.

> I was municipal president in 2001, and there were various weddings that year. The costumbre is that the municipal president has to start the dance. The people here admired me and many of them congratulated me on what a good job I did. Of course, thank God, my father provided me with a good education, and I know well the culture of the town. One elderly lady asked me if I was going to dance. I told her, "Of course, Tia! But I'm going to do it with my five senses and not with the bottle in my hand and that won't take anything away from it." Here I was [at the fiesta] and most of them thought I was going to leave or not even come in the first place. One person asked me if I was going to skip the fiesta. I asked him why would I skip it? It turns out there were rumors about whether I would

or wouldn't go on that day or if I even knew how to dance. I do dance the *son* music that plays here, and I showed them. Everyone had their mouths wide open, since I danced well, and I was not drunk. I danced because it was the custom of the town and it made the people happy that I honored it because my mother told me many years ago that if the *presidente* didn't dance, there wouldn't be a party because everyone would leave. No, I tell you, I didn't skip this custom.[127]

Pastor López Llaguno's interview emphasizes his full participation in the fiesta without drinking. He danced while sober, with his *cinco sentidos* (full senses) not intoxicated and, therefore, took part in the dance more seriously than the typical festival revelers. Although he was a Protestant, López Llaguno was able to maintain meaningful roles in the community. The fact that over 10 percent of municipal presidents in Oaxaca today are Protestants suggests that Protestants are finding ways to negotiate custom with religious beliefs as they increasingly take on political roles of importance in their communities.[128] SIL missionaries also played a key role in publishing Zapotec reading material and providing access to health care, which complicates the common assertion that the SIL divided indigenous communities. López Llaguno was able to negotiate his Protestant beliefs with tradition. As his interview attests, the SIL is positively remembered in Yatzachi to this day. To defend itself from criticism that it was an imperialistic organization, the SIL often invited well-known Mexican intellectuals, activists, or indigenous peoples to speak on their behalf.

SIL Responds

Shortly after the Colegio de Etnólogos y Antropólogos Sociales's (National College of Ethnologists and Social Anthropologists, CEAS) 1975 condemnation of the organization, the president of SIL Mexico, John Alsop, sent the national news journal *Proceso* three letters from indigenous men in San Juan Atepec and Ixtlán de Juárez, Oaxaca, defending the presence of the SIL. Two supporters, Simón Pérez and Amós Hernández, claimed that the SIL missionaries taught them to defend their rights and to live a better quality of life.[129] Pérez and Hernández compared the positive contributions the SIL made to Atepec to improvements Benito Juárez brought in modernizing Mexico in the mid-nineteenth century. Mario Villalobos Villalobos wrote that from the time that he was nine years old, he had had a close relationship with the SIL missionaries in Atepec. He described how they taught him to read in Zapotec. He closed his letter by stating that those who criticize the SIL missionaries in Oaxaca did not really know them.[130]

Responding to criticism of SIL work in Oaxaca, Mexican ethnographer Iñigo Laviada cited SIL missionary Walter Miller's forty years of labor in Mixe communities. Laviada complained in December 1978 that clueless Mexico City journalists engaged in old tropes linking US missionaries like Miller to espionage, despite never having set foot in an indigenous village. Laviada, who conducted his research in the Mixes region and knew Miller personally, wrote this in response to a November 1978 article in Mexico City's *Excélsior* that insinuated SIL missionaries gave out free lunches to Oaxacan schoolchildren because they want "to fatten the children up and convert them into fuel for airplanes."[131]

SIL missionary Barbara Hollenbach offers a similar defense of the SIL's impact on indigenous communities. Hollenbach and her husband Bruce were SIL linguists in the Juxtlahuaca Triqui zone of Oaxaca from 1960 to 1980. The Hollenbachs returned to Oaxaca again in 1996 to work in the Mixtec community of Magdalena Peñasco, Tlaxiaco. Hollenbach mentioned false accusations that SIL employees heard during their tenure in Oaxaca:

> Accusations that get recycled are that we are stealing their language and making big money selling it in the US, that we are testing drugs for US pharmaceutical companies, that we are sterilizing Indian women to keep the population down, that we are kidnapping people and turning their bodies into rocket fuel, and that we work for the CIA.... In fact, when my husband and I got to Tlaxiaco [in 1996], the rumor was that we were spies for sub-comandante Marcos. I think my aptitude for "spy" on a scale of zero to ten would be something like minus two.[132]

Hollenbach also defended the SIL against the common accusation that it tried to destroy local customs. According to Hollenbach, such changes had little to do with the SIL. Hollenbach stated:

The introduction of schools has also had considerable influence, but I think roads have done more, partly by letting the outside world in, but mainly by letting the indigenous people leave for periods of time and see other customs and places. Another huge factor in the past decade or two is media, first the radio, then TV and satellite TV, and now the Internet. There is virtually nothing in the media to promote indigenous languages or culture, and the influences are in general far from healthy.[133]

Hollenbach touches on several key criticisms of the SIL in Latin America. Her observations about other factors besides Protestantism changing indigenous customs are important. There certainly were divisions and significant changes in Oaxacan communities prior to the arrival of SIL missionaries; to argue otherwise discounts indigenous agency. But at the same time, while Protestantism in itself might not have caused the extensive changes detractors claimed, the SIL did have powerful and long-lasting connections within and outside of Mexico. Additionally, while the SIL denied its links to US politics, W. C. Townsend met regularly with US presidents and senators.[134] While there is little documented evidence to link SIL Mexico to any ties with the CIA, it is not hard to understand why Mexican politicians, activists, or local leaders associated the SIL with the US government's covert actions in Guatemala, Chile, and Bolivia to usurp socialist regimes. The SIL prided itself on its good rapport with Latin American government officials, many of whom in the late 1970s were right-wing military dictators.[135]

INI/SEP Response

As a result of the mounting questionable exposés of the SIL's purported CIA connections and the lobbying of Mexico City anthropologists, INI officials acted quickly in 1979.[136] SEP director Fernando Solana Morales appointed Salomón Nahmad Sittón, director of the Department of Indigenous Affairs, to evaluate the benefits or risks of SEP's continued partnership with the SIL. In his June 19, 1979, memorandum to Solana, Nahmad Sittón advised the immediate cancellation of the SEP-SIL bilingual education agreement.[137] Nahmad Sittón warned that pending journalistic revelations of the SIL's ties to the CIA and petroleum companies would be comparable to Watergate.[138]

If SEP continued to work with the SIL, SEP would face fierce criticism in the national and international arenas. Nahmad Sittón asserted that any SIL linguistic work underway in indigenous communities could immediately be transferred to SEP's Department of Indigenous Affairs. It should, he argued, be Mexican bilingual promoters, not North Americans, designing public education curricula for indigenous children.[139]

Along with his recommendation that SEP sever its ties with the North American organization, Nahmad Sittón assured his superiors that he had contacted the Cárdenas family to inform them that SEP and INI no longer desired collaboration with the SIL. This was a delicate matter because, at the time, Amalia Cárdenas, General Cárdenas's widow, was the honorary president of the SIL in Mexico. She and her son, Cuauhtémoc Cárdenas, future Partido de la Revolución Democrática (Party of the Democratic Revolution, PRD) presidential candidate, had appeared at several SIL events. For example, in June 1977, the Cárdenas family traveled to Waxhaw, North Carolina, to inaugurate the SIL's Mexico-Cárdenas Museum, which one Mexico City journalist described as "a symbol of goodwill and friendship between two neighboring countries."[140] Despite such a close relationship, Nahmad Sittón reported that the Cárdenas family understood the political firestorm surrounding the SIL and would sever their ties with the organization.

Losing the Cárdenas family's backing was a crucial blow to the SIL's legitimacy in Mexico. The organization prided itself on its relationship with the Cárdenas family stretching back to 1935 and saw Cárdenas as a close friend. In fact, the most popular display at the Mexico-Cárdenas Museum is the 1938 blue Chevrolet automobile that "Don Lázaro" donated to Townsend for his fieldwork excursions.[141] Townsend's support of Cárdenas's decision to nationalize Mexican oil in 1938 put him at odds with Protestant donors in the United States who branded the Cardenista administration as socialist. After his presidency, Cárdenas and Townsend remained close friends. Lázaro and Amalia Cárdenas served as best man and matron of honor in Townsend's second marriage, to Elaine Mielke, in 1946; the ceremony took place in the Cárdenas home along Lake Pátzcuaro, Michoacán.[142] Furthermore, in 1952, Townsend wrote a hagiographic biography of Cárdenas, reviewed by the *New York Times*. An opportune second edition was published in 1979, just as the SIL was wearing out its welcome in Mexico. Townsend's collaboration with the Mexican government since 1935 earned him the Aguila award in 1978, the highest honor a foreigner can receive from the Mexican government. This close relationship with the government changed in one quick year because of the efforts of Mexican scholars.

The academics of the Mexico City–based CEAS used the framework of internal colonialism to describe SIL's influence on indigenous communities in Latin America. CEAS's involvement began in 1975, when anthropologist Jesús Ángel Ochoa Zazueta labeled the SIL a "pseudo-scientific imperialist organization" in his eighty-five-page condemnation of the SIL.[143] Signed by thirty prominent Mexican anthropologists, it concluded with a demand that all government entities, individual researchers, and activists working on cultural projects in indigenous communities denounce the SIL and its activities and support its immediate suspension.[144] In early September 1979, the CEAS led an organized opposition movement against the SIL. Finally, on September 21, in response to Nahmad Sittón's recommendations and the CEAS protests and press campaigns, SEP formally severed the bilingual education contract with the SIL that dated back to 1951.

A special edition of *Proceso* in October of 1979 followed CEAS's denunciation of the SEP-SIL contract. The lead articles argued that the SIL undermined indigenous traditions in Oaxaca and fostered violent confrontations between evangelical Protestants and Catholics.[145] The *Proceso* special issue contained several interviews with community leaders and indigenous educators throughout Oaxaca. Opponents of the SIL focused on its negative impact on indigenous culture through its insistence on individualism, not collectivism. Eliseo Pérez García, legal representative for Indigenous Affairs in the Sierra Juárez, Oaxaca, complained that the SIL destroyed converts' participation in tequio. He wrote, "To this, the gringos state that there is not an Article in the Mexican Constitution that obliges Mexicans to contribute to tequio. They [the gringos] say tequio goes against God and that we should respect private property. Many of us are opposed to them but the truth is that these [Mexican converts] side with the Bible [over tequio]."[146] Pérez García's assertion speaks to the overarching argument against Protestantism in indigenous communities in that it prioritizes individualism over collectivism.

Nationalism and anti-imperialism also played important roles in the rapid demise of the SIL. Mexicans who converted to Protestantism and befriended missionaries were called "malinchistas," or "sellouts," a reference to conquistador Hernán Cortés's indigenous translator and mistress, La Malinche. For example, Santiago Salazar, coordinator of the Spanish Language Pilot Plan in the Mixteca, complained that in San Juan Mixtepec, there was an American known as "Uncle Tom" who became involved in all town activities. However, he concluded, "The indigenous people also are to blame for letting foreigners or white people impact the community. Unfortunately, 'el malinchismo' still causes us much damage."[147] Again, converting to Protestantism undermined not just indigenous cultures but also Mexican nationalism.

Other Oaxacan opponents to the SIL focused on the SIL's monopoly of bilingual education. Cándido Coheto Martínez, later State Coordinator of Indigenous Education, looked back at the conflict in Santiago Yosondúa to exemplify why SEP teachers, not missionaries, should be in charge of bilingual education:

> It is false that bilingual education advocates are not qualified to develop the linguistics field. Our promoters have prepared bilingual primers of very high quality, but we need support.... While the SIL is given translation contracts for bilingual textbooks, our [INI/SEP] work is not recognized and we are abandoned [by government entities].[148]

Flor Vásquez, regional advocate for Zapotec communities of the Central Valleys, agreed with Coheto Martínez: "Despite the many shortcomings, our work has greater significance than that developed by members of SIL, because they don't know us [indigenous Oaxacans] intimately. We talk to our people in our native language and, at the same time, teach them Spanish. But not as the missionaries that try to make us forget our language in search of a divine peace and other non-existent paradises."[149] Vásquez's statement makes it clear that Native indigenous language speakers—not North American missionaries—should be in control of empowering Mexico's indigenous people through culturally sensitive programs, not Bible study. INI and SEP agreed.

Nahmad Sittón and other prominent Mexican anthropologists such as Margarita Nolasco, Guillermo Bonfil Batalla, and Rodolfo Stavenhagen argued that the SIL's school primers taught indigenous children to be submissive and to adopt "el american way of life."[150] For example, primers designed for Chinantec-speaking children in northern Oaxaca near the Veracruz border teach Chinantec children to be respectful of authority and mind their social status; in "Juan Tonto," "Foolish Juan" always did the opposite of "Juan Listo" or "Intelligent Juan." In another primer, "El Carbonero Vengador," "the Avenging Coalman" caught indigenous customers stealing from him, instead of paying for individual orders. Both primers conveyed messages that the indigenous person was childlike and that one had to respect the rights of private property and businesses or else pay the consequences.[151]

In such primers, indigenous people were always depicted as laborers, and mestizos were their honest but firm employers who required them to dress appropriately in Western clothing and follow all directions. Indigenous protagonists who had not adapted new ways were depicted as always carrying a bottle of aguardiente and dressed in tattered manta fabric clothing with palm hats. These primers were published in 1978 and suggest that the SIL (and SEP) still had not made the transition from 1950s era primers, such as the Mixtec "Jica ri escuela" (I Go to School) in which the young boy humbly greets his mestizo teacher and learns the basics about sickness prevention and hygiene. In the late 1970s' indigenous rights climate, INI officials wanted to transition to a bilingual education program that affirmed indigenous cultures, autonomy, and self-determination. The embarrassment for the Mexican government, according to Nahmad Sittón, was that such aforementioned SIL primers were stamped with INI and SEP seals of approval.[152]

Another critique Mexican anthropologists had of the SIL's educational manuals in Oaxaca was that the cooking recipes directed at indigenous women were not possible with the basic stoves available in rural Oaxaca, nor were they culturally sensitive to local diets. For example, pancakes for breakfast and peanut butter and jelly sandwiches for lunch were not staple menus for Oaxacan family cuisine and often called for ingredients that were unavailable, unaffordable, or unappetizing to rural people.[153]

To reverse what he called cultural ethnocide, Nahmad Sittón pushed for INI to train and send its own workers to do outreach to indigenous communities, not North Americans.[154] By 1980, INI had eighty-five Centros de Coordinador Indígenistas (Indigenist Coordinating Centers, CCI) in Mexico. This was a substantial increase from the beginnings in 1951, when there were just two Centros de Coordinador in the whole country, eleven centers in 1970, and sixty-four centers in 1975.[155] In Oaxaca, there were twenty centers in 1980, an increase from just three in 1954. In 1980, INI began to devote a greater share of its budget to recruitment and training of Native (bilingual) education advocates.[156] As INI programming grew, the SIL scaled down its own, but it did not ever fully withdraw from Mexico.

SIL in Oaxaca, Post-1979

SIL's exodus from Mexico was a prolonged and contested process. Many linguists were still in the midst of fieldwork and asked for additional time. Despite being in Mexico for forty-three years, the SIL still had barely completed half of its proposed translations, a goal that would have rendered their stay indefinite.[157] About half of the total SIL employees already had legal residency in Mexico, making the nonrenewal of work visas difficult to enforce. In addition, Townsend used his remaining connections with respected Mexican politicians and intellectuals to appeal SEP's decision and stall the organization's departure.[158] As an immediate measure to satisfy the CEAS accusations of secret training in clandestine zones of southern Mexico, the SIL closed its "Jungle Camp" in the Lacandón rain forest of Chiapas.[159]

The most visible post-1979 denunciations against the SIL took place in Oaxaca. Between 1936 and 1979, SIL linguist-missionaries had worked in thirty Oaxacan communities, studying variants of the Cuicateco, Chinanteco, Chontal, Huave, Mazateco, Mixe, Mixtec, Triqui, and Zapotec languages. According to the 1975 census, over 11 percent of Oaxacans were monolingual in an indigenous language only, thus Oaxaca remained an important linguistic zone. In 1979, the SIL had 372 employees in the country, 92 of whom were in Oaxaca.[160] Missionary-linguists still aspired to work on New Testament translations for sixty-two more Oaxacan dialects.[161]

Despite the SEP-SIL contract severance, the Oaxacan headquarters at Mitla continued operating normally. Mitla directors John Lind and Alan Jamieson proceeded with scheduled linguistics workshops. A visiting reporter from *Proceso*, Ignacio Ramírez, described SIL's Mitla "base" as an ostentatious example of Yankee imperialism. He noted the American-style housing units, with fences to separate each individual lawn; California, Virginia, North Carolina, Arizona, and Texas license plates on cars in the driveways; and the exclusive playground with shiny slides and monkey bars for linguists' children. As one Mitla resident complained, "The gringos own practically the whole hill up there."[162] The SIL's decision to continue working in Oaxaca led to more conflicts in the 1980s.

Beginning in 1983, Oaxacan indigenous rights networks and and the Unión Nacional de Padres de Familia (National Parents Association) launched a series of public complaints against the SIL's continued presence in Oaxaca. On March 23, 1983, *Novedades* reported that Oaxacan indigenous activists encouraged President Miguel de la Madrid Hurtado to issue an edict demanding the SIL's departure.[163] Despite Fernando Solana Morales's elimination of the SIL-SEP contract on September 21, 1979, SIL linguists continued their work throughout the 570 municipalities of Oaxaca.[164]

President de la Madrid made a much-anticipated visit to Oaxaca to share his commitment to indigenous communities and to show respect for cultural preservation. His visit was planned to coincide with President Benito Juárez's national holiday of March 21. He outlined his administration's vision for social and economic programs in indigenous zones of Mexico, comparing the resilient strength of Oaxacans to its most famous native son. In honor of Juárez's legacy, he pledged 493 million pesos to Governor Pedro Vásquez Colmenares for development programs in indigenous zones.[165] That sum, combined with Vásquez Colmenares's proposal to invest 563 million pesos in creating public highways in rural zones, was the largest investment for development outside of the state capital or tourist zones along the coast.

Newly inaugurated in December 1982, de la Madrid set forth his agenda for indigenous Mexico during that spring Oaxaca visit: "Mexico's indigenous policy should not be a policy for indigenous people but rather with indigenous people. We want to hear proposals from indigenous people and have them actively participate in relevant programs. We want indigenous Oaxacans to be the authors, not the objects of state and federal programs."[166] De la Madrid's vision represented a striking overhaul from the original architects of Mexican indigenism who saw themselves as benevolent fathers of indigenous peoples who would transition into mestizos. Part of this commitment to indigenous Mexico meant the ouster of the SIL. On the campaign trail, in his *consultas populares* (public meetings), de la Madrid bluntly stated that the only thing the SIL had accomplished in indigenous villages was to "impose the truth of the white man."[167]

In a visit to the Mixteca Baja town of Laguna de Guadalupe in Juxtlahuaca, de la Madrid ordered remaining SIL missionaries to leave Oaxaca. The Unión Nacional de Padres de Familia praised de la Madrid's enforcement of the SIL's departure from Oaxaca.[168] Association president José Ortiz Arana stated that "religious sects, especially the North American SIL, have as an objective to divide our indigenous communities and eliminate their customs and beliefs."[169] De la Madrid agreed. In his speech to Laguna de Guadalupe residents, he warned: "We are Mexicans because of our indigenous roots, and if we allow the loss of these indigenous cultures, we will be denying all Mexicans their heritage."[170]

A popular political cartoon published in Oaxaca City's *Noticias* the day after de la Madrid's visit perhaps best sums up the SIL persona non grata status in Oaxaca (fig. 13). The cartoon depicts an indigenous person in tattered clothing, representing the state of Oaxaca, who is having his feet washed. The dirty water or perhaps mud coming off of his filthy feet represents the expected departure of the SIL from Oaxaca. The cartoon by Ortiz Ramírez is titled "Lavatorio" or "Washroom." Here, the artist might simply mean "bathroom," or he might be making a larger criticism of the SIL's penchant for recruiting native language speakers to help them in their language laboratories as they translate the New Testament. Thus, the scene depicted could easily take place in one of SIL's high-tech language facilities such as the Mitla base. Another way to interpret the drawing is in the context of semana santa, Holy Week. Easter was on April 3 in 1983, just over a week following the publication of Ortiz Ramírez's cartoon. So, it is not inconceivable that the scene depicts Maundy Thursday as recorded by John 13:1–17, in which Jesus washes the apostles' feet before the Last Supper. This event is an important holy day for Catholics, and it is especially celebrated in Oaxaca, with all villagers attending mass together and marching in feast day processions.[171] Oaxaca was ridding itself of the SIL's sins.

Another cartoon by the same artist depicts the SIL as Satan, and President Miguel de la Madrid Hurtado (MMH) as the archangel Michael (fig. 14). As in the previous one, this cartoon coincides with de la Madrid's visit to Oaxaca, when he had harsh words for the organization. We see that the Oaxacan campesino (peasant) is stuck in the middle, impoverished, and in tattered clothes, like the indigenous person depicted in the previous cartoon. It is as if the campesino is caught between two powerful forces, neither beneficial.

Figure 13. Political cartoon celebrating the SIL's (ILV in Spanish) imminent departure from Oaxaca. *Noticias*, March 22, 1983. Courtesy of Hemeroteca Pública de Oaxaca.

Perhaps referencing Revelation 12:7–9, de la Madrid raises his sword to slay Satan (the SIL), who is hiding behind the wall. The campesino is trying to pull de la Madrid into Oaxaca to deal with the SIL situation. The peasant is suffering from Mexico's severe economic crisis, which began in 1982 and would last most of the 1980s. It particularly affected Oaxaca, which was also experiencing a major agricultural crisis. The campesino is clutching a document attesting to his bankruptcy, perhaps suggesting that his community is a victim of the SIL's monopoly of the Oaxacan social, religious, and economic arenas.

Despite de la Madrid's strong pleas for the SIL to leave Oaxaca during his March 1983 visit, and various congressional meetings in 1984, the SIL pressed on. This presence occasionally garnered protests from organizations aligned with leftist organizations that viewed the SIL as an obstacle to indigenous campesino political organizing. In addition, despite affirming the

Figure 14. A destitute Oaxacan campesino caught between Archangel Michael (President Miguel de la Madrid Hurtado) and Satan (ILV/SIL). *Noticias*, March 23, 1983. Courtesy of Hemeroteca Pública de Oaxaca.

importance of the preservation of native languages, the SIL rigidly avoided association with grassroots indigenous rights' coalitions, which used indigenous identity to frame their challenges to the state throughout the 1970s and 1980s.[172] As an example, the Oaxacan State Public Security cited a 1984 demonstration of eighty Mixtecs from Huertilla in Huajuapan de León, in Oaxaca City's zocalo (main plaza).[173] During the protest, participants used a microphone to chant "Out with the Gringos" as they marched with four different banners demanding the release of political prisoners and solidarity with the Organización Campesina Revolucionaria (Revolutionary Peasant Organization).[174] The protesters especially demanded the release of La Huertilla's municipal president, Zarafin Estrada Zurita, and the immediate departure of the SIL from the Mixteca region.[175]

Despite all the public protests and press campaigns such as the ones just described, Mexico never formally expelled the SIL. Instead, the SIL lost one of its key buildings in Mexico City; it already belonged to the Mexican government. Yet, perhaps most damaging, they permanently lost their prestigious textbook contract. Many SIL personnel relocated temporarily to Catalina, Arizona, until the fall of 1985. With Mexico's economic crisis at its peak and minimal confidence left in de la Madrid's leadership after his botched handling of the 1985 Mexico City earthquake, the attacks against *imperialismo yankee* faded to the background. SIL linguists started working again, albeit without Mexican government support.

Indigenous Rights and Language Revitalization

Anthropologist Henning Siverts argued in 1969 that only "romantic intellectuals and certain idealistic absentee politicians" use a shared sense of "Indianhood" to describe the 800,000 Tzotzil and Tzeltal highland Maya.[176] But this was changing. Encouraged by the slight democratic opening following the 1968 student movement and influenced by "participatory indigenism," indigenous communities asserted demands for self-determination and autonomy in Mexico.[177] In the 1970s, Mexican indigenous rights leaders were in the nascent stage of molding a pan-indigenous movement. This unification stressed the shared struggles of Native Mexicans. While no actual indigenous people attended the original Barbados Conference, it was the seed for Mexico's First National Congress of Indigenous Peoples in 1975.[178] In 1981, the Coalición Obrera Campesina Estudiantil del Istmo (Coalition of Workers, Peasants, and Students of the Isthmus, COCEI) a radical Zapotec political movement based in Juchitán, became the first indigenous party to win control of a municipal government.[179]

Native languages played an important role in indigenous rights movements.[180] In the 1980s, a new generation of anthropologists and indigenous activists promoted the reclamation and revitalization of Native languages, cultures, and traditions.[181] INI ethnolinguist Eduardo García Santiago lamented the dearth of publications in Mixtec. In his 1982 *Clases Sociales y Grupos Étnicos en Yosondúa*, he noted that SIL missionaries had published the only local stories and legends written in the Mixtec language: "Aside from those publications, nothing of Mixtec history or culture existed in the predominantly Mixtec-speaking Tlaxiaco district."[182] Through the reclamation of indigenous languages, García Santiago hoped for national and international indigenous solidarity.

> When the Indian knows his true history, when he is able to write his own history and reclaim its truth without feeling shame, we will then be able to identify with our true history, and that will be our first step toward the national liberation of Indian people. When we have taken this important step, we can then take the next step which will be the unity of our ethnic group for future relations with Indians all over this country and the world, that way forming a group of ideas that will allow us to fight against the oppression that we've been subjected to.[183]

Santiago García's vision was a noticeable change in the conceptualization of indigenous identity, moving from localized to pan-indigenous. However, having a standardized language per ethnic group remains an obstacle for the movement's cohesion, considering the vast number and differences in indigenous languages and cultures.

Ayuujk (Mixe) ethnologist Juan Carlos Reyes Gómez agrees with García Santiago about the lack of language publications by Native linguists. He also notes the challenges Native linguists face. Reyes states: "As long as it's not us, the actual Native speakers, leading language programs, we won't be able to ensure the preservation of our languages."[184] For example, there are dozens of indigenous rights organizations that are currently struggling to agree on a standard alphabet for each of Oaxaca's sixteen ethnic groupings. Reyes Gómez founded a civil society organization dedicated to promoting a standard Mixe language. A challenge it faces in the Mixe region of Oaxaca's Sierra Norte is that there are over twenty-two local dialects of Mixe, making it difficult to form one standard alphabet, which is Reyes Gómez's goal. He said the SIL has always opposed that idea because the dialects are sufficiently different enough to require separate translations. Reyes Gómez maintains that while many of the dialects are different enough, they must standardize in order for more publications in Mixe to reach Mixe communities and for bilingual teachers to be able to design better quality, in-depth curriculums. Reyes Gómez acknowledged the foundational work the SIL did in valorizing indigenous languages. He noted that when he first trained as a linguist in the late 1980s, he used SIL dictionaries and scholarly publications to understand

Mixe syntax and grammar rules. But at the same time, Reyes Gómez argued that the language revitalization movement has to happen from within, and it must not have any obligations to religious affiliations that could serve to divide communities.[185]

Reyes Gómez's participation in Mixe language preservation organizations brings up a key dilemma that indigenous activists, anthropologists, and the SIL continue to disagree over today. Linguist-activists like Reyes Gómez argue that having twenty-two different dialects of Mixe in Oaxaca prevents a unified pan-Mixe organization from developing and strengthening Mixe demands to the state and federal governments. The SIL's practice of translating religious and other Mixe literature into dozens of variants contributes to Mixe language disunity. The debate over whether to standardize the individual variants of each of Oaxaca's sixteen distinct indigenous languages is an ongoing issue in revitalization movements today.

Founded in Tlaxiaco, Oaxaca, in 1989 to preserve the Mixtec language, the independent Ve'e Tu'un Savi (House of the Voice of the Rain) organizes language symposiums to unite Mixtecs from the coast, highlands, and lowlands. Ve'e Tu'un Savi is also transnational, serving Mixtec migrants living in Tijuana and southern California. The organization uses a standardized alphabet for Mixtec's roughly fifty-four variants.[186] However, Mixtecs opposed to a uniform alphabet argue that standardization takes away from the important nuances of each dialect. As the Mixtec and Mixe revitalization movements in Oaxaca suggest, language can be a political tool that can concomitantly harm and bolster identity movements.

Since 1951, the SIL has published a volume every four years that keeps a running tally on all living languages in the world.[187] *Ethnologue* was originally designed as a guide for Protestant missionaries learning about rare languages before starting a mission site. It is now a go-to guide for social workers, healthcare providers, law enforcement, US State Department officials, and anthropologists preparing for fieldwork in new communities. However, what a researcher counts or does not count as a separate language has cultural and political ramifications.[188] In 2005, *Ethnologue* listed fifty-four different indigenous languages in Guatemala, whereas non-SIL Guatemalan linguists had documented eighteen.[189] This drastic difference illustrates a common critique of the SIL. By dividing language families into so many different dialects, it discouraged pan-ethnic or pan-indigenous organizing.

In the highlands of Guatemala, modern Mayan political movements want to condense all recognized dialects of the Mayan language into one lingua franca: Cakchiquel. However, a major problem within the pan-Mayan movement, similar to the one Reyes Gómez mentioned for Mixe in Oaxaca, is deciding which variant to privilege. Which regional Mayan language becomes the archetype for all Mayans to follow? Inevitably, some communities will feel marginalized. Losing one's language has significant cultural and identity implications; affirming one's native language can be a core component of indigenous identity. Should linguists invent a comprehensive dialect that combines aspects of all of the languages? The advantage of having one pan-Mayan language is that it could be recognized as an official language of Guatemala and gain recognition on par with the Spanish language at government functions. It's dubious the Guatemalan government would have the resources or desire to provide official documents in dozens of different Mayan languages. Anthropologist Kay B. Warren has traced this debate in her studies on pan-Mayan activism in Guatemala. Recognizing the power dynamics at stake, she warns: "In the question for standardization, scientific knowledge is playing a key role in the historical reconstruction of tradition and the mediation of what otherwise might be endless disputes between actual communities based on loyalty to place and ancestors."[190] SIL missionary-linguists' application of a scientific formula to languages had deeply significant cultural and political implications.

Conclusion

The SIL's presence in Oaxaca is long, contested, and complex. Many Oaxacans are surprised they still operate in Oaxaca.[191] In the community of Yosondúa, the expulsion of the SIL in 1977 was publicized as a watershed example of indigenous autonomy and resistance to outside penetration of their community. In Yatzachi, the SIL's long history resulted in a more favorable memory of the organization. The controversial presence of the SIL in Oaxaca shaped a new generation of bilingual educators who believed that language revitalization should come from within the community, not with any religious strings attached. The SIL's headquarters at Mitla continues its operations, though the playground equipment is rusty and many of the housing units are empty most of the year, partly because of new technology. With digital sound recorders and transcription software, many SIL linguists are able to finish translation work at the SIL International Linguistics Center in Dallas, Texas, instead of working on the Mitla Center's outdated IBM computers.

While researching at Mitla's Jaime Torres Bodet Library, I was astonished to find shelf after shelf of New Testament translations in local variations of Mixtec, Zapotec, Mazatec, Triqui, Chinanteco, Cuicateco, and Chocho. The language proficiency of the SIL missionaries was impressive. At the same time, the SIL's work was too long of a process to be effective in immediately preserving languages. Translating the New Testament into every single community dialect required an SIL missionary to live in one indigenous community for at least a decade. The SIL maintains that, by laboriously translating all languages including local variants, the organization is validating and valorizing localized ethnolinguistic identities. Pan-indigenous revitalization movements argue that the SIL's method is impractical and leads to ethnic fragmentation.

Yet as much as INI and SEP bilingual education advocates have criticized the quality of SIL translations, they are still often the only dictionaries or primers from marginalized communities in Oaxaca.[192] Of the former INI bilingual education advocates whom I interviewed, the majority affirmed that if it had not been for the SIL, some of the older myths and legends would perhaps never have been recorded. Yet, because of the convenience of using the SIL for so many decades, INI and SEP lacked the funds and support to train larger generations of its own bilingual promoters prior to 1979.[193]

Protestantism breaks down social hierarchies and encourages ordinary community members to lead a Bible study or build a church. Subsequently, mechanisms that keep a community running, such as tequio and cargo, are disrupted by Protestant conversion. Yet, some Protestant converts have found ways to negotiate clashes between tradition and religious conversion. In Yatzachi, Telésforo López Llaguno was initially ridiculed for leaving his religion and giving up drinking. He managed to negotiate cargo responsibilities with his religious values. Protestantism also operated as a door, allowing outsiders (missionaries or INI officials) symbolically and physically to enter traditionally closed villages. The mixed nature of outside intervention was apparent in Yosondúa, where an SIL missionary couple's activities threatened the authorities concerned with protecting pre-Hispanic sacred spaces. Santiago Ojeda countered that Protestantism actually reinforced indigenous identity, by teaching Yosondúans to read in their native tongue.

The SIL's entrenched presence in indigenous communities overlapped into discussions of indigenous rights and autonomy in Oaxaca. On one hand, the SIL argued that it was promoting indigenous identity and culture by recording these languages and affirming the importance of regional dialects. On the other hand, SIL opponents argued that by encouraging Protestants to not participate in feast days and tequio assignments for the Church, the SIL was unraveling centuries of traditions and social adhesion. Additionally, from the national government's point of view, accusations of Protestant neoimperialism bandied about by social scientists were far more damaging to the PRI's hegemony than a handful of Mexican Protestant families angry at the state for not backing individual religious rights. The following chapter examines the reaction of the Catholic Church to Protestant organizations, especially during the 1970s and 1980s. When Pope John Paul II visited Oaxaca in early 1979, the SIL was still operating there, albeit controversially.

CHAPTER FIVE

Liberation Theology, Indigenous Rights, and Nationalism

> I would like to meet with you one by one to tell you: come back to the fold of the church, your mother.
>
> —POPE JOHN PAUL II IN MEXICO CITY, 1990

JOHN PAUL II made headlines when he traveled to Mexico in January of 1979. His weeklong schedule revolved around his invitation to address the Third General Conference of Latin American Bishops in Puebla City, south of the capital. The ambitious trip also included visits to Oaxaca in the southwest, the central western state of Guanajuato, and, finally, Nuevo León in northern Mexico. Mexico City reporters described the crowds coming out to greet Pope John Paul II as "a human river of people."[1]

The Mexican tour drew attention for several reasons. It was John Paul II's first international trip since his election to the papacy in September of 1978. He was the first pope to visit Mexico and only the second to visit Latin America. The press was curious about the first non-Italian pope in centuries. He was relatively young and an avid exerciser, requesting a stationary bicycle in his accommodations abroad.[2] His papacy also represented an important crossroads for the Vatican. At the Puebla conference, he dealt with the discord between the institutional and the grassroots church over liberation theology. John Paul II went to a country that was passionately Catholic but also politically cut off from the Vatican. Finally, he entered Mexico at a time of shifting conceptualizations of Native peoples' role in the nation-state.

During the 1970s and 1980s, the Catholic Church increasingly became concerned with Protestant growth, pejoratively referring to the trend as "the invasion of the sects."[3] Oaxacan and Chiapan bishops worried that Protestant competition weakened indigenous communities at a time when they collectively needed to unite against state repression. For the bishops, stemming the tide of Protestantism became synonymous with fighting for indigenous rights. Despite the PRI's focus on participatory indigenism in the 1970s and 1980s, violence against Native peoples was rampant in southern Mexico. The popular church saw liberation theology as a strategy in defending indigenous struggles for autonomy.

The Vatican's changing strategies toward Protestant growth illustrated a wide spectrum of responses the Catholic Church had to religious competition. John Paul II visited Mexico five times, his last trip culminating with the canonization of the indigenous peasant Juan Diego as a saint. By examining the national and local context of John Paul II's trip to Mexico in 1979, this chapter reveals the complications arising when nationalism, indigenous rights, liberation theology, and foreign relations all intersect.

Liberation Theology in Latin America

The Second Vatican Council (1962–1965) generated new ways of thinking about the role of the Catholic Church in contemporary society. How could the Church engage a world saddled with very real and present issues such as famine, nuclear weapons, or military dictatorships? Reforms included encouragement of ecumenism, prioritizing vernacular languages over Latin, and reassessment of modernity.[4] During the 1968 Second General Conference of Latin American Bishops (CELAM, Consejo Episcopal Latinoamericano), in Medellín, Colombia, participants produced several documents laying out how the Church would empower those seeking liberation from political repression, poverty, or social injustice.[5] Peruvian priest Gustavo Gutiérrez later coined the phrase "liberation theology."

Stemming from the foundational scholarship of Gutiérrez, Latin American bishops pushed for a preferential option for the poor in their ministries. Catholic clergy and laypeople worked together to radically alter the structural inequalities in poor and especially indigenous regions of Latin

America. This meant consciousness-raising—following educator Paulo Freire's model—and activism.[6] Christian base communities (Comunidades Eclesiales de Base, CEBs), empowered (often poor) laypeople to read the Gospel and apply its teachings to their own contemporary struggles.

Liberation theology brought mixed reactions in the region.[7] Some Latin American bishops embraced much of it—Bishop Samuel Ruiz of San Cristóbal de las Casas, Chiapas, Mexico, Archbishop Paulo Evaristo Cardenal Arns of São Paulo, Brazil, and Archbishop Oscar Romero of San Salvador, El Salvador—while Archbishop Alfonso López Trujillo of Medellín, Colombia, opposed it, citing the danger of "parallel" churches incorporating elements of Marxism.[8] Ultimately, liberation theology played a profound role in how the institutional Catholic Church and the popular church interacted.

Discussions of liberation theology demonstrated different interpretations of the Church's place in modern society, heightening divisions between the institutional and popular church. By "popular church," I mean how religion was practiced regionally and often at the grassroots level, integrating local traditions and culture; a church shaped by the people. By "institutional," I mean the Church hierarchy, particularly mandates emanating from Rome, concerned with preservation of uniformity of doctrine and practice. To be clear, the institutional church valued the role of the popular church—Vatican II reforms and later encyclicals issued by Paul VI and John Paul II supported local religious traditions and emphases. However, the institutional church's job is to set the universal pulse of the church. Some strains of liberation theology challenged this universality.[9]

Yet the Vatican did not wholly reject liberation theology. Pope John Paul II's growing concerns about it suggest the institutional church feared linking its doctrinal mission with a social and political message. In other words, the overlap between some liberation theology practices and Marxism was clearly problematic. For example, Vatican documents compiled by Cardinal Joseph Ratzinger (later Pope Benedict XVI) in the early 1980s condemned revolutionary activism by the clergy and cautioned that some strains of liberation theology were Marxist.[10] In that same decade, the Vatican temporarily silenced Brazilian theologian Leonardo Boff and publicly scolded priest and Sandinista Minister of Culture Ernesto Cardenal.

Whether or not John Paul II was too rigid on liberation theology remains a subject of contentious debates in the field of religious history.[11] He grew up in Communist Poland and perhaps did not grasp the nuances of liberation theology in Latin America, which he sometimes interpreted as inseparable from Marxism. Yet, because John Paul II's message, by the mid-1980s and the early 1990s, clearly criticized neoliberalism and emphasized liberationist agendas such as human rights in Latin America, his legacy on liberation theology is contested.[12]

Detailing the deep complexities of John Paul II's interpretation of liberation theology is beyond this study's aims. However, most scholars agree that between Medellín in 1968 and Puebla in 1979, the Vatican worried liberation theology overshadowed the core of the Church's teachings on the nature of salvation and the Church.[13] Given the Church's extremely restricted role in Castro's Cuba and the growing strength of the Sandinista movement in Nicaragua, the Vatican sought to distance itself from revolution. Reacting to these challenges, Pope Paul VI laid out the Vatican's conceptualization of the Church's place in social justice movements in a couple of important statements. In 1975, he called for the Church to uphold its commitment to transcendence, which is to say that the Church did not define itself by a social or political message, as liberation theology praxis prioritized.[14] In other words, it sought to balance a pursuit of social justice without reducing it to a more or less exclusive focus. Thus, Pope John Paul II wanted to recalibrate the levels of how liberation theology was playing out in Latin America.

The 1979 Conference of Latin American Bishops in Puebla re-examined liberation theology's impact on the region, exposing rifts between the institutional and popular church. In his address, John Paul II warned the episcopacy against boiling their ministries down to a single political or economic ideology. He clearly did not intend a blanket condemnation of the theology—he backed the preferential option for the poor—but was leery of Marxist interpretations of the theology. In fact, Pope John Paul II built on Paul VI's recommendations that the core of the Church's teachings should be ministry in accordance with the Gospel, not politics. By promoting conservative Alfonso López de Trujillo to Archbishop of Medellín in 1979, Pope John Paul II began to regain Vatican control over the Latin American episcopacy.[15]

Despite the institutional church's support of the more conservative factions of CELAM, theologians such as Leonardo Boff and Gustavo Gutiérrez influenced the final documents coming out of Puebla. Not permitted to attend, but writing commentaries off-site, they helped shape the documents to reflect a progressive strain, not the more traditional views of CELAM General Secretary Archbishop López Trujillo.[16] While the institutional church feared linking its mission with a political leaning, some bishops argued that the Church had to be political to stop repression.[17] These debates were noticeable to non-Catholic attendees of CELAM. Mexican Episcopal Church Bishop José Saucedo wrote that while liberation theology was a "thorn in the Church's side," he thought the Church allowed enough diversity of opinions to work through it.[18] This diversity of opinions often played out regionally in Latin America.

In southern Mexico, liberation theology has an important history beginning with support of agrarian and indigenous movements in the 1970s and ultimately providing some of the ideological framework for the 1994 Zapatista uprising.[19] Progressive-leaning bishops representing the pastoral region known as Pacífico Sur[20] promoted liberation theology in isolated indigenous regions by sponsoring CEBs and ministering to Central American refugees fleeing state repression in their own nations.[21] In Mexico, Pope John Paul II promised to stand with Native peoples of the Americas. However, from the popular church's perspective, the pope was naïve about the deep-seated problems they faced. Oaxaca would be his testing ground.

International Relations, Participatory Indigenism, and Anticlericalism

Nationalism was at the forefront of Mexico's foreign policy in the late 1970s. Mexican President José López Portillo had to handle the pope's January 1979 trip delicately. The visit was a chance to promote Mexico to the world: Hundreds of international journalists arrived in the days leading up to the historic visit. Many reporters highlighted Mexico's booming oil and natural gas industry. In fact, the following month, President Jimmy Carter would visit Mexico, determined to improve trade relations, especially in the wake of the United States' energy crisis.[22] Moreover, the United States viewed Mexico as an ally in democracy—albeit flawed—while right-wing military regimes controlled much of South America and Castro's Cuba continued to export revolutionary socialism to the region. President Carter praised the Mexican government for also being "gran amigo" with the United States.

Addressing the Mexican Congress on February 16, he acknowledged the tenets of Mexican nationalism surrounding subsoil rights. He stated, "We understand clearly that the Mexican oil resources are the national patrimony of the Mexican people, to be developed and used and sold as Mexico sees fit."[23] In previous interactions, López Portillo had insinuated that the United States still had a "big brother" approach to Mexico, instead of seeing the two nations as equals.[24] Given the oil crisis spurred by the Iranian Revolution, the Carter administration hoped to benefit from Mexico's recent windfall: Economists estimated that Mexico potentially had over two hundred billion barrels of oil in 1979.[25] While the actual oil reserves in Mexico turned out to be much lower—and overspending on the oil industry brought massive inflation by the mid-1980s—President López Portillo was able to command the attention of the Carter and Ronald Reagan administrations.[26]

Journalists, however, linked the nation's dependence on Roman Catholicism with its concomitant reliance on North American financial support. A political cartoon from *Fogonazo*, a Oaxaca City local paper, on January 10, 1979, with a caption of "First comes *el papa*," is particularly insightful regarding this paradox. The pope looked humble, with empty pockets, but clearly had spiritual support to offer the Mexican nation. The other panel of the cartoon reads, "Later comes *el papá*," showing Jimmy Carter coming to Mexico with loads of money to offer Mexico in exchange, perhaps, for natural resources. In other words, Carter was a paternal figure on which Mexico was dependent: He was the benefactor. The year 1979 was a time to contemplate Mexico's relationship with religious organizations, as well as its dependence on the US economy.

That year, the López Portillo administration severed its long history with the Protestant Summer Institute of Linguistics, citing its incompatibility with Mexican nationalism. Would the pope's visit represent neocolonialism? Or, was it a chance to repair relations with the Church and find common ground? The 1917 Mexican Constitution was vehemently anticlerical: Clergy were not supposed to wear religious garb in public, could not vote, and churches were the property of the nation. Despite the *arreglos* (agreements) of 1929 ending the Cristero conflict, church-state relations in Mexico remained strained; Mexico did not re-establish relations with the Vatican until the Carlos Salinas administration in 1992.[27] Nonetheless, Pope John Paul II's 1979 trip laid the groundwork for restoring formal diplomacy between the states.

The 1970s were also a complicated time in Mexico for state relations with

Native communities. A new generation of social scientists questioned official nationalism and saw indigenous identity not as exclusively Mexican but rather as linked to the historic struggles of indigenous communities globally.[28] As we saw in Chapter Four, Latin American anthropologists produced the 1971 Declaration of Barbados, tracing the long history of exploitation of Native lands and peoples.[29] The authors demanded the liberation of indigenous peoples, the commitment of anthropologists to activist scholarship, and the immediate departure of foreign missionaries from indigenous communities.[30]

Building on this premise, Mexican anthropologists challenged notions of *indigenismo nacional*, which had called for indigenous peoples' integration into the fabric of Mexican political and cultural life. Thus, the INI's traditional policies of Native incorporation by the adaptation of Spanish and by becoming culturally mestizo now collided with anthropological ideologies that backed indigenous peoples in forging their own destinies within the nation-state.[31] Consequently, the Luis Echeverría and López Portillo administrations emphasized "participatory indigenism" in their relations with indigenous communities.[32]

Taking advantage of this new policy in national politics, many Native communities asserted their rights to autonomy and control over natural resources in the late 1970s.[33] One recurring theme in national and local conversations about rights to autonomy was the presence of foreigners in indigenous communities, particularly religious personnel. This issue is readily apparent in the way state INI and political officials reacted to the pope's visit to Oaxaca.

Local INI officials were quick to criticize the tone of the pope's visit. For example, outreach worker Cándido Coheto Martínez, who later became the State Coordinator of Indigenous Education, stated indigenous people suffered persecution beginning with the Spanish conquest.[34] He further ruminated in *El Diario*, a Oaxaca City–based paper, "If the pope really cared about supporting indigenous peoples in Latin America, he would make a statement about indigenous rights to autonomy and self-determination at CELAM."[35] Coheto Martínez also criticized the government for using indigenous peoples for charming folkloric representations for tourists but not caring otherwise. He hoped the pope's visit would not represent that same contradiction. Pope John Paul II, Coheto Martínez wagered, should already notice how in Mexico, and globally, there were extreme inequalities and even ethnocide against indigenous peoples. Coheto Martínez's criticism of the pope's visit aligns with criticism in the previous chapter on the SIL: Missionaries failed to acknowledge the systemic obstacles facing Native peoples. To be clear, Pope John Paul II would go on to produce encyclicals defending Native peoples' rights in the 1990s. But certainly for Coheto Martínez, religious officials' promises came too little and too late.

Because of Mexico's anticlerical constitution, President López Portillo carefully planned his interactions with John Paul II. Perhaps as a conciliatory measure, he invited the pope for a private meeting (not a state dinner) at the Los Pinos presidential residence.[36] As López Portillo earlier exhorted about the pope's visit and its potential conflict with Mexico's strict policy of separation of church and state: "It would be a test of the courtesy, the gentlemanly behavior, the pride, the dignity, the confidence that Mexico had in itself and in its institutions, while always respecting Mexico's constitution."[37] Accordingly, López Portillo offered to pay the fine for Pope John Paul II wearing his pontifical garments in Mexico.[38]

The Oaxacan state government also debated how it would respond to John Paul II's visit. An early January 1979 editorial in *Carteles del Sur* stated that the pope's visit was not violating Mexico's protocol for state visits. In fact, it argued that some of the concerns were blown out of proportion, as the Vatican clearly knew that Mexico was a secular state. Furthermore, the paper stressed how it was an honor to have such an illustrious visitor to Mexico, and especially to Oaxaca. *Carteles del Sur* referenced the statement by the Secretary of the Interior, who noted that citizens enjoy "broad liberties" that give Mexicans the freedom to enjoy many rights, including those of religion. The newspaper argued there were many Mexican Catholics (especially in Oaxaca) delighted with the pope's visit, and Mexico should be respectful of that.[39] The editorial commended John Paul II for standing with indigenous peoples in Oaxaca.

The *Carteles del Sur* article also mentioned that the pope's visit was a time for the Mexican government to seriously examine the plight of the country's indigenous peoples. The editorial reminded its readers that the whole reason the pope chose to perform a mass in Cuilapan, Oaxaca, was to draw attention to indigenous people. Thus, Pope John Paul II's visit should be a time to celebrate Oaxaca's indigenous heritage. Yet reporting of the pope's trip also acknowledged the inherent conflict with the region's social needs. Political cartoons made fun of all the resources allocated for the pope's visit when Oaxaca's indigenous people lacked basic necessities.

Some local papers even speculated that Oaxaca City might not have enough hotels or restaurants to feed the thousands of visitors due to arrive at the end of January. Yet for its part, the Oaxacan tourism sector enthusiastically promoted the pope's visit as an economic boon for the state. The director of state tourism reported that it would bring one hundred million pesos to Oaxaca, including hotel accommodations for tourists, foreign press, and visiting religious officials. Major companies such as Bancomer Bank advertised the pope's visit by taking out full-page newspaper ads listing not just its services but also the complete radio and television schedule of coverage for the pope's visit.[40]

Ultimately, the state government treated the pope like any other important visitor. However, to maintain church-state separation, Oaxacan governor Eliseo Jiménez Ruíz did not attend any of the religious ceremonies. Government spokespeople reminded Oaxacans of President Benito Juárez's call for separation of church and state but maintained that the governor could be respectful of both Oaxaca's most important reformer and the visiting dignitary. As a compromise, the governor met the pope briefly at the airport and presented him with two volumes on Oaxaca's indigenous history, written by a nineteenth-century Catholic priest.[41] He did not, however, accompany the pope to Cuilapan, about fifteen miles from the airport.

Cuilapan is the site of an old Dominican monastery from the early colonial period. The unfinished structure lays on top of a Zapotec sacred space. In 1979, the grounds easily accommodated thousands of indigenous people from across the region who attended the open-air mass.[42] Indigenous representative Esteban Hernández greeted the pope in Zapotec and presented him with a cassette tape with the same greeting recorded in fifteen indigenous languages of Oaxaca and Chiapas.[43] Inviting Hernández to the altar symbolized the merging of the institutional and grassroots church's effort to show it stood with Latin American indigenous peoples.

After receiving a variety of gifts from the seven regions of Oaxaca, including ceramics, embroidered shirts, and chocolate, John Paul II began his homily.[44] He emphasized Native peoples' important cultural heritage while also praising the colonial-era Dominican missionaries who evangelized Oaxaca.[45] Additionally, Pope John Paul II (like his predecessor Paul VI had promised Colombian peasants during the second CELAM meeting in 1968) wanted "to be in solidarity with your cause, which is the cause of humble people, of the poor."[46] In a sense, Pope John Paul II backed agrarian reform, a contentious issue in Oaxaca in the 1970s.[47] However, Pope John Paul II also warned his audience against "harbor[ing] feelings of hatred and violence."[48] He concluded, "The Pope wants to be your voice, the voice of those who cannot speak."[49]

The Mexico City reporters covering the Oaxacan visit made countless references to the Tower of Babel at the Cuilapan mass, given the diversity of languages spoken at the mass. Other reporters focused on how the pope, or "el Padrecito Blanco," was allegedly the first white man to visit Cuilapan since the conquest. Such exaggerated references fed into old tropes about the sixteenth-century Spanish conquest of Native Mexicans, especially the legend of Quetzalcoatl, the Aztec deity conquistador Hernán Cortés allegedly resembled.[50]

Following the huge outdoor mass, the pope headed back to Oaxaca City for a procession through the streets surrounding Oaxaca City's zocalo (plaza) in an open-roofed car.[51] After a mass at Oaxaca City's main cathedral, replete with more indigenous folkloric dance and presentations, Pope John Paul II flew back to Mexico City by late afternoon.[52]

The pope's visit to Oaxaca illustrates the intersection of the institutional church and the popular church. Vatican policy certainly wanted better lives for indigenous peoples, but it did not support the methods of liberationist priests. John Paul II assured the predominantly Mixtec and Zapotec audience that he stood with oppressed Christians throughout the world. But by criticizing the more radical tenets of liberation theology at the CELAM meeting, Pope John Paul II was also limiting the power of the popular church in Mexico while progressive bishops were working to condemn state violence against Native peoples. Of course, from the Vatican perspective, the popular church was not above criticism and worried about the focus on political ideologies at the expense of ministry.

This surely was a complicated premise for the Archbishop of Oaxaca who helped organize the pope's Oaxaca tour. Bartolomé Carrasco was a staunch follower of liberation theology, speaking daily of the social and political injustice rampant in Oaxaca. Archbishop Carrasco embraced Oaxaca's version of popular Catholicism—its localized sets of symbols and syncretic rituals, which operated as "a salient tool of resistance" to marginalization.⁵³ Throughout the 1970s and 1980s, the Pacífico Sur bishops advocated for the collective rights of indigenous peoples in Oaxaca and Chiapas, even as the national Mexican episcopacy and the Vatican continued to clamp down on the progressive church in Latin America.⁵⁴ The Pacífico Sur Region represented Oaxaca and Chiapas, Mexico's poorest and most heavily indigenous regions, including thousands of Mayan refugees fleeing from civil war–ridden Guatemala.

Pope John Paul II, in the early years of his papacy, did not fully understand the lived experiences of Latin American clergy who saw poverty, exploitative working conditions, and forced displacement as the most pressing issues facing Latin American Catholics. There was also a strong strain of Mexican nationalism among Catholic and Protestant clergy and resentment over the power of the institutional Catholic Church. As one Jesuit priest at CELAM put it after the Puebla meeting, "Before trying to evangelize Latin American societies, the church should convert itself, getting rid of its own riches and privileges."⁵⁵ Anglican Bishop José Saucuedo also critiqued the stark contrast between the well-heeled dress of those attending the pope's mass at the Basilica of the Virgin of Guadalupe in Mexico City and the poverty of the crowds waiting outside. The contrast of the Church's wealth and power with the struggles of Native communities in Oaxaca was also apparent in press coverage of the pope's visit.

Political cartoons from leftist Mexican papers made light of the fact that caciques (local mestizo political bosses) would embrace Mexican peasants on the day of the pope's visit and yet not really change at all. For example, Oaxaca City's *Carteles del Sur* depicted a cacique greeting an indigenous man as "hermano indígena," or "my indigenous brother," with open arms (fig. 15). But the next day, the cacique kicks the indigenous man to the ground, belittling him as an "indio jijo" or "Indian son of a bitch."

Political cartoons also reflected the contradictions in how Mexico marketed itself during the pope's visit. The four states and Districto Federal had major governance issues in 1979: dozens of student strikes and university shutdowns in Jalisco alone, corruption in Nuevo León, and Oaxaca's five hundred thousand Native people living in abject poverty. In one cartoon entitled "Juan Pablo II Superestrella," or "John Paul II Superstar," the pope walks toward the governors and the Mexico City mayor with open arms.

Figure 15. Caricature of the Day. *Carteles del Sur*, January 31, 1979. Courtesy of Hemeroteca Pública de Oaxaca and Claudio Sánchez Islas.

Each political official carries something unique to his region: molé from Oaxaca, Santa Clara candies from Puebla, the golden key to the city of Mexico City. However, each political official discourteously does not extend the gifts to the pope. Perhaps they keep the gifts to themselves, much like they treat their citizens. A frog at the bottom of the cartoon admonishes the officials for their cold treatment of Juan Pablo II, contrasting with the Mexican people, who warmly welcomed him. The frog scolds "Lo cortés no quita lo creyente," "Courtesy does not inhibit the believer," which is a play on a Mexican popular expression "Lo cortés no quita lo valiente," "Courtesy does not inhibit bravery." In other words, being a secular public official does not necessarily mean one cannot be personally religious or excited for the pope's visit. The cartoon also hints at the idea that Pope John Paul II was the first white man to conquer the Zapotec region spiritually since the time of Hernán Cortés. The Oaxacan governor, for example, carries a codice (codex) reading "Quetzalcoatl," a reference to the myth that the Aztecs mistook Cortés for their most important deity, a god rumored to be light-skinned in

Figure 16. John Paul II, Superstar. *El Universal*, January 28, 1979. Courtesy of *El Universal*.

appearance. By referring to the conquest era, the artist might also be implying that Mexican politicians are *malinchistas* (sellouts), similar to La Malinche (Doña Marina), Cortés's indigenous partner and translator. The cartoon might also be insinuating that while the governors had to feign inhospitality because of Mexico's secular traditions, the men fawned over seeing the charismatic pope.

Political cartoons also spoke to the poverty and social issues still facing Oaxacans, regardless of the pope's visit. In one, a campesino couple in Oaxaca wear tattered clothes and reminisce about the pope's visit. The campesino stated "with all the hustle and bustle" of his whirlwind visit, "the Pope saw what it is like to love God in Indian territory." The old phrase "vió lo que es amar a Dios en tierra de Indios" means to learn to love God through difficult situations or hard times. The saying has its roots in the colonial era when settlers complained that it was nearly impossible for Spaniards to be successful in indigenous regions. In other words, one has to overcome challenges in

Figure 17. He left! *El Universal*, February 1, 1979. Courtesy of *El Universal*.

foreign lands or new situations. At the end of the cartoon, the caption concludes "Se fue" (He left), meaning the pope departed Oaxaca, perhaps after seeing all the struggles. The campesino couple, shown in tattered clothing, have no choice but to stay.

Mexican reporters also questioned the ethics of shelling out lots of money for the pope's visit when Mixtecs often faced food and water shortages in their communities.[56] An article in *El Universal* mentioned how politicians and caciques used Native peoples as "political trampolines" when it was advantageous to the politician's or landowner's cause. For example, one political cartoon showed López Portillo lamenting the pope's departure at the end of January; the president is lonely and looking for companionship in the deserted Mexico City airport. But a moment later, he goes back to his old ways, making friends again with big business, politicians, and the media, all represented as the Seven Deadly Sins.[57]

Just as the pope's visit was a Rorschach test for Vatican-Mexican relations, it also illuminated how the Catholic Church hierarchy risked losing touch with the struggles of the poor and disenfranchised. John Paul II assured the audience at Cuilapan that he stood with oppressed Christians throughout the world. However, the pope's criticism of liberation theology during the 1979 CELAM meeting made it clear that he did not approve of how "the preferential option for the poor" was playing out in indigenous regions of Latin America, even if later in his career social justice became the cornerstone of his papacy.

Obispos de la Región Pacífico Sur

Throughout the 1980s, the Pacífico Sur bishops advocated for collective rights of indigenous peoples in Oaxaca and Chiapas.[58] While these bishops often clashed with the national episcopacy and even the Vatican, the institutional church and the grassroots church in Oaxaca agreed in one critical area. Protestant growth was a threat to the vitality of the Church in what was arguably the most Catholic region of the world. Throughout the 1980s, the southern episcopacy argued that sectas weakened indigenous communities at a time when they needed to use collective rights to unite against state violence. Under assault from modernization, migration, and religious fragmentation, liberationists emphasized how leaving the Catholic Church was not just an act of religious dissension but also an attack against indigenous and communal identity.

Headed by Archbishop Bartolomé Carrasco of Oaxaca City from 1976 until 1992, the Pacífico Sur made rights of indigenous peoples the cornerstone of its ministry. Throughout the 1970s and the 1980s, Catholic bishops spoke publicly against the repression of indigenous Chiapanecos and Oaxaqueños. The Pacífico Sur challenged the overall conservative leaning of the Mexican national episcopacy by promoting liberation theology.[59] Horrified by the repression of Guatemalan Mayans during the neighboring country's 1960–1992 civil war, and seeing similar social, political, and economic inequalities in Mexico, the episcopacy sought to expose violations of indigenous rights in Oaxaca and Chiapas.[60]

Agrarianism had long been a contentious issue especially in indigenous zones, where earlier reforms never took hold. The populist administrations of Lázaro Cárdenas (1934–1940) and Luis Echeverría (1970–1976) engaged in agrarian reform programs (land distribution, credit loans, irrigation systems, fertilizer) for landless peasants, earning them the support of indigenous populations in rural southern Mexico.[61] Part of this reform included land distribution in Chiapas's Lacandón jungle region; the very place where the Neo-Zapatistas formed a movement that would lead to revolution by 1994. Yet the López Portillo presidency (1976–1982) sided with private landowners in agrarian disputes, erasing many of the gains indigenous communities made. Thus, the state's clientalistic partnership wore off by the late 1970s as indigenous communities increasingly started questioning their second-class citizenship in Mexico.[62] The state responded with violence.

On December 15, 1978, Arturo Lona Reyes, bishop of Tehuantepec, Oaxaca, and president of the Episcopal Commission for Indians, wrote a letter asking President López Portillo to condemn paramilitary violence in Oaxaca. The letter outlined a horrific case of violence against indigenous leaders in Puxmetacan, Mixes, that was a microcosm for what happened throughout southern Mexico. Lona Reyes described the murder of eight indigenous Mixe leaders who were asking for the restoration of ejidal (communal) land that rightfully belonged to the community but was fraudulently controlled by a former state deputy. The former deputy had assistance from a private army and a small plane in his attack; Lona Reyes believed they belonged to the Mexican military. The bishop placed the murder of the indigenous leaders in Puxmetacan, Mixes, within the larger picture of state violence in Mexico.

> The victims are always the same. Indians and the peasants who struggle for their rights. . . . Mexico is following the road of violence, repressions, and massacres of innocent people—situations of violence that do not differ from the most repressive countries of Latin America. . . . For this reason, in the name of the Gospel and the basic human rights of our indigenous and peasants peoples who are being crushed by violence, I urgently call on all Mexicans but especially on those who govern our country, that they satisfactorily clarify these acts, punish the culpable individuals, and devise necessary structural mechanisms to guarantee not only nonviolence against the weakest members of our society but justice and effective peace for all.[63]

Throughout the 1970s and 1980s, the Pacífico Sur condemned violence against participants in the agrarian reform movements sweeping the region.

Similar to late nineteenth-century Oaxacan Catholics linking Protestantism to North American imperialism in Mexico, Pacífico Sur bishops also sought to associate North American agendas and values with Protestant *sectas* in their evangelization of indigenous communities. In 1982, the Bishops complained that *sectas* like Mormons and Jehovah's Witnesses persuaded indigenous Mexicans that the ways of the North Americans "are better, more intelligent and stronger. . . . Because of the presence of these propagators, there have been deaths, burning of [saints'] images, and arson in our chapels."[64] The Pacífico Sur bishops would later draw a comparison between the US religious right's influences in Central America, especially in Guatemala, where President Efraín Ríos Montt enjoyed a close relationship with US televangelists, not to mention the Reagan administration.[65]

The Pacífico Sur collectively warned about the rise of *sectas* in southern Mexico. The bishops complained, "It's gotten to the point that some of these sectarians have become municipal authorities."[66] The bishops were particularly concerned that Mexico could soon be following the same road to Protestantism as Guatemala.

> It is becoming increasingly alarming in this region that, parallel to the social explosion going on in Central America with Protestantism, Protestant sects are multiplying and springing up over there. The *sectas* say they need to lead Christians to God since, according to them, Catholic priests are preoccupied with mundane matters, not spiritual ones. This division, manipulation, and social weakening that these sects cause in the *Pueblo* is anti-patriotic and suggests what might also happen here when social tensions will boil over their limits. Is the problem moving to southern Mexico from Central America? Why are they [sect leaders] using the same tactics [as in Guatemala]? This proselytizing, as we have seen elsewhere, aggravates tensions and sharpens disagreements that already are volatile here.[67]

The bishops were most likely referring to the sharp rise of evangelical Protestantism in Guatemala during its civil war. Between 1982 and 1983, Ríos Montt engaged in a scorched earth campaign designed to eradicate the Guerilla Army of the Poor (Ejército Guerrillero de los Pobres).[68] Ríos Montt, a

Church of the Word pastor and aid recipient from American right-wing televangelists, compared his assault against the guerrillas as a Christian crusade to root out Satan and advance the Kingdom of God.[69] This new type of Christian citizenship emboldened powerful political leaders.[70] Moreover, Ríos Montt received economic and military support from the Reagan administration, which viewed his Guatemalan presidency as an ally in curbing socialist threats in Cold War Central America.

Throughout the early 1980s, thousands of Mayans fled over the Mexican border to escape the violence of the civil war. These refugees hoped to migrate to the United States or to resettle in Chiapas where Mayan Mam populations had straddled the Guatemalan-Mexican border for centuries. This migration exemplified religious divisions as well. Catholics tended to side with the guerrilla rebels, whereas supporters of Ríos Montt often converted to evangelical Protestantism; most refugees identified as Catholic. In 1984, the Guatemalan military attacked one of the refugee camps on Mexican soil, infuriating the Pacífico Sur bishops. Ostensibly to protect the refugees, the Mexican Department of the Interior favored relocating Guatemalan citizens outside of Chiapas.[71] While on the surface, that might have seemed like a good idea, Pacífico Sur bishops argued that the state was doing that to weaken the ministry work they were doing with Mayans in southern Mexico.[72] Moreover, the shared language and cultural traditions among Guatemalan and Chiapan Mayans was a significant reason to welcome the refugees to Chiapas, not resettle them to underpopulated Campeche.[73] To that end, protecting the forty-six thousand Mayan refugees in southern Mexico became an important objective.[74]

Friction between Pacífico Sur bishops and the Mexican government intensified during the Guatemalan refugee crisis. The Pacífico Sur bishops ministered to the refugees, issued letters encouraging the state to give them political asylum, and set up refugee shelters. Concerned that some of the Guatemalans might sympathize with some of Mexico's own radical peasant movements, the Mexican Department of the Interior monitored the actions of Catholic clergy in the region. It particularly focused on Bishop Samuel Ruiz in San Cristóbal de las Casas, Chiapas.

Serving from 1960 to 2000, Bishop Ruiz exemplified the liberationist bent of the Pacífico Sur pastoral region. A dynamic speaker at the 1968 Medellín CELAM conference, Ruiz established CEBs, encouraged the translation of bibles and church liturgy into Mayan dialects like Tzeltal and Tzotzil, and trained Native people to serve as catechists in Chiapas.[75] Ruiz empowered Mayans about their rights to dignity in the face of poverty, exploitation by coffee plantation landowners, and political repression.[76] In the 1980s, Ruiz ministered to the Mayan Guatemalan refugees, encouraging priests in the border city of Tapachula, Chiapas, to instruct migration officers about the political violence facing the refugees if they were turned away. The Mexican military accused Ruiz of "harboring guerillas."[77] In 1984, army intelligence reported that Ruiz had two thousand Guatemalan refugees living on his personal land, "La Gloria," near the border. Hiding out among those refugees, the report suggested, were Chiapan peasant organizers who might be recruiting for their own guerrilla uprising.[78]

Throughout the 1970s and 1980s, Mayan peasants in Ruiz's diocese organized against the caciques (landowners) for better pay and working conditions. They also demanded agrarian reform by occupying large properties. In 1974, Ruiz organized the first Indigenous Peoples' Congress in Chiapas.[79] While the populist Luis Echeverría administration endorsed indigenous congresses, Ruiz pushed boundaries by insisting that indigenous people of Chiapas (not government officials or ladinos, non-Indians) plan the event.[80]

The Zapatista National Liberation Army (Ejército Zapatista de Liberación Nacional, EZLN) revolutionary movement credited their early ideologies as stemming from liberationist activism introduced by Ruiz. The EZLN protested constitutional changes ending ejidal land rights, Emiliano Zapata's legacy from the Mexican Revolution. In 1992, President Carlos Salinas's administration (1988–1994) declared an end of ejidal land distribution originally guaranteed in the 1917 Constitution and long a cornerstone of local autonomy. These new Zapatistas opposed other neoliberal economic policies such as the North American Free Trade Agreement (NAFTA) that drove out smalltime corn growers. It is not a coincidence that the Zapatista revolt began on the very first day of NAFTA's implementation.

Soon after the January 1, 1994, uprising, Archbishop Ruiz developed the National Commission on Mediation to broker dialogue between the PRI government and the Zapatistas, ultimately leading to the San Andrés Accords in 1996, mostly ending the armed conflict.[81] PRI politicians, landowners, and some bishops of the national episcopacy wanted Ruiz punished for getting involved in politics and "fomenting class war."[82] Large landowners and

Chiapan political officials pejoratively called him the "Red Bishop" of Chiapas.[83] Many Protestants from San Pedro Chenalhó and San Juan Chamula tried to stay out of the conflict, but some sided with the state PRI government in 1994.[84] However, this political division in Chiapas was complicated because PRI-supporting traditionalist Catholic leadership exiled Protestants from San Juan Chamula in the 1970s.

Ecumenicism in southern Mexico remained a contentious issue for Catholic clergy. The Second Vatican Council had called for more interdenominational dialogue; indeed, Latin American Protestant clergy attended the Puebla conference and collaborated with Catholic bishops on how Catholicism could work with Protestant churches. Nonetheless, Anglican bishop José Saucedo reported feeling shocked by the remaining "great ignorance of and/or general indifference" the bishops expressed toward Protestantism. Anglican Bishop Saucedo noted how workshop attendees lumped all non-Catholic groups together and that he spent most of the conference explaining who he was and what Anglicanism was. He was relieved when a bishop referenced the Vatican II statement on ecumenicalism, which especially highlighted the close relationship and shared traditions between Catholics and Anglicans.[85] But the bishops in the southern episcopacy were far more concerned with fast-growing groups such as Pentecostals, Seventh-day Adventists, and Jehovah's Witnesses than with Anglicans.

The Oaxacan bishops saw clear divisions in indigenous communities overwhelmed by Protestantism. Because of sectarianism caused by sectas, the Bishops argued, violence, gloom, and social chaos were becoming ever-present in Oaxacan pueblos.[86] However, Oaxacan Archbishop Carrasco was careful to differentiate between "secta" and historic denominations that participated in the World Council of Churches. "Not all of the Protestants act in the same manner.... The sects generally have neither a body of doctrine nor organization hierarchy, and they are extremely aggressive against the doctrines and the practices of the Catholic Church. But out of the denominations represented in the World Council, some contribute sincerely to ecumenical dialogue and collaborate regularly with us."[87] The issue dividing Catholics and Protestants in southern Mexico mostly focused on local traditions that drove usos y costumbres. Some of these customs involved ritualistic consumption of alcohol.

The Pacífico Sur disliked secta criticism of patron saint's day fiestas. The

Oaxacan hierarchy certainly agreed that alcoholism was a serious problem in indigenous communities. It also understood that some syncretic rituals practiced in indigenous communities were borderline sacrilegious. However, in their pastoral guide, they warned local priests to be wary of the sectas' approach.

> Religious sects assail people and alcoholic communities with fundamental, paternalistic attitudes and frightening threats against the drinkers. Many times this does successfully distance people from alcohol. But unfortunately, all those who are recipients of these aggressions from the sects turn to a totally individualistic life, separated not just from alcohol, but also specifically isolating themselves from the economic, social, political, and cultural commitments that the historical processes requires for the liberation of the *pueblos*. While combating alcoholism is laudable, the means by which the sects go about achieving this and the limited outcomes are not pastorally best for these individuals.[88]

Therefore, the bishops acknowledged the negative impact alcoholism had in the pueblos. However, along with the requirement that secta adherents stop drinking, they also adopted other attitudes and habits that prevented these communities from fighting for their basic human rights. By isolating themselves politically, socially, culturally, and economically from their neighbors, secta members could not unite under one umbrella of resistance as Christians or as members of an indigenous group to combat state violence. Empowerment of the people, as the manual implied, was clearly an important tenet of liberation theology. For the most part, sectas question community traditions that do not fit into their new religious worldview. The Catholic Church, Archbishop Carrasco argued, served as an advocate for repressed and vulnerable groups, in contrast to sectas who supported the military. Religious violence is an ongoing problem in Chiapas and Oaxaca.[89]

The Pacífico Sur bishops often drew connections between repression in Latin America and global causes, including Poland's Solidarity movement. Pope John Paul II spoke often about Polish resistance to communism; the Solidarity movement of the early 1980s would be close to his heart. In his homily on January 31, 1982, Oaxacan Archbishop Carrasco posited that the repression against Polish Catholic workers was similar to the human rights violations in Guatemala and El Salvador. Carrasco also reiterated his preference for the poor and the underrepresented in Oaxaca.[90] By highlighting the plight of Polish dockworkers, the progressive church demonstrated that Catholics had to take a political stance to bring about social justice. The popular church hoped that Catholic activism against the communist Polish United Workers' Party might encourage Mexico's institutional church to speak out against authoritarianism in its own ruling party, the PRI.

On February 1, 1982, Pacífico Sur organized a march in Oaxaca City, starting from La Iglesia de los Pobres (Church of the Poor) near the baseball stadium in the northern part of the city and ending up near the main cathedral in Oaxaca City's central zocalo. Thousands of Oaxacans carried banners stating that today they stood with John Paul II and the People of Poland. But tomorrow they wanted John Paul II to stand with Mexico and Central American victims. They carried banners of the Mexican flag, the Polish flag, and the Vatican flag.[91] After a moment of silence for Polish dissidents in prison, Archbishop Carrasco noted that when John Paul II visited Oaxaca in 1979, he spoke about keeping the faith even in the face of struggle. Carrasco noted that just like Solidarity movement leaders kept Catholic faith at the forefront of their struggle against the communist government, so too did Native peoples of southern Mexico invoke liberation theology in their own social justice movements.

Since Archbishop Carrasco's retirement in 1993, Oaxaca's archdiocese has been generally conservative, with some important exceptions.[92] Both the popular and institutional Catholic Church have run into problems with the PRI state political party. Religious identity took on a political meaning during recent protest movements in the state. Protestant organizations supported the beleaguered *sexenio* of PRI governor Ulises Ruiz Ortiz (2004–2010). In 2006, following the formation of the Popular Assembly of the Peoples of Oaxaca (Asamblea Popular de los Pueblos de Oaxaca, APPO), the archbishop's office remained neutral, ultimately playing the role of mediator between the protesters and the governor's office. APPO emerged as a protest to the state government's use of excessive force during the 2006 Oaxacan teachers' strike. It was a coalition of three hundred Oaxacan organizations fighting the state government for six months, during which twenty-three civilians died.[93] Consequently, tension developed between Governor Ruiz Ortiz and the Catholic Church—Ruiz Ortiz accused the archdiocese of siding with APPO.⁹⁴ At various points, APPO protesters in Oaxaca City received shelter from Catholic churches. However, the Confraternidad de Pastores Cristianos Evangélicos del Estado de Oaxaca (Confraternity of Evangelical Christian Pastors of Oaxaca, COPACEO) backed Governor Ruiz Ortiz. The competition between the Catholic Church and Protestantism was now playing out on the state political field.

Founded in 1987, COPACEO is the most powerful non-Catholic religious advocacy organization in Oaxaca.⁹⁵ While many Oaxacans called for the governor's resignation in 2006, COPACEO served as an important political ally for Governor Ruiz Ortiz, holding rallies for him. The Oaxacan archdiocese's Director of the Commission on Peace and Justice, Father Wilfrido Mayrén Peláez—popularly known as Padre Ubi—compared "los aleyuas" (Catholics sometimes use the term *the hallelujahs* to describe Evangelical Christians) collaboration with Ruis Ortiz during the APPO movement to Protestant support of Guatemalan President Efraín Montt while he carried out his scorched earth policy. Ríos Montt, Padre Ubi explained, had "a secret agreement with Protestant groups to persecute and attack the [popular] Catholic Church committed to the people and the defense of the poor."⁹⁶ Padre Ubi described receiving death threats for the Oaxacan archdiocese's protection of the teacher protesters.⁹⁷

At the same time, the Catholic Church in Oaxaca was not just leery of los aleyuas. It also feared splintering of Catholics in the 1980s. By "splintering," I mean Catholic groups that were starting to question the traditions and organization of Native communities, many of them eventually becoming Pentecostal. In Oaxaca, there were plenty of prolonged conflicts involving "traditional" Catholics against "modern" Catholics. In the Central Valley Zapotec community of San Antonino Castillo, two different Catholic groups fought for control of the local parish.⁹⁸ At issue in San Antonino was who could determine how local Catholicism was practiced. The majority of the community who wanted the mayordomos to continue collecting money for saints' day fiestas supported one group, Los Honorables, led by Father Elpidio Ramírez. On the other side were Los Cruzados (Those of the Cross), who wanted to drastically change the way saints' days were celebrated. Los Cruzados was a charismatic prayer group with seventeen branches throughout Oaxaca.⁹⁹ The group's leader in San Antonino, Father Marcelino Sánchez Hernández, attracted a large following of teenagers in the community and brought in outside visitors.

In 1983, Marcelino Sánchez Hernández, popularly called Padre Marcelino, and his young supporters argued that the town spent too much time and precious resources on the fiesta system and was forgetting the true meaning of the sacraments.[100] Elders in the community sent a petition to the Secretary General's office, complaining that Padre Marcelino's supporters had little experience in organizing the local church and that they were trying to eradicate costumbres by criticizing the town's patron saint day fiesta.[101] They asked that the traditionalists and their priest have primary control of the church inventory and cultural norms in the community.

This example suggests that some segments of the Oaxacan Catholic base did not approve of money spent by the religious cofradías (brotherhoods) that drove local Catholicism. It also points to changing social dynamics in the community. Young people had taken their elders to task for allocating money for the town's feast day celebration, preferring the funds spent elsewhere. The community elders argued that the youth had no right to question tradition. In this case, the traditionalists won. Archbishop Carrasco intervened to support Father Ramírez over Padre Marcelino, and so did the Oaxacan state authorities, who mentioned in a report that Marcelino's group appeared to attract individuals of questionable morals, including homosexuals and "mujeres de la vida galante" (prostitutes).[102] Given the fierce opposition to the changes and new social dynamics this group represented, perhaps it is not surprising that many members of Los Cruzados throughout Oaxaca later were the first in their villages to convert to Pentecostalism.[103] Like the competition between traditional and modernist Catholics, competition from Pentecostal and Restorationist Christians (Seventh-day Adventists, Jehovah's Witnesses, Mormons, or Luz del Mundo) was a deep concern for the institutional and grassroots church in Oaxaca.

Growing Challenges to Catholicism

Concern about sectas' growth was the main theme of the Catholic Church's national episcopal conference in Toluca, Mexico, in 1988. Alluding to the conference's main themes, the Oaxacan archdiocese expressed concern about Protestant groups dividing Mexican communities and spreading a "doctrine totally foreign to what was proposed by Christ."[104] The Oaxacan archdiocese, with its progressive archbishop Carrasco, preferred to depict Christ as a fighter for social justice; Christians should not have to wait for the second coming of Christ to experience His righteousness. The archdiocese blamed groups such as the Jehovah's Witnesses for creating serious problems in Oaxaca by dividing communities and taking advantage of illiterate people. Oaxacan archdiocese spokesman Daniel Quiroga Dorantes stated: "This is a situation of concern to the Catholic Church because it does not want a struggle or bloodshed between native people who are easy prey for the Protestant sects because of their poor living conditions."[105] The archdiocese noted: "The Church is not worried about losing followers, what it's worried about is the damage that these groups cause in the communities."[106] The competition from Christian rivals was "as vexing to the Vatican" as the spread of liberation theology in previous decades.[107]

In May of 1990, Pope John Paul II traveled to Mexico for the second of his five trips to the nation. During his tour of the southern states, John Paul II repeatedly blamed Catholic bishops and priests for not offering enough outreach to the Mexicans who had "broken the link of saving grace, joining the sects."[108] At his largest open-air mass in Mexico City, John Paul II directed a special message to Mexican Protestants: "I would like to meet with you one by one to tell you: come back to the fold of the church, your mother."[109] By providing a more personalized outreach, the pope hoped to regain former parishioners.

At the conclusion of another visit in 1999, John Paul II warned the Mexican National Episcopacy, "The success of proselytism by sects and new religious groups cannot be ignored. Pastoral policies will have to be revised, so that each particular church can offer the faithful more personalized religious care."[110] This approach was a core component to Pope John Paul II's "New Evangelization" campaign meant to rekindle the appeal of Catholicism and reaffirm that Catholicism possesses the fullness of the "true Christian" religion.[111] Of course, the Church had been ecumenical since Vatican II; however, this was an approach to remind Catholics that the Church was still there for them, even if they had dabbled in other faiths. A real challenge, however, was the lack of ordained clergy.

In the 1980s, the Catholic Church in southern Mexico was hemorrhaging followers at alarming rates, mostly due to its perpetual shortage of priests and the explosion of evangelical Protestant denominations in high-poverty regions. To that end, the Catholic Church was particularly concerned with reaching indigenous populations in remote zones.[112] Catholic priests in rural Mexican zones often only offered mass once a month in individual parishes.[113] The extensive educational prerequisites for seminary training, the vows of celibacy, and diminishing economic resources made it difficult for the Mexican Catholic Church—as in other regions—to ordain enough priests. In isolated areas, Catholic deacons, catechists, and nuns took on the role of priests, with deacons performing all sacraments except reconciliation or last rites. Even if deacons are not by canon law permitted to say Mass (apart from the homily and Gospel reading), they often did it in high-need areas.[114] In Chiapas, for example, Native deacons outnumber priests four to one.[115] Yet the institutional church was also leery of Bishop Ruiz's strategies; he ordained thousands of Native deacons, some whom practiced syncretic Catholicism.

In contrast, Pentecostal leaders trained their new ministers fast and frequently with few formal requirements.[116] These churches responded intimately to the local needs of communities.[117] In fact, while the most visible Pentecostal denomination right now in Latin America is the Assemblies of God, 80 percent of Pentecostals belong to small nondenominational churches.[118] The Catholic Church tried to impede this growth in Mexico by publishing short, simple pamphlets with the rhetorical question in bold font, "Who founded your church?"[119] The flier was directed toward former Catholics who had converted to other Christian denominations, included a list of twenty-eight denominations from Adventist to the YMCA, and listed the year the church was established, the place, and the founder. For example, Jehovah's Witness is listed as founded by Charles T. Russell in Philadelphia in 1876, the Pentecostals in 1905 in Los Angeles, and La Luz del Mundo (Light of the World) as founded in 1926 in Guadalajara, Mexico, by Aarón Joaquín Flores. However, the document lists "Catholic" at the bottom of the list with its founder as Jesus Christ in Israel, in the year 33. The message is clear here: Catholicism is the only *true* Church for Mexicans. The bottom of the flier invites fallen Catholics to "Come back, without fear! The Church is waiting for you with open arms to meet again with Christ."[120] This was part of the papacy's New Evangelism movement, dedicated to rekindle the excitement of being Catholic and perhaps regain Catholics who had left the church.

Despite the New Evangelization campaign, Protestantism continues to make huge gains in Mexico. In 1990, 89.7 percent of Mexicans identified as Catholic.[121] In the 2010 census, 82.7 percent of Mexicans reported they were Catholic.[122] Sociologist Roberto J. Blancarte estimates that 1,300 Mexican Catholics left the Church each day between 2000 and 2010.[123] In contrast, Protestantism (combining historical, Pentecostal, and alternative denominations) almost doubled. In 2000, there were six million Protestants in Mexico; they registered at just under eleven million in 2010.[124] Today, the archdiocese of Oaxaca estimates that 83 percent of its zone is Catholic.[125] While Mexican Protestantism still lags behind Guatemala or El Salvador, for example, the concentration of Pentecostals in poor, indigenous communities of southern Mexico is significant. The southern states make up just 13 percent of Mexico's population; yet it is where almost 25 percent of the nation's Protestants reside.[126]

Conclusion

The pope's 1979 visit challenged notions of Mexican nationalism but ultimately paved the way for the restoration of diplomatic relations with the Vatican in 1992. It also brought issues of indigenous rights to the forefront in the national press as Mexico City and international reporters observed firsthand the marginalized condition of indigenous communities such as Cuilapan. The pope's visit also served as a practice run for President Carter's state visit the next month, hence strengthening international relations.

Yet what the 1979 papal trip did not do was resolve the break within the church over liberation theology. This discord would last until the late 1980s, until the breakdown of the Soviet Union and the decline of the Sandinista Revolution in Nicaragua by 1990. The Cold War over, and the political context changed, liberation theology's main messages seemed less threatening. In Pope John Paul II's trips to Mexico in the 1990s, the fear of Marxist influences retreated and the pope became more concerned about "la invasion de las sectas," particularly in indigenous zones. Linking devotion to the Virgin Mary to indigenous spirituality remained an important theme, one that united the popular and institutional churches. The Virgin of Guadalupe remains Mexico's most iconic symbol of Catholicism, national identity, and cultural pride. Pope John Paul II bequeathed a gold crown to the brown-skinned virgin statue when he first visited her Mexico City basilica in 1979. In homilies spanning five papal visits to Mexico, he alluded often to the indigenous peasant to whom she appeared in 1531, calling out to him in his native Náhuatl. Juan Diego's 2002 canonization was a way for the institutional church to embrace indigenous rights at a time when it more than ever needed to hold on to Latin American Catholics.[127]

John Paul II's trip to Mexico in 1979 illuminates the trajectory of the popular and institutional churches' views on liberation theology, indigenous struggles for autonomy, and Protestant growth in Latin America. These issues remain ongoing between the popular and institutional church but with some differences. Pope Francis, elected in 2013, is intimately familiar with the challenges of Protestant growth in Latin America. Instead of warning about "la invasión de las sectas," the Argentine Pope has peppered his homilies and encyclicals with acknowledgement of the ties binding Catholics and Protestants together, not the differences separating them.[128] As the first Latin American pontiff, and as a Jesuit with a complex understanding of the nuances of liberation theology in Latin America, Pope Francis seeks to rekindle some of the social justice commitments of the progressive Catholic Church in Latin America.

CHAPTER SIX

"Here the People Rule"

Customary Law and State Formation

COMPETING NOTIONS OF tradition continued to dominate religious conflict cases of the 1980s. In contrast to the earlier cases involving mainline denominations, these newer conflicts almost exclusively dealt with the influx of new Protestant denominations. At present, nonmainline Protestant and alternative Christian congregations, often referred to as sectas, make up the fastest growing denominations in Mexico. As we saw in Chapter Five, the Mexican Catholic Church continued to voice its opposition to Protestantism as the invasion of the sects from North America. This trend has led to continued religious conflicts in Oaxaca in a period of significant migration and social unrest.

Endemic poverty and an agricultural crisis spurred mass migration from Oaxaca throughout the 1980s. As a result, many indigenous communities were increasingly left with a shrunken pool of available citizens for tequio projects and cargo positions, the very core of a community's identity. Oaxaca's PRI state government, concerned in the 1980s about campesino mobilizations in the Central Valleys, Zapotec radicalism in Juchitán, and the increasing gains of the leftist Partido de la Revolución Democrática (Party of the Democratic Revolution, PRD) in rural areas, sought to retain its control of indigenous Oaxacan communities by strengthening its commitment to usos y costumbres. It is within this complex and volatile milieu that indigenous Oaxacans chose to expel Pentecostals and Jehovah's Witnesses from their communities.

This chapter examines the intersection of local, state, and federal government authority in religious conflicts in Oaxaca. I analyze Oaxacan religious conflicts within the context of major shifts in economic and political life in the 1980s, paying particular attention to two prolonged religious conflict cases in Oaxaca's Sierra region.[1] Pentecostals and Jehovah's Witnesses in the Sierra region were not just religious dissidents but also agents of sociopolitical change. By abstaining from tequio assignments, Protestant converts challenged religious rituals and sought to modify their communities' ethos. Ultimately, the reach of the state was limited and, at times, ambiguous.

With the establishment of the Department of Religious Affairs (Departamento de Asuntos Religiosos, DAR) office in 1976, all Mexican states were expected to mediate instances of religious intolerance. The DAR attempted to adjudicate religious conflicts and keep track of religious building permits, saving the Mexican Attorney General's office from being saturated with religious intolerance cases. Between 1976 and 1992, the DAR documented 352 reported cases of religious intolerance in Oaxaca.[2] These cases ranged from verbal attacks to destruction of property to death threats and homicide. In the formal complaints submitted to the DAR during the 1980s, tradition, respect for municipal authority, and threats to citizenship (both the local and national conceptualizations) are the familiar premises used to protest the growth of the sectas.

In Oaxaca, the state government vacillated between supporting usos y costumbres and the rights of Protestants. The state government found itself obligated to enforce two opposing mandates: individual guarantees of freedom of religion and local self-government enshrined in usos y costumbres. In many cases, the state government ultimately decided that constitutional law trumped customary law, but this often came too late to make a difference to the victims of religious conflict. In the principal case studies of this chapter, complaints to the state government revolved around Protestant abstention from tequio or cargo positions. Conflicts between customary and constitutional law can be seen as attempts by locals to defend their communities by strengthening local autonomy and using tradition to counter outside influences. An important external influence during the 1980s was the rising rate of migration.

Migration

Throughout the 1980s, whether migrants or non-Catholics could still be considered ciudadanos was a burning question in many usos y costumbres communities. Should Zapotecan *busbois* (busboys) in Los Angeles or Mixtec *pineros* (timber workers) in Oregon's Willamette Valley still contribute toward tequio? Were they still community citizens? They were, after all, in a transnational space often organizing with paisanos from their Native communities or regions of Oaxaca. Did community members who converted to Protestantism also have to be responsible for tequio? What were the legal repercussions if they did not contribute?

Indigenous Oaxacans outnumber mestizos exponentially in terms of migration to the United States. Although the state of Oaxaca ranked sixth in overall migration to the United States in 2004, Oaxaca is still number one in indigenous migration; Zapotecs are the largest ethnic group to migrate.[3] Like migration, religious conversion is also an "agent of sociopolitical change."[4] Rejecting traditional obligations like tequio and cargo has effectively altered community dynamics. However, while many Catholic migrants managed to strengthen indigenous identity and hence Catholic rituals through migration, evangelical and alternative Christians challenged a core element of indigenous communal identity: syncretic Catholicism.

Oaxacan migration to the United States surged in the 1970s and 1980s, later than other regions of Mexico. During the bracero program between 1942 and 1964, only a small percentage of indigenous Oaxacans took agricultural jobs in the United States.[5] More frequently, especially beginning in the 1930s, they migrated to Veracruz to work on coffee or sugar plantations, to northern Oaxaca to do mining work, or to Mexico City for factory jobs.[6] By the mid-1960s, Oaxacan migrants headed to Baja, California, to work in the San Quintín Valley's agro-export industry or to work in Tijuana's nascent maquiladoras. In the 1970s, Oaxaca's agricultural crisis particularly affected indigenous communities.[7] In Oaxaca's Mixteca region the cost of the fertilizer required for a small milpa (corn plot) often exceeded the market value of the corn itself.[8] As Mexico's foreign debt soared and southern Mexico's agricultural crisis worsened, Oaxacan migration to the United States accelerated.[9] The choice for indigenous Oaxacans was "migrate or starve."[10] The population of Oaxacans in California swelled so high in the 1980s that anthropologist Michael Kearney coined the term *Oaxacalifornia* to describe the transnational migrant community.[11]

Kearney argues that it was within this transnational space that indigenous Oaxacans strengthened their own indigenous identity by founding rights organizations with other Zapotecs or Mixtecs from Oaxaca. Similarly, Protestants abstaining from religious rituals threaten and often alter social structure in their home communities. Yet, by doing so, they also strengthen and share their own identities as cristianos with indigenous peoples from other communities, as well as with mestizos and foreigners. The formation of this transnational identity mirrored trends in the United States as well. Migrating to the United States meant encountering a multireligious nation. Protestants currently make up over 46.5 percent of the US population; Catholics make up 20.8 percent of the population.[12] Overall, 22 percent of Latinos in the United States identify as Protestant.[13] Today 10 percent of New Yorkers are Pentecostals, of whom 33 percent are Latinos.[14]

Oaxacan migration to other regions of Mexico and the United States during the 1970s and 1980s helped pave the way for conversion to evangelical Protestantism. Journalist Sam Quinones described the popularity of Protestantism in Mixtec communities along the US-Mexican border: "The new churches are symbols of economic success, of modernity, of the monumental power and attraction of the United States. The adoption of a Protestant faith is almost standard issue in leaving Oaxaca for a future."[15] Once away from their traditional villages, Oaxacans living in Tijuana often had to adjust to different legal codes and a plethora of religious worship options. Luis Guerrero from the Mixtec village of Santa María Asunción described that it was not until he left Oaxaca that he understood the difference between constitutional rights and customary law. Guerrero stated: "Earthly law allows you to speak up for your rights with the police, the bosses.... In the villages... the local authorities pressure them to fulfill tradition. They want them to put on traditional parties.... Our children have no shoes because of tradition. We came here to leave all that behind."[16]

Quinones's essay on conversion at the border also conveys how Protestantism was not just a spiritual choice; migration paired with conversion meant a rupture in traditional social organization. While absentee villagers faced peer pressure to return to their communities when it was their turn to serve prestigious cargo positions (such as mayordomo of the fiesta or town mayor), they could also potentially send money in place of service, or they could decide not to support traditional fiestas.[17] In fact, remittances from migrants are, after tourism, Oaxaca's greatest revenue.[18] For communities with small populations, such revenue can both bolster and potentially destroy community adhesion.[19] Remittances help with local development projects (building a road, church renovation, irrigation) and also reaffirm the importance of the patron saint fiestas by sponsoring key aspects of it and/or timing their returns to the village to coincide with the town's fiesta.[20] Migrants with more cash flow than typical villagers also contribute to the growing competition over *quinceañera* and wedding celebrations.[21]

Migration changed hierarchies and status in the community and brought new ways of thinking about economic investments that might benefit individuals rather than the whole community.[22] At the same time, in communities where participation in tequio was followed rigidly, municipal leaders had the authority to sanction dissenters (whether for religious reasons or migratory status). Communitarian privileges often include farming on ejidal land, using the corn mill, access to public utilities, and voting in asamblea.

A migrant would still want to retain those aforementioned rights if he planned to return to his native village or if he left family members behind. Today, 40 percent of native-born Oaxacans have worked in the United States.[23] But, for important rites of passage (baptism of children, marriage, burial), they come back to the village.[24] Protestantism and migration certainly do not always go together; however, the local and global factors that led Oaxacans to migrate often were the very same influences that led them to convert: poverty and exposure to new markets and ways of thinking.[25] Oaxacans who both migrated and converted to Protestantism could experience both spiritual and social repercussions.

Migration can also mean freedom from village boundaries and expectations. "Dissenters" from the Zapotec community of San Agustín Yatareni who criticized the labor and financial expenses associated with tequio and cargo use migration to Poughkeepsie, New York, as an escape valve. Once free from the tequio and cargo restrictions, "dissenter" migrants focus on individual, not collective, advancement. The same can be true of religious conversion. For example, in Yatareni, Seventh-day Adventists make up a large percentage of the migrants who criticize the "quema de dinero" or "burning of money" on fiestas. By questioning every aspect of existing social structure in Yatareni, Adventists are stigmatized even more than men who leave their village wives for American girlfriends or stop sending money home to their families.[26] In Yatareni, Catholics relegate Adventists to the lowest cargos and the most onerous tequio assignments. Adventists struggle to balance their religious commitments while retaining community respect, which mostly is judged upon tequio performance and cargo participation, many of which are related to Catholic Church activities the Adventists no longer support.[27]

Tequio Conflicts

The complaints about tequios' religious assignments often dealt with Evangelicals' refusal to help repair local Catholic churches. While the majority of complaints against tequio in the 1980s cited religious beliefs, not all the cases are about religious incompatibility with tequio. Rather, the 1980s reveal a shifting interest in individual rights, the entrance of capitalism into village economies, and globalization. This section examines general opposition to tequio assignments before focusing on religiously based conflict cases.

Individualism, territorial boundaries, and capitalism all broke down the centrality of tequio in many Oaxacan communities in the 1980s. For example, in 1982, Jenaro Ramírez Ríos complained that he did not want to be treated like a peón, a physical laborer.[28] A resident of the Mixteca Alta community of San José Ayuquila, Huajuapan de León, Ramírez Ríos explained to governor Pedro Vásquez Colmenares that he contributed funds annually for community development projects. He resented being ordered to do physical labor once a week when he believed he had already done his part for the community. Ramírez Ríos, himself a former mayor of San José Ayuquila, asked the governor how his predecessor, Governor Eliseo Jiménez Ruíz, would feel if Vásquez Colmenares asked him to labor as a peón after serving six years as governor of Oaxaca. To further his characterization of tequio service as onerous, he also mentioned that the mayor of San José Ayuquila ordered elderly female residents to do tequio service, a practice he considered to be reprehensible.

In another case, in the Zapotec district of Tlacolula, Manuel Bautista

Aguilar complained to state authorities that he was required to perform tequio in his native town, Teotitlán del Valle, Tlacolula, but also in San Francisco Tutla, a small village just outside of Oaxaca City where he had purchased a small parcel of land for his daughter. In his 1981 complaint to Tutla authorities, Bautista Aguilar argued that his teenage daughter was not able to do physical labor and should be exempted altogether from the tequio. Instead, San Francisco Tutla reassigned the tequio responsibility to him, despite the fact that he resided in Teotitlán. He now had two concurrent tequio obligations, making it difficult for him to commute eighteen miles daily to sell his handwoven serapes (blankets) in Oaxaca City's market. Bautista Aguilar worked independently selling his textiles and did quite well, as is evidenced by his ability to invest in property closer to Oaxaca City. Serving in daylong tequios took him away from the job that provided for his family. To that end, he asked the Tutla authorities to exempt him from all tequios. Although he opted out for professional reasons, his justification had much in common with evangelical opposition to customary laws. He argued that the federal Mexican Constitution made no mention of customary law and he labeled tequio as comparable to Mexico's porfiriato exploitative hacienda labor systems.[29] In this example, Bautista Aguilar was a professional weaver who saw mobility as a way to improve his life, and the traditions of these communities were pulling him back. The entrance of capitalism and globalization into these villages caused resentments and friction.

Since independence, and especially after the Mexican Revolution and the advent of ejidal land distribution, territorial boundaries were constantly in dispute and often led to violent inter-and intra-village conflicts. Ausencio Ramírez Gijon in the coastal district of Juquila complained that, as a resident of one of the rancherías (small villages) of San Juan Lachao municipality, he should not have to complete tequios that only benefited the *cabecera municipal* (the county seat).[30] His complaint speaks to the fragmented and constantly shifting boundaries of municipalities that increased in the 1970s with more land distributions resulting from President Luis Echeverría's agrarian reform policy.[31] Ramírez Gijon's ranchería, Armonía, legally pertained to San Juan Lachao but had little interaction or history with the municipal seat.[32] He felt that the municipal government's reliance on the outer village was excessive and unjust to his family, who would never reap the benefits of the collective tequios commissioned for the township's center.

Issues of tradition continued to dominate conflict cases of the 1980s. Yet the 1980s' conflicts also dealt with the onslaught of new sectas and non-mainline groups. In the Zapotec town of Santiago Choapam, municipal mayor Efraín Cruz Orozco explained to the Oaxacan Secretary of State Carlos Hernández Underwood on January 29, 1982: "We have a careful agreement in this town that there is no other religion than the one that's already here."[33] He added that new religious groups brought divisions and conflicts because they did not contribute to tequio assignments or serve positions along the cargo hierarchical ladder. Most significantly, he complained that secta (he did not specify denomination) members went door to door each week handing out religious "propaganda," something never done before in his community. With the proliferation of fringe Christian denominations in 1980s Oaxaca, house calls became a common pattern in communities' religious tapestries. Within this growth trajectory, the highest conversion percentages were to Pentecostal and alternative denominations (Jehovah's Witnesses, Mormons, Adventists). In other cases, complaints to the state government were ostensibly about tequio but really were reactions to the social and cultural changes corresponding with rapid religious change.

San Juan Juquila Mixes

San Juan Juquila Mixes is a municipality located in the northern part of the district of Yautepec in the Sierra Sur region of Oaxaca, bordering just south of the Sierra Norte district of Mixes.[34] Residents trace the community's first exposure to Protestantism to when a SIL missionary arrived to translate the Bible into the Mixe language in 1937.[35] Many of the earliest Protestants remember playing basketball with missionary Walter S. Miller's sons and learning to read in Bible study class.[36] For decades, Miller was the lone missionary in San Juan Juquila Mixes; transportation to Oaxaca City took a few days by horse since most of the roads were impassable by truck. Since the 1970 completion of a highway connecting San Juan Juquila Mixes more directly with Oaxaca City and Ixtepec in the Isthmus, Pentecostal, Adventist, and Jehovah's Witness hermanos visited the community more frequently.[37] At the same time, young teenagers in the 1970s started to leave San Juan

Juquila Mixes to go to high school in neighboring towns or in Oaxaca City.[38] By 1980, there were eight hundred Catholics and approximately sixty Jehovah's Witnesses in San Juan Juquila Mixes.[39]

At present, Jehovah's Witnesses are the largest alternative Christian religion in Oaxaca. Jehovah's Witnesses also merit special attention because their core beliefs are radically different from both mainline and evangelical Protestant denominations. While they are classified in the Mexican census as a biblically based religion, Witnesses are on the margins of Christianity. Jehovah's Witnesses challenge not just religious norms but also civil government, school districts, and health-care providers. Witnesses, for the most part, do not donate blood or accept transfusions, celebrate civil or religious holidays, enroll in the military, participate in electoral elections, or salute the national flag.[40]

San Juan Juquila Mixes is a prime example of a conflict over secta nonparticipation in tequios that benefited the Catholic Church. In the early 1980s, an active Jehovah's Witness minority refused to participate in some key tequio assignments. The municipal government responded by fining the Jehovah's Witnesses, incarcerating some of them, and, finally, by threatening to expel all Jehovah's Witnesses from the community. The Oaxacan state government sided with the Jehovah's Witnesses but ultimately could do little to change the town's social and religious customs.

In a March 24, 1981, letter to Governor Pedro Vásquez Colmenares, San Juan Juquila Mixes mayor Félix Tiburcio Espina complained that Jehovah's Witnesses in his town destroyed community social adhesion.[41] The mayor stressed the significance of tequio: "As you know, for centuries our communities have cherished a practice of free service in which the residents collaborate in activities that are of importance to the town."[42] He argued that without tequio his administration would be unable to offer basic services to town residents. The mayor concluded that since the state and federal governments did not provide sufficient funds for local development, his town would be in dire straits without the full participation of all San Juan Juquila Mixes residents in tequio. While Tiburcio Espina acknowledged that the Mexican Constitution protected San Juan Juquila Mixes residents, he argued that tequio was not about law but about tradition: "Mr. Governor, centuries before the Mexican Constitution even existed, there has been a tradition of this kind of exchange in the indigenous communities of Oaxaca."[43] Without full cooperation of all ciudadanos, the municipal government, he claimed, would "suffer a severe collapse."[44]

The municipal authorities based their opposition to the Jehovah's Witnesses on the familiar premises seen in Chapters Three and Four: tradition, respect for government, and threats from outsiders, particularly foreigners.[45] The difference is that the federal- and state-supported government in the 1980s was not backing community expulsions of non-Catholics; Oaxacan state officials consistently sided with the Witnesses despite the authorities' accusations that the Witnesses were "anarquistas."[46] On April 22, 1981, Carlos Hernández Underwood, Oaxaca's Secretary of State, sent a memo to state investigator Jesus Martínez Álvarez to examine the municipal mayor's charges against the Jehovah's Witnesses.

The municipal authorities wrote another letter of complaint on February 4, 1982, responding to the DAR's proposed mediation session. Tiburcio Espina complained that the Jehovah's Witness men used religion "like a trampoline" so that they did not have to contribute to collective work projects such as the road the town was currently building.[47] For Tiburcio Espina, the problem was not about his office violating Article 24 of the Constitution (which guaranteed religious freedom) but rather a case of the Witnesses not contributing to road projects that benefited the whole community.[48]

Later that month, Tiburcio Espina framed the conflict in San Juan Juquila Mixes as a case of powerful Witness outsiders taking advantage of indigenous peoples. He described himself as a humble and illiterate indigenous man who had worked his way up the cargo ladder through dedication to his town and loyalty to the PRI government. He threatened to resign from his position and hand in the keys to the governor if the Jehovah's Witnesses did not leave the community. Tiburcio Espina pleaded: "The Jehovah's Witnesses laugh at us because they say they have your support because we are ILLITERATE AND POOR and because they are supported by a very powerful American organization. These factors permit them to agitate our people and divide the town."[49] Tiburcio Espina included the transcript from an open assembly where his municipal coauthorities asked community members if they should disown tradition to accommodate the *testigos*' needs. "At that point the assembly energetically shouted that you could not erase traditions just because a few people dedicate themselves to dividing the community for personal profit."[50] Finally, he claimed that the Witnesses were "bringing a series of lies and falsities [to the DAR], even forging the signatures of his accomplices in the Jehovah's Witness religion."[51] The Witnesses countered the mayor's accusations.

Witnesses Conrado Espina's and Victor Vásquez Barceló's letters of complaint suggest that they would not support activities that benefited the Catholic Church since it was of no use to them. From the municipal mayor's point of view, this stance was equivalent to rejecting the collective identity of the community; they had practiced syncretic Catholicism for five centuries, who were the Jehovah's Witnesses to break this tradition? The church in the center of town was the core of community identity; its sacredness stretched beyond the physical space and into the symbolic rituals and movements it represented.[52] The Witnesses were attempting to create their own sacred space and sense of community, which in turn affected new social organization and identity in San Juan Juquila Mixes.

The Oaxacan state government issued several letters to the community advising that they compromise with the Jehovah's Witnesses. In March of 1982, the department sent a government mediator from the DAR to San Juan Juquila to investigate. Investigator Saúl Jiménez Crispin wrote that it was obvious that the municipal officials refused to acknowledge that what they were doing violated religious freedom in Mexico. Instead, Jiménez Crispin complained that the mayor called a public assembly, despite the DAR's recommendation that they choose three representatives from each religion to privately negotiate their differences instead of in a large forum. Jiménez Crispin reported that the asamblea meeting dragged on in the burning sun for over two hours, all in Mixe, which he could not understand. The eight hundred Catholics at the asamblea held large banners that stated, "Religion is free—Catholic, Apostolic and Roman," while the sixty Jehovah's Witnesses held one declaring "Religion is free—Jehovah's Witnesses." Jiménez Crispin further reported that a dozen Catholic women in San Juan Juquila Mixes rushed toward the Jehovah's Witnesses trying to hit them and knock down their sign.[53]

Jiménez Crispin described how a negotiation following the public asamblea with three Jehovah's Witnesses and three Catholics initially resulted in a compromise: Both parties would respect the religious beliefs of the other. However, it was short-lived: "While the announcement was being made, individuals from the Catholic group began to hurl insulting words toward myself and the Oaxacan state government; one could hear such hurtful phrases as these. 'Con dinero baila el perro' [Money makes the world go around] and 'Aquí mande el pueblo' [Here the people rule]."[54] Jiménez Crispin tried to teach town members about the Mexican Constitution and let them know that what they were debating was anachronistic; Article 24 of the Constitution already ensured religious freedom, so their protests over the Jehovah's Witness presence held no credibility. However, the conflict was not about belief but rather the fulfillment of town duties.

Jiménez Crispin reported that a bilingual teacher, Professor Zamora, acted as an intermediary between himself and Mayor Tiburcio Espina, who the DAR investigator noted either did not understand Spanish or was "feigning ignorance" when he met with him.[55] The professor did not acknowledge Jiménez Crispin's presence and dominated the asamblea, arguing that "Jehovah's Witnesses poisoned the youth of the town, they brought exotic ideas, and they were against local customs."[56] The asamblea broke out in applause when Zamora concluded that the only way to resolve the situation was for the Witnesses to leave either "por las buenas o por las malas" [either voluntarily or by force].[57] Professor Zamora took over the meeting and the Catholics applauded him each time he asked that the government confiscate the properties of these "dangerous people" before the people in the town took action themselves.[58]

At the close of the meeting, Jiménez Crispin asked Jehovah's Witnesses Victor Vásquez Barceló and Conrado Espina to provide the Jehovah's Witnesses' point of view. Vásquez Barceló argued that the Witnesses were not "poisoning the youth in the town" but rather helping them become literate.[59] He showed copies of the secular literacy materials his congregation donated to local families and he also provided receipts for contributions Witnesses had made for capital developments. While they did not give money toward activities for the Catholic Church or fiestas, they did give money toward other types of community projects. Vásquez Barceló's statement went ignored since "the Catholics were too fanatical and did not listen to reason, all they did was insult the members of the Jehovah's Witnesses."[60] Later, Conrado Espina affirmed that the Jehovah's Witnesses were consistently eager to collaborate in everything that was beneficial for the town as a whole, but they would not give any money when the collection was for painting the Catholic church or other liturgical expenses.

Jiménez Crispin complained that the teacher and the mayor spoke in Mixe the whole time and refused to sign the agreement. However, Jiménez Crispin noted, the mayor was well able to convey the following ultimatum in Spanish: "Tell your government that here the people rule and if you don't get rid of these Jehovah's Witnesses we are going to close the Municipal office and the state government can do whatever it pleases."[61] The Mixe men's use of their native language earlier served to perhaps confuse or undermine state authorities. A frustrated Jiménez Crispin concluded that despite having spent an entire day with the community, no solution was reached, mostly, Jiménez Crispin argued, because of Professor Zamora's manipulation of the community by "taking advantage of the ignorance and the fanaticism of this poor town of San Juan Juquila Mixes, Yautepec, Oaxaca."[62]

In response, the state judicial attorney ordered the municipal authorities to come to the state capitol building in Oaxaca City for a mediation session set for April 5, 1982. The Jehovah's Witnesses attended, but the mayor and his coauthorities claimed that they received the notice too late. The conflict continued throughout the 1980s before subsiding in the late 1990s when more community members converted to the Jehovah's Witness denomination and other non-Catholic congregations competed for recognition. As of 2010, the municipality of San Juan Juquila Mixes had a population of roughly 3,500, of which about 10 percent were Jehovah's Witnesses.[63] Overall, the town is now 15 percent non-Catholic.[64]

The threat of outsiders invading the community was a common formula to use. The Witnesses pushed back against this contention by emphasizing their past contributions to community tequio and monetary contributions for secular events. The local community men were the Salón del Reino (Kingdom Hall) leaders, not North Americans. The Witnesses either converted after spending time in Oaxaca City working or attending school outside of the village or they were returning migrants. Furthermore, the Jehovah's Witnesses were respectful of tequio obligations but did not comply when local authorities mixed Catholicism with civil obligations.

Perhaps what made interactions with the Jehovah's Witness faith dramatically different than dealing with mainline Protestants is that the Jehovah's Witness religion is designed to remove members from the constraints of secular society and focus them in preparation for the apocalypse, which is why witnessing to new members is such an essential component of the

Jehovah's Witness faith. For example, members distribute the well-known *Despertad!* (Awake!) or *Atalaya* (Watchtower) bulletin warning people of the rapidly approaching doomsday. In fact, Jehovah's Witness conversion also affects local political leadership differently than mainline denominations. Whereas Tlacochahuayan Baptists took on active political roles in the community, Jehovah's Witnesses limited their political participation, preferring to remove themselves from the secular realm. Mexican Jehovah's Witnesses do not salute the political flag, enroll in the military, or sing the national anthem, as they believe that their only true allegiance is to God.

The Oaxacan state government supported the rights of the Jehovah's Witnesses to abstain from tequio and attempted to conduct a series of mediation sessions with DAR representatives. The Jehovah's Witnesses in San Juan Juquila Mixes respected their obligations to contribute to projects that benefited the whole town. To that end, they did procure receipts for monetary donations and purchases they had made for the town. In their version of the conflict, they were actually strengthening education and capital development in San Juan Juquila. These converts challenged social organization and communal adhesion by refraining from certain tequio projects. Yet while conversion to a secta may have been the visible conflict, the underlying issue in San Juan Juquila Mixes was about local power dynamics and the strength of customary law.

San Juan Tabaá, Villa Alta, Sierra Norte

Pentecostalism emerged as a strain of evangelical Protestantism that enthusiastically calls for a direct relationship with the Holy Spirit through glossolalia, or speaking in tongues, as experienced by the apostles on Pentecost Sunday.[65] Pentecostalism also entails faith healing and prophesies. However, the key difference between Pentecostalism and mainstream Protestant churches is that, while it can represent a particular denomination, Assemblies of God being the most visible one, Pentecostalism is "an umbrella term used to describe evangelical Protestants sharing certain theological and organizational features."[66] While Pentecostalism in Latin America was essentially an offshoot of twentieth-century North American missionary movements, its practice in Latin America by marginalized groups such as indigenous peoples, urban poor, and women represents Latin America's "first popular manifestation of Protestantism."[67] Pentecostalism spread to Hispanics living in the United States not long after its birth in Los Angeles, California, in 1906 at the Azusa Street Revival.[68] The earliest Pentecostal congregations registered in Mexico included Iglesia Apostólica de la Fe en Cristo Jesús, Iglesia Cristiana Espiritual, Iglesia del Evangelio Completo, and Asambleas de Dios in the 1920s.[69] Pentecostal conflicts with Catholic majorities were a pressing issue in Oaxacan communities, especially San Juan Tabaá.

San Juan Tabaá Pentecostals believe the first Protestant in their town was a former bracero worker. Nicolás Ortiz Marcos, once a devout Catholic leader in the community, converted in the United States and returned to his community to conduct Bible study classes in his home.[70] Like San Juan Juquila, Mixes, the Zapotec community of San Juan Tabaá in the district of Villa Alta, Sierra Norte, also hosted a SIL missionary beginning in 1947, and early evangélicos formed a Bible study group with them in 1950.[71] In 1970, they built their own Pentecostal church, Esmirna, named for the biblical city in modern-day Turkey. The church was part of the Movimiento Iglesia Evangélica Pentecostés Independiente (MIEPI), currently one of the fastest growing Pentecostal churches in southern Mexico. Mexican Valente Aponte González founded MIEPI in 1930 in Mexico City. As of 2002, MIEPI had 751 centers in 27 Mexican states, primarily along the border and in southern Mexico.[72]

Conflicts between Protestants and municipal leadership often began over customary law regulations. Pentecostals in San Juan Tabaá were inevitably outvoted in public asambleas. In these meetings, elders convened with ciudadanos in good standing in the community to vote on tequios and community policies. In June 1983, San Juan Tabaá Pentecostals started petitioning state and federal offices. In their letters to Oaxacan governor Pedro Vásquez Colmenares, they complained about Catholics forcing them to help renovate the Catholic church in Tabaá. The municipal authorities threatened the thirty-eight Pentecostal families living in Tabaá with expulsion, prohibition from using the communal corn grinder, and lynching if they did not contribute to the project while using the familiar argument that their town had always practiced collective rituals.[73] Additionally, since San Juan Tabaá was one of the oldest villages in the entire Sierra Norte region of Oaxaca, the municipal authorities felt strongly about the renovation project.⁷⁴ The church had to be maintained and respected; it was the heart of the community.

Municipal president Juan B. Castellanos Morales stated that, through collective work, their ancestors had persevered against hardships for centuries, an example Tabaeños wanted to emulate, not renounce. Castellanos Morales had a long list of complaints about the Pentecostals. "The worst part is that they destroy our youth by teaching them to ridicule our Indigenous culture and encouraging this new generation to rebel against authorities."⁷⁵ Finally, he asserted that the Pentecostal pastors were brainwashing their followers through hypnotism and the promise of miracles "and that's how they achieved the blind confidence in this religion."⁷⁶ By describing the alleged use of "magic" during their services, Castellanos Morales was most likely reacting to the exuberant style of Pentecostal worship that celebrated the Holy Spirit. The municipal mayor might have been purposely confusing the Pentecostals with deadly cults such as Jim Jones's Peoples Temple to insinuate that his paisanos were at risk of being manipulated by their church leaders in dangerous ways.

Castellanos Morales demanded that the state governor's office intervene and punish the "negligent" villagers who confused religion with public obligations such as cargo and tequio. The municipal president's complaint attests to how boundaries between public and private, civic and religious were blurred in indigenous communities. Catholicism was such an integral part of community life that breaking from it meant also breaking from the community ethos. The municipal president himself did not realize how blurred the boundaries between civil and religious obligations were when he accused the evangélicos of not honoring their public duties. The evangélicos were opting not to participate in tequio, but they were doing so because they rejected giving funds or labor toward the renovation of the Catholic church. In contrast, the municipal president saw the renovation of the Catholic church not as a religious duty but as a community obligation to support the preservation of an ancient Dominican church. Castellanos Morales concluded that, unless the dissenters started contributing toward the church renovation, they would be expelled from the community.

Castellanos Morales was confident in his mandate; the Church of San Juan Tabaá was *patrimonio nacional*, and his municipal government was charged with keeping it up to date despite the fact that it received insufficient funds from the state government. Castellanos Morales alluded to rising inflation in Mexico by "taking into account the crisis we are experiencing due to the high cost of living, we decided to organize the project 50 percent by tequio, the only means possible."[77] In other words, Castellanos Morales's government could not afford to bring in professional laborers to do the whole church renovation; much of it would have to be done by organized volunteer groups in the community.

For their part, the evangélicos, as with the Jehovah's Witnesses in San Juan Juquila, provided evidence of their contributions to the construction of a *telesecundaria* (satellite high school) in 1981. Furthermore, the evangelicals mentioned that other hermanos who had migrated to Oaxaca City or other regions of Mexico still paid fees toward tequio and sent tax money in to help subsidize the corn mill and other development projects in the community even though they were not benefiting from them daily. Pentecostal leader Pablo Fabián Mendoza also mentioned that it was the evangélicos who had led the collection for money to bring electricity to the town, thus demonstrating their commitment to progress.[78] Fabián Mendoza further brought up the absurdity of the renovation project by noting that its projected cost totaled over three million pesos, a staggering sum considering the poverty in the region. The municipal authorities required local residents to pay one thousand pesos each and migrants living in Mexico City up to ten thousand pesos for the renovation. The Pentecostal elders described it as bleeding the community members dry.[79]

On March 6, 1983, the town gathered at an asamblea to discuss the tequio project. During the meeting, the Pentecostals rejected the proposed project despite severe pressure from their Catholic neighbors. Fabián Mendoza said that some San Juan Tabaá members got close to them and threatened to lynch the Pentecostal hermanos if they did not contribute to the collective project. The community as a whole voted to restrict the Pentecostals from grinding corn at the nixtamal, accessing irrigation water for their crops, and accessing electricity; to revoke their rights to ejidal lands, delete their names from the Civil Registry; and to threaten to strip them of membership to the *tienda campesina* (communal goods store) if they continued to oppose the needs of the town. Fabián Mendoza also mentioned that the town authorities had advised the telesecundaria to ban evangelical children from attending, but the school principal did not comply.[80]

On March 22, 1983, the municipal authorities wrote a letter to President Miguel de la Madrid asserting that the conflict in San Juan Tabaá was not a case of religious intolerance by Catholics. Municipal authorities respected religious freedom and were only concerned with preserving the sixteenth-century Dominican church in their community; it held colonial paintings that were part of their cultural heritage. They mentioned that, because of the 1983 economic crisis in Mexico, they knew that the project would not get much federal or state funding.[81] Therefore, the municipal authorities made up the difference by asking each family in the community to donate money and physical labor toward fixing the roof. The mayor claimed that fifty Pentecostal families refused to contribute. Without the Pentecostal money or labor, finishing up the 3.5 million peso renovation project would be difficult.

Furthermore, similar to San Juan Juquila, the Tabaá mayor labeled the Pentecostals a "toxic" presence in the town. Mayor Castellanos Morales praised de la Madrid's willingness to listen to the needs of indigenous groups and commended his strong words against the continued presence of the SIL in Oaxaca during his March 1983 visit.[82] The letter accused Pentecostals not just in their community but also throughout the Zapotec Sierra of encouraging their followers to rebel against the villages' customs in order to get out of doing tequio. The Catholics in San Juan Tabaá hinted that some remaining SIL missionaries in the Zapotec region also criticized tequio in Oaxaca and perhaps were responsible for the contempt of Pentecostals in the region toward performing tequio.[83]

The Tabaá case played out over a series of petitions back and forth between the municipal mayor's office, the Oaxacan Religious Affairs Department, the Pentecostals in San Juan Tabaá and Mexico City, and the Religious Affairs main office in Mexico City. On May 23, 1983, Mayor Castellanos Morales sent a bilateral compromise signed by the Catholics in the town and a dozen evangelical families stating they would contribute to future tequios, including ones related to the Catholic church. Noticeably, the document declared that Pentecostals outside of San Juan Tabaá held no right to appeal tequio matters. Of course, the same would not be true for migrants living in the United States who were Catholic. Catholic migrants did not serve in tequios while they were away. They still contributed in other ways and maintained communication by telephone, letters, and through familial intermediaries with the municipal government.

One Tabaeño migrant, Gerardo Mendoza García, particularly rejected the municipal authorities' treatment of the Pentecostals. Exposed to evangelical Protestant teachings while growing up in San Juan Tabaá, Mendoza García formally converted to Pentecostalism in 1978 while working in Mexico City. Even though Mendoza García lived most of the year in Mexico City, he still had a plot of land where he grew coffee and he depended on it for extra income. He also identified with San Juan Tabaá, not Mexico City, as his true home. Mendoza García, twenty-six years old in 1983 and living in Mexico City, described the prevalent Pentecostal opinion regarding the Catholic church's renovation project: "We did not ask for their help when we built ours, so why did we have to help with theirs?,"[84] Mendoza García explained. "Because I came frequently from Mexico City to visit the evangelical church and the pastor, the town mayor blamed me as the principal agitator, that I was the reason for all of the problems, that I was telling the evangelicals not to collaborate, that I was the problem. So, they grabbed me and locked me up like a criminal."[85] Mendoza García's role in the conflict suggests that while he had migrated to Mexico City for work, he remained committed to the Pentecostal congregation in his community. For the municipal leaders in the community, Mendoza García was an outsider and his influence over other evangelicals in the community was a threat. His example also supports my contention that once evangelicals left their home communities and learned "constitutional" law, they came back to support the interests of evangelicals in their native communities. They also identified with other Pentecostals in new locations. When Mendoza García heard of the conflict in his community, he "automatically supported his hermanos" despite living in Mexico City.[86] He attended mandatory mediation sessions in the Oaxaca City governor's office along with the San Juan Tabaá evangelical leaders and the municipal authorities. He also brought Mexico City Pentecostal advocates with him for support. "And so that's when they started to say that they were the ones who ruled in the town, that it did not matter what they said in Oaxaca City or Mexico City. . . . No, they said, this time we are going to be the ones who make the law. We are the law. . . . We want you to support us with repairing the Catholic Church. Whether you want to or you don't want to, it doesn't matter."[87] In this example, the supremacy of local authority over individuals' choices is readily apparent.

Aware of the volatile situation in San Juan Tabaá, CONEDEF wrote a letter of complaint to Governor Pedro Vásquez Colmenares. Evangelical

Defense Committee President Ramón Urirre complained that he had helped the Oaxacan state government negotiate an agreement in April between the Catholic municipal authorities and the Evangelical families that both groups would support each other in tequios, meaning that the Catholics might occasionally have to help in a tequio for the Pentecostal church. The agreement was never implemented, and evangelical homes and crops continued to be damaged as Catholics threw stones at their windows and denied them access to irrigation water.[88] At least ten of the thirty-eight evangelical families left San Juan Tabaá, afraid of being shot at since everyone was armed.[89] The Pentecostal leaders earlier had suggested that the army come in and persuade the town members to hand in their arms. Evangelical president Ramón Urirre complained that the state police came in to check out the damaged homes but did nothing about the violence.[90]

Mendoza García used legal channels in Mexico City to protest evangélico persecution in Oaxaca. He brought his case all the way to the national DAR office in Mexico City. On September 8, 1983, Mexico City official Maria Emilia Farias Mackey wrote a memo to Governor Pedro Vásquez Colmenares of Oaxaca stating that the mayor of San Juan Tabaá illegally charged Mendoza García and other evangelicals with a fine of eight thousand pesos when they chose not to participate in the church renovation tequio. After this, the Oaxacan Attorney General's office entered the conflict by writing a memo on October 3, 1983, asking Oaxacan investigators to monitor the town. Mendoza García's case continued to attract the attention of the Oaxacan state government throughout 1984.

On February 5, 1984, the new San Juan Tabaá mayor Serafín Bautista Cruz called a general assembly to discuss the fate of Mendoza García. Mendoza García was charged with committing crimes "against the social norms at the heart of the community."[91] His family advised him not to dispute the charges: "They said let them take everything, you will still have God."[92] Mendoza García then recalled the night Catholic townspeople tried to lynch him.

> My brother-in-laws and other hermanos grabbed me and told me to run, that people were coming for me. We ran to the coffee plantation. The air was practically pushing me forward as I ran. We kept running and weaving between the coffee plants. We found a bench and pushed it against the fence, and I jumped over. They were now fifty people

following us calling my name, looking for me, but I had left the plantation. I ran and ran. I crossed a small creek on a board, slipping the whole time until I found a path on the other side. There was a family friend that lived off the path a little bit. They hid me in their outhouse. From there I could hear people calling out, looking for me. I stayed in there for I don't know, maybe two hours. By then, the people were gone. Then I walked back home a different way, entering the town through the back, maybe at 1:30 in the morning, but I'm not sure. My family and lots of hermanos from the church were at the house crying, thinking I had died. They thanked God that nothing had happened to me, nothing. And that's what happened. So, after that, we went to bed, calm and everything. They called me to the municipal hall again the next day, but it was different. It was light out so I knew people weren't going to try to grab me. The municipal authorities told me they were going to guard the roads that night so that townspeople wouldn't come after me again. But I think they were really watching the roads so that I wouldn't escape town, right? I didn't do anything and I slept fine after that. I slept peacefully because you know the saying, "If you have nothing to hide, you have nothing to fear."[93]

But the following day, the municipal authorities called together another asamblea. Mendoza García described it as a meeting of just Catholic men, mostly the friends and family of the municipal mayor, not the whole community. A dozen Evangelical hermanos were sentenced to two nights in the local jail for not contributing toward the church fees. Mendoza García was officially expelled. As a *persona foránea* or stranger he was no longer eligible to serve municipal positions or obligated to contribute to community services such as tequio; he was no longer recognized as a native Tabaeño. Mendoza García described his reaction when he was officially expelled:

Well, maybe because the Lord gave me strength, when they told me they were writing up a document to have me expelled from the town, I answered them back. I said, "You know what, why you don't write in that document that I'm expelled from not just the town, but from Oaxaca, and all of Mexico? You know, I want to go see new places, different places. So, then don't just ban me from the town, ban me from the whole Mexican

Republic. Since you are trying to get rid of me, why should I have to go live in Oaxaca City? It doesn't make sense. Why don't you make it the whole country?"[94]

Mendoza García's challenge to Tabaá authorities suggests that he knew the local government ultimately did not have the constitutional right to ban him from San Juan Tabaá, let alone Mexico.

On February 15, 1984, the Oaxacan Attorney General's office sent a memo to Mendoza García and to the mayor José E. Bautista Fabián ordering them to attend mediation at the governor's palace on May 5, 1984. Though he attended the required mediation meetings, what municipal authorities agreed to in Oaxaca City meant nothing in the community. Mendoza García said that even with all his legal and spiritual support from Mexico City and Oaxaca City, nothing changed. He recalled:

> I left my town [in 1984] and maybe came back four or five years later. I had nothing left there, no land, no house. They took the ejidal property and houses from all of my family who were evangelicals. I didn't try to get my house back, I let it go, and I stayed with my wife's family. No one said anything to me about not being allowed back in. But things are still the same. If an Evangelical man wants to marry a Catholic girl, the Evangelical has to pay 30,000 pesos to the municipal government since they know that the new couple won't contribute to most of the tequios that revolve around the Catholic Church. If the groom doesn't pay the fee, he'll lose his right to ejidal property. So, what happens in many cases is that evangelicals go back to being Catholic when they want to marry, at least nominally. That's how San Juan Tabaá is trying to get rid of Evangelicals.[95]

However, Mendoza García noted that the Protestants in the town keep growing in numbers. The monetary fines and social ostracism have only served to make the religion even more appealing to Tabaeños.[96] Mendoza García was officially expelled from the community, but the Tabaá Pentecostals could remain in the village as long as they promised not to recruit new members openly and paid fees in place of doing tequios that violated their religious convictions. Yet, as Mendoza García's testimony suggests, the monetary fines often had the opposite outcome.[97]

The cases in San Juan Tabaá and San Juan Juquila both speak to the question of citizenship. In many usos y costumbres communities, indigenous peoples refer to themselves as ciudadanos (citizens), meaning members of the community with special obligations and privileges.[98] In both San Juan Tabaá and San Juan Juquila, converts were still expected to contribute toward collective work projects and monetary donations involving the Catholic Church. Migrants were expected to do the same. Yet, migrant evangélicos like Mendoza García could be more of a threat to community solidarity than absent Catholics who looked forward to coming home and participating in the fiestas.

Conclusion

These conflict cases have demonstrated that power resided at the community level. Sometimes Protestants negotiated their new beliefs with traditional obligations and rituals, but whether they are expelled, fined, or victims of violence, it was determined in the local realm. The state government might have feuding parties sign an agreement to respect one another's religious beliefs. However, an official paper from Oaxaca City had limited authority in their home communities because "aquí mande el pueblo" [here the people rule].[99]

In remote regions of Oaxaca, leaders have retained considerable political authority since the colonial era. Local officials tried to negotiate with the colonial and then Mexican governments to maintain a small degree of autonomy, which allowed indigenous communities to assert agency either through local governance patterns or the benefit of distance from the capital city, and thus maintain religious and traditional continuity. This continuity is seen in both the cases discussed in this chapter. In San Juan Juquila Mixes, the municipal mayor threatened to close down his municipal office if the Oaxacan state government did not support his edict that every San Juan Juquilan contribute toward the renovation of the community's Catholic church. Here, we see the fluidity between sacred, political, and communal space as a constant theme in local municipal governments' commitment to maintaining the structural viability of colonial-era Catholic churches both as local and national cultural patrimony and as a central symbol of indigenous identity.

This chapter has also demonstrated how modernization, education, and migration to other regions of Mexico and often the United States led to changes in social and economic hierarchies in the community. Instead of remaining loyal to community adhesion, Pentecostals and other alternative Christians sought different types of religious connections that prevailed over their connections to local identity. Their actions challenged Catholic communal rituals but also sought (perhaps indirectly initially) to change their communities' ethos as a whole.

Converting to las sectas defied community cohesion much more saliently than the conversion to mainline Protestantism. By building churches and providing outreach in their community, evangélicos created not just their own religious space but also a new, unsanctioned social space. As a result, they no longer needed the Catholic Church to manage their social, economic, and spiritual needs. Evangélicos also were able to maintain, reclaim, or strengthen an indigenous identity through migration, education, and religious change that united them with indigenous citizens throughout Oaxaca, Mexico, and the United States, as is evident in theoretical conceptualizations of space such as Oaxacalifornia.[100] While local leaders argued that conversion disrupted centuries-old traditions and community adhesion, conversion also produced a new type of identity unconstrained by territorial borders.

CONCLUSION

Reimagining Communities

IN NOVEMBER 2008, Oaxaca City hosted a Luis Palau festival. Originally from Argentina, Palau is nicknamed the "Billy Graham of Latin America" for the size and popularity of his revival meetings.[1] Oaxacan evangélicos in white Palau T-shirts cheered and waved white Palau flags along the busy Niños Héroes thoroughfare as the delegation entered the city.[2] Three hundred and fifty Protestant churches and 170,000 Oaxacans attended the free outdoor festival. Two thousand volunteers reached out to prospective converts at Christian rock concerts, children's bouncy worlds, and during health screenings.[3] The Luis Palau "Good Music and Good News" tour was the largest evangelical event in the state's history.[4]

Palau's presence in Oaxaca speaks to the strength of the state's evangelical Protestant movement. Palau only visits areas with large potential audiences, and he requires local churches to fund-raise to cover the festival's expenses. In the weeks following the event, Catholics complained about state funds spent on hosting the event and letting Palau take over the city.[5] Additionally, they argued that it was a violation of the separation of church and state, since the governor closed public schools so that young children could attend the event.[6] Opponents also suggested that Oaxacan governor Ulises Ruiz Ortiz, a Pentecostal and PRI member, had political motives in supporting the event.[7] *Noticias* published a prominent photograph of the governor with Palau's family.[8] Local Pentecostal churches sponsored the evangelical pastor. However, Ruiz Ortiz and his cabinet hosted dinners, meetings, and prayer services with Palau, collaborating with the pastor in social services outreach campaigns throughout the state.⁹

Ruiz Ortiz's supporters staunchly disagreed that the politician favored Palau's programming. In fact, the COPACEO insisted that the festival's use of a public space paralleled Catholic events.¹⁰ For evangélicos, perhaps the road closings and fanfare given to Palau's visit shared much in common with Pope John Paul II's historic trip. However, Governor Eliseo Jiménez Ruíz only tepidly participated in the pope's 1979 visit. Aside from a brief airport meeting, Jiménez Ruíz recused himself from the religious celebrations, reflecting his support of Mexico's strict church-state relations.

In 1992, President Carlos Salinas amended the anticlerical provisions of the 1917 Constitution. Religious organizations could now be civil associations, new church buildings no longer belonged to the government, clergy could wear religious habits in public and vote in elections, and registered groups could host public processions and activities. Additionally, Mexico reinstated its diplomatic relations with the Vatican, smoothing sixty years of strained relations following the Cristero War. Essentially, the Catholic Church regained its legal and social rights.¹¹ These religious reforms also led to less bureaucratic red tape in opening new Protestant churches. Yet religion was not the only government deregulation in the early 1990s.

Neoliberal reforms threatened ejidal land distribution, long a cornerstone of local autonomy. President Salinas revised communal land ownership guarantees in Article 27 of the Constitution. Within this reform, the Mexican government attempted to give preference to corporations and global trade agreements at the expense of marginalized communities. On January 1, 1994, the very day NAFTA went into effect, Chiapan Mayans rose up to demand autonomy and essentially "the right to have rights" in the modern nation-state. Faced with the Zapatista Revolution and persistent indigenous agitation for collective rights throughout Latin America, the Mexican government debated indigenous autonomy and self-determination at the regional level.¹² The 1996 San Andrés Peace Accords with the Zapatistas promised to forge a path toward a new relationship between indigenous peoples and the state through local autonomy and a focus on multicultural education.¹³ However, the proposed amendment calling for indigenous rights to autonomy and self-determination never passed the federal government. Ultimately, a watered-down version of it is articulated in Article 2 of the

Constitution, declaring Mexico a multicultural nation.[14] In contrast, the Oaxacan state government implemented indigenous rights legislation.

Oaxaca's PRI-controlled government, concerned earlier in the 1980s about campesino mobilizations in the Central Valleys, Zapotec radicalism in Juchitán, and the increasing gains of the leftist PRD in rural areas, sought to retain its control of indigenous communities by strengthening its commitment to usos y costumbres. The PRI in the 1990s recognized the benefits of the "politics of recognition."[15] For example, Governor Diódoro Carrasco Altamirano (1992–1998) knew that collaboration and consultation (padded with neocorporatism) were more effective in governing Oaxaca's sixteen distinct indigenous groups than top-down rule.[16] Thus, looking to avoid its own indigenous uprising in a region where leftist guerrilla groups were starting to operate, the Oaxacan state congress formally legalized usos y costumbres by 1998.[17]

The core of the "Law of the Rights of Indigenous Peoples and Communities of the State of Oaxaca" promises respect for indigenous autonomy, defined as self-determination over legal and electoral norms, land, natural resources, education, language, worldview, and customs, among other guarantees.[18] This also extended to municipal elections whereby communities could decide whether to allow national parties to have a presence in their municipality.[19] In place of the party system with private paper ballots, communities could vote openly in public asamblea as they traditionally had done, and the state honors the results.

Although the "Law of the Rights of Indigenous Peoples" is thoughtful and innovative in its commitment to indigenous peoples' cultural rights, the guarantees are also somewhat ambivalent. For example, Article 27 states that indigenous people have the right to perform their traditional religious ceremonies as they see fit; however, it also states that such practices must not violate existing religious freedom legislation. Moreover, Article 43 guarantees communities the right to preserve customary tequio work projects, but Article 44 adds that the state government will mediate in instances of conflicts between community members and tequio obligations. In sum, usos y costumbres legislation is at odds with religious tolerance and nondiscrimination provisions guaranteed in state and national legislation.[20]

Ultimately, local rights to autonomy are often more salient than the state or national laws. Thus, public asamblea can potentially exclude women or individuals lacking ciudadano de bien status from taking part in the shared governance process.[21] Those practices contradict state law but reflect customary governance norms. Within the local context of community citizenship, questioning usos y costumbres is tantamount to subordinating ancient traditions and customs for the perceived benefit of outsiders.[22] Religious conflicts remain volatile in Oaxaca as converts continue to challenge the parameters of the tequio and the cargo systems enshrined in customary law.

For over a century, Catholic and Protestant Oaxacans have fought to define rights and norms in their communities. On the surface, such conflicts are about religious beliefs, but a more nuanced look reveals they are also about who or what determines local, regional, and national identities. Converts chose not to participate consistently or abstained altogether from the cargo system. The tradition was a fusion of civil-religious obligations that their new faiths did not support. For Catholics, converts threatened communal adhesion, leaving their communities vulnerable to outside penetration from North American missionary organizations, the Mexican state, or exploitative companies. While my book suggests that Protestants and Catholics sometimes are able to negotiate compromises over tequio obligations, acceptance often followed protracted struggles over where power resided in the community.[23]

These cases have explored the role of the Mexican state in Native communities. Even with the threat of intervention by state authorities, local leaders still held much power over the social-religious realm. Elders who had worked their way up the cargo ladder through decades of service rejected a new relationship with the state whereby individuals, not a leader representing the pueblo, could get the government's attention through filing a complaint in the legal system. Furthermore, this study has demonstrated the inability of the larger state, at both the state and national levels, to enforce the Constitution. Despite the mediation of the Department of Religious Affairs, many conflicts in Oaxaca evidence the ineffectiveness of state power over local rule. The legalization of usos y costumbres governance in 1998 decreased the state government's ability to enforce the individual rights of indigenous Protestants. The friction between customary and constitutional law creates a legal vacuum into which the protection of the state comes too little or too late for expelled Protestants.

As my conflict cases have demonstrated, power resides primarily in the community. Sometimes Protestants negotiated their new beliefs with traditional obligations and rituals, but whether they faced expulsion, fines, or violence, their fate was determined in the local realm. The state government might have feuding parties sign an agreement to respect one another's religious beliefs. However, as these cases demonstrate, an official paper from Oaxaca City had limited authority in their home communities because "aquí manda el pueblo" [here the people rule].[24] Even with the threat of intervention by state authorities, customary rule still held much power over the social-religious realm.

These conflicts also express the conceptualization of sacred space in both the physical and imaginary realms. Late nineteenth-century missionary Lucius Smith purchased a former Catholic Church building, complaining of its "large and ugly crucifixes," where he would rather see a bare cross, illustrating the Protestant preference for simple worship styles and emphasis on Christ's resurrection. Protestant services in former Catholic spaces caused confusion and resentment. The Oaxacan archdiocese warned Catholics against entering *templos evangélicos*, even if they were historically Catholic churches.

In 1926, Samuel Juárez García established a Baptist congregation in his Zapotec hometown. Today, Baptist families are working to rebuild the crumbling church's lone remaining facade in remembrance of the minister's legacy. Ongoing disputes with a Catholic neighbor over the boundaries of the property have slowed the plans. Yet Baptists continue to meet on the original grounds and advance a collective and social memory of the late pastor as a crucial indigenous Protestant martyr.

The fluidity between sacred, political, and communal spaces is also a constant theme in local municipal governments' commitment to maintaining the structural viability of colonial-era Catholic churches both as local and national cultural patrimony and as a central symbol of identity in indigenous communities. While various political, academic, and religious institutions claimed to speak "for" them, indigenous leaders wrote letters of protest to state and federal authorities over Protestantism's impact on community life. For example, Tabaeño municipal authorities argued that all ciudadanos had to contribute funds and labor toward a church renovation project because it was the oldest Dominican church in the Sierra Norte region of Oaxaca and contained valuable sixteenth-century religious paintings and statues. For the local municipal authorities, participating in the tequio was not just about honoring a sacred space but also about one's civic duty to protect shared cultural patrimony at the center of the community.

Local leaders also argued that conversion disrupted centuries-old traditions and community adhesion. In San Juan Juquila, the response to non-Catholics abstaining from key tequio projects illustrated the strength of customary over constitutional law. When a government mediator tried to settle the dispute in favor of individual rights to religious freedom, Mayor Félix Tiburcio Espina warned: "Tell your government that here the people rule and if you don't get rid of these Jehovah's Witnesses we are going to close the Municipal office and the state government can do whatever it pleases."[25] Protestantism violated the social norms at the heart of their communities' identity—tequio and cargo—leading to violence and divisions.

The historical production of political and religious spaces in Oaxacan communities has also changed over time from a shared local identity to a more regional, national, and increasingly transnational one. Evangélicos maintained, reclaimed, or strengthened transregional and transnational indigenous identity through migration, education, and religious change that united them with indigenous citizens throughout Oaxaca, Mexico, and the United States. Conversion also produced a new type of identity unconstrained by territorial borders. During the 1950s, for example, a national evangelical defense network issued pleas across Mexico and the United States for support of Protestants entangled in conflicts. Protestantism challenges community norms and communal cohesion, breaking Protestants from the binds of tradition and propelling them into a larger national and transnational arena. It is in this "imagined community" where Protestants are hosting, as sociologist David Martin put it, "their very own *fiesta*."[26]

Through preservation of pre-Hispanic and colonial-era rituals, Catholic Oaxacans maintain an intimate connection to ancestors, representing a syncretic and popular Catholicism. Protestants may identify with this strong connection to language and culture, arguing that as evangélicos, they strengthen indigenous identity; Protestant converts often study and integrate their local languages as they work on religious tracts and Bible translations; additionally, they are rejecting a form of Christianity brought in by Spanish colonizers. In contrast, majority Catholics argued that Protestantism reflected North American values; furthermore, collective rights trumped individual rights to religious freedom. Such local conflicts arose as part of a larger debate centering on indigenous rights, nationalism, and the bitter legacy of US intervention in Latin America.

For its part, the Mexican state sought to project an image of itself as a protector of indigenous rights in Oaxaca. While intervening in conflict cases between indigenous authorities and Protestant converts, the PRI often ceded to the collective rights arguments. The Oaxacan state's concession in 1998 to permit a degree of local autonomy rule via usos y costumbres challenged the long-standing belief in the monolithic and authoritarian character of the postrevolutionary party-state. Local autonomy in Oaxaca, thus, demonstrated compromise among the state-PRI and Native actors in a way that undermined the idea of authoritarian rule. The Mexican state was certainly a key player in religious disputes, but the parameters of Protestantism were ultimately determined at the local level where el pueblo (the people) ruled.

Of course, ambiguous legal jurisdictions could also work to the state's advantage sometimes. In a sense, the competing legalities could please both the local community and the state: Each entity felt that they were in charge. Perhaps that represents a continuation of Native people's abilities to carve out a degree of autonomy in the post-conquest period. Or perhaps it represents the shrewdness of the ruling party in its interactions with Native communities spanning 1920s assimilationist approaches to embracing multiculturalism in the 1990s.

Oaxaca's PRI remained undefeated at the statewide level from 1930 through 2010. Regional threats chipped away at the state PRI—notably the success of the COCEI Zapotec party in Juchitán's municipal elections in 1981. However, the state government's refusal to recognize the COCEI led to almost a decade of civil unrest in the Isthmus region. Looking to avoid unrest over past demands for political representation and community autonomy, PRI officials in the 1990s preferred co-opting and negotiating with Native communities. Hence, offering leaders a degree of local governance became preferential to watching opposition parties (such as the conservative Partido de Acción Nacional, PRD, COCEI, etc.) make gains in the region. Yet Governor Ulises Ruiz Ortiz's disastrous term left a legacy of state violence against the 2006 teachers' strike. Surprising pundits but probably not Oaxacans observing firsthand the PRI's waning popularity, opposition candidate Gabino Cué Monteagudo won the gubernatorial race in 2010. However, his successor, Alejandro Murat Hinojosa, the polished PRIista son of former governor José Murat, is in power until 2022.[27] How the "New PRI" negotiates issues of customary governance will be important to analyze.

On September 7, 2017, a massive 8.2 magnitude earthquake struck Oaxaca. The Zapotec city of Juchitán was one of the worst hit zones. Once the center of a violent showdown between the state PRI and the local COCEI party, Juchitán is particularly worried about government aid from Oaxaca City reaching the far-flung Isthmus region. Given the history of the PRI's nonrecognition of COCEI's political victories, coupled with a general distrust of government funds actually reaching the most peripheral zones, civil society organizations and private agencies are driving much of the local recovery effort.[28] In all of this, transnational Christian organizations will surely play a role in rebuilding Juchitán's infrastructure, especially since the isthmus is a region rapidly shifting from Catholicism to Pentecostalism.

Attesting to Protestantism's massive rise in Latin America, the Pew Research Center notes that while just one out of ten Latin Americans was raised Protestant, almost one in five Latin Americans today practice Protestantism.[29] Additionally, approximately 22 percent of Latinos in the United States currently identify as Protestant, mainly Pentecostal.[30] While Latino Catholics still make up a solid third of all Roman Catholics in the United States, they are rapidly shifting to strains of Pentecostalism. Perhaps not surprisingly, 50 percent of Latino Catholics also identify as part of the Catholic Charismatic Renewal (CCR), a movement emerging in the late 1960s.[31] CCR is very similar to Pentecostal worship style: Glossolalia, hand clapping or shouting, a more personalized relationship with God, and laypeople—especially women—leading prayer groups are central components of the meetings. Ultimately, what US Latinos collectively see in CCR or Pentecostalism is a new sense of belonging and community that Oaxacan converts once sought, whether in the Mixteca region, Mexico City, Tijuana, Oaxacalifornia, or Poughkeepsie, New York. Through their identification as evangélicos, they united across political, geographic, and ethnic borders. In the process, they redefined what it meant to be indigenous, to be Mexican, and to be Christian.

Notes

Introduction

1. Lawrence P. Van Slyke, as quoted in Wheeler, *Modern Missions in Mexico*, 280–81.
2. Efraín Cruz Orozco to Oaxacan Secretary General, "Relacionados con Tequios," January 29, 1982, 1/131.7 (1–30) 82/333 (AGEPEO). All translations are my own unless otherwise noted.
3. See Yashar, *Contesting Citizenship in Latin America*, for an analysis of struggles over integration of collective rights and autonomy in Bolivia, Ecuador, and Peru. Yashar argues that postliberal changes in conceptualizations of citizenship "politicized indigenous identities precisely because they unwittingly challenged enclaves of local autonomy that had gone largely unrecognized by the state" (8). Kevin Lewis O'Neill describes the intersection of democracy and neo-Pentecostalism as a new form of Christian citizenship in *City of God*, 331–32n2.
4. Throughout this book I use the term *indigenous peoples* to refer in general to Native peoples in Oaxaca. I recognize that this term is one historically imposed upon Natives during the conquest period. When available, I try to refer to Oaxacans by their individual ethnic groupings. I also recognize that indigenous identity cannot boil down to an essentialist list of markers such as language or dress. Instead, I interpret identity in a more fluid sense and see it as especially strengthened or even reconstructed during times of resistance to outsiders.
5. Yashar, *Contesting Citizenship in Latin America*, 292.
6. Article 27 of the 1917 Constitution declared that land was property of the nation (with some exceptions), hence limiting church land ownership. Article 130 denied priests and ministers the right to participate in the political sphere; clergy could not hold office or speak about politics from the pulpit.

7. Historian Jason Dormady argues that the evangelical Protestant denomination Luz del Mundo (LDM) got along with the newly formed Partido Revolucionario Institucional (PRI) government partially because of LDM's founder's service in the Mexican Revolution and "mutual dislike of the Catholic Church" (*Primitive Revolution*, 45). For more on LDM's history, see de la Torre, *Los hijos de la luz*.
8. See Wheeler, *Modern Missions in Mexico*, 256–83, for Presbyterian interest in opening schools and increasing missionary work in indigenous Mexico.
9. Oaxaca is divided into eight geographic regions.
10. Instituto Nacional de Estadística y Geografía (INEGI), *Censo de población y Vivienda*, 1895. Pew Research Center, *Religion in Latin America*, 17.
11. "Where Angels Fear to Tread: Evangelicals Are Swooping on Long-Ignored Regions," *Economist*, May 24, 2012.
12. INEGI, *Censo de Población y Vivienda*, 2000, and *Censo de Población y Vivienda*, 2010. See also Gross, "Pentecostal Congregations and Religious Competition in Rural Mexico," for a discussion of Protestant growth in southern Mexico, especially Oaxaca. In "Protestantism and Modernity," Gross examines Oaxaca's Protestant growth rate.
13. INEGI, *Censo de Población y Vivienda*, 2010.
14. Political scientists Timothy J. Steigenga and Edward L. Cleary detail the difficulty with Protestant terminology in the introduction to their edited volume, *Conversion of a Continent*, 7–9. Political scientist Anthony Gill, in his article "The Struggle to Be Soul Provider," argues that *Protestant*, though a problematic term, is still the most useful way to describe non-Catholic Christians in Latin America (36–37n4). Economist Amy Sherman notes that "'Evangelical' is basically synonymous with 'Protestant'" in Guatemala (*Soul of Development*, ix). Anthropologist Toomas Gross also uses the sweeping category of "Protestant" to refer to non-Catholic Mexican Christians in "Pentecostal Congregations and Religious Competition in Rural Mexico" (106–7n1). Expressing frustration with Protestant classification terminology, anthropologist Kevin L. O'Neill states: "'Denomination' is an ethnographically unhelpful category in postwar Guatemala" (*Secure the Soul*, 210n11).
15. These labels speak to their intimate and personal relationship to Jesus Christ and each other as opposed to the more hierarchical Father/Priest and children/parishioners relationship in Catholicism. By excluding Catholics from the rubric of Christianity, they are emphasizing their personal, Christ-centered worship as opposed to Catholics, who include the pope and the saints as essential components of their belief system.
16. I use the term *alternative Christians* to describe Adventists, Mormons, and Jehovah's Witnesses. Other historians use the term *restorationist Christians*. I want to acknowledge that while they are indeed Christians, their beliefs and practices put them outside the parameters of mainstream Christianity. See

sociologist Bryan R. Wilson, *Social Dimensions of Sectarianism*, for a discussion of the term *sect*. For the recent political-religious debate over whether Mormons are Christians, see David S. Reynolds, "Why Evangelicals Don't Like Mormons," *New York Times*, January 25, 2012.
17. Pew Research Center, *Religion in Latin America*.
18. For background on the historical significance of the cargo system, see Chance and Taylor, "Cofradías and Cargos." In contrast to Chance and Taylor, Carole Nagengast and Michael Kearney describe tequio as "an ancient system of obligation that has been utilized by the Aztecs and Mixtecs for community projects," in "Mixtec Ethnicity," 89. See also Loewe, *Maya or Mestizo?*, for an excellent discussion of the cargo system's contested history in Oaxaca, and Greenberg, "Sanctity and Resistance in Closed Corporate Indigenous Communities."
19. Works focusing on religion and state formation include Purnell, *Popular Movements and State Formation in Revolutionary Mexico*; Becker, *Setting the Virgin on Fire*; Hartch, *Missionaries of the State*; and Fallaw, *Religion and State Formation in Postrevolutionary Mexico*.
20. Article 3 called for the secularization of schools; Article 24 guaranteed religious freedom in Mexico but limited public displays of religious activities; Article 27 declared land, water, and subsoil rights the property of the nation; Article 123 guaranteed workers the right to form a union; and Article 130 restricted religious officials' participation in political life.
21. Lewis, "Mexico's National Indigenist Institute," 612. See also Dawson, "From Models for the Nation to Model Citizens."
22. See Adrian Bantjes's discussion of revolutionary ideology that equated defanaticization campaigns with the "spiritual liberation" Mexico's indigenous peoples needed in "Idolatry and Iconoclasm in Revolutionary Mexico," 93.
23. Hartch, *Missionaries of the State*, 21–24.
24. Participatory indigenism meant more inclusion of and greater sensitivity toward Native peoples' traditions in government policies. It also included training indigenous people for professional civil service and educational positions. See N. Gutiérrez, *Nationalist Myths and Ethnic Identities*.
25. Saúl Jiménez Crispin to Justiniano Carballido González, Attorney General, Oaxaca, February 15, 1982, box 140, file 162.6 San Juan Juquila Mixes, Yautepec, Oaxaca, collection: Asuntos Agrarios (AGEPEO).
26. See Knight, "Weight of the State in Modern Mexico," and Knight, "Cardenismo."
27. See Gilly, *El Cardenismo, una utopia Mexicana*, for a hagiographic look at Cárdenas's role in shaping Mexico's social, economic, and political gains of the postrevolutionary period. See Carey's *Plaza of Sacrifices* for a gendered study of PRI's crackdown on the student movement.
28. The seminal historiographical contribution in re-examining twentieth-century

state formation is Joseph and Nugent, *Everyday Forms of State Formation*. For how state interests interact with local rule, see B. Smith, *Pistoleros and Popular Movements*, and Gillingham and Smith, *Dictablanda*. See also Lenti, *Redeeming the Revolution*, for an analysis of how PRI embraced the labor movement to gain legitimacy following criticism of state violence against the student movement.

29. B. Smith, *Pistoleros and Popular Movements*, 10–11.
30. Gillingham and Smith, *Dictablanda*, 11–13.
31. Historian Francie R. Chassen-López places Oaxaca at the center of revolutionary activity, revising the hitherto emphasis on central and northern Mexican events, which relegated Oaxaca as an insignificant backwater; see *From Liberal to Revolutionary Oaxaca*. See also B. Smith's description of how "a view from the south" provides new and important ways of examining state formation (*Pistoleros*, 14–15).
32. Scholars have taken different historical, spiritual, economic, and gender-based approaches to examining what David Martin aptly refers to as the explosion of Protestantism in late twentieth–century Latin America. For the foundational scholarship on the rise of Protestantism in Latin America, see Stoll, *Is Latin America Turning Protestant?*; Garrard-Burnett, *On Earth as It Is in Heaven*; Martin, *Tongues of Fire*; and Chesnut, *Competitive Spirits*. For a groundbreaking early study of the history of the transnational Iglesia Apostólica Pentecostal denomination in Mexico and California, see Gaxiola, *La Serpiente y La Paloma*. Gaxiola's work is especially important because he analyzes the differences between "Oneness" Pentecostals and "Tridentine" Pentecostals. He also was one of the first Latino Pentecostals to have a PhD in theology, hence bridging the gap between institutional accounts of church growth and scholarly ones. For scholarship specifically on Mexican Protestantism, see Bastian, *Protestantismo y Sociedad en México*; Marroquín, *El Conflicto Religioso*; and Bowen, *Evangelism and Apostasy*. For Protestantism's impact on indigenous communities, see Dow, "Expansion of Protestantism in Mexico"; Garma Navarro, *Protestantismo en una comunidad Totonaca de Puebla*; and Gross, "Protestantism and Modernity." Examining Protestantism at the macro level is a recent trend in political science scholarship; see Timothy J. Steigenga and Edward L. Cleary's volume *Conversion of a Continent* for an excellent source on how scholars across the social sciences debate the impact religious pluralism has had in modern Latin America. Likewise, historian Todd Hartch's recent work *The Rebirth of Latin American Christianity* places Protestant growth in Mexico within the larger context of Latin American, African, and Asian religious pluralism movements. Martin Lindhardt's edited volume *New Ways of Being Pentecostal in Latin America* also contributes important ways to view the bigger picture of religious transformation. However, comprehensive noninstitutional historical studies on Protestantism in Oaxaca are still deficient.

33. Stoll, review of *Holy Saints and Fiery Preachers*, 595–96.
34. See Levine, *Religion and Political Conflict in Latin America*; Sigmund, *Liberation Theology at the Crossroads*; and Klaiber, *Church, Dictatorships, and Democracy in Latin America*.
35. For the foundational work on the *cristiada*, see historian Jean Meyer's *Cristero Rebellion*. See also Meyer, *El conflicto religioso en Oaxaca*, for a regional example of *cristero* and post-cristero violence in Oaxaca. See also Bantjes, "Idolatry and Iconoclasm in Revolutionary Mexico."
36. Dormady, *Primitive Revolution*.
37. Anthropologist Mary I. O'Connor's *Mixtec Evangelicals* offers an excellent field study comparing the socioeconomic levels of Catholics to Pentecostals in four villages in the Mixteca Alta region, but historical scholarship on Protestant growth in rural Mexico is still understudied.
38. My approach follows the work of Florencia Mallon's and Daniel James's groundbreaking inclusion of oral histories in their work on Mapuche activism and Argentine unionism, respectively (Mallon, *Courage Tastes of Blood*; Reuque Paillalef and Mallon, *When a Flower Was Reborn*; James, *Doña María's Story*). I strive to follow Lynn Abrams's conceptualization of oral history as representing "the product of a struggle for dominance of a particular interpretation of an event or period" (Abrams, *Oral History Theory*, 97).
39. See Les W. Field, "Who Are the Indians?," for an excellent synthesis of the different schools of thought on defining indigenous identity.
40. See Stephen, "Creation and Re-Creation of Ethnicity," 18, 33.
41. Hobsbawm, "Introduction: Inventing Traditions," 2–3. As a comparative example, Navajo historian Jennifer Nez Denetdale argues that notions of precontact gender roles are at times reimagined and reconstructed to limit women's representation in contemporary Native government. See Denetdale, "Securing the Navajo National Boundaries." See also Denetdale, *Reclaiming Diné History*.
42. By "syncretic," I mean blending elements of pre-Hispanic religious traditions into Catholic religiosity. As an example, the celebration of Saint John the Baptist in San Juan Mixtepec integrates elements of Mixtec ritual and spirituality into the rooster beheading ceremony. Enculturated Catholicism is another way to express this cultural fusion.
43. Bastian, *Los Disidentes*, and Bastian, "Disidencia religiosa en el campo mexicano."
44. See Brusco, *Reformation of Machismo*, and Nash, "Protestantism in an Indian Village in the Western Highlands of Guatemala," for arguments that conversion to Protestantism decreases alcoholism and reduces domestic violence.
45. Economist Amy Sherman describes behavioral changes that set Protestant converts apart from traditional Catholics in *The Soul of Development*, 45–49.
46. In *Los Disidentes*, Bastian describes how religious conversion and the development of pro-Mexican Revolution ideology went hand in hand as Protestant

networks weakened traditional Catholic power brokers, especially by promoting new ways of thinking about civic values and patriotism.

47. B. Anderson, *Imagined Communities*, 198–99.
48. Kearney, "Transnational Oaxacan Indigenous Identity," 175.
49. In *Making a Difference in a Globalized World*, anthropologist Laurie A. Occhipinti describes the connections between a rural western Pennsylvania Presbyterian church and a small rural church in Sabaneta, northwest Dominican Republic.
50. See Hartch, *Missionaries of the State*, and Garrard-Burnett, *Protestantism in Guatemala*. In contrast, historian Jean-Pierre Bastian is adamant that Protestant growth is not a result of North American imperialism (see *La mutación religiosa de América Latina*).
51. Given the documented economic and political connections between the United States and military dictators in many Latin American countries during the 1970s and the early 1980s, it is not surprising that political scientists, anthropologists, and human rights activists churned out early and frequent denunciations of Protestant organizations in Latin America, especially the Summer Institute of Linguistics. For a sampling of literature condemning Protestant organizations such as the SIL, see Hvalkof and Aaby, *Is God an American?*; Stoll, *Fishers of Men or Founders of Empire?*; and Hart, "Story of the Wycliffe Translators."
52. Garrard-Burnett, "'Like a Mighty Rushing Wind.'" See also Ramírez, *Migrating Faith*, 201.
53. Michael Kearney, Carole Nagengast, Jonathan Fox and Gaspar Rivera-Salgado, Lynn Stephen, and Carmen Martínez Novo have tracked indigenous Oaxacan migration to California, Washington, and Oregon while often focusing on how indigenous identities are used to frame protests for safer working conditions or improved living arrangements. Kearney, "Effects of Transnational Culture, Economy, and Migration"; Nagengast and Kearney, "Mixtec Ethnicity"; Fox and Rivera-Salgado, *Indigenous Migrants in the United States*; Stephen, *Transborder Lives*; and Martínez Novo, *Who Defines Indigenous?*.
54. See, for example, Rivera-Salgado's "Transnational Political Strategies," and Cohen, *Culture of Migration in Southern Mexico*. See also Ruiz-Navarro, "New Guadalupanos."
55. See Gross, "Farewell to Fiestas and Saints?," for an argument that the fiesta system in Oaxaca is actually growing in symbolic and physical importance because of the rise of Protestant churches.
56. Anthropologist Mary I. O'Connor's *Mixtec Evangelicals* is an important addition to the literature, complementing sociologist Toomas Gross's "Pentecostal Congregations and Religious Competition in Rural Mexico."
57. Social scientists also use the term *neo-Christian* to categorize Mormons and Jehovah's Witnesses. See Steigenga and Cleary, *Conversion of a Continent*, 9.

Daniel Ramírez describes Mexican Apostolics as non-Trinitarian Pentecostals in *Migrating Faith*, 214n13.

58. Borland, "That's Not What I Said," 321.
59. The Instituto Nacional Indigenista (INI) was also founded in 1948. In Chapter Four, I analyze INI's collaboration with Protestant organizations such as the SIL in modernizing indigenous communities.
60. Michael Novak, "The Case against Liberation Theology," *New York Times*, October 21, 1984.
61. Saúl Jiménez Crispin to Justiniano Carballido González, Attorney General, Oaxaca, February 15, 1982, file: San Juan Juquila Mixes, Yautepec, Oaxaca, collection: Asuntos Agrarios (AGEPEO).
62. Scholars remain divided over whether usos y costumbres is truly a vestige of pre-Hispanic governance or a colonial institution. For an argument supporting the colonial implementation of the cargo system, see Chance and Taylor, "Cofradías and Cargos." In contrast to Chance and Taylor, Nagengast and Kearney describe tequio as "an ancient system of obligation that has been utilized by the Aztecs and Mixtecs for community projects" ("Mixtec Ethnicity," 89). See also Greenberg, "Sanctity and Resistance in Closed Corporate Indigenous Communities," for a discussion of the fiesta system and civil-religious hierarchies.
63. For a discussion of usos y costumbres legislation as a reaction to the Zapatista movement in 1994, see Eisenstadt and Ríos, "Multicultural Institutions, Distributional Politics, and Postelectoral Mobilization in Indigenous Mexico."

Chapter One

1. The Religious Freedom Act of 1860 was a significant and controversial departure from the 1824 Constitution's treatment of the Catholic Church, which placed Catholicism as the state religion. The Federal Constitution of the Mexican United States, October 4, 1824, stated: "The Religion of the Mexican Nation, is, and will be perpetually, the Roman Catholic Apostolic. The Nation will protect it by wise and just laws, and prohibit the exercise of any other religion whatsoever." The 1857 Liberal Constitution limited Catholic Church landholdings, clerical privileges, and essentially legalized Protestantism.
2. Benito Juárez, as quoted in Sierra, *Juárez, su obra y su tiempo*, 546.
3. See Bliss, *Concise History of Missions*, 99–109, for background of US missionary organizations in late nineteenth-century Latin America. See Orozco, "Not to Be Called Christians," for US Protestant missionaries' perceptions of Catholicism in Mexico.
4. See William Green, "A Trip to the Land of the Mixtecos," *Gospel in All Lands*, March 1891, 105–10, for a description of the first Evangelical Society in Oaxaca, in 1871.

5. Schwaller, *History of the Catholic Church in Latin America*, 174. See also Schmitt, "American Protestant Missionaries and the Díaz Regime in Mexico."
6. Schwaller, *History of the Catholic Church in Latin America*, 175.
7. See William Green, "A Trip to the Land of the Mixtecos," *Gospel in All Lands*, March 1891, 109, for the early history of Methodism in Oaxaca.
8. Clark and Clark, *Gospel in Latin Lands*, 190.
9. Treviño Osuna, *Historia de los trabajos Bautistas en México*, 32.
10. Rankin, *Twenty Years among the Mexicans*, 198–99.
11. Clark and Clark, *Gospel in Latin Lands*, 191.
12. Rankin, *Twenty Years among the Mexicans*, 213–14.
13. Rankin suggests that Protestant churches were labeled "Evangelical," as that term corresponded with the Mexican idea of gospel church. Rankin, 165.
14. Rankin, 157–58.
15. J. W. Butler, *History of the Methodist Episcopal Church in Mexico*, 130. See also William Green, "A Trip to the Land of the Mixtecos," *Gospel in All Lands*, March 1891, 109, for a description of the first Evangelical Society in Oaxaca, in 1871.
16. *La Victoria: Periódico Oficial del Gobierno del Estado de Oaxaca*, August 3, 1871.
17. Lucius C. Smith, "Our Mission in Oaxaca," *Gospel in All Lands*, May 1892, 252, and J. W. Butler, *History of the Methodist Episcopal Church in Mexico*, 131.
18. Lucius C. Smith, "The People of the State of Oaxaca, Mexico," *Gospel in All Lands*, April 1893, 147.
19. The Jesuits turned the Templo de la Compañía over to the archdiocese when the order was expelled from Spanish America in 1767. It then was used by the Order of the Immaculate Conception nuns until 1867 when the property was expropriated in compliance with Benito Juárez's 1856 Lerdo Law, which limited collective landholding. Local vendors, civic organizations, and Protestants used office, retail, and meeting spaces in the immense property at various times. See Secretario de Desarrollo Urbano y Ecología, *Oaxaca*, 119, 159–61.
20. "Importantes advertencias a los católicos," *La Hoja del Pueblo*, December 8, 1883.
21. "D. Matías Romero y los Protestantes," *La Voz de la Verdad*, April 4, 1897.
22. "La propaganda protestante en México," *La Hoja del Pueblo*, January 8, 1884.
23. "Una Manifestación," *La Hoja del Pueblo*, January 1, 1884.
24. "La Bandera del Evangelio," *La Hoja del Pueblo*, February 1, 1884.
25. "Importantes advertencias á los católicos," *La Hoja del Pueblo*, December 8, 1883.
26. "Una Manifestación," *La Hoja del Pueblo*, January 1, 1884.
27. *Annual Report of the Missionary Society, Sunday-School Union and Tract Society of the Methodist Episcopal Church*, 1890, 279.
28. See Chassen-López, *From Liberal to Revolutionary Oaxaca*, 308–10, for a more

detailed account of Liberal Governor José Esperón's (1872–1876) expropriation of Catholic Church and indigenous communal landholdings.
29. J. W. Butler, *History of the Methodist Episcopal Church in Mexico*, 132.
30. J. W. Butler, 130.
31. J. W. Butler, 141.
32. Bishop C. C. McCabe, "Letter from Mexico," *Northern Christian Advocate*, January 24, 1900.
33. J. W. Butler, *History of the Methodist Episcopal Church in Mexico*, 133.
34. See Bastian, *Protestantismo y sociedad en México*, for Protestant missionary work along railroad routes. See also Hurst, *History of Methodism*, 218. Author interview with Pastor Jaime García, March 15, 2010, Xoxocotlán, Oaxaca.
35. Lucius C. Smith, "A Tour in the State of Oaxaca, Mexico," *Gospel in All Lands*, August 1892, 391.
36. J. W. Butler, *History of the Methodist Episcopal Church in Mexico*, 131.
37. Lucius C. Smith, "Our Mission in Oaxaca," *Gospel in All Lands*, 1894, 252.
38. Lucius C. Smith, "Our Mission in Oaxaca," *Gospel in All Lands*, 1894, 252.
39. Lucius C. Smith, "A Tour in the State of Oaxaca, Mexico," *Gospel in All Lands*, 391–92.
40. "Sketches of Deceased Methodist Episcopal Missionaries," *Gospel in All Lands*, January 1901, 272.
41. "Mission of the Methodist Episcopal Church," *Gospel in All Lands*, March 1893.
42. Lucius Smith, "A Market Day in Oaxaca," *Gospel in All Lands*, March 1894, 109–10.
43. Hurst, *History of Methodism*, 199.
44. Lucius C. Smith, "A Tour in the State of Oaxaca, Mexico," *Gospel in All Lands*, August 1892, 391. US anthropologist Frederick Starr narrated his 1899 railroad journey from Tehuacán, Puebla, to Cuicatlán in *In Indian Mexico*. See especially pages 259–71 for Starr's stereotypical "indigenous physical type" genre photographs but also his rich descriptions of Mazatecan, Cuicatec, and Chinantec villages.
45. Chassen-López, *From Liberal to Revolutionary Oaxaca*, 456–57.
46. Lucius C. Smith, "A Tour in the State of Oaxaca, Mexico," *Gospel in All Lands*, August 1892, 392.
47. See Rubén Ruiz Guerra's chapter on Methodist schools in *New People*, 144–87.
48. "The Benefits of Educating Women," *El Abogado Cristiano Ilustrado*, November 10, 1887.
49. Rev. J. M. Euroza, "Oaxaca District of the Mexico Methodist Conference," *Gospel in All Lands*, January 1901, 490.
50. Lucius C. Smith, "A Tour in the State of Oaxaca, Mexico," *Gospel in All Lands*, August 1892, 392.
51. Lucius C. Smith, "The People of the State of Oaxaca, Mexico," *Gospel in All Lands*, April 1893, 148.

52. Jennings and Sellen, *Real Fake*, 94–96.
53. Starr, *In Indian Mexico*, 4.
54. Smith had a doctorate in theology from Boston University. His first missionary trip was to Santiago, Chile, under William Taylor's missionary project in 1878. Following the death of his first wife, he married an English woman who was born in Chile of Methodist missionary parents. Together, they set off for Mexico in 1884. See "Sketches of Deceased Methodist Episcopal Missionaries," *Gospel in All Lands*, January 1901, 272–73.
55. Conzatti, "En Memorium," in Conzatti and Smith, *Flora Sinóptica Mexicana*, 207.
56. Rev. Dr. Hayes, "Rev. Lucins [sic] C. Smith," *Northern Christian Advocate*, February 12, 1896; "En Memoriam," *El Abogado Cristiano Ilustrado*, April 1, 1896.
57. Bishop C. C. McCabe, "Letter from Mexico," *Northern Christian Advocate*, January 24, 1900.
58. The coverage of his passing in Oaxaca's official government paper makes no mention of a previous injury. See "Sensible Pérdida," *Périodico Ofícial del Gobierno del Estado de Oaxaca*, March 17, 1896. See also "Sketches of Deceased Methodist Episcopal Missionaries," *Gospel in All Lands*, January 1901, 272.
59. Bishop C. C. McCabe, "Letter from Mexico," *Northern Christian Advocate*, January 24, 1900.
60. J. W. Butler, *History of the Methodist Episcopal Church in Mexico*, 135.
61. J. W. Butler, 135.
62. Protestant missionaries often criticized cockfighting, bullfighting, and boxing as vicious vices in which spectators wasted money on gambling and drinking. Instead, missionaries promoted team sports.
63. "Oaxaca District," *Annual Report of the Missionary Society*, Sunday-School Union and Tract Society of the Methodist Episcopal Church, for the Year 1909, 1909, 450–51.
64. Chassen-López, "Benito Juárez de Maza of Oaxaca," 23.
65. M. Overmyer-Velázquez, *Visions of the Emerald City*, 96.
66. Báez, *Compendio de Historia de Oaxaca*.
67. *Oaxaca Herald*, July 11, 1909, and J. W. Butler, *History of the Methodist Episcopal Church in Mexico*, 138.
68. *Oaxaca Herald*, April 11, 1909.
69. J. W. Butler, *History of the Methodist Episcopal Church in Mexico*, 129. See also the *Mexican Mining Journal*, January 1909, 9–11, for information about Mexican mining prospects in prerevolutionary Oaxaca.
70. "Labor Cheap and Plentiful," *Oaxaca Herald*, March 10, 1907.
71. "The Gold-Filled Hills of Mexico," *Index*, December 14, 1907.
72. "The Way They Look at It Up North," *Oaxaca Herald*, July 21, 1907.
73. "Church Building Fund," *Oaxaca Herald*, April 28, 1907.
74. "An American School," *Oaxaca Herald*, June 28, 1908.

75. "Working against Odds," *Spirit of Missions*, vol. 74, 1909, 409.
76. "Working against Odds," *Spirit of Missions*, vol. 74, 1909, 409.
77. "Working against Odds," *Spirit of Missions*, vol. 74, 1909, 409.
78. "Church Supper, Dance, and Garden Party Thursday," *Oaxaca Herald*, November 17, 1907. Hamer also made the news in the United States for the 160 tons of silver shipped from his Oaxaca mine to the United States. "Train Load of Bullion," *Prescott Evening Courier*, March 4, 1907.
79. "Church Supper, Dance, and Garden Party Thursday," *Oaxaca Herald*, November 17, 1907.
80. See also Yohn, *Contest of Faiths*, for background on roles of missionary women. See Arrom, *Volunteering for a Cause*, for an examination of the role of Catholic women volunteers in helping the poor.
81. "Church Building Fund," *Oaxaca Herald*, April 28, 1907.
82. Arrom, *Volunteering for a Cause*, 93.
83. See "Services Today," *Oaxaca Herald*, May 19, 1907, and "Jackpots Go to Church," *Oaxaca Herald*, May 3, 1908.
84. "Organ Here for Church," *Oaxaca Herald*, September 8, 1907.
85. See B. T. Smith, "Anticlericalism, Politics, and Freemasonry in Mexico, 1920–1940," for more on the relationship between Protestantism and Masonry.
86. "New Rooms for the Church," *Oaxaca Herald*, February 16, 1908.
87. "Celebrate Holy Week with All Solemnity," *Oaxaca Herald*, March 24, 1907.
88. *Oaxaca Herald*, April 4, 1909.
89. In Oaxaca he is associated with animals since he grew up on a farm and believed in treating work animals with compassion. While Saint Francis of Assisi is more clearly associated with animals, perhaps it is a regional tradition to honor San Ramón de Nonato as a caretaker of draft animals.
90. See Larumbe, "Así era Oaxaca," for a description of San Ramón de Nonato celebrations at La Merced Church.
91. Parmenter, *Lawrence in Oaxaca*, 40.
92. For more on traditions associated with La Virgen de la Soledad, see Graziano, *Miraculous Images and Votive Offerings*, 30, 143.
93. *Oaxaca Herald*, December 15, 1908.
94. See Wright-Rios, *Revolutions in Mexican Catholicism*, 43–47 and 73–82, for a discussion of Archbishop Gillow's role in revamping Oaxacan Catholicism and further description of the week-long festivities.
95. "Prominent Catholics Coming," *Oaxaca Herald*, January 10, 1909; Russ Harruff, "The Story of Oaxaca's Patron Saint," *Oaxaca Herald*, January 17, 1909.
96. On styles of Catholic worship of different images of La Virgen, see Graziano, *Miraculous Images and Votive Offerings in Mexico*.
97. *Oaxaca Herald*, January 31, 1909.
98. *Oaxaca Herald*, February 14, 1909.
99. "Our Religious (?) Press," *Oaxaca Herald*, December 5, 1909.

100. See Baldwin, *Protestants and the Mexican Revolution*.
101. Chassen-López, *From Liberal to Revolutionary Oaxaca*, 456–57, 504.
102. J. W. Butler, *History of the Methodist Episcopal Church in Mexico*, 138.
103. J. W. Butler, 138.
104. "Fue Amparado el Presbítero Rickards," *Heraldo de México*, July 2, 1926. See also Parmenter, *Lawrence in Oaxaca*, 37–38.

Chapter Two

1. Wheeler, *Modern Missions in Mexico*, 29.
2. Wheeler, *Modern Missions in Mexico*, 22–23.
3. Founded in 1903, the National Baptist Convention of Mexico was financially supported by northern Baptist boards of the United States. See Rudd, *Practical Mystic*, for a detailed analysis of board agendas in Mexico.
4. For the seminal Protestant publication in the genre of historic Christian martyrdom, see John Foxe's 1563 work, *Foxe's Book of Martyrs*. For a comparative look at late nineteenth-century Protestant competition with Catholicism in Korea, see Oak, *Making of Korean Christianity*, 20–25.
5. Samuel Juárez García, "Entre los zapotecos," *El Atalaya Bautista*, August 2, 1923.
6. See Abrams, *Oral History Theory*, 78–105, for her discussion on the oral historian's use of memory as a source.
7. Prominent Protestant leaders included Congregationalist revolutionary leader Pascual Orozco Jr., Baptist senator Jonás García, and Ministry of Education director Presbyterian Moisés Sáenz. See Baldwin, *Protestants and the Mexican Revolution*, 132–42, for a more detailed description of Protestant Mexicans in Revolutionary and postrevolutionary positions of importance.
8. See Garduño, *Misiones Culturales*, for the political and educational ideologies behind the "crusades against ignorance." See Jackson Albarran, *Seen and Heard in Mexico*, 234–41, for a discussion of the Ministry of Education's Children's Literacy Army and its role in "revolutionary civilizing missions." See also Beezley, "Creating a Revolutionary Culture," for an analysis of the Cultural Missions program.
9. See Adrian Bantjes's discussion of revolutionary ideology that equated defanaticization campaigns with the "spiritual liberation" Mexico's indigenous peoples needed to achieve economic progress in "Idolatry and Iconoclasm in Revolutionary Mexico," 93.
10. See J. C. Anderson, *Evangelical Saga*, 114–17, for an analysis of the early debates within the CNBM over foreign vs. national missionaries.
11. Rudd, *Practical Mystic*, 96.
12. Rudd, 96.

13. Treviño Osuna, *Historia de los trabajos bautistas en México*, 367.
14. Josué G. Bautista, "Historia de las misiones Bautistas entre los Indios de México," *El Atalaya Bautista*, December 1, 1921.
15. Juárez García first worked with General Missionary Representative Rudd under the auspices of the American Baptist Home Mission Society before signing with the Convención Nacional Bautista de México in October of 1920. Treviño Osuna, *Historia de los trabajos Bautistas en México*, 368–69.
16. See Howard Benjamin Grose, ed., *Baptist Home Mission Monthly*, January 1909, and de la Mora Rivas, *100 Biografías de Pastores Bautistas Mexicanos*, 53–54, for brief biographical sketches of Váldez and Juárez García, respectively.
17. Mercedes S. de Bautista, "Una Carta Interesante," *El Atalaya Bautista*, November 4, 1920.
18. Juárez García, "Entre los Zapotecos," *El Atalaya Bautista*, January 1, 1922; de la Mora Rivas, *100 Biografías de Pastores Bautistas Mexicanos*, 53–54.
19. Juárez García, "Entre los Zapotecos," *El Atalaya Bautista*, January 1, 1922.
20. See Poole, "An Image of 'Our Indian,'" for a discussion of postrevolutionary intellectual and political manipulation of Oaxaca's ethnic diversity to promote the state's interests.
21. B. T. Smith, *Pistoleros and Popular Movements*, 49–50.
22. Juárez García, "Informe Anual de la Junta Misionera: La obra entre los Indios," *El Atalaya Bautista*, July 15, 1921.
23. Juárez García, "Entre los Zapotecos," *El Atalaya Bautista*, August 2, 1923.
24. Juárez García, "Entre los Zapotecos," *El Atalaya Bautista*, August 2, 1923.
25. Juárez García, "Entre los Zapotecos," *El Atalaya Bautista*, April 21, 1921.
26. Juárez García, "Entre los Zapotecos," *El Atalaya Bautista*, April 21, 1921.
27. Juárez García, "Entre los Zapotecos," *El Atalaya Bautista*, April 21, 1921.
28. Juárez García, "Entre los Zapotecos," *El Atalaya Bautista*, March 15, 1921.
29. Juárez García, "Entre los Zapotecos," *El Atalaya Bautista*, March 15, 1921.
30. Juárez García, "Entre los Zapotecos," *El Atalaya Bautista*, March 15, 1921.
31. Barabas, *Dones, dueños y santos*, 71.
32. Writing at the same time Juárez García began his work in Oaxaca, renowned novelist and journalist Martín Luis Guzmán stated: "Since then—since the Conquest or since pre-Hispanic times, it's the same thing—the Indian is there, submissive and prostrate, indifferent to good and evil, without a conscience, with his soul converted into a rudimentary button, incapable of even hope" ("La Inconsciencia Moral del Indígena," *El Universal*, March 3, 1921).
33. Rudd, *Practical Mystic*, 112.
34. See Pool, *Guadalupan Controversies in Mexico*, for a survey of the major arguments disputing her miraculous apparition in 1531.
35. Juárez García, "Entre Los Zapotecas," *El Atalaya Bautista*, April 21, 1921.
36. Juárez García, "Informe," *El Atalaya Bautista*, January 23, 1923.
37. Juárez García, "Informe," *El Atalaya Bautista*, January 23, 1923.

38. According to Rudd's journal, the Protestant *velada* (evening performance) to celebrate the centennial was a great success and helped unify the four thousand Protestants in attendance as Mexicans. Margaret Rudd notes that this was the largest public gathering of Protestants in Mexico ever. Rudd, *Practical Mystic*, 120.
39. Juárez García, "Informe Anual de la Junta Misionera: La obra entre los Indios," *El Atalaya Bautista*, July 15, 1921.
40. Rudd, *Practical Mystic*, 121.
41. Alejandro Treviño Osuna, "Convención Nacional Bautista de México: Por Nuestros Campos," *El Atalaya Bautista*, May 5, 1921.
42. Juárez García, "Informe Anual de la Junta Misionera: La obra entre los Indios," *El Atalaya Bautista*, July 15, 1921. Miguel Alfaro's mission with the Tarasca ran simultaneously with Juárez García's mission.
43. Juárez García, "Informe Anual de la Junta Misionera: La obra entre los Indios," *El Atalaya Bautista*, July 15, 1921, and "Entre los Zapotecas," *El Atalaya Bautista*, April 21, 1921.
44. Juárez García, "Capilla Bautista de Tlacochahuaya, Oaxaca," *El Atalaya Bautista*, July 29, 1926.
45. Reverend J. W. Bain, "Woman's Power in Saving the West," *Baptist Home Mission Monthly*, April 1887, 126. Beaver, *American Protestant Women in World Mission*, 13–57. See also Yohn, *Contest of Faiths*, for a comparison of Presbyterian female missionaries working in Hispano-Catholic communities of northern New Mexico; Olcott, *Revolutionary Women in Post-Revolutionary Mexico*, 13.
46. "Nuestra Capilla en Tlacochahuaya," *El Atalaya Bautista*, August 12, 1926.
47. Esther G. de Montes, "Un Llamado a la Mujer Cristiana Mexicana," *El Atalaya Bautista*, January 17, 1922.
48. Unión Femenil y Del Hogar, *El Atalaya Bautista*, January 1922.
49. Esther G. de Montes, "Un Llamado a la Mujer Cristiana Mexicana," *El Atalaya Bautista*, January 17, 1922.
50. Esther G. de Montes, "Un Llamado a la Mujer Cristiana Mexicana," *El Atalaya Bautista*, January 17, 1922.
51. "A Raíz de la Convención Nacional," *El Atalaya Bautista*, November 11, 1922.
52. Amada T. de García, "Capilla de Tlacochahuaya," *El Atalaya Bautista*, November 26, 1925.
53. For background on the historical significance of the cargo system, see Chance and Taylor, "Cofradías and Cargos."
54. Juárez García, "Capilla Bautista de Tlacochahuaya, Oaxaca," *El Atalaya Bautista*, July 29, 1926.
55. Juárez García, "Capilla Bautista de Tlacochahuaya, Oaxaca," *El Atalaya Bautista*, July 29, 1926.
56. E. Borocio, "Nuestra Capilla de Tlacochahuaya," *El Atalaya Bautista*, August 12, 1926.

57. "Costumbres Típicas de los Zapotecas," Unión Femenil y Del Hogar, *El Atalaya Bautista*, June 17, 1926.
58. "Costumbres Típicas de los Zapotecas," Unión Femenil y Del Hogar, *El Atalaya Bautista*, June 17, 1926.
59. See Gallaher, "Role of Protestant Missionaries in Mexico's Indigenous Awakening," for a discussion of conversion to Protestantism stemming from free access to missionary clinics. For Seventh-day Adventist health clinics in Mexico, see C. E. Conwell, "The Need of Medical Missions in Mexico," *Medical Missionary*, November 1913.
60. Ironically, some of the very practices the Baptist women condemned, such as saving umbilical cords, are currently expensive and highly recommended medical practices in the Western world.
61. "Costumbres Típicas de los Zapotecas," Unión Femenil y Del Hogar, *El Atalaya Bautista*, June 17, 1926. For further background on Zapotec traditional healing practices, see Stephen, *Zapotec Women*, and Barabas, *Dones, dueños y santos*.
62. "Costumbres Típicas de los Zapotecas," Unión Femenil y Del Hogar, *El Atalaya Bautista*, June 17, 1926.
63. "Costumbres Típicas de los Zapotecas," Unión Femenil y Del Hogar, *El Atalaya Bautista*, June 17, 1926.
64. "Costumbres Típicas de los Zapotecas," Unión Femenil y Del Hogar, *El Atalaya Bautista*, June 17, 1926. "¡Quiera el Señor bendecir su obra entre los indios, para que, iluminados por el Evangelio de paz, pueda levantarse esa raza, digna de mejor suerte, libre del fanatismo y la ignorancia que la hunden en la miseria!"
65. See Lewis, *Hall of Mirrors*, 172–73, for her conceptualization of sanctioned/unsanctioned spaces in colonial Mexico and the roles of Spaniards, mestizos, and indigenous peoples in creating, negotiating, and disputing these domains.
66. Moisés Arévalo, "La misión entre los Zapotecos," *El Atalaya Bautista*, October 2, 1926.
67. José Vasconcelos, a Oaxacan and the first secretary of public education from 1921 to 1924, promised his support for a railroad connection between Oaxaca City and Tehuantepec in his presidential campaign of 1929. However, the connecting line never materialized. See Bastian, *Protestantismo y sociedad en México*, for greater detail on the correlation between Protestant missionary work along railroad routes and mining company stations. Finally, see also Wheeler, *Modern Missions in Mexico*, 16–17, for a brief discussion of Oaxaca City's foreign (and mostly Protestant) mineworker population prior to the 1910 Revolution.
68. For background on the 1914 Cincinnati plan, including original missionary territorial maps from the historic conference, see Wheeler, *Modern Missions in Mexico*, 118–34.
69. Reverend L. P. Van Slyke, quoted in Wheeler, *Modern Missions in Mexico*, 276–77.

70. Van Slyke, quoted in Wheeler, 276–77.
71. Juárez García, "Informe que rinde el Comisionado para hacer la visita a los hermanos de Tapachula, Chiapas, México, que así lo solicitaron," *El Atalaya Bautista*, April 7, 1927.
72. This Baptist-Presbyterian rivalry could have had nineteenth-century roots. Melinda Rankin, a Presbyterian and the first US missionary to establish a mission in northern Mexico, competed with British American Baptist missionary Thomas Westrup over converts in the 1860s. See Rankin, *Twenty Years among the Mexicans*, and Patterson, *Century of Baptist Work in Mexico*.
73. Juárez García, "No es de Extrañarse," *El Atalaya Bautista*, May 7, 1927.
74. Juárez García, "No es de Extrañarse," *El Atalaya Bautista*, May 7, 1927.
75. See Ricard, *Spiritual Conquest of Mexico*, for a discussion of missionary zones and competition between religious orders in colonial Mexico.
76. Bantjes, "Idolatry and Iconoclasm in Revolutionary Mexico," 88.
77. Plutarco Elías Calles, as quoted in Knight, "Revolutionary Anticlericalism," 30.
78. Therefore, confronting the impossibility of practicing our sacred ministry under the conditions imposed by this decree, and, after having consulted the Most Holy Father, His Holiness the Pope, and with his ratification, we order that after July 31, until we order otherwise, all religious services requiring the intervention of priests shall be suspended in all the churches of the country.... We advise you, beloved sons, that this is not meant to impose on you the grave penalty of interdiction, but we merely intend to use the only weapon at present at our disposal to protest against the anti-religious clauses of the Constitution and the laws hereby sanctioned. ("Text of Pastoral Letter from Mexican Episcopate," *New York Times*, July 26, 1926)
79. For the foundational work on the cristiada, see historian Jean Meyer's *The Cristero Rebellion*. See also Meyer, *El conflicto religioso en Oaxaca*, for a regional example of cristero and postcristero violence in Oaxaca.
80. Knights of Columbus, "Martyrs of Christ the King Reliquary Present at Papal Mass in Mexico," *Columbia*, May 2012, 7.
81. Meyer, *El conflicto religioso en Oaxaca*, 3.
82. See Hartch, *Missionaries of the State*, for an in-depth analysis of the relationship of the Mexican government with Protestant missionary organizations such as the Summer Institute of Linguistics.
83. Meyer, *El conflicto religioso en Oaxaca*, 54–55.
84. "La entrega de los templos a los juntas vecinales se lleva a cabo," *El Informador*, September 28, 1934.
85. "Los Campesinos Vigilarán que se cumpla la ley de cultos," *El Oaxaqueño*, October, 31, 1934.
86. "La Iglesia y la cuestión social," *El Oaxaqueño*, January 30, 1935.
87. "Visita Pastoral," *Boletín Oficial y Revista Eclesiástica de Antequera*, September 1923.

88. "Visita Pastoral," *Boletín Oficial y Revista Eclesiástica de Antequera*, September 1923.
89. See Meyer, "Religious Conflict and Catholic Resistance in 1930s Oaxaca," for background information on religious conflict in Cardenista Oaxaca.
90. Eliseo Manzano, *Samuel J. García, Mártir de Tlacochahuaya*, 1958, pamphlet, Seminario Teológico Bautista G. H. Lacy, Oaxaca City.
91. Elvira Cruz García, interview with the author, Tlacochahuaya, Oaxaca, October 2, 2009.
92. "Pugna política en Tlacochahuaya: Se atribuye la intranquilidad al Sr. S. J. García," *El Informador*, January 1, 1935.
93. "Misiones Culturales enviadas a Oaxaca por mandato expreso del Presidente Cárdenas para desarrollar labor efectiva en las comunidades indígenas," *El Oaxaqueño*, September 14, 1937.
94. See Bastian, *Los disidentes*, for a discussion of the relationship between Masonry and Protestantism.
95. "Asesinato Cometido en Tlacochahuaya: Un grupo de hombres Asaltó a Damián Ángeles," *El Informador*, October 4, 1934.
96. Collections: Dirección Jurídica y de Gobierno, Pleitos Religiosos, Tlacochahuaya, 1934 (AGEPEO).
97. "Pugna política en Tlacochahuaya: Se atribuye la intranquilidad al Sr. S. J. García," *El Informador*, January 1, 1935.
98. Eliseo Manzano, *Samuel J. García, Mártir de Tlacochahuaya*, 1958, pamphlet, Seminario Teológico Bautista G. H. Lacy, Oaxaca City.
99. Salomón Hernández Juárez, interview with author, Tlacochahuaya, Oaxaca, March 14, 2010.
100. Elvira Cruz García, interview with author, Tlacochahuaya, Oaxaca, October 2, 2009. "Y esto lo que pasó allí yo lo sé por mi Mama, porque mi Mama fue el molino en esta hora, si, molino de Ixtelmala."
101. Cruz García interview.
102. Cruz García interview.
103. Olcott, quoting the Mexican Agrarian Department pamphlet "¡Despertar Lagunero!," in *Revolutionary Women in Postrevolutionary Mexico*, 148. Olcott also quotes an Agrarian Department official who described how rural women cheered: "Here are the mills! Away with the metates!" Olcott, 148. See also Olcott, "Politics of Opportunity," for a discussion of Cárdenas's attempt to integrate rural women into the postrevolutionary state. Finally, Dawn Keremitsis, "Del metate al molino," traces how the Catholic Church and men initially criticized the new molino technology as inappropriate for women's work. However, Keremitsis also questions whether the arrival of Cárdenas's rural development program actually helped liberate women from their familial obligations by freeing them to work outside of the home (287, 302).
104. "Como Fue El Sangriento Motín Que Ocurrió En Un Pueblo De Oaxaca," *El*

Continental, October, 13 1935. See also *Periódico Oficial del Gobierno del Estado de Oaxaca*, October 1935.

105. CNBM ran the G. H. Lacy Baptist Seminary in Tlacolula, Oaxaca, from 1938 to 1943, before it moved to Puebla and then finally returned to Xoxocotlán, just outside the city of Oaxaca in 1960. However, the CNBM did not re-establish missionary work in Tlacochahuaya until 2005. See also "Recuperación de la obra," *La Luz Bautista*, April 19, 2007.
106. See also Bonner, *We Will Not Be Stopped*, for an overview of evangelical indigenous martyrdom in Chiapas written for a North American missionary audience.
107. For an analysis of corn as a symbol of indigenous identity in southern Mexico, see Barabas, *Dones, dueños y santos*, 64–65.
108. Angela López Martínez, as quoted in Stephen, ¡*Zapata Lives!*, 304.
109. Vaughan, *Cultural Politics in Revolution*, 42.
110. On the relationship between respectable masculinity and Protestant conversion, see Kent, *Converting Women*, and Brusco, *Reformation of Machismo*. For a discussion of the postrevolutionary masculine ideals for Mexican men, see Olcott, *Revolutionary Women in Postrevolutionary Mexico*, 18–19. Olcott notes that postrevolutionary governments advocated team sports like baseball and basketball over boxing or cockfighting as respectable forms of masculine recreation (19).
111. Carlos Martínez, interview with author, Tlacochahuaya, Oaxaca, September 30, 2009.
112. For a discussion of Protestant conversion and individualism, see Greenberg, "Sanctity and Resistance in Closed Corporate Indigenous Communities."
113. Joseph Lee discusses a similar conflict with missionaries' disruption of customary law and rituals with respect to ancestor shrines and communal water work in South China during the 1890s. Discussing Presbyterians' reluctance to financially support traditional celebrations in a former ancestral temple in the Hainan Province, Lee concludes: "Whenever Christian identity took precedence over communal identity, confrontation with the non-Christians was only a matter of time." Lee, *Bible and the Gun*, 124, 153.
114. David Naglieri, "Freedom Is Our Lives," *Columbia*, May 2012, 10.
115. Yannakakis, *Art of Being In-Between*, 1–2, 127.
116. Abrams, *Oral History Theory*, 100–101.
117. Abrams, 101.
118. Cruz García, interview with the author, Tlacochahuaya, Oaxaca, October 2, 2009.

Chapter Three

1. Arturo Rivera, Cuicatlán, Oaxaca, telegram to Governor Alfonso Pérez Gasca, May 13, 1958, box 136, file 160, collection: Pleitos Religiosos (AGEPEO).
2. See Chassen-López, *From Liberal to Revolutionary Oaxaca*, 73–76, for a

background to the introduction of telegraph lines, railroad stations, street lighting, and telephone connections in Porfiriato Oaxaca. While by the time of the 1910 Revolution parts of Oaxaca were considerably modernized, it is important to remember that some indigenous villages did not receive, for example, electricity until the 1950s and 1960s or sometimes even later.

3. See Young, "Cincinnati Plan and the National Presbyterian Church of Mexico," for the national implications of the plan and the lack of agency given to Mexican Presbyterian or Methodist ministers in the 1914 meetings.
4. De la Luz García, *El Movimiento Pentecostal*, 211–12.
5. The Instituto Nacional Indigenista (INI) was also founded in 1948. In Chapter Four, I analyze INI's collaboration with Protestant organizations such as the Summer Institute of Linguistics (SIL) in modernizing indigenous communities.
6. In 1950, Protestants composed 1.33 percent of the Mexican population. In 1960, Protestants made up 1.66 percent of the Mexican population. INEGI, *Censo de Población y Vivienda*, 1950, 1960.
7. Methodist writer and famed journalist Gonzalo Báez-Camargo intensely covered the Tepeji conflict as the Mexican correspondent for the US biweekly *Christian Century*. See Báez-Camargo, "Punish Mob for Attack on Chapel," *Christian Century*, September 2, 1953, for Báez-Camargo's on-the-ground account. For more analysis of Ruiz Cortines's intervention in Hidalgo, see L. Scott, *Salt of the Earth*, 46, and Hartch, *Missionaries of the State*, 77–79.
8. Lindy Scott argues that Catholic-State relations improved tremendously under the Ávila Camacho administration because of his un-Cardenista statement of "Soy un creyente" or "I am a believer." In other words, Catholicism came back in fashion after the 1920–1940 postrevolutionary anticlericalism period. Additionally, even though subsequent President Miguel Alemán's mother was a Presbyterian, Scott maintains that the Catholic Church experienced a further rebirth during Alemán's term. Despite Mexico's burgeoning Protestant population, Alemán did next to nothing in cases of religious intolerance. L. Scott, *Salt of the Earth*, 44–45. Of course, Ruiz Cortines's intervention against the Catholic factory workers can also be viewed as an example of the president's militant stance on union strikes in Mexico. See Middlebrook, *Paradox of Revolution*, for an analysis of labor union repression in the late 1950s under Ruiz Cortines and especially during López Mateos's administration.
9. Hartch, *Missionaries of the State*, 77.
10. See Hartch, *Missionaries of the State*, 77–79, for more background on Ruiz Cortines's administration and religious tolerance.
11. L. Scott, *Salt of the Earth*, 46.
12. "Asuntos relativos del Comité Nacional Evangélico de Defensa," 1957–1960, box 136, file 160, collection: Pleitos Religiosos (AGEPEO).
13. Agapito Ramos Ramírez to Cándido Ramírez, "Asuntos relativos del Comité

Nacional Evangélico de Defensa," Santa María del Mar, Juchitán, March 27, 1957, box 140, file 1192 (AGEPEO).

14. Ramos Ramírez to Ramírez, "Asuntos relativos del Comité Nacional Evangélico de Defensa" (AGEPEO).
15. Ramos Ramírez to Cándido Ramírez, "Asuntos relativos del Comité Nacional Evangélico de Defensa" (AGEPEO).
16. Guillermo Martínez León to Agapito Ramos Ramírez, June 20, 1957, box 140, file 1192 (AGEPEO).
17. De la Luz García, *El Movimiento Pentecostal*, 211–22.
18. Guzmán vociferously spoke out against Catholic Parents Associations who annually protested government textbooks produced for primary schools. Catholic groups opposed the treatment of the Church in lessons on the Mexican Revolution. See Paul P. Kennedy, "Mexico Winning Textbook Fight," *New York Times*, March 12, 1963.
19. Manuel Donato Valencia Arriaga to Waldo Altamirano, July 25, 1946, and Altamirano to Governor Edmundo Sánchez Cano, August 21, 1946, box 343/(17)/23 (AGEPEO).
20. Ricardo Armas Pacheco, Minister of Justice, Cuicatlán, to Governor Alfonso Pérez Gasca, May 15, 1958, 4/149 (3) "58"/1083, collection: Relativo a la Construcción de un templo protestante en Cuicatlán (AGEPEO).
21. Arturo Rivera et al., to Governor Pérez Gasca, May 3, 1958, 1/149 (3) "58"/1083 (AGEPEO).
22. Rivera et al., to Governor Pérez Gasca, May 21, 1958, box 136, file 160 (AGEPEO).
23. Agapito Ramos Ramírez to Governor Pérez Gasca, August 27, 1958, box 136, file 160 (AGEPEO).
24. Enrique Sánchez to Oaxacan Secretary of State, September 15, 1958, box 136, file 160 (AGEPEO).
25. Public Justice Minister Pacheco Armas to Attorney General Jesús Rojas Villavicencio, May 2, 1961, box 136, file 160 (AGEPEO).
26. Public Justice Minister Pacheco Armas to Attorney General Jesús Rojas Villavicencio, June 23, 1961, box 136, file 160 (AGEPEO).
27. Methodists had actually worked in Cuicatlán since the 1890s but, because of the implementation of the Plan de Cincinnati in 1914, the Presbyterians received missions in southern Mexico and the Methodists took the north. See Vázquez, *Los que sembraron con lágrimas*, 238–39, for a summary of which Presbyterian missionaries arrived in Oaxaca beginning in 1920.
28. Presbyterian Church Ministers Epifanio Contreras, Saúl Velasco, Luís Rosa Torres, and Samuel Vásquez to Governor Rodolfo Brena Torres, August 21, 1964, box 136, file 160, 1958–1964 (AGEPEO).
29. Presbyterian leader José Ponce Hernández to Governor Brena Torres, April 22, 1961, box 136, file 160, 1958–1964 (AGEPEO).

30. José Espina Sánchez et al., "Carta de Testimonio," April 24, 1961, Cuicatlán, Oaxaca (AGEPEO).
31. José Ponce Hernández et al., Presbyterian collective letter to Governor Pérez Gasca, April 22, 1961 (AGEPEO).
32. For studies on the link between North American imperialism and Protestantism, see Pérez and Robinson, *La misión detras de la misión*, and Colby and Dennett, *Thy Will Be Done*.
33. Arturo Rivera et al., to Cuicatlán Municipal Mayor, June 8, 1964, 4/143.1 (3) "63"/1920 (AGEPEO).
34. Rivera et al., to Cuicatlán Municipal Mayor (AGEPEO).
35. Rivera et al., to Cuicatlán Municipal Mayor (AGEPEO).
36. Rivera et al., to Cuicatlán Municipal Mayor (AGEPEO).
37. For early postrevolutionary Protestant critiques of Catholicism, see Bantjes, "Idolatry and Iconoclasm in Revolutionary Mexico," and Browning, *Roman Christianity in Latin America*.
38. Oaxaca City Secretary General Cutberto Chagoya to Tristan Canales Valverde in the Ministry of the Interior's office in Mexico City, August 24, 1964, 4/143.1 (3) "63"/1920 (AGEPEO).
39. Rubén Pérez Peña to Adrian Zavala Ramírez, Gregorio Oropeza Carrera, and Alberto Mendoza Roque, March 19, 1965, Cuicatlán, 2/343 (17) 76 (AGEPEO). Political Constitution of the United Mexican States, 1917, Article 24, as translated into English: "Every man is free to pursue the religious belief that best suits him, and to practice its ceremonies, devotions or cults, as long as they do not constitute a crime. Congress cannot dictate laws that establish or abolish any given religion. Ordinarily, all religious acts will be practiced in temples, and those that extraordinarily are practiced outside temples must adhere to law."
40. Oaxacan subsecretary of state Guillermo Martínez León finally sent the official permit with Cuicatlán mayor José Villacanas Linares's approval signature to Cuicatlán Presbyterian leaders Joel Ponce Hernández and Emiliano M. Brena González on July 1, 1968.
41. Felipe Sánchez Muñiz, Elder Director of Iglesia Cristiana Interdenominacional, to Governor Brena Torres, May 18, 1960, 4/143.0 (16) "60"/1634 (AGEPEO).
42. Felipe Sánchez Muñiz to Gov. Pérez Gasca, May 18, 1960, box 136, file 160 (AGEPEO).
43. Universal Declaration of Human Rights, Article 18. "Everyone has the right to freedom of thought, conscience and religion; this right includes freedom to change his religion or belief, and freedom, either alone or in community with others and in public or private, to manifest his religion or belief in teaching, practice, worship and observance." Timoteo Ortega López, telegram to Oaxacan Governor, May 31, 1960, box 136, file 160 (AGEPEO).
44. Iglesia de Tlaltenco, Texmeluacan Puebla, telegram to Oaxacan governor, June 3,

1960, box 136, file 160, collection: Asuntos relativos del Comité Nacional Evangelico de Defensa (AGEPEO).
45. Guillermo Martínez León to Oaxacan State Attorney General, June 2, 1960, 4/143.0 (16) "60"/1639, box 136, file 160 (AGEPEO).
46. Martínez León to Attorney General (AGEPEO).
47. Martínez León to Attorney General (AGEPEO). Martínez León pasted the full content of Article 24 into the text of his letter to the municipal mayor of Coyula: "Everyone is free to profess the religious beliefs of his choice and free to practice the ceremonies, devotions or religious acts of worship, in the churches or in the private home, as long as it doesn't constitute a crime or disrespect of the law. All acts of public religious worship should be celebrated precisely within the churches which will always be under the vigilance of the authorities."
48. Pastor Jaime García, interview with author, Xoxocotlán, Oaxaca, March 15, 2010. García mentioned the arrival of telegraph lines in rural Oaxaca as essential in uniting Protestants. For the foundational literature on social movement theory, consult McAdam, McCarthy, and Zald, *Comparative Perspectives on Social Movements*.
49. Feliciano Hernández Jiménez to Guillermo Martínez León, Oaxacan Subsecretary of State, March 11, 1963, 4/143.1 (3) "63"/300, box 136, file 160 (AGEPEO).
50. Feliciano Hernández Jiménez to Guillermo Martínez León, Oaxacan Subsecretary of State, February 10, 1963, 4/143.1 (3) "63"/292, box 136, file 160 (AGEPEO).
51. Feliciano Hernández Jiménez to Guillermo Martínez León, Oaxacan Subsecretary of State, March 11, 1965, 4/143.1 (3) "63"/239, box 136, file 160 (AGEPEO).
52. Hernández Jiménez to Martínez León, March 11, 1965 (AGEPEO).
53. Hernández Jiménez to Martínez León, February 10, 1963 (AGEPEO).
54. Hernández Jiménez to Martínez León, March 11, 1965 (AGEPEO).
55. Hernández Jiménez to Martínez León, March 11, 1965 (AGEPEO).
56. See Bowen, *Evangelism and Apostasy*; Rivera Farfán, *Diversidad religiosa y conflicto en Chiapas*; and Bonner, *We Will Not Be Stopped*.
57. Antonio Serrano, Andrés Serrano, and Francisco Rodríguez to Oaxacan Attorney General, March 31, 1964, 4/143.1 (3) "63" 292, file: Asuntos Religosos (AGEPEO).
58. Serrano, Serrano, and Rodríguez to Attorney General, March 31, 1964 (AGEPEO).
59. Serrano, Serrano, and Rodríguez to Attorney General, March 31, 1964 (AGEPEO).
60. Hernández Jiménez to Martínez León, March 11, 1965 (AGEPEO).
61. Bartolo Hernández López, interview with author, Yolotepec de la Paz, Yosondúa, Oaxaca, September 10, 2008.
62. On braceros, see Fox, "Indigenous Mexican Migrants," 163. See Stephen,

Transborder Lives, 96–97 and 108–12, for her oral histories with ex-braceros in Teotitlán del Valle and San Agustín Atenango, Oaxaca. In Teotitlán del Valle, 25 percent of adult males did participate in the bracero program, higher than average for Oaxacan indigenous villages. Stephen also discusses internal Oaxacan and Mexican migration patterns for Zapotecs of the Central Valleys and Mixtecs of the Mixteca Alta. See also Durand Alcántara, *La lucha campesina en Oaxaca y Guerrero, 1978–1987*, 152, for statistics on Mixtec internal and external migration in the 1970s and 1980s. Finally, see Barabas and Bartolomé, *Dinámicas culturales*, 39–41, for background on Mixtec, Zapotec, and Triqui migration patterns. Barabas and Bartolomé demonstrate that Oaxacan migration to the United States did not take off in significant numbers until the 1970s.

63. Fox, "Indigenous Mexican Migrants," 163; Bartolo Hernández López, interview with author, Yolotepec de la Paz, Yosondúa, Oaxaca, September 10, 2008.
64. Bartolo Hernández López to Governor Pérez Gasca, July 7, 1957, 4/140 (24) "57"/1637 (AGEPEO).
65. Hernández López to Pérez Gasca, July 7, 1957 (AGEPEO).
66. Bartolo Hernández López, interview with author, Yolotepec de la Paz, Yosondúa, Oaxaca, September 10, 2008.
67. Francisco Jiménez, Félix Hernández, and Tereso Hernández to Public Minister of Justice, Tlaxiaco, October 7, 1958, Municipal Archive of Santiago Yosondúa, Tlaxiaco, Oaxaca.
68. Bartolo Hernández López to Tadeo García Gatica, September 10, 1958, Municipal Archive of Santiago Yosondúa, Tlaxiaco, Oaxaca.
69. "Indígenas de Yolotepec se quejan hasta la presidente de la República," *El Universal*, August 16, 1958.
70. Bartolo Hernández López to President Ruiz Cortines, July 7, 1957, Municipal Archive of Santiago Yosondúa, Tlaxiaco, Oaxaca.
71. Miguel García Cruz to Tadeo García Gatica, August 18, 1958, Municipal Archive of Santiago Yosondúa, Tlaxiaco, Oaxaca.
72. Francisco Jiménez, Yolotepec de la Paz, Yosondúa, to Yosondúa Municipal President, Tadeo García Gatica, July 27, 1958, Municipal Archive of Santiago Yosondúa, Tlaxiaco, Oaxaca.
73. Bartolo Hernández López, interview with author, Yolotepec de la Paz, Yosondúa, Oaxaca, September 10, 2008.
74. For the growing literature on the role of social media in contemporary movements, see Van De Donk, *Cyberprotest*; Earl and Kimport, *Digitally Enabled Social Change*; and Snow, *Blackwell Companion to Social Movements*.
75. Sociologist Max Weber's 1904 *The Protestant Ethic and the Spirit of Capitalism* started a conversation on the links between "Ascetic Protestantism" and individual wealth. See Lehmann, "Friends and Foes," for a good discussion of the austere spending behaviors that Weber deemed Protestant in nature.

Chapter Four

1. Wallis and Bennett, *Two Thousand Tongues to Go*, 54–55; Pike, "William Cameron Townsend"; Israel Shenker, "Expert Linguist Spreads the Word with Missionary Zeal," *New York Times*, June 21, 1969.
2. Hart, "Story of the Wycliffe Translators," 16; Ochoa Zazueta, "El Instituto Lingüístico del Verano," 2; Colegio de Etnólogos y Antropólogos Sociales, *Dominación Ideológica y Ciencia Social*, 7–8.
3. Salomón Nahmad Sittón to Fernando Solana, "Memorándum Confidencial," June 19, 1979, Personal Archive of Salomón Nahmad Sittón (SNS), Centro de Investigaciones y Estudios Superiores en Antropología Social, Oaxaca City.
4. See Overmyer-Velázquez, *Folkloric Poverty*, for a critical take on PRI's political agenda in promoting multiculturalism.
5. Colegio de Etnólogos y Antropólogos Sociales, *Dominación ideológica y ciencia social*, 11.
6. Nolasco, "Educación Indígena," 253. See also Nahmad Sittón, "Oaxaca y el CIESAS."
7. See Muñoz, *Stand Up and Fight*, for background on participatory indigenismo during the Echeverría presidency.
8. Galeano, *Las venas abiertas de América Latina*.
9. Oaxaca is divided into eight geographic regions. The Mixteca region is enclosed by two mountain ranges in western Oaxaca, bordering with the Mexican states of Guerrero and Puebla. The Mixteca has seven districts: Juxtlahuaca, Silacayoapan, Huajuapan, Coixtlahuaca, Teposcolula, Tlaxiaco, and Nochixtlán. The Mixteca Alta and Baja are composed primarily of ethnically Mixtec peoples with minor populations of Triqui and Cuicatec peoples. La Sierra Norte is located in northeastern Oaxaca, nestled between the Central Valleys and the Papaloapan region and sharing its easternmost border with the state of Veracruz. La Sierra Norte is divided into three districts: Ixtlán de Juárez, Mixes, and Villa Alta. Zapotecs primarily make up the districts of Ixtlán de Juárez and Villa Alta, while there is a significant Chinantec population in Ixtlán de Juárez. The Mixes district is populated by ethnically Mixe people. See the map in figure 1 for the locations of districts, languages spoken, and ethnic groups of the southwestern state of Oaxaca.
10. Svelmoe, *New Vision for Missions*, 7–8.
11. Steven, *Thousand Trails*, 20–21.
12. Central American Mission was founded in 1890 by Congregationalist minister C. I. Scofield. The minister was supported by American coffee investors in Costa Rica who wanted to convert their local workers to evangelical Christianity.
13. See Clarence W. Hall, "Two Thousand Tongues to Go," *Reader's Digest*, August 1958, 197. See also Benge and Benge, *Cameron Townsend*, 57.
14. Benge and Benge, *Cameron Townsend*, 97.

15. For a history of Protestantism in Guatemala, see Garrard-Burnett, *Protestantism in Guatemala*. For a background to W. C. Townsend's early missionary work in Guatemala, see Svelmoe, *New Vision for Missions*, and Benge and Benge, *Cameron Townsend*.
16. Benge and Benge, *Cameron Townsend*, 108.
17. Steven, *Doorway to the World*, 7–8.
18. Wallis and Bennett, *Two Thousand Tongues to Go*, 54.
19. Israel Shenker, "Expert Linguist Spreads the Word with Missionary Zeal," *New York Times*, June 21, 1969.
20. S. F. Lewis, "Mexico's National Indigenist Institute," 612.
21. S. F. Lewis, "Mexico's National Indigenist Institute," 612.
22. For background to the establishment of DAAI and INAH in Mexico, see Sámano Rentería, "El Indigenismo institucionalizado en México," 145–47. See also Kemper, "From Nationalism to Internationalism." For an argument on connections between indigenism and racism in Mexico, see Knight, "Racism, Revolution, and Indigenismo." For a different take to Knight's on the paternalistic leanings of indigenismo, see Dawson, "From Models for the Nation to Model Citizens."
23. S. F. Lewis, "Mexico's National Indigenist Institute," 612.
24. Lázaro Cárdenas, General Population Law, as quoted in Overmyer-Velázquez, *Beyond la Frontera*, 274.
25. Svelmoe, *New Vision for Missions*, 241.
26. See Steven, *Doorway to the World*, 41–44, for background on Townsend's decision to give the SIL a secular name outside of the United States.
27. William C. Townsend to President Lázaro Cárdenas, April 7, 1936, volume 1338, file 710.1/1598, folder 1, Archivo General de la Nación (AGN); Townsend to President Cárdenas, December 22, 1936, volume 1338, file 710.1/1598, folder 3 (AGN); Genaro Vásquez, Department of Labor, to Luis I. Rodríguez, Secretary to President Cárdenas, January 29, 1936, volume 1338, file 710.1/1590, folder 5 (AGN).
28. Hartch, *Missionaries of the State*, 7. See also Steven, *Doorway to the World*, 39–41, for linguist Ken Pike's memory of the Seventh Inter-American Scientific Congress in Mexico City, 1935.
29. Svelmoe, *New Vision for Missions*, 247.
30. Hartch, *Missionaries of the State*, 4–5. See also Steven, *Doorway to the World*, 40.
31. Svelmoe, *New Vision for Missions*, 247. See also Steven, *Doorway to the World*, 71–72, for an in-depth description of SIL linguists Eunice Pike and Florence Hansen's translation work in the Mazatecan region of Oaxaca.
32. Townsend to Lázaro Cárdenas, January 29, 1936, volume 1338, file 710.1/1598, folder 5 (AGN).
33. Svelmoe, *New Vision for Missions*, 270–73; Steven, Doorway to the World, 52–53.

34. Steven, *Doorway to the World*, 120–21.
35. Stoll, "Summer Institute of Linguistics and Indigenous Movements," 90.
36. Townsend, *Truth about Mexico's Oil*, 83–85.
37. Hefley and Hefley, *Uncle Cam*, 110.
38. See Cowan, "Report of the Activities of the Summer Institute of Linguistics," 5, for original contract. The *Boletín Indigenista* collection resides at the Jaime Torres Bodet Library, Summer Institute of Linguistics (SIL/ILV), Mitla, Oaxaca.
39. Colegio de Etnólogos y Antropólogos Sociales, *Dominación Ideológica y Ciencia Social*, 31.
40. Wright, "Gift of Tongues," 18.
41. As anthropologist David Stoll said of the SIL's inherent contradictions with its "nonsectarian" identity: "This will-o'-the-wisp is supposed to restrain zealous translators, distinguish SIL from other evangelical missions, and surmount the church-state objection to its contracts. Yet Wycliffe always has assured home supporters that it works with other evangelical missions and that translation produces new evangelical congregations." Stoll, *Fishers of Men or Founders of Empire?*, 75.
42. Wright, "Gift of Tongues," 19.
43. W. C. Cameron, "Notes on Spiritual Work for WBT Fieldworkers, 1948," in *Mexican Branch Handbook* (Santa Ana, CA: Wycliffe Bible Translators, 1956), as quoted in Stoll, *Fishers of Men or Founders of Empire?*, 75–76.
44. Stoll, *Fishers of Men or Founders of Empire?*, 76.
45. Clarence W. Hall, "Two Thousand Tongues to Go," *Reader's Digest*, August 1958, 215.
46. Stoll, *Fishers of Men or Founders of Empire?*, 79.
47. Doremus, "Indigenism, Mestizaje, and National Identity in Mexico," 375–76.
48. For Mexico's rapid economic initiatives in the 1940s and 1950s, see Newcomer, *Reconciling Modernity*.
49. Sánchez, "New Era in the Department of Indian Affairs," 47.
50. Sánchez, "New Era in the Department of Indian Affairs," 47.
51. For an anthropological discussion of state attempts to promote Mexican nationalism in the Yucatán, see Loewe, *Maya or Mestizo*.
52. McIntosh, "Activities of the Summer Institute of Linguistics for the Year 1953," 5.
53. McIntosh, "Activities of the Summer Institute of Linguistics for the Year 1953," 7.
54. See Smith and Smith, *One More Mountain to Climb*, for a personal account of the couple's work in the Chinantec village of Ojitlan, Oaxaca.
55. Wright, "Gift of Tongues," 20.
56. Benge and Benge, *Cameron Townsend*, 109; Slocum and Holmes, *Who Brought the Word*, 45.

57. Israel Shenker, "Expert Linguist Spreads the Word with Missionary Zeal," *New York Times*, June 21, 1969.
58. Sámano Rentería, "El Indigenismo institucionalizado en México," 142; Stephen, *¡Zapata Lives!*, 332.
59. See Gamio, "Consideraciones sobre el problema indígena en América," and "Dialogue on Indian Questions." See also Caso, "Definición del indio y lo indio."
60. See Doremus, "Indigenism, Mestizaje, and National Identity in Mexico," for a discussion of Caso's and Gamio's creation of official indigenismo.
61. President Luis Echeverría Álvarez made an attempt to attract former student protesters and leftist intellectuals to serve in his PRI cabinet. See Carey, *Plaza of Sacrifices*, 154–57, for a discussion of the so-called democratic opening during the Echeverría administration (1970–1976).
62. Warman et al., *De eso que llaman antropología mexicana*, 57.
63. Bartolomé, Bonfil Batalla, and Bonilla, "Declaration of Barbados."
64. See Varese "Memories of Solidarity," for his personal account of the conference and its impact on indigenous rights movements.
65. Bartolomé, Bonfil Batalla, and Bonilla, "Declaration of Barbados," 268.
66. See Bartolomé, *Procesos interculturales*, 315–32, for background on the subsequent declarations and Mexican indigenous congresses in which he and other Mexican anthropologists participated in the 1970s.
67. Bartolomé, Bonfil Batalla, and Bonilla, "Declaration of Barbados," 268.
68. Marx, *Communist Manifesto*.
69. Bartolomé, Bonfil Batalla, and Bonilla, "Declaration of Barbados," 268.
70. Nolasco, "Educación Indígena," 253. See also Nahmad Sittón, "Oaxaca y el CIESAS."
71. See Margarita Nolasco's and Salomón Nahmad Sittón's Mexican senate hearings testimonies, "Aclaraciones sobre lo expuesto ante la comisión de asuntos indígenas del Senado de la Republica referente al I.L.V.," transcribed in *Licitud Conforme a Derecho de las Demandas de las Comunidades Indígenas*, 1983 (SNS).
72. Bowen, *Evangelism and Apostasy*, 169.
73. See Pallares, *Peasant Struggles to Indigenous Resistance*, 176–77, for a discussion of the links between pan-ethnic organizing in Ecuador and the expulsion of the SIL in 1981. Pallares also links anti-SIL rhetoric to Ecuadorian nationalism that was bulwarked by indigenous cultures, not assimilation.
74. Hvalkof and Aaby, "No Tobacco, No Hallelujah," in Hvalkof and Aaby, *Is God an American?*, 185.
75. Hvalkof and Aaby, "No Tobacco, No Hallelujah," in Hvalkof and Aaby, *Is God an American?*, 185.
76. Israel Shenker, "Expert Linguist Spreads the Word with Missionary Zeal," *New York Times*, June 21, 1969.

77. Clarence W. Hall, "Two Thousand Tongues to Go," *Reader's Digest*, August 1958, 205.
78. In 1936, Ken Pike became the first SIL missionary in a Mixtec community. His sister Eunice Pike and Florence Henderson started in the Mazateca region that same year and Walter Miller worked in the Mixe region from 1938 until his death in 1978.
79. Israel Shenker, "Expert Linguist Spreads the Word with Missionary Zeal," *New York Times*, June 21, 1969. See also E. Farris, *Nuevo Testamento*.
80. K. Farris, "When God Directs the Play," *Presbyterian Church in America CEP*, July 1, 1989, https://archive.pcacdm.org/when-god-directs-the-play/.
81. Searle Hoogshagen, a SIL missionary in the Mixe region, described a similar suspicion in Coatlán. The former missionary recalled: "During our first weeks in the village, it was obvious that the people—especially the women—were afraid of us. When I would walk up or down the street the women would hastily get their children into the house. We later learned that they had heard rumors that Protestants ate babies." Searle Hoogshagen, *Missionary Monthly*, January 1, 1996, 6.
82. Kathryn Farris, "Asking Others to Have Faith When We Didn't," *Presbyterian Church in America CEP*, March 1, 1990, https://archive.pcacdm.org/asking-others-to-have-faith-when-we-didnt-have/.
83. Individuals suspicious of SIL motives in native language acquisition might have been referring to the use of Native American languages for message coding during World War II. The Navajo language was used in the Pacific Rim by the US marines; it was the one code that the Japanese could not break. The idea to use Navajo was suggested by Philip Johnston, the son of Protestant missionaries who grew up on a Navajo reservation. Fluent in Navajo, Johnston was a top advisor to the marines and recruited Navajo men to serve in the program. In 1968, the State Department released declassified documents from World War II acknowledging the crucial service of Navajo code breakers. See Iverson and Roessel, *Diné*, 183. See also Paul, *Navajo Code Talkers*, 7–10. Suspicion of Americans' motives for learning indigenous languages is not limited to US missionaries abroad. Title VI Foreign Language and Area Studies (FLAS) language programs for US graduate students came under scrutiny following the September 11 attacks in 2001. One University of Michigan language professor discouraged her students from accepting FLAS funding for less commonly taught languages, fearing that the Defense Department would ask them to be informants. See Jodie Morse, "No Spooks, Please. We're Academics," *Time*, October 15, 2001.
84. Kathryn Farris, "Asking Others to Have Faith When We Didn't," *Presbyterian Church in America CEP*, March 1, 1990, https://archive.pcacdm.org/asking-others-to-have-faith-when-we-didnt-have/.
85. Kathryn Farris, "Do You Really Care, Lord?," *Presbyterian Journal*, September 7, 1977, 10–11.

86. Kathryn Farris, "Do You Really Care, Lord?," *Presbyterian Journal*, September 7, 1977, 10–11.
87. Kathryn Farris, "Asking Others to Have Faith When We Didn't." *Presbyterian Church in America CEP*, March 1, 1990, https://archive.pcacdm.org/asking-others-to-have-faith-when-we-didnt-have/.
88. E. Farris, *Nuevo Testamento en Mixteco de Yosondúa*.
89. Isidoro Santiago Ojeda, interview with author, Yosondúa, Oaxaca, September 15, 2010.
90. Searle Hoogshagen, "Mixe Evangelical Churches: Leadership Training," *Missionary Monthly*, March 1997, 12.
91. Isidoro Santiago Ojeda, interview with author, Yosondúa, Oaxaca, September 15, 2010.
92. See E. Farris, "Syntactic Sketch of Yosondúa Mixtec"; K. Farris, *Diccionario básico del mixteco de Yosondúa, Oaxaca*.
93. See Terraciano, *Mixtecs of Colonial Oaxaca*, 416n3.
94. Martínez Cruz and Farris, *Cuando Cárdenas Visitó Nuestro Pueblo*.
95. Leal, "La visita de Lázaro Cárdenas," 15.
96. See Mantecón, "Lázaro Cárdenas en la memoria colectiva," for a discussion of collective memory surrounding Cárdenas's populist legacy.
97. For background on the Balsas River project that brought the former president to the Mixteca in 1970, see W. C. Townsend's biography, *Lázaro Cárdenas*, 393–97.
98. See Kiddle and Muñoz, "Introduction," for a discussion of Cardenista populism.
99. Alan Riding, "Mexico Trying to Lead Indians into World but Save Traditions," *New York Times*, December 26, 1975.
100. Muñoz credits the emergence of effective indigenous mobilization to the Echeverría administration's "participatory indigenismo." See Muñoz, "Populism, Indigenismo, and Indigenous Mobilization," 124–25. See also Muñoz's latest monograph on the subject, *Stand Up and Fight*, for background on participatory indigenismo during the Echeverría presidency.
101. Muñoz, "Populism, Indigenismo, and Indigenous Mobilization," 132–33.
102. Stephen, *¡Zapata Lives!*, 332.
103. See Domínguez, "Las demandas de los indios."
104. Flaviano Nicolás López, Sabino Sánchez Rosas, Ismael A. Osorio Rosas, Francisco Martínez Velasco, Juan Alcalá García, and Cándido V. Coheto Martínez, "Acta de los indios de Oaxaca," Yosondúa, June 27, 1977 (SNS).
105. López et al., "Acta de los indios de Oaxaca" (SNS).
106. López et al., "Acta de los indios de Oaxaca" (SNS).
107. López et al., "Acta de los indios de Oaxaca" (SNS).
108. A similar accusation occurred in La Laguna de Guadalupe, Chicahuaxtla, where SIL missionaries Robert Langacre and Claudio Good worked on Mixtec New

Testament translations. The missionaries left the community in 1981 and their church, according to anthropologist Carlos Durand Alcántara, "was turned into a middle school that benefited 257 students, instead of a handful of Protestants." Durand Alcántara also accused SIL missionaries in general of stealing precious geological formations as well as being spies. Specifically in La Laguna de Guadalupe, Durand Alcántara hints that the SIL missionaries flaunted their material wealth by building a home with two floors, something unheard of in La Laguna prior to the missionaries' arrival. See Durand Alcántara, *La lucha campesina en Oaxaca y Guerrero*, 50–53, for his criticism of the SIL in the Mixteca.

109. Isidoro Santiago Ojeda, interview with author, Yosondúa, Oaxaca, September 15, 2010.
110. "Edwin R. Farris" memorial, Find a Grave, https://www.findagrave.com/memorial/85039104.
111. Wheeler, *Modern Missions in Mexico*, 264.
112. Lawrence P. Van Slyke, as quoted in Wheeler, *Modern Missions in Mexico*, 280–81. See also "Rev. L. P. Van Slyke Works for More Than Two Years on Translation of British Scholar's Book into Spanish," *Nunda News*, April 28, 1960, for a report on Van Slyke's subsequent missionary activities and academic pursuits after serving as a missionary in Oaxaca from 1920 to 1936. In the article, Van Slyke mentions his goal of making Protestant scholarly and theological works available to Latin American Protestants.
113. Leal, "That Each May Hear in His Own Tongue," 340, 350.
114. Leal, "Problems in Zapotec Translation." In 1954 he also published with his wife Mary, "Noun Possession in Villa Alta Zapotec."
115. Leal, "That Each May Hear in His Own Tongue," 350.
116. Leal, *Mary*, 17.
117. Box 118, file 159, folder 2/22383, June 5, 1973 (AGEPEO).
118. The Leals arrived at Yatzachi in 1937. For a personal account of their experience in Yatzachi, see Leal, *Mary*. See also "Otis Leal, Dear Senior Missionary," Calvary Church, http://www.calvarylife.org/.
119. Many SIL missionaries investigated the customs behind witchcraft in the hope of eradicating the beliefs surrounding it. In 1963, William Townsend reported with satisfaction: "Witchcraft, killings, superstition, ignorance, fear and sickness are giving way before the Light of the Word, literacy, medicine and contact with the best in the outside world." Townsend, "Tribes, Tongues and Translators," 8; Butler, "Un relato de la hechicería en los pueblos zapotecos de la sierra en el distrito de Villa Alta"; Davis, "Cuicatec Tales about Witchcraft"; and Pike, "Texts on Mazatec Food Witchcraft."
120. Telésforo López Llaguno, interview with author, Yatzachi el Bajo, Oaxaca, May 5, 2011.
121. For a background on the SIL/WBT's Jungle Aviation and Radio Services (JAARS), which was created in 1948, see Slocum and Holmes, "Airman's Halo."

122. López Llaguno, interview with author.
123. López Llaguno, interview with author.
124. López Llaguno, interview with author.
125. López Llaguno, interview with author.
126. López Llaguno, interview with author.
127. López Llaguno, interview with author.
128. See Lipp, *Mixe of Oaxaca*, 52, for a discussion of the adaptations and reduced emphasis on Mixe rituals because of Protestant conversion. See also Instituto Nacional Indigenista, *Los Mixtecos de la Sierra*, for a brief discussion of the fading cargo system in Protestant Mixtec communities.
129. "Tres indígenas defienden al ILV," *Proceso*, October 1, 1979, 6.
130. "Tres indígenas defienden al ILV," *Proceso*, October 1, 1979, 6.
131. Iñigo Laviada, *Excélsior*, December 7, 1978.
132. Barbara Hollenbach, e-mail message to author, July 25, 2009.
133. Hollenbach, e-mail to author.
134. Benge and Benge, *Cameron Townsend*, 9–11, 213–14.
135. Benthall, "Summer Institute of Linguistics," 3.
136. In a widely cited 1973 NACLA article, anthropologist Laurie Hart argued that the SIL "pacified" indigenous communities with the Gospel so that multinational companies could exploit valuable uranium, petroleum, and lithium deposits. Hart, "Story of the Wycliffe Translators." See Hartch, *Missionaries of the State*, 147–49, for a discussion of the impact of Hart's article on anthropologists globally. See John Alsop, "No despreciamos al indígena," *Proceso*, October 1, 1979, for a refutation of the CIA/SIL connections. For SIL instructions to missionaries on how to handle false accusations of espionage, see Johnson, "Some Common Allegations and Fine Answers," 58–59.
137. Salomón Nahmad Sittón to Fernando Solana Morales, "Memorándum Confidencial," June 19, 1979 (SNS). While Nahmad Sittón headed the investigation, he was assisted by the general director of INAH Guillermo Bonfil Batalla, SEP cultural director Rodolfo Stavenhagen, and INI director Ignacio Ovalle Fernández.
138. Nahmad Sittón was referring to Charlotte Dennett's research for *Thy Will Be Done*, which claimed Nelson Rockefeller's business ties to the SIL and the CIA.
139. See Field, "Global Indigenous Movements," 230–36, for a discussion of the debate over recognition of Native languages at the official and local levels.
140. Pedro Gringoire, *Excélsior*, June 21, 1977. It is worth noting that "Pedro Gringoire" was the pseudonym for Methodist writer Gonzalo Báez-Camargo. Under that name he worked for fifty years as a reporter for *Excélsior*, often writing favorable articles for the SIL. See Mondragón, *Like Leaven in the Dough*, 152n3.
141. "Mexico Cardenas Museum," North Carolina Digital Collections, State Library of North Carolina, http://cdm16062.contentdm.oclc.org/cdm/singleitem/collection/p16062coll8/id/6148/rec/5.

142. Benge and Benge, *Cameron Townsend*, 185.
143. Ochoa Zazueta, "El Instituto Lingüístico del Verano," 2.
144. Ochoa Zazueta, "El Instituto Lingüístico del Verano," 81.
145. Ignacio Ramírez, "Oaxaca: El ILV disgrega grupos, suprime tradiciones, provoca pleitos," *Proceso*, October 8, 1979, 21–22.
146. Ramírez, "Oaxaca," 21.
147. Ramírez, "Oaxaca," 22.
148. Ramírez, "Oaxaca," 22.
149. Ramírez, "Oaxaca," 22.
150. Margarita Nolasco, "Aclaraciones sobre lo expuesto ante la comisión de Asuntos Indígenas del Senado de la República referente al ILV," May 1983, 1 (SNS).
151. "El Carbonero Vengador," 1978, Chinantec, Jaime Torres Bodet Library, Summer Institute of Linguistics (SIL/ILV); "Juan Tonto: Cuentos folklóricos," 1978, Chinantec, Tepetotutla, Jaime Torres Bodet Library, Summer Institute of Linguistics (SIL/ILV).
152. Salomón Nahmad Sittón, "Aclaraciones sobre lo expuesto ante la comisión de Asuntos Indígenas del Senado de la República referente al ILV," May 1983, 3 (SNS).
153. For example, see Lucía López de Policarpo, Angélica Salvador Policarpo, Inéz M. Butler, eds., *Goncho pastel: vamos a hacer pasteles; recetas para hornear pasteles y galletas*, 1972, Jaime Torres Bodet Library, Summer Institute of Linguistics (SIL/ILV).
154. Benthall, "Summer Institute of Linguistics," 3.
155. Alan Riding, "Mexico Trying to Lead Indians into World But Save Traditions," *New York Times*, December 26, 1975.
156. Rámon Hernández López, *La Educación para los Pueblos Indígenas de México*, Ministry of Education training literature, México City, 2000, Centro de Coordinación Indígena (CCI) Archive, Tlaxiaco, Oaxaca; Rámon Hernández López, interview with author, San Agustín Tlacotepec, August 15, 2008.
157. Guillermo Correa e Ignacio Ramírez, "Los indígenas exigen respeto a su cultura," *Proceso*, October 15, 1979.
158. Todd Hartch notes the SIL's temporary success in appealing to President José López Portillo directly in 1982. After all, López Portillo had approved Townsend's 1978 Águila award presented by the Mexican embassy to acknowledge his forty-two years of service in Mexico. Hartch describes the resiliency of the SIL; despite all the condemnations, they managed to keep running in Mexico. Hartch, *Missionaries of the State*, 152–53, 162.
159. Earl Adams, "The End of an Era: Closing Up Jungle Camp," April 11, 1980, as cited in Hartch, *Missionaries of the State*, 157, 214n69.
160. Colegio de Etnólogos y Antropólogos Sociales, *Dominación Ideológica y Ciencia Social*, 33.

161. Ignacio Ramírez, "El ILV anuncia en Oaxaca que seguirá su labor," *Proceso*, October 15, 1979, 28.
162. Ramírez, "El ILV anuncia en Oaxaca que seguirá su labor," 28.
163. Oaxaca City's *Noticias* offered wide coverage of de la Madrid's visit, particularly his stance on the SIL. "MMH Testimonio el Clamor Que Exige la Expulsión del ILV," *Noticias*, March 22, 1983; "Clamor Indígena en contra del ILV," *Noticias*, March 23, 1983.
164. Roberto Santiago and Marcos León, "El ILV, Instrumento de Penetración y Espionaje de los Estados Unidos: Proporcione la División Política de los 570 municipios," *Noticias*, February 22, 1982.
165. Miguel Ángel Ramírez, "Respeto y preservación de su identidad cultural," *El Día: Vocero del Pueblo Mexicano*, March 23, 1983; "Fuerte Inversión para las Zonas Indígenas," *El Nacional*, March 23, 1983.
166. Miguel Ángel Ramírez, "Respeto y preservación de su identidad cultural," *El Día: Vocero del Pueblo Mexicano*, March 23, 1983.
167. Elena Gallegos, "Desde el Poder se Prohijó al Lingüístico," *El Sol de México*, March 23, 1983. See also Zanetta, *Influence of the World Bank*, 108–10, for a description of Madrid's campaign strategies.
168. Lauro López López, "Apoyo a la medida de expulsar de manera definitiva al ILV," *El Día: Vocero del Pueblo Mexicano*, March 23, 1983.
169. López López, "Apoyo a la medida de expulsar de manera definitiva al ILV."
170. Miguel Ángel Ramírez, "Respeto y preservación de su identidad cultural," *El Día: Vocero del Pueblo Mexicano*, March 23, 1983.
171. For a recent photographic essay on Holy Thursday's typical celebration in the Zapotec community of Teotitlán del Valle, see Norma Hawthorne, "Portrait Photography Workshop: Maundy Thursday in Oaxaca," *Oaxaca Cultural Navigator: Norma Schafer*, April 6, 2012, http://oaxacaculture.com/2012/04/portrait-photography-workshop-maundy-thursday-in-oaxaca/.
172. See Rubin, *Decentering the Regime*, for an analysis of the radical Zapotec COCEI in Juchitán.
173. State Public Security Office, Memorandum to Governor of Oaxaca, June 4, 1984, box 100, file 160 (AGEPEO).
174. Original Spanish on selected banners: "Solución inmediata a problema de La Huertilla." "No más apoyo al ILV." "Fuera Gringos de Oaxaca." "Basto de engaños al pueblo." "Libertad presos políticos O.O.C.R."
175. State Public Security Office to Governor of Oaxaca, June 4, 1984, box 100, file 160 (AGEPEO).
176. Siverts, "Ethnic Stability and Boundary Dynamics in Southern Mexico," 115, 116.
177. Fox, Rivera, and Stephen, "Indigenous Rights and Self-Determination in Mexico." See also Muñoz, *Stand Up and Fight*.
178. See Muñoz, "Populism, Indigenismo, and Indigenous Mobilization," for an in-depth discussion of the congress's impact on shaping INI policy.

179. In his study of Zapotec resistance in Juchitán, Oaxaca, Jeffrey Rubin demonstrates that the Coalición Obrera Campesina Estudiantil del Istmo (COCEI) organizers in the 1970s were models to whom the 1994 Zapatista leaders gave credit. See Rubin, *Decentering the Regime*.
180. See Campbell, *Zapotec Renaissance*, for a discussion of the Coalition of Workers, Peasants, and Students of the Isthmus's (COCEI) success in encouraging Zapotec language production.
181. See Bonfil Batalla, *México Profundo*.
182. García Santiago, *Clases Sociales y Grupos Étnicos en Yosondúa*, 120–21.
183. García Santiago, *Clases Sociales y Grupos Étnicos en Yosondúa*, 99–100.
184. Juan Carlos Reyes Gómez, interview with author, Oaxaca de Juárez, September 20, 2010. Reyes Gómez is the director of the Integral Intercultural Language Academy of Oaxaca and the director of the Department of Mixe Culture in Oaxaca.
185. Juan Carlos Reyes Gómez, interview with author, Oaxaca de Juárez, September 20, 2010.
186. Bertha Rodríguez, "Mixtec Alphabet, Ndusu Tu'un Savi," Centro Binacional para el Desarrollo Indígena Oaxaqueño, June 7, 2009, http://centrobinacional.org/2009/06/mixtec-alphabet-ndusu-tu%E2%80%99un-savi/; Rufino Domínguez Santos, "VIII Congreso de Tu'un Savi," Frente Indigena de Organizaciones Binacionales, June 13, 2005, http://fiob.org/2005/06/viii-congreso-vee-tuun-savi/.
187. "World," Ethnologue: Languages of the World, https://www.ethnologue.com/world.
188. Michael Erard, "How Linguists and Missionaries Share a Bible of 6,912 Languages," *New York Times*, July 19, 2005.
189. Michael Erard, "How Linguists and Missionaries Share a Bible of 6,912 Languages," *New York Times*, July 19, 2005.
190. Warren, *Indigenous Movements and Their Critics*, 58–59.
191. Juan Carlos Reyes Gómez, interview with author, Oaxaca de Juárez, September 20, 2010.
192. In *Missionaries of the State*, historian Todd Hartch comes to the same conclusion.
193. Cándido Coheto Martínez, interview with author, Oaxaca de Juárez, December 1, 2009.

Chapter Five

1. *El Universal*, January 28, 1979.
2. "México recibe el Papa a las 13 Hrs," *El Sol de México*, January 26, 1979; photograph caption reads "Papa Deportista."
3. "La invasión de las sectas" is a phrase used by the institutional Catholic Church and lay Catholics in Latin America to describe the growth of

Notes to Pages 132–134

evangelical Protestantism. David Stoll, *Is Latin America Turning Protestant*, 1–23, offers an excellent overview of evangelical Protestant inroads in Latin America. See Guerra Gómez, *Las sectas y su invasión del mundo hispano*; Consejo Episcopal Latino Americano, *Sectas en América Latina*; and Ganuza, *Las Sectas nos Invaden*, for condemnations of "las sectas" published by Catholic presses. See Saldaña, *De sectas a sectas*, for a collection of papers presented at a 1987 Oaxacan symposium focused on the growth of sects in Oaxaca. The participants ranged from sociologists from Benito Juárez Autonomous University to indigenous community leaders from Zapotec and Chatino communities. The participants argued sects—whether Baptist or Jehovah's Witnesses—were destroying Oaxacan communities. Finally, see Alfredo Silletta *Las Sectas Invaden La Argentina*, for a South American example.

4. Levine, *Religion and Political Conflict in Latin America*, 12–14.
5. On the Medellín Conference, see Rourke, *Roots of Pope Francis's Social and Political Thought*, 47–50. For an overview of liberation theology, see Berryman, *Liberation Theology*, and C. Smith, *Emergence of Liberation Theology*.
6. Gutiérrez, *Theology of Liberation*; Boff, *Introducing Liberation Theology*; and Freire, *Pedagogy of the Oppressed*.
7. George Vecsey, "In Latin America, 'Liberation Theology' Pulls Both Ways: The Bishops' Meeting Begins," *New York Times*, January 28, 1979.
8. Pontifical Council for the Family, "Reflection by Cardinal Alfonso López Trujillo." See also Warren Hoge, "Papal Visit Divides Catholics in Brazil: Factions Jockey for Endorsement of Varying Strands of Doctrine," *New York Times*, April 27, 1980.
9. As Prefect of the Sacred Congregation for the Doctrine of Faith, Cardinal Joseph Ratzinger published criticisms of liberation theology; see his 1984, "Instruction on Certain Aspects of the 'Theology of Liberation.'"
10. Marlise Simons, "Vatican Study Expected to Caution Activist Priests," *New York Times*, September 2, 1984.
11. Levine, *Religion and Political Conflict in Latin America*, and Sigmund, *Liberation Theology at the Crossroads*.
12. The shift in Pope John Paul II's view toward Liberation Theology is evident in his 1986 Letter to Brazilian Bishops. By the early 1990s, Pope John Paul II produced strong decrees on the church's role in promoting social justice. See Juan de Onis, "Pope's Tour Reflects Church's New Activist Role for the Poor," *Los Angeles Times*, June 28, 1986.
13. See Rourke, *Roots of Pope Francis's Social and Political Thought*, for an analysis of different emphases in Medellín (58–59) and Pueba (78–81).
14. Paul VI, *Evangelii Nuntiandi*, Vatican website, December 8, 1975, 62, http://w2.vatican.va/content/paul-vi/en/apost_exhortations/documents/hf_p-vi_exh_19751208_evangelii-nuntiandi.html.

15. González Gary, "Poder y presiones de la iglesia," 255. See also López Trujillo's 1985 "Declaration of Los Andes."
16. Rourke, *Roots of Pope Francis's Social and Political Thought*, 79–81. George Vecsey, "'Outsiders' Swayed Latin Church Talks: Prominent Theologians, Kept Out of Bishops' Mexican Session, Had an Activist Influence," *New York Times*, February 18, 1979.
17. Warren Hoge, "Papal Visit Divides Catholics in Brazil: Factions Jockey for Endorsement of Varying Strands of Doctrine," *New York Times*, April 27, 1980.
18. See José G. Saucedo, "Comments and Reflections on Puebla, 1979," *Living Church*, April 8, 1979, 9–11.
19. See Hayden, "In Chiapas," and Stahler-Sholk, "Resisting Neoliberal Homogenization." For Oaxaca, see Rubin, *Decentering the Regime*.
20. The Regional Pacífico Sur Episcopacy includes the archdiocese of Oaxaca (Oaxaca City and surrounding Central Valley towns), Huautula, Mixes, Puerto Escondido, Tehuantepec, and Tuxtepec; in Chiapas: San Cristóbal de las Casas, Tapachula, and Tuxtla Gutiérrez.
21. For an examination of CEBS in Oaxaca, see MacNabb and Rees, "Liberation or Theology?."
22. Richard Halloran, "Mexico Figuring Prominently in U. S. Energy Calculations," *Fort Myers News-Press*, January 7, 1979.
23. Jimmy Carter, "Mexico City, Mexico Remarks before the Mexican Congress," February 16, 1979, *American Presidency Project*, http://www.presidency.ucsb.edu/ws/?pid=31927.
24. Jeff Nesmith, "Presidents Begin Neighborly Talks," *Palm Beach Post*, February 15, 1979; Martin Tolchin, "A New Seriousness in Washington's Approach to Mexico," *New York Times*, February 19, 1979; James Reston, "Despite All Those Barbs, Carter Succeeded," *Akron Beacon Journal*, February 19, 1979.
25. "Ronald Reagan and Mexico's López Portillo: The Climate Is Good: Can They Usher in a New Era?," *Florida Today*, October 4, 1981; Alan Riding, "The Mixed Blessings of Mexico's Oil," *New York Times*, January 11, 1981.
26. Some economists, however, doubted Mexico's ability to solve the United States' energy crisis (Ernest Conine, "U. S. Shouldn't Count on Mexican Oil," *Clarion-Ledger*, October 26, 1979). Initial excitement over Mexico's increased production of oil during the López Portillo administration wore off by the end of his administration. Government economists no doubt exaggerated the amount of reserves, overspending on credit. When oil prices tanked in the early 1980s, Mexico's foreign debt skyrocketed, eventually resulting in massive currency inflation and lower wages. Lenti, *Redeeming the Revolution*, 280; Davis, *Urban Leviathan*, 240–41; Sheppard, *Persistent Revolution*, 65–67.
27. See "Ley de Asociaciones Religiosas y Culto Público," July 15, 1992, http://www.diputados.gob.mx/LeyesBiblio/pdf/24_171215.pdf.
28. Warman et al., *De eso que llaman antropología mexicana*, 57.

29. See Bartolomé, *Procesos interculturales*, 315–32, for background on the subsequent declarations and Mexican indigenous congresses in which he and other Mexican anthropologists participated in the 1970s.
30. Bartolomé, Bonfil Batalla, and Bonilla, "Declaration of Barbados."
31. Nolasco, "Educación Indígena," 253; Nahmad Sittón, "Oaxaca y el CIESAS."
32. Stephen, *¡Zapata Lives!*, 332. See especially Muñoz, *Stand Up and Fight*, for background on participatory indigenismo during the Echeverría presidency.
33. See Domínguez, "Las demandas de los indios."
34. Domínguez, "Las demandas de los indios."
35. Ángel Coronel, *Fogonazo*, January 7, 1979.
36. Ángel Gomez Granados, "Por una hora hablaron el Presidente de México y su Santidad de Justicia y de Paz en el Mundo," *El Universal*, January 27, 1979.
37. Fernando Rivera Arteaga, "El Polaco que Vino de Roma," *El Sol de México*, January 30, 1979.
38. Tim Golden, "Mexico Ending Church Restraints after 70 Years of Official Hostility," *New York Times*, December 20, 1991.
39. "Cordialidad Mexicana ante la visita Papa," editorial, *Carteles del Sur*, January 20, 1979.
40. "Bancomer," *El Universal*, January 26, 1979.
41. "El Gobernador recibió al Papa en el aeropuerto," *Carteles del Sur*, January 30, 1979.
42. "Recibe Hoy Oaxaca a Juan Pablo II," *Oaxaca Gráfico*, January 29, 1979; Alejandro Reyes Sánchez, "El Papa en Cuilapan," *Noticias*, January 16, 1979; "Muchos Muchos Miles de Indígenas," *Carteles del Sur*, January 30, 1979.
43. Jorge Aviles Randolph, "Esteban Hernández, en Zapoteco, Hablará de los Indios al Papa," *El Universal*, January 29, 1979.
44. "¡Juan Pablo II Vitoreado en Oaxaca!," *Oaxaca Gráfico*, January 30, 1979; Perea, *El Papa en México*, 157.
45. John Paul II, *John Paul II in Mexico*, 93.
46. John Paul II, *John Paul II in Mexico*, 96.
47. See Zafra, "Problemática agraria en Oaxaca," for an analysis of the Coalition of Workers, Peasants, and Students of Oaxaca (COCEO) and land reform in the early 1970s; see Rubin, *Decentering the Regime*, for an analysis of the Coalition of Workers, Peasants, and Students of the Isthmus (COCEI) in the late 1970s.
48. John Paul II, *John Paul II in Mexico*, 96–97.
49. Perea, *El Papa en México*, 161.
50. C. Townsend, "Burying the White Gods."
51. John Paul II, *John Paul II in Mexico*, 99.
52. Manuel del Castillo, "Bendijo Tripulación, Avión, y Hasta la Bitácora de Vuelo," *El Sol de Mexico*, January 30, 1979.
53. Norget, "Progressive Theology and Popular Religiosity in Oaxaca, Mexico," 93.
54. Sheppard, *Persistent Revolution*, 197; Michael Novak, "The Case against Liberation Theology," *New York Times*, October 21, 1984.

55. "La Iglesia debe despojarse de sus privilegios y sus riquezas," *El Universal*, January 31, 1979.
56. Juan Rodríguez, "Ellos no Tienen ni Agua para Beber: Los Mixtecos y Mixes Están Aprendiendo a Odiar por el Derroche en la Ciudades," *El Universal*, January 28, 1979.
57. Abel Quezada, "Volviendo a Empezar," *El Universal*, February 1, 1979.
58. Michael Novak, "The Case against Liberation Theology," *New York Times*, October 21, 1984.
59. González Gary, "Poder y presiones de la iglesia," 263, 291.
60. "Growing Repression in Mexico."
61. See Barry, *Free Trade and the Farm Crisis in Mexico*, for an examination of the negative recursions of NAFTA in southern Mexico. Barry also gives the history of the failure of twentieth-century populism in adequately meeting the needs of indigenous communities.
62. Clientalism refers to state patronage of various constituencies, whether it is union organizations, the peasantry, or indigenous peoples. The 1970s and 1980s brought the emergence of Mexico's civil society: Following the 1985 earthquake in Mexico City, a leftist opposition party almost stripped the PRI of its leadership in the 1988 election. In Oaxaca, broad opposition movements founded in the 1970s such as the Coalición Obrera Campesina Estudiantil de Oaxaca (COCEO) and the Coalición Obrera Campesina Esudiantil del Istmo (COCEI) fought for agrarian reform and a greater voice in politics, including recognition of Zapotec cultural traditions. Harvey, *Chiapas Rebellion*, 131.
63. Lona Reyes, "Violence against the Indians in Oaxaca."
64. Bartolomé Carrasco Briseño, Jesús C. Alba, Samuel Ruiz García, Arturo Lona Reyes, and Hermenegildo Ramírez, "Vivir Cristianamente el Compromiso Político," February 27, 1982, 222–23, collection: Obispos de la Región Pacífico Sur, Archivo Histórico de la Arquidiócesis de Oaxaca (AHAO).
65. See Stoll, *Is Latin America Turning Protestant*, for background to the US religious right's ties to Central America in the 1980s. See also Steigenga, "Politics of Pentecostalized Religion." See O'Neill, *City of God*, for insight into a Guatemalan megachurch's strategy to evangelize Mexico and Mexican migrants living in Chicago.
66. Carrasco Briseño et al., "Vivir Cristianamente el Compromiso Político," 222–23 (AHAO).
67. Carrasco Briseño et al., "Vivir Cristianamente el Compromiso Político," 218 (AHAO).
68. See Garrard-Burnett, *Terror in the Land of the Holy Spirit*, for an excellent account of Montt's use of evangelical Protestantism to justify the slaughter of Mayan guerillas.
69. See Marlise Simons, "Latin America's New Gospel," *New York Times*, November 7, 1982, for an investigative report of Ríos Montt's leadership role in the

evangelical Christian "Church of the Word" in Guatemala. See also Robert Lindsey, "Church Denies It Has Political Goals in Guatemala," *New York Times*, August 14, 1983.
70. Kevin Lewis O'Neill explores the term "Christian citizenship" in his monograph *City of God*. See especially his treatment of the Ríos Montt regime (23–24).
71. Stolen, *Guatemalans in the Aftermath of Violence*, 121–22.
72. M. C. García, *Seeking Refuge*, 59–61.
73. Carlos Fazio, "2,500 guatemaltecos huyen de El Chupadero y se reubican en Chiapas," *Proceso*, June 30, 1984. Valencia, *Guatemalan Refugees in Mexico*, 8–9.
74. In 1984, the Pacífico Sur bishops wrote "On the Situation of the Refugees." See Valencia, *Guatemalan Refugees in Mexico*, 79.
75. Moksnes, *Maya Exodus*, 64–66.
76. Moksnes, *Maya Exodus*, 66.
77. Report from General Brig. Commander Sixto Ruben Mendoza, Chiapas, to National Defense Secretary, D. F., March 14, 1984, 547–48, expediate A, collection 36/a Zona Militar, National Security Archive (NSA).
78. Inteligencia, S-2, 1984, "Estudio de Estado Mayor," 545–48 (NSA).
79. Sheppard, *Persistent Revolution*, 197. See also Moksnes, *Maya Exodus*, 66–67.
80. Kampwirth, *Women and Guerrilla Movements*, 96.
81. Moksnes, *Maya Exodus*, 202, 220.
82. Klaiber, *Church, Dictatorships, and Democracy*, 260–61. In 1995, the Chiapan governor, Eduardo Robledo Rincón, demanded Ruiz's ouster; see Anthony DePalma, "The 'Dear Father' of Mexican Indians Is the 'Assassin Bishop' to His Foes," *New York Times*, February 19, 1995. Mexico's apostolic delegate, Girolamo Prigione, tried to have Ruiz removed as bishop at various points. See Klaiber, *Church, Dictatorships, and Democracy*, 260–61; Camp, *Crossing Swords*, 231–33.
83. M. C. Garcia, *Seeking Refuge*, 73.
84. See Eber, "'Buscando una nueva vida,'" 140–41, 146.
85. See José G. Saucedo, "Comments and Reflections on Puebla, 1979," *Living Church*, April 8, 1979, 9–11.
86. Carrasco Briseño et al., "Vivir Cristianamente el Compromiso Político," 218 (AHAO).
87. Carrasco Briseño et al., "Vivir Cristianamente el Compromiso Político," 223 (AHAO).
88. Carrasco Briseño et al., "Vivir Cristianamente el Compromiso Político," 477 (AHAO).
89. Molly Moore, "Religions Collide in Mexico's South," *Washington Post*, February 6, 1996.
90. Roberto Santiago, "Testimonio de libertad y paz de la grey Católica," *Noticias*, February 1, 1982.

91. Roberto Santiago, "Testimonio de libertad y paz de la grey Católica," *Noticias*, February 1, 1982.
92. See Norget, "Progressive Theology and Popular Religiosity," 92, 99.
93. See Stephen, *We Are the Face of Oaxaca*, 116–17.
94. Padre Ubi, interview with author, Colonia Xocimilco, Oaxaca City, April 2010. Padre Ubi compared the state government's violence against the protesters to Efraín Ríos Montt's scorched earth policy in Guatemala. Gustavo Castillo, "Sin aviso, se suspendieron las garantías en Oaxaca," *La Jornada*, December 2, 2016, http://www.jornada.unam.mx/2006/12/03/index.php?section=politica&article=003n1pol.
95. Gross, "Pentecostal Congregations and Religious Competition," 97.
96. Gustavo Castillo, "Sin aviso, se suspendieron las garantías en Oaxaca," *La Jornada*, December 2, 2016, http://www.jornada.unam.mx/2006/12/03/index.php?section=politica&article=003n1pol.
97. Padre Ubi, interview with author, Colonia Xochimilco, Oaxaca City, April 2010.
98. Toribio Santiago Patéos et al., to Juan Antonino Santiago, Mayor, San Antonillo, March 6, 1983, box 140, file 162.6, collection: Asuntos Agrarios (AGEPEO).
99. Marroquín, *El Conflicto Religioso*, 93.
100. David Nicolás Vásquez Velasco to Justiniano Carballido, Director Jurídico y de Gobierno, Oaxaca, June 20, 1983, box 140, file 162.6, file: San Antonino Velasco, Ocotlán, Oaxaca, collection: Asuntos Agrarios (AGEPEO).
101. Mayor Juan Antonino Santiago to Jesús Martínez, Secretario General del Despacho, Oaxaca, June 14, 1983, box 140, file 162.6, file: San Antonino Velasco, Octolán, Oaxaca, collection: Asuntos Agrarios (AGEPEO).
102. Perfecto Mora Ravelo to Justiniano Carballido Gonzalez, June 17, 1983, San Antonino Castillo, box 140, file 162.6, folder: San Antonino Velasco, Octolán Oaxaca, Dirección Jurídica, collection: Asuntos Agrarios (AGEPEO).
103. Marroquín, *El Botín Sagrado*, 49.
104. Abraham Cruz, "Desestabilizan los Protestantes," *El Imparcial*, April 16, 1988.
105. Cruz, "Desestabilizan los Protestantes."
106. Cruz, "Desestabilizan los Protestantes."
107. Alessandra Stanley, "Pope Is Returning to Mexico with New Target: Capitalism," *New York Times*, January 22, 1999.
108. Larry Rohter, "Pope, in Mexico, Faces Rising Protestant Tide," *New York Times*, May 12, 1990.
109. Rohter, "Pope, in Mexico, Faces Rising Protestant Tide."
110. Alessandra Stanley, quoting John Paul II's 1990 statement, in "Pope Urges Bishops to Minister to the Rich," *New York Times*, January 24, 1999. See also Clyde Haberman, "Speak Out on Social Issues, Pope Tells Mexico Bishops," *New York Times*, May 13, 1990.
111. John Paul II, "New Evangelization." See also Norget, "Progressive Theology and

Popular Religiosity," 100–103, for a discussion of the strained relationship between the New Evangelization campaign and popular religiosity in the archdiocese of Oaxaca post-1992. Finally, see Edward L. Cleary, "John Paul Cries 'Wolf': Misreading the Pentecostals," *Commonweal*, November 20, 1992, 7–8.

112. Pope John Paul II, "The Task of the Latin American Bishops," *Origins*, March 24, 1983. For more on the New Evangelization campaign, see Peterson and Vásquez, "New Evangelization in Latin American Perspective."

113. Sociologist Enrique Marroquín notes that as of 1992, the archdiocese of Oaxaca had only 160 ordained priests. That meant that one parish priest could be responsible for ministering from fifteen to up to eighty small communities, an overwhelming task. Marroquín, *El Botín Sagrado*, 42.

114. See Marroquín, *El Botín Sagrado*, 41–45, for a description of rivalries between nuns, priests, and catechists in rural zones of Oaxaca.

115. In 2001, the Vatican restricted the diocese of San Cristóbal de las Casas, Chiapas, from ordaining new indigenous deacons. The Vatican argued that under former bishop Samuel Ruiz, the deacons became too numerous and acted, at times, independently of the Catholic Church. Diego Cevallos, "Mexico: Vatican Incomprehension Stymies Pastoral Plan in Chiapas," Inter Press Service, January 29, 2007, http://www.ipsnews.net/2007/01/mexico-vatican-incomprehension-stymies-pastoral-plan-in-chiapas/. See also Ginger Thompson, "Vatican Curbing Deacons in Mexico," *New York Times*, March 12, 2002.

116. C. Smith, Introduction, *Latin American Religion in Motion*, 10.

117. Gabriel Xantomila, "Crecimiento exponencial de evangelistas," *El Heraldo de Chiapas*, December 14, 2015, http://www.oem.com.mx/elmexicano/notas/n4028059.htm.

118. David Gonzalez, "House Afire: A Sliver of a Storefront, a Faith on the Rise," *New York Times*, January 14, 2007.

119. "¿Quien fundó tu iglesia?," Mexican National Episcopacy, 1993. I am indebted to Father Enrique Marroquín for giving me copies of the episcopacies' re-evangelization pamphlets from the early 1990s.

120. "¡Volved, pues sin miedo! La Iglesia os espera con los brazos abiertos para reencontraros con Cristo," Mexican National Episcopacy, 1993.

121. "Religious Diversity Is Increasing in Mexico," *Geo-Mexico: The Geography and Dynamics of Modern Mexico* (blog), May 28, 2011, http://geo-Mexico.com/?p=4056.

122. INEGI, *Censo de Población y Vivienda*, 2010.

123. Julian Rodríguez Marin, "More Than 1,000 Mexicans Leave Catholic Church Daily, Expert Says," *Latin American Herald Tribune*, April 3, 2010, http://www.laht.com/article.asp?ArticleId=390745&CategoryId=14091.

124. INEGI, *Censo de Población y Vivienda*, 2010.

125. "Statistics," Archdiocese of Antequera, Oaxaca, http://www.catholic-hierarchy.org/diocese/dante.html#stats, accessed September 24, 2017.

126. Gross, "Pentecostal Congregations and Religious Competition in Rural Mexico," 89.
127. See Frank Bruni and Ginger Thompson, "Bolstering Faith of Indians, Pope Gives Mexico a Saint," *New York Times*, August 1, 2002, for a discussion of indigenous culture in Mexico and its relationship with Catholic and Protestant faiths at the time of Juan Diego's canonization mass, and Daniel J. Wakin, "At St. Patrick's, a Fragment of an Aztec Saint's Cloak," *New York Times*, December 6, 2003, for discussion of Juan Diego's transnational importance.
128. John Stonestreet, "Pope Francis' Visit Reminds Us: Catholics and Protestants Can and Should Stand Shoulder to Shoulder," *Christianity Today*, October 2, 2015, http://www.cnsnews.com/commentary/john-stonestreet/paradoxes-pope-francis.

Chapter Six

1. See Figure 1, Map of the Eight Regions of Oaxaca.
2. Marroquín, *El Conflicto Religioso*, 54.
3. Velásquez, "Migrant Communities, Gender, and Political Power," 483.
4. Velásquez, "Migrant Communities, Gender, and Political Power," 486. See Barabas and Bartolomé, "Los sistemas normativos frente a las nuevas alternativas religiosas en Oaxaca," 110, for a brief discussion on the connection between migration to the United States and the spread of Pentecostal churches in Oaxaca.
5. On braceros, see Fox, "Indigenous Mexican Migrants," 163. See Stephen, *Transborder Lives*, 96–97 and 108–12, for her oral histories with ex-braceros in Teotitlán del Valle and San Agustín Atenango, Oaxaca. In Teotitlán del Valle, 25 percent of adult males did participate in the bracero program, which is higher than average for Oaxacan indigenous villages. Stephen also discusses internal Oaxacan and Mexican migration patterns for Zapotecs of the Central Valleys and Mixtecs of the Mixteca Alta. See also Durand Alcántara, *La lucha campesina en Oaxaca y Guerrero*, 152, for statistics on Mixtec internal and external migration in the 1970s and 1980s. Finally, see Barabas and Bartolomé, *Dinámicas culturales*, 39–41, for background to Mixtec, Zapotec, and Triqui migration patterns. Barabas and Bartolomé demonstrate that Oaxacan migration to the United States did not take off in significant numbers until the 1970s. Douglas Massey puts the number of Oaxacan braceros at less than 5 percent in Cohen, *Culture of Migration in Southern Mexico*, 60.
6. Fox, "Indigenous Mexican Migrants," 163; Bartolo Hernández, interview with author, Yolotepec de la Paz, Yosondúa, Oaxaca, September 10, 2008.
7. See Simon, "Crisis in el Campo," for a discussion of the failed "Green Revolution" in Mexico. Simon demonstrates that President Luis Echeverría's support

of chemical fertilizers for southern Mexico was a death sentence for Oaxacan agriculture; the land became depleted and eroded within just a few annual harvests.
8. Simon, "Crisis in el Campo," 37–38.
9. Alan Riding, "Inflation, the Scourge of Latin America, Takes Hold in Mexico; Domestic Ills," *New York Times*, August 2, 1974, and "Mexico's Gloomy Economy," *New York Times*, April 12, 1982. See Montes García, "Los conflictos religiosos en Oaxaca," for an argument on the inverse correlation between the failing agricultural sector and the rise of Protestantism. See Whitt, "Mexican Peso Crisis." See also Gates, *In Default*, for a case study of the agricultural crisis stemming from the debt crisis in Campeche, Mexico. Finally, see Teichman, *Policy-Making in Mexico*, for a background to Mexico's national recession during the Miguel de la Madrid 1982–1988 administration.
10. Eric Schlosser, "In the Strawberry Fields," *Atlantic*, November 1995, http://www.theatlantic.com/magazine/archive/1995/11/in-the-strawberry-fields/5754/.
11. Fox, "Indigenous Mexican Migrants," 174. See Rivera-Salgado, "Welcome to Oaxacalifornia," for background to indigenous Oaxacan transborder political and labor organizing in the 1980s and 1990s. See Nagengast and Kearney, "Mixtec Ethnicity," for an analysis on how indigenous Oaxacans use their ethnic identity to unite and protest deplorable living and working conditions in northern Mexico and California.
12. "America's Changing Religious Landscape," Pew Research Center, Religion & Public Life, http://www.pewforum.org/2015/05/12/americas-changing-religious-landscape/.
13. Pew Research Center, *Religion in Latin America*.
14. David Gonzalez, "House Afire: A Sliver of a Storefront, a Faith on the Rise," *New York Times*, January 14, 2007. See also Espinosa, *Latino Pentecostals in America*, 269–70.
15. Quinones, *True Tales from Another Mexico*, 110.
16. Quinones, 111.
17. Michael Kearney and Federico Besserer discuss the use of substitutes to fulfill cargo positions. However, they underline the fact that many communities still prefer that the migrant physically return to the village to fulfill his obligation. See Kearney and Besserer, "Oaxacan Municipal Governance in Transnational Context," 452–53.
18. See Cohen, "Transnational Migration in Rural Oaxaca," for background on how remittances are allocated in a Zapotec community.
19. See VanWey, Tucker, and McConnell, "Community Organization, Migration and Remittances in Oaxaca," for a quantitative study on the economic and political impact of remittances to Zapotec communities.
20. See Stephen, *Transborder Lives*, 48–59, for a discussion of how migration cycles affected mayordomías.

21. See Mountz and Wright, "Daily Life in the Transnational Migrant Community," 416–17, for an analysis of fiesta competition in a Zapotec migrant-sending community. See also Gross, "Farewell to Fiestas and Saints?," for an argument that the fiesta system in Oaxaca is actually growing in symbolic and physical importance because of the rise of Protestant churches. Finally, see Cohen, "Transnational Migration in Rural Oaxaca," for his survey on a Zapotec migrant-sending village where expenditures on fiestas or luxury items such as televisions were relatively low compared to the home improvements and business opportunities available for returning migrants with savings.
22. James C. Scott's article "Prestige as the Public Discourse of Domination" suggests that while wealth can run out, the person's respected status in the community does not. Hence, status, not wealth, is still more important for maintaining prestige in one's community.
23. Cohen, *Culture of Migration in Southern Mexico*, 6.
24. See Barabas and Bartolomé, "Los que se van al Norte," for recent statistics on internal and external Oaxacan migration.
25. Gastón Espinosa notes that of the 7.5 percent of the Mexican population who have migrated to the United States, 15 percent of them are Protestant ("Brown Moses," 384). His research on Latino Pentecostalism in the United States also suggests that Mexican migrants are being converted by Mexican American Pentecostals with their own churches, not by Anglo-Americans as is popularly suggested in scholarship. Rather, Espinosa posits, "There is also a long tradition of indigenous, independent, and autonomous Latino Protestant churches that are completely run by and for the Mexican American and Latino community" (289).
26. Mountz, "Daily Life in the Transnational Migrant Community," 422–23.
27. Seventh-day Adventists are classified as biblical and nonevangelical in the Mexican census, along with Mormons and Jehovah's Witnesses. Adventists do not work on Saturdays, so this has affected their ability to complete weekend tequio assignments. Jehovah's Witnesses do not celebrate any type of religious, familial, or civil holiday celebrations.
28. Jenaro Ramírez Ríos to Governor Pedro Vásquez Colmenares, May 7, 1982, box 118, file 161, collection: Relacionados con Tequios (AGEPEO).
29. Manuel Bautista Aguilar to Municipal Authority, San Francisco Tutla, March 23, 1982, box 118, file 161, collection: Relacionados con Tequios (AGEPEO).
30. Ausencio Ramírez Gijon to Mayor Hipoleto García Pacheco of San Lachao, May 20, 1982, box 118, file 161 (AGEPEO).
31. See Dennis, *Intervillage Conflict in Oaxaca*, for a solid analysis of agrarian conflicts in the Central Valleys of Oaxaca.
32. See Dennis, *Intervillage Conflict*, 127–48, for a discussion of similar conflicts regarding *agencia* rights in the Zapotec district of Etla.
33. Efraín Cruz Orozco to Oaxacan Secretary General, "Relacionados con Tequios," January 29, 1982, 1/131.7 (1–30) 82/333 (AGEPEO).

34. The Sierra Sur region of Oaxaca is south of the Sierra Norte, south of the Central Valleys and bordered by the La Costa region to the west and the Isthmus region to the east.
35. SIL missionary Walter S. Miller stayed in the community for two decades before moving onto another Mixe community where he stayed until his death in 1978. He was a well-respected publisher on Mixe linguistics and often served as a guide for anthropologists and the occasional mycologists seeking María Sabina's hallucinogenic mushrooms. See Miller, "El tonalamatl mixe y los hongos sagrados," and *Cuentos Mixes*.
36. "Missionary to Tribe in Mexico to Preach," *Dallas Morning News*, October 8, 1938; Ladislao Domínguez, "Origen de la iglesia evangélica en la región Mixe," *Hablando en Voz alta* (blog), June 29, 2010, http://jonathancruz747.blogspot.com/2010/06/una-historia-en-nada-conocida.html.
37. Lipp, *Mixe of Oaxaca*, 147.
38. Ladislao Domínguez, "Una historia en nada conocida," *Hablando en un voz alto* (blog), June 29, 2010, http://jonathancruz747.blogspot.com/2010/06/una-historia-en-nada-conocida.html.
39. Saúl Jiménez Crispin to Justiniano Carballido González, Attorney General, Oaxaca, February 15, 1982, box 140, file 162.6, collection: Asuntos Agrarios (AGEPEO).
40. I say "generally" because Jehovah's Witnesses are also advised to follow their consciences in making personal health and social decisions.
41. Félix Tiburcio Espina to Governor Pedro Vásquez Colmenares, March 24, 1981, box 140, file 162.6, collection: Asuntos Agrarios (AGEPEO).
42. Tiburcio Espina to Colmenares, March 24, 1981 (AGEPEO).
43. Tiburcio Espina to Colmenares, March 24, 1981 (AGEPEO).
44. Tiburcio Espina to Colmenares, March 24, 1981 (AGEPEO).
45. Félix Tiburcio Espina to Governor Pedro Vásquez Colmenares, February 28, 1982, box 140, file 162.6, collection: Asuntos Agrarios (AGEPEO).
46. Tiburcio Espina et al., to Vásquez Colmenares, February 4, 1982, box 140, file 162.6, collection: Asuntos Agrarios (AGEPEO).
47. Tiburcio Espina et al., to Colmenares, February 4, 1982 (AGEPEO).
48. Tiburcio Espina et al., to Colmenares, February 4, 1982 (AGEPEO).
49. Tiburcio Espina to Colmenares, February 28, 1982 (AGEPEO).
50. Saúl Jiménez Crispin to Justiniano Carballido González, Attorney General, Oaxaca, February 15, 1982, box 140, file 162.6, collection: Asuntos Agrarios (AGEPEO).
51. Tiburcio Espina and PRI Committee, San Juan Juquila, Mixes, to Governor Vásquez Colmenares, February 4, 1982, box 140, file 162.6, collection: Asuntos Agrarios (AGEPEO).
52. Sociologist Olga Montes García notes in her study on religious conflicts in Oaxaca that patron saint day fiestas are not just about celebrating a Catholic

saint but are really a celebration of the community itself; it is a time to renew and reaffirm customs and traditions. Montes García, "Las dinámicas de los conflictos religiosos en Oaxaca," 163.

53. Saúl Jiménez Crispin to Justiniano Carballido González, Attorney General, Oaxaca, February 15, 1982, box 140, file 162.6, collection: Asuntos Agrarios (AGEPEO).
54. Jiménez Crispin to Carballido González, February 15, 1982 (AGEPEO).
55. Jiménez Crispin to Carballido González, February 15, 1982 (AGEPEO).
56. Jiménez Crispin to Carballido González, February 15, 1982 (AGEPEO).
57. Jiménez Crispin to Carballido González, February 15, 1982 (AGEPEO).
58. Jiménez Crispin to Carballido González, February 15, 1982 (AGEPEO).
59. Jiménez Crispin to Carballido González, February 15, 1982 (AGEPEO).
60. Jiménez Crispin to Carballido González, February 15, 1982 (AGEPEO).
61. Jiménez Crispin to Carballido González, February 15, 1982 (AGEPEO).
62. Jiménez Crispin to Carballido González, February 15, 1982 (AGEPEO).
63. San Juan Juquila Mixes Plan Municipal de Desarrollo 2010, https://www.finanzasoaxaca.gob.mx/pdf/inversion_publica/pmds/08_10/200.pdf.
64. Comisión Nacional Para el Desarrollo de los Pueblos Indígenas, "Indicadores sociodemográficos de la población total y la población indígena por municipio, 2000," http://www.cdi.gob.mx/cedulas/2000/OAXA/20200-00.pdf.
65. See Luke, Book of Acts of the Apostles, 2:1–13, "The Holy Spirit Comes at Pentecost."
66. Gill, *Rendering unto Caesar*, 83.
67. Martin, *Tongues of Fire*, 53.
68. Officially, Pentecostalism started in 1901 in Topeka, Kansas. But in terms of popularizing the religion and attracting significant followers, many scholars credit the African American preacher William Seymour as its more important disseminator. Seymour led a series of revivals in downtown Los Angeles in 1906. See Robeck, Azusa Street Mission and Revival, for background on Seymour and his connection to Mexican Americans in Los Angeles. See Petersen, "Azusa Street Mission and Latin American Pentecostalism," 66–67. See also Espinosa, "'God Made a Miracle in My Life.'" See also Espinosa, "Brown Moses," for background on Latino involvement in the Azusa Street Revival. Finally, see also Espinosa, *Latino Pentecostals in America*.
69. See de la Luz García, *El Movimiento Pentecostal en México*, and D. Ramírez, *Migrating Faith*.
70. Gerardo Mendoza García, interview with author, Oaxaca City, Oaxaca, December 1, 2009.
71. Gerardo Mendoza García, interview with author, Oaxaca City, Oaxaca, December 1, 2009.
72. Hernández Hernández, "El cambio religiosos en México," 69.
73. Alejandro Sobarzo Loaiza to Pedro Vásquez Colmenares, August 2, 1983, file 2/347/15704 (AGEPEO).

74. See Yannakakis, *Art of Being In-Between*, for background to Catholicism and political rule in Native communities of the Sierra Norte.
75. Mayor Juan B. Castellanos Morales to Governor Pedro Vásquez Colmenares, March 8, 1983, folder 41, San Juan Tabaá, Villa Alta (AGEPEO).
76. Castellanos Morales to Colmenares, March 8, 1983 (AGEPEO).
77. Juan B. Castellanos Morales et al., "Decree by the Community of San Juan Tabaá," March 7, 1983, file 143.1/Dirección Jurídica del Gobierno (AGEPEO).
78. Pablo Fabián Mendoza to Governor Pedro Vásquez Colmenares, March 9, 1983, file 143.1/Dirección Jurídica del Gobierno (AGEPEO).
79. As Mountz and Wright demonstrate in "Daily Life in a Transnational Migrant Community," and Gross depicts in "Farewell to Fiestas and Saints?," migrants are taxed at higher rates, are expected to make larger contributions to their home communities, and are often assigned the most prestigious and expensive cargo positions upon return to the community.
80. Pablo Fabián Mendoza to Governor Pedro Vásquez Colmenares, March 9, 1983, file 143.1/Dirección Jurídica del Gobierno (AGEPEO).
81. Juan B. Castellanos Morales to President Miguel de la Madrid Hurtado, March 22, 1983, file 143.1, collection: Dirección Jurídica del Gobierno (AGEPEO).
82. Castellanos Morales to President Miguel de la Madrid, March 22, 1983 (AGEPEO).
83. Castellanos Morales to President Miguel de la Madrid, March 22, 1983 (AGEPEO).
84. Gerardo Mendoza García, interview with author, Oaxaca City, Oaxaca, December 1, 2009.
85. Mendoza García, interview with author.
86. Mendoza García, interview with author.
87. Mendoza García, interview with author.
88. Ramón Urirre to Governor Pedro Vásquez Colmenares, May 26, 1983, 143.1/Dirección Jurídica del Gobierno (AGEPEO).
89. Pablo Fabián Mendoza to Governor Pedro Vásquez Colmenares, April 29, 1983, 143.1/Dirección Jurídica del Gobierno (AGEPEO).
90. Ramón Urirre to Governor Pedro Vásquez Colmenares, May 26, 1983, 143.1/Dirección Jurídica del Gobierno (AGEPEO).
91. Serafín Bautista Cruz et al., *Acta de San Juan Tabaá*, February 5, 1984, 143.1/Dirección Jurídica del Gobierno (AGEPEO).
92. Gerardo Mendoza García, interview with author, Oaxaca City, Oaxaca, December 1, 2009.
93. Mendoza García, interview with author.
94. Mendoza García, interview with author.
95. Mendoza García, interview with author.
96. Mendoza García, interview with author.
97. Mendoza García, interview with author.

98. See Nader, *Harmony Ideology,* for ethnography on customary law and social organization in a Zapotec community in the Sierra Norte.
99. Saúl Jiménez Crispin to Carballido González, Attorney General, Oaxaca, February 15, 1982, file: San Juan Juquila Mixes, Yautepec, Oaxaca, collection: Asuntos Agrarios (AGEPEO).
100. See Kearney, "Effects of Transnational Culture, Economy, and Migration," for a description of the political-geographic-symbolic space known as Oaxacalifornia.

Conclusion

1. Bascuti, *Luis Palau,* 111.
2. I walked past the Palau supporters each afternoon in the days leading up to the festival on the busy Calzada Niños Héroes.
3. "Más de 150 mil personas en festival con Luis Palau en México," Noticia Cristiana, November 27, 2008, http://www.noticiacristiana.com/iglesia/2008/11/mas-de-150-mil-personas-en-festival-con-luis-palau-en-mexico.html.
4. "Past Events," Luis Palau Association, http://legacy.palau.org/past-events/oaxaca-press-release.
5. See eduard1230, "Luis Palau en Oaxaca (el negocio de la fe) No apto para Cristianos Evangélicos," YouTube video, 2:55, posted November 16, 2008, https://www.youtube.com/watch?v=IIhhrsWIHLA. See also "Católicos en México cuestionan al predicador Luis Palau por dudoso manejo de recursos," Noticia Cristiana, November 12, 2008, http://www.noticiacristiana.com/iglesia/2008/11/catolicos-en-mexico-cuestionan-al-predicador-luis-palau-por-dudoso-manejo-de-recursos.html. For footage of the 2008 festival, see Luis Palau, "Festival Oaxaca-Huatulco Mexico," YouTube video, 5:13, February 2, 2017, https://www.youtube.com/watch?v=goVuyqmn2qA. Palau's recent festival in Manhattan's Central Park followed a similar pattern to his Oaxaca gathering; see Ileana Najarro, "Thousands Gather at Evangelical Event in Central Park," *New York Times,* July 11, 2015.
6. Isidoro Yescas, "Totalmente laicos," *Noticias,* September 14, 2010.
7. "El Comercio de la Fe: Ulises, PRI, Fanáticos Religiosos y su Abuelo: Los modernos fariseos en Oaxaca, México," ¡Todo el Poder al Pueblo!, November 19, 2008, http://todoelpoderalpueblo.blogspot.com/2008/11/el-comercio-de-la-fe-ulises-pri.html.
8. "Refrenda URO su respeto a las asociaciones civiles y religiosas," *Noticias,* November 12, 2008.
9. Luis Palau Association, "Luis Palau Reaches 150,000 in Southern Mexico," Oregon Faith Report, November 19, 2008, http://oregonfaithreport.com/2008/11/luis-palau-reach-150000-in-southern-mexico/.

10. "Más de 150 mil personas en festival con Luis Palau en México," Noticia Cristiana, November 27, 2008, http://www.noticiacristiana.com/iglesia/2008/11/mas-de-150-mil-personas-en-festival-con-luis-palau-en-mexico.html. "Católicos en México cuestionan al predicador Luis Palau por dudoso manejo de recursos," Noticia Cristiana, November 12, 2008, http://www.noticiacristiana.com/iglesia/2008/11/catolicos-en-mexico-cuestionan-al-predicador-luis-palau-por-dudoso-manejo-de-recursos.html.
11. Gill, "Politics of Regulating Religion in Mexico."
12. The year 1992, the five hundredth anniversary of Columbus's "discovery" of the Americas, was important for pan-indigenous organizing across the Americas. See Yashar, *Contesting Citizenship in Latin America*, for a discussion of how framing social movements by indigenous identities has been successful for movements in Bolivia and Ecuador.
13. Wortham, *Indigenous Media in Mexico*, 25–26; Nash, "Fiesta of the Word," 263, 267.
14. Speed and Collier, "Limiting Indigenous Autonomy in Chiapas," 883.
15. Anaya Muñoz, "Emergence and Development of the Politics of Recognition," 601.
16. Anaya Muñoz, "Emergence and Development of the Politics of Recognition," 606–7.
17. On the Ejército Popular Revolucionario (Popular Revolutionary Army) in Oaxaca and Guerrero, see Illades, *Conflict, Domination and Violence*, 69–70; Hector Tobar, "A Small Guerrilla Band Is Waging War in Mexico," *Los Angeles Times*, September 20, 2007; and Andrés Becerril, "ÉPR: una lucha de dos décadas; afirma tener presencia en todo el país," *Excélsior*, June 28, 2016.
18. "Ley de derechos de los pueblos y comunidades indígenas del estado de Oaxaca," http://www.diputados.gob.mx/comisiones/asunindi/oaxregla.pdf.
19. On usos y costumbres legislation in Oaxaca, see O'Connor, *Mixtec Evangelicals*, 7.
20. "Ley de derechos de los pueblos y comunidades indígenas del estado de Oaxaca," http://www.diputados.gob.mx/comisiones/asunindi/oaxregla.pdf.
21. Political Scientist Todd Eisenstadt explores the controversy over communitarian rights in *Politics, Identity, and Mexico's Indigenous Rights Movements*. He cites a 2010 study suggesting that 70 percent of Oaxaca's usos y costumbres communities do not permit women to vote in public asamblea (113).
22. Sociologist Kurt Bowen remarks, "Evangelical refusal to participate in tequio was an undeniable rebellion against a key element of traditional village life." Bowen, *Evangelism and Apostasy*, 188.
23. See Kahn, *All Religions Are Good in Tzintzuntzan*, for examples of positive Catholic-Protestant relations in Michoacán.
24. Saúl Jiménez Crispin to Justiniano Carballido González, Attorney General, Oaxaca, February 15, 1982, file: San Juan Juquila Mixes, Yautepec, Oaxaca, collection: Asuntos Agrarios (AGEPEO).

25. Jiménez Crispin to Carballido González, February 15, 1982 (AGEPEO).
26. David Martin, as quoted in Garrard-Burnett and Stoll, *Rethinking Protestantism in Latin America*, 285.
27. Daniel Hernández, "In Mexico Elections, PRI Makes Gains but Appears to Lose 3 Key States," *Los Angeles Times*, July 5, 2010; Louise Story and Alejandra Xanic von Bertrab, "Mexican Political Family Has Close Ties to Ruling Party, and Homes in the U.S.," *New York Times*, February 10, 2015.
28. Paulina Villegas and Elisabeth Malkin, "As Mexico Earthquake Aid Mounts, Many Fear It Will Be Diverted," *New York Times*, September 12, 2017.
29. Pew Research Center, *Religion in Latin America*, 7.
30. Pew Research Center, "Shifting Religious Identity of Latinos in the United States," 5.
31. Matovina, *Latino Catholicism*, 116–18. See also DeAnda, "History, Renewal and El Camino de La Leche," 141–43.

Bibliography

Archives and Research Libraries

Archivo del Poder Judicial de Oaxaca (APJO), Oaxaca City
    Juzgado de Tlacolula
Archivo General de la Nación (AGN), Mexico City
    Ramo Gobernación
    Ramo Presidentes
Archivo General del Poder Ejecutivo del Estado de Oaxaca (AGEPEO), Oaxaca City
    Dirección Jurídica y de Gobierno
    Pleitos Religiosos
    Asuntos Agrarios
    Asuntos Indígenas
Archivo Histórico de la Arquidiócesis de Oaxaca (AHAO), Oaxaca City
    Cartas Pastorales
    Obispos Mexicanos de la Región Pacífico Sur (OPASUR)
Biblioteca Francisco de Burgoa, Oaxaca City
    Luís Castañeda Guzmán Collection
Centro Coordinador Indigenista (CCI) Archive, Tlaxiaco, Oaxaca
    Acervo Documental
Centro de Investigaciones y Estudios Superiores en Antropología Social, (CIESAS), Unidad
    Pacífico Sur, Biblioteca Oaxaca City
    Salomón Nahmad Sitton (SNS) Archive
Comisión Nacional de Pueblos Indígenas de México (CDI/formerly INI)
    Archivo Histórico, Mexico City
    Biblioteca Juan Rulfo

Comisión Nacional de Pueblos Indígenas de México (CDI/formerly INI)
    Biblioteca Pública, Oaxaca City
Fundación Cultural Bustamante Vasconcelos, Oaxaca City
Hemeroteca de la Universidad Autónoma Benito Juárez de Oaxaca (UABJO)
Hemeroteca Nacional de México, Universidad Nacional Autónoma de México
    (UNAM), Mexico City
Hemeroteca Pública de Oaxaca Nestor Sánchez, Oaxaca City
Instituto Nacional de Estadística y Geografía (INEGI), Oaxaca City
Jaime Torres Bodet Library, Mitla, Oaxaca, Summer Institute of Linguistics Archive
National Security Archive (NSA), https://nsarchive.gwu.edu/
PEW Research Center http://www.pewforum.org/
Presbyterian Historical Society, Philadelphia
    Biographical Sketches of Ministers and Missionaries
Secretaría de Educación Pública (SEP), Mexico City
    Departamento de Educación Indígena
Tlacochahuaya Municipal Archive
    Acervo Documental
Tlaxiaco Municipal Archive
    Acervo Documental
University of Texas
    Nettie Lee Benson Latin American Collection
Yosondúa Municipal Archive
    Acervo Documental

Interviews

Cándido Coheto Martínez, interview with author, Oaxaca de Juárez, December 1, 2009
Elvira Cruz García, interview with author, Tlacochahuaya, Oaxaca, October 2, 2009
Pastor Jaime García, interview with author, Xoxocotlán, Oaxaca, March 15, 2010
Salomón Hernández Juárez, interview with author, Tlacochahuaya, Oaxaca, March 14, 2010
Bartolo Hernández López, interview with author, Yolotepec de la Paz, Oaxaca September 10, 2008
Ramón Hernández López, interview with author, San Agustín Tlacotepec, August 15, 2008
Barbara Hollenbach, e-mail message to author, July 25, 2009
Flaviano Nicolás López, interview with author, Yosondúa, Oaxaca, November 7, 2008
Telésforo López Llaguno, interview with author, Yatzachi el Bajo, Oaxaca, May 5, 2011
Enrique Marroquín, interview with author, Guadalajara, March 25, 2009
Carlos Martínez, interview with author, Tlacochahuaya, Oaxaca, September 30, 2009

Father Wilfrido Mayrén Peláez, interview with author, Xochimilco, Oaxaca, April 3, 2010
Gerardo Mendoza García, interview with author, Oaxaca de Juárez, December 1, 2009
Juan Carlos Reyes Gómez, interview with author, Oaxaca de Juárez, September 20, 2010
Joaquín Rodríguez Palacios, interview with author, Oaxaca de Juárez, September 10, 2010
Isidoro Santiago Ojeda, interview with author, Yosondúa, Oaxaca, September 15, 2010
Padre Ubi, interview with author, Colonia Xochimilco, Oaxaca City, April 2010

Newspapers and Periodicals

El Abogado Cristiano Ilustrado
Akron Beacon Journal
Annual Report of the Missionary Society, Sunday-School Union and Tract Society of the Methodist Episcopal Church
El Atalaya Bautista
Atlantic
Baptist Home Mission Monthly
Bisbee Daily Review
Boletín Oficial y Revista Eclesiástica de Antequera
Carteles del Sur
Christian Century
Christianity Today
Clarion-Ledger
Columbia
Commonweal
El Continental
Dallas Morning News
El Día: Vocero del Pueblo Mexicano
Economist
Excélsior
Florida Today
Fogonazo
Fort Myers News-Press
Gospel in All Lands
El Heraldo de Chiapas
Heraldo de México
La Hoja del Pueblo
El Imparcial
Index

El Informador
La Jornada
Latin American Herald Tribune
Living Church
Los Angeles Times
La Luz Bautista
Medical Missionary
Mexican Mining Journal
Missionary Monthly
El Nacional
New York Times
Northern Christian Advocate
Noticias
Nunda News
Oaxaca Gráfico
Oaxaca Herald
El Oaxaqueño
Origins
Palm Beach Post
Periódico Oficial del Gobierno del Estado de Oaxaca
Presbyterian Journal
Prescott Evening Courier
Proceso
Reader's Digest
El Sol de México
Spirit of Missions
Time
El Universal
La Victoria: Periódico Oficial del Gobierno del Estado de Oaxaca
La Voz de la Verdad
Washington Post

Published Sources

Abrams, Lynn. *Oral History Theory*. New York: Routledge, 2010.

Anaya Muñoz, Alejandro. "The Emergence and Development of the Politics of Recognition of Cultural Diversity and Indigenous Peoples' Rights in Mexico: Chiapas and Oaxaca in Comparative Perspective." *Journal of Latin American Studies* 37, no. 3 (August 2005): 585–610.

Anderson, Benedict. *Imagined Communities: Reflections on the Origin and Spread of Nationalism*. London: Verso, 1991.

Anderson, Justice C. *An Evangelical Saga: Baptists and Their Precursors in Latin America*. Longwood, FL: Xulon Press, 2005.

Arrom, Silvia Marina. *Volunteering for a Cause: Gender, Faith, and Charity in Mexico from the Reform to the Revolution*. Albuquerque: University of New Mexico Press, 2016.

Báez, Victoriano D. *Compendio de Historia de Oaxaca*. Oaxaca City: Talleres Tipográficos de Julián S. Soto, 1909.

Baldwin, Deborah. *Protestants and the Mexican Revolution: Missionaries, Ministers, and Social Change*. Urbana, IL: University of Illinois Press, 1990.

Bantjes, Adrian. "Idolatry and Iconoclasm in Revolutionary Mexico." *Mexican Studies/Estudios Mexicanos* 13, no. 1 (Winter 1997): 87–120.

Barabas, Alicia. *Dones, dueños y santos: Ensayo sobre religiones en Oaxaca*. México City: INAH, 2006.

Barabas, Alicia, and Miguel Bartolomé. "Los que se van al Norte: La migración indígena en Oaxaca." In *Dinámicas culturales: Religiones y migración en Oaxaca*, edited by Alicia Barabas and Miguel Bartolomé, 23–98. Oaxaca City: Centro INAH, 2010.

———. "Los sistemas normativos frente a las nuevas alternativas religiosas en Oaxaca." In *Dinámicas culturales: Religiones y migración en Oaxaca*, edited by Alicia Barabas and Miguel Bartolomé, 99–174. Oaxaca City: Centro INAH, 2010.

Barabas, Alicia, and Miguel Bartolomé, eds. *Dinámicas culturales: Religiones y migración en Oaxaca*. Oaxaca City: Centro INAH, 2010.

Barry, Tom. *Free Trade and the Farm Crisis in Mexico*. Boston: South End Press, 1995.

Bartolomé, Miguel. *Procesos interculturales: Antropología del pluralismo cultural en América Latina*. México City: Siglo XXI Editores, 2006.

Bartolomé, Miguel, Guillermo Bonfil Batalla, and Victor Daniel Bonilla. "The Declaration of Barbados: For the Liberation of the Indians." *Current Anthropology* 14, no. 3 (June 1973): 268–69.

Bascuti, Ellen. *Luis Palau: Evangelist to the World*. Uhrichsville, OH: Barbour Publishing, 2000.

Bastian, Jean-Pierre. "Disidencia religiosa en el campo mexicano." In *Religión y Política en México*, 177–92. San Diego: Centro de Estudios México-Estados Unidos, 1985.

———. *La mutación religiosa de América Latina*. México City: Fondo de Cultura Económica, 1997.

———. *Los Disidentes: Sociedades Protestantes y Revolución en México, 1872–1911*. México City: Fondo de Cultura Económica, 1989.

———. *Protestantismo y sociedad en México*. México City: Casa Unida de Publicaciones, 1983.

Beaver, R. Pierce. *American Protestant Women in World Mission: A History of the First Feminist Movement in North America*. Grand Rapids, MI: Eerdmans, 1968.

Becker, Marjorie. *Setting the Virgin on Fire: Lázaro Cárdenas, Michoacán Peasants, and the Redemption of the Mexican Revolution*. Berkeley: University of California Press, 1995.

Beezley, William H. "Creating a Revolutionary Culture: Vasconcelos, Indians, Anthropologists, and Calendar Girls." In *A Companion to Mexican History and Culture*, edited by William H. Beezley, 420–38. Malden, MA: Wiley-Blackwell, 2011.

Benge, Janet, and Geoff Benge. *Cameron Townsend: Good News in Every Language*. Seattle: YWAM Publishing, 1998.

Benthall, Jonathan. "The Summer Institute of Linguistics." *Royal Anthropological Institute News* 53 (December 1982): 1–5.

Berryman, Phillip. *Liberation Theology*. Philadelphia: Temple University Press, 1987.

Bliss, Edwin. *A Concise History of Missions*. New York: Fleming H. Revell, 1897.

Boff, Leonardo. *Introducing Liberation Theology*. Maryknoll, NY: Orbis Books, 1987.

Bonfil Batalla, Guillermo. *México Profundo: Reclaiming a Civilization*. Austin: University of Texas Press, 1996.

Bonner, Arthur. *We Will Not Be Stopped: Evangelical Persecution, Catholicism and Zapatismo in Chiapas, Mexico*. Boca Raton, FL: Universal Publishers, 1998.

Borland, Katherine. "That's Not What I Said: Interpretive Conflict in Oral Narrative Research." In *The Oral History Reader*, edited by Robert Perks and Alistair Thomson, 320–33. New York: Routledge, 1998.

Bowen, Kurt. *Evangelism and Apostasy: The Evolution and Impact of Evangelicals in Modern Mexico*. Montreal: McGill-Queen's University Press, 1996.

Browning, Webster E. *Roman Christianity in Latin America*. Grand Rapids, MI: Fleming H. Revell Company, 1924.

Brusco, Elizabeth. *The Reformation of Machismo: Evangelical Conversion and Gender in Colombia*. Austin: University of Texas Press, 1995.

Butler, Inez M. "Un relato de la hechicería en los pueblos zapotecos de la sierra en el distrito de Villa Alta." *Tlalocan* 9 (1982): 249–55.

Butler, John Wesley. *History of the Methodist Episcopal Church in Mexico: Personal Reminiscences, Present Conditions and Future Outlook*. New York: The Methodist Book Concern, 1918.

Camp, Roderic Ai. *Crossing Swords: Politics and Religion in Mexico*. New York: Oxford University Press, 1997.

Campbell, Howard. *Zapotec Renaissance: Ethnic Politics and Cultural Revivalism in Southern Mexico*. Albuquerque: University of New Mexico Press, 1995.

Carey, Elaine. *Plaza of Sacrifices: Gender, Power and Terror in 1968 Mexico*. Albuquerque: University of New Mexico Press, 2005.

Caso, Alfonso. "Definición del indio y lo indio." *América Indígena* 8, no. 4 (1948): 239–47.

Chance, John K., and William B. Taylor. "Cofradías and Cargos: An Historical Perspective on the Mesoamerican Civil-Religious Hierarchy." *American Ethnologist* 12, no. 1 (1985): 1–26.

Chassen-López, Francie R. "Benito Juárez de Maza of Oaxaca." In *State Governors in the Mexican Revolution, 1910–1952: Portraits in Conflict, Courage and Corruption*, edited by Jurgen Buchenau and William Beezley, 19–42. New York: Rowman and Littlefield, 2009.

———. *From Liberal to Revolutionary Oaxaca: The View from the South, Mexico 1867–1911*. University Park: Pennsylvania State University Press, 2004.

Chesnut, R. Andrew. *Competitive Spirits: Latin America's New Religious Economy*. New York: Oxford University Press, 2007.

Clark, Francis E., and Harriet A. Clark. *The Gospel in Latin Lands: Outline Studies of Protestant Work in the Latin Countries of Europe and America*. New York: The MacMillan Company, 1909.

Cohen, Jeffrey H. *The Culture of Migration in Southern Mexico*. Austin: University of Texas Press, 2004.

———. "Transnational Migration in Rural Oaxaca, Mexico: Dependency, Development, and the Household." *American Anthropologist* 103, no. 4 (December 2001): 954–67.

Colby, Gerard, and Charlotte Dennett. *Thy Will Be Done: The Conquest of the Amazon, Nelson Rockefeller and Evangelism in the Age of Oil*. New York: HarperCollins, 1996.

Colegio de Etnólogos y Antropólogos Sociales. *Dominación Ideológica y Ciencia Social: El ILV en México*. México City: Nueva Cultura, 1979.

Consejo Episcopal Latino Americano (CELAM). *Sectas en América Latina*. Guatemala City: Imprenta Gutenberg, 1982.

Conzatti, Cassiano, and Lucius Smith. *Flora Sinóptica Mexicana*. Oaxaca, Mexico: Imprenta de Lorenzo San-German, 1896.

Cowan, George M. "Report of the Activities of the Summer Institute of Linguistics in México for the Year 1951." *Boletín Indigenista* 12, no. 2 (1952): 1–8.

Davis, Diane. *Urban Leviathan: Mexico City in the Twentieth Century*. Philadelphia: Temple University Press, 2010.

Davis, Marjorie. "Cuicatec Tales about Witchcraft." *Tlalocan* 4 (1963): 197–203.

Dawson, Alexander S. "From Models for the Nation to Model Citizens: Indigenismo and the 'Revindication' of the Mexican Indian, 1920–1940." *Journal of Latin American Studies* 30, no. 2 (May 1998): 279–308.

DeAnda, Neomi. "History, Renewal and El Camino de La Leche." In *Pentecostals and Charismatics in Latin American and Latino Communities*, edited by Néstor Medina and Sammy Alfaro, 141–56. New York: Palgrave and Macmillan, 2015.

de la Luz García, Deyssy Jael. *El Movimiento Pentecostal en México: La Iglesia de Dios, 1926–1948*. México City: La Editorial Manda, 2010.

de la Mora Rivas, Fernando. *100 Biografías de Pastores Bautistas Mexicanos*. México City: Convención Nacional Bautista de México, 2004.

de la Torre, Renée. *Los hijos de la luz: Discurso, identidad y poder en La Luz del Mundo*. Guadalajara: Universidad de Guadalajara, 2000.

Denetdale, Jennifer Nez. *Reclaiming Diné History*. Tucson: University of Arizona Press, 2007.

———. "Securing the Navajo National Boundaries: War, Patriotism, Tradition, and the Diné Marriage Act of 2005." *Wicazō Sa Review* 2, no. 2 (Fall 2009): 131–48.

Dennis, Philip A. *Intervillage Conflict in Oaxaca*. New Brunswick, NJ: Rutgers University Press, 1987.

Domínguez, Genaro. "Las demandas de los indios." In *INI 40 Años*, 261–64. México City: INI, 1988.

Doremus, Anne. "Indigenism, Mestizaje, and National Identity in Mexico during the 1940s and the 1950s." *Mexican Studies/Estudios Mexicanos* 17, no. 2 (Summer 2001): 375–402.

Dormady, Jason. *Primitive Revolution: Restorationist Religion and the Idea of the Mexican Revolution, 1940–1968*. Albuquerque: University of New Mexico Press, 2011.

Dow, James. "The Expansion of Protestantism in Mexico: An Anthropological View." *Anthropological Quarterly* 78, no. 4 (2005): 827–50.

Durand Alcántara, Carlos. *La lucha campesina en Oaxaca y Guerrero, 1978–1987*. Puebla, Mexico: Costa-Amic Editores, 1989.

Earl, Jennifer, and Katrina Kimport. *Digitally Enabled Social Change: Activism in the Internet Age*. Cambridge, MA: MIT Press, 2011.

Eber, Christine. "'Buscando una nueva vida': Liberation through Autonomy in San Pedro Chenalhó, 1970–1998." In *Mayan Lives, Mayan Utopias: The Indigenous Peoples of Chiapas and the Zapatista Rebellion*, edited by Jan Rus, 135–60. Lanham, MD: Rowman and Littlefield, 2003.

Eisenstadt, Todd A. *Politics, Identity, and Mexico's Indigenous Rights Movements*. New York: Cambridge University Press, 2011.

Eisenstadt, Todd A., and Viridiana Ríos. "Multicultural Institutions, Distributional Politics, and Postelectoral Mobilization in Indigenous Mexico." *Latin American Politics and Society* 56, no. 2 (2014): 70–92.

Espinosa, Gastón. "Brown Moses: Francisco Olazabal and Mexican American Pentecostal Healing in the Borderlands." In *Mexican American Religions: Spirituality, Activism, and Culture*, edited by Gastón Espinosa and Mario T. García, 263–95. Durham, NC: Duke University Press, 2008.

———. "'God Made a Miracle in My Life': Latino Pentecostal Healing in the Borderlands." In *Religion and Healing in America*, edited by Linda L. Barnes and Susan S. Sered, 123–38. New York: Oxford University Press, 2005.

———. *Latino Pentecostals in America: Faith and Politics in Action*. Cambridge, MA: Harvard University Press, 2014.

Fallaw, Ben. *Religion and State Formation in Postrevolutionary Mexico*. Durham, NC: Duke University Press, 2013.

Farris, Edwin. *Nuevo Testamento. En Mixteco de Yosondúa y en Español*. México City: World Home Bible League and Liga del Sembrador, 1988.

———. "A Syntactic Sketch of Yosondúa Mixtec." In *Studies in the Syntax of Mixtecan Languages*, edited by Henry Bradley and Barbara E. Hollenbach, 1–171. Dallas: Summer Institute of Linguistics and the University of Texas at Arlington, 1992.

Farris, Kathryn. *Diccionario básico del mixteco de Yosondúa, Oaxaca*. México City: Instituto Lingüístico de Verano, 2002.

Field, Les W. "Global Indigenous Movements: Convergence and Differentiation in the Face of the Twenty-First-Century State." In *Border Crossings: Transnational Americanist Anthropology*, edited by Kathleen S. Fine-Dare, 230–46. Lincoln: University of Nebraska Press, 2009.

———."Who Are the Indians? Reconceptualizing Indigenous Identity, Resistance, and the Role of Social Science in Latin America." *Latin America Research Review* 29, no. 3 (1994): 237–48.

Fox, Jonathan. "Indigenous Mexican Migrants." In *Beyond La Frontera: The History of Mexico-U. S. Migration*, edited by Mark Overmyer-Velázquez, 161–78. New York: Oxford University Press, 2011.

Fox, Jonathan, and Gaspar Rivera-Salgado, eds. *Indigenous Mexican Migrants in the United States*. La Jolla, CA: Center for U.S.-Mexican Studies, University of California–San Diego, 2004.

Fox, Jonathan, Gaspar Rivera, and Lynn Stephen. "Indigenous Rights and Self-Determination in Mexico." *Cultural Survival Quarterly* 23, no. 1 (Spring 1999): 23–26.

Foxe, John. *Foxe's Book of Martyrs: A History of the Lives, Sufferings, and Deaths of the Early Christian and Protestant Martyrs*. Newberry, FL: Bridge-Logos Publishers, 2001.

Freire, Paulo. *Pedagogy of the Oppressed*. New York: Herder and Herder, 1970.

Galeano, Eduardo. *Las venas abiertas de América Latina*. México City: Siglo CCI Editores, 1971.

Gallaher, Carolyn. "The Role of Protestant Missionaries in Mexico's Indigenous Awakening." *Bulletin of Latin American Research* 26, no. 1 (2007): 88–111.

Gamio, Manuel. "Consideraciones sobre el problema indígena en América." *América Indígena* 2, no. 2 (1942): 15–19.

———. "Dialogue on Indian Questions." *Boletín Indigenista* 14, no. 4 (1954): 233–39.

Ganuza, Juan Miguel. *Las Sectas nos Invaden*. Ediciones Paulinas, 1983.

García, Maria Cristina. *Seeking Refuge: Central American Migration to Mexico, the United States, and Canada*. Berkeley: University of California Press, 2006.

García Santiago, Eduardo. *Clases Sociales y Grupos Étnicos en Yosondúa*. INI, 1982.

Garduño, Blanca. *Misiones Culturales: los años utópicos, 1920–1938*. México City: Consejo Nacional para la Cultura y las Artes, 1999.

Garma Navarro, Carlos. *Protestantismo en una comunidad Totonaca de Puebla*. México City: Instituto Nacional Indigenista, 1987.

Garrard-Burnett, Virginia, ed. "'Like a Mighty Rushing Wind': The Growth of

Protestantism in Contemporary Latin America." In *Religion and Society in Latin America: Interpretive Essays from Conquest to Present*, edited by Lee M. Penyak and Walter J. Petry, 190–206. Maryknoll, NY: Orbis Books, 2009.

——. *On Earth as It Is in Heaven: Religion in Modern Latin America*. Wilmington, DE: Scholarly Resources, 2000.

——. *Protestantism in Guatemala: Living in the New Jerusalem*. Austin: University of Texas Press, 1998.

——. *Terror in the Land of the Holy Spirit: Guatemala under General Efrain Rios Montt, 1982–1983*. New York: Oxford University Press, 2011.

Garrard-Burnett, Virginia, and David Stoll, eds. *Rethinking Protestantism in Latin America*. Philadelphia: Temple University Press, 1993.

Gates, Marilyn. *In Default: Peasants, the Debt Crisis, and the Agricultural Challenge in Mexico*. Boulder, CO: Westview Press, 1993.

Gaxiola, Manuel J. *La serpiente y la paloma*. Pasadena, CA: W. Carey Library, 1970.

Gill, Anthony. "The Politics of Regulating Religion in Mexico: The 1992 Constitutional Reforms in Historical Context." *Journal of Church and State* 41, no. 4 (Autumn 1999): 761–94.

——. *Rendering unto Caesar: The Catholic Church and the State in Latin America*. Chicago: University of Chicago Press, 1998.

——. "The Struggle to Be Soul Provider: Catholic Responses to Protestant Growth in Latin America." In *Latin American Religion in Motion*, edited by Christian Smith and Joshua Prokopy, 16–41. New York: Routledge, 1999.

Gillingham, Paul, and Benjamin Smith. *Dictablanda: Politics, Work and Culture in Mexico, 1938–1968*. Durham, NC: Duke University Press, 2014.

Gilly, Adolfo. *El Cardenismo, una utopia Mexicana*. México City: Cal y Arena, 1994.

González Gary, Óscar. "Poder y presiones de la iglesia." In *México ante la crisis: El impacto social y cultural, las alternativas*, edited by Pablo González Casanova, 238–94. México City: Siglo XXI Press, 1985.

Graziano, Frank. *Miraculous Images and Votive Offerings in Mexico*. New York: Oxford University Press, 2016.

Greenberg, James B. "Sanctity and Resistance in Closed Corporate Indigenous Communities: Coffee Money, Violence, and Ritual Organization in Chatino Communities in Oaxaca." In *Class, Politics and Popular Religion in Mexico and Central America*, edited by Lynn Stephen and James Dow, 95–114. Society for Latin American Publication Series, vol. 10. Washington, DC: American Anthropological Association, 1990.

Gross, Toomas. "Farewell to Fiestas and Saints? Changing Catholic Practices in Contemporary Rural Oaxaca." *Journal of Ethnology and Folkloristics* 3, no. 1 (2009): 3–19.

——. "Pentecostal Congregations and Religious Competition in Rural Mexico." In *New Ways of Being Pentecostal in Latin America*, edited by Mark Lindhardt, 87–110. Lanham, MD: Lexington Books, 2016.

———. "Protestantism and Modernity: The Implications of Religious Change in Contemporary Rural Oaxaca." *Sociology of Religion* 64, no. 4 (2003): 479–98.
"Growing Repression in Mexico." *LADOC* 8, no. 2 (November/December 1977): 19–22.
Guerra Gómez, Manuel. *Las sectas y su invasión del mundo hispano: una guía.* Pamplona, Spain: Ediciones Universidad de Navarra, 2003.
Gutiérrez, Gustavo. *A Theology of Liberation.* Maryknoll, NY: Orbis Books, 1973.
Gutiérrez, Natividad. *Nationalist Myths and Ethnic Identities: Indigenous Intellectuals and the Mexican State.* Lincoln: University of Nebraska Press, 2015.
Hart, Laurie. "Story of the Wycliffe Translators: Pacifying the Last Frontiers." *NACLA* 10 (December 1973): 15–31.
Hartch, Todd. *Missionaries of the State: The Summer Institute of Linguistics, State Formation, and Indigenous Mexico, 1935–1985.* Tuscaloosa: University of Alabama Press, 2006.
———. *The Prophet of Cuernavaca: Ivan Illich and the Crisis of the West.* New York: Oxford University Press, 2015.
———. *The Rebirth of Latin American Christianity.* New York: Oxford University Press, 2014.
Harvey, Neil. *The Chiapas Rebellion: The Struggle for Land and Democracy.* Durham: Duke University Press, 1998.
Hayden, Tom. "In Chiapas." In *The Zapatista Reader*, edited by Tom Hayden, 93–96. New York: Nation Books, 2002.
Hefley, James, and Marti Hefley. *Uncle Cam: The Story of William Cameron Townsend.* Huntington Beach, CA: Wycliffe Bible Translators, 1984.
Hernández Hernández, Alberto. "El cambio religiosos en México: crecimiento y auge del pentecostalismo." In *Más Allá del Espíritu: Actores, Acciones y Prácticas en Iglesias Pentecostales*, edited by Carolina Rivera Farfán and Elizabeth Juárez Cerdi, 53–90. Zamora, México: El Colegio de Michoacán, 2007.
Hobsbawm, Eric. "Introduction: Inventing Traditions." In *The Invention of Tradition*, edited by Eric Hobsbawm and Terence Ranger, 1–14. Cambridge: Cambridge University Press, 1983.
Hurst, John Fletcher. *The History of Methodism.* New York: Eaton and Mains, 1904.
Hvalkof, Søren, and Peter Aaby. *Is God an American? An Anthropological Perspective on the Missionary Work of the Summer Institute of Linguistics.* Copenhagen: International Work Group for Indigenous Affairs, 1981.
Illades, Carlos. *Conflict, Domination and Violence: Episodes in Mexican Social History.* New York: Berghahn Books, 2017.
Instituto Nacional de Estadística y Geografía (INEGI). *Censo de Población y Vivienda*, 1895–2010.
Instituto Nacional Indigenista. *Los Mixtecos de la Sierra.* México City: INI, 1982.
Iverson, Peter, and Monty Roessel. *Diné: A History of the Navajos.* Albuquerque: University of New Mexico Press, 2002.

Jackson Albarran, Elena. *Seen and Heard in Mexico: Children and Revolutionary Cultural Nationalism*. Lincoln: University of Nebraska Press, 2015.

James, Daniel. *Doña María's Story: Life History, Memory, and Political Identity*. Durham, NC: Duke University Press, 2001.

Jennings, Justin, and Adam T. Sellen, eds. *Real Fake: The Story of a Zapotec Urn*. Toronto, Ontario: Royal Ontario Museum, 2018.

John Paul II. *John Paul II in Mexico: Collected Speeches*. New York: HarperCollins, 1979.

———. "The New Evangelization: Homily of Blessed John Paul II in Mexico." Veracruz, Mexico, 1990. Vatican website. http://www.jp2shrine.org/jp/en/ev/jpii.html.

Johnson, Don. "Some Common Allegations and Fine Answers." In *Best of Both Worlds: A Handbook in International Relations*, edited by Richard Pittman, 58–61. Waxhaw, NC: Summer Institute of Linguistics, 1988.

Joseph, Gilbert M., and Daniel Nugent, eds. *Everyday Forms of State Formation: Revolution and the Negotiation of Rule in Modern Mexico*. Durham, NC: Duke University Press, 1994.

Kahn, Peter. *All Religions Are Good in Tzintzuntzan: Evangelicals in Catholic Mexico*. Austin: University of Texas Press, 2003.

Kampwirth, Karen. *Women and Guerrilla Movements: Nicaragua, El Salvador, Chiapas, Cuba*. University Park: Pennsylvania State University Press, 2002.

Kearney, Michael. "The Effects of Transnational Culture, Economy, and Migration of Mixtec Ethnic Identity in Oaxacalifornia." In *The Bubbling Cauldron: Race, Ethnicity and the Urban Crisis*, edited by Michael Peter Smith, 226–43. Minneapolis: University of Minnesota Press, 1995.

———. "Transnational Oaxacan Indigenous Identity: The Case of Mixtecs and Zapotecs." *Identities* 7, no. 2 (2000): 173–95.

Kearney, Michael, and Federico Besserer. "Oaxacan Municipal Governance in Transnational Context." In *Indigenous Mexican Migrants in the United States*, edited by Jonathan Fox and Gaspar Rivera-Salgado, 449–66. La Jolla, CA: Center for US-Mexican Studies, 2004.

Kemper, Robert. "From Nationalism to Internationalism: The Development of Mexican Anthropology." In *The Social Contexts of American Ethnology*, edited by June Helm, 139–56. Washington, DC: Proceedings of the American Ethnological Society, 1984.

Kent, Eliza F. *Converting Women: Gender and Protestant Christianity in Colonial South India*. New York: Oxford University Press, 2004.

Keremitsis, Dawn. "Del metate al molino: la mujer mexicana de 1910 a 1940." In *Historia Mexicana* 33, no. 2 (October–December 1983): 285–302.

Kiddle, Amelia M., and María L. O. Muñoz, eds. "Introduction: Men of the People: Lázaro Cárdenas, Luis Echeverría, and Revolutionary Populism." In *Populism in Twentieth Century Mexico: The Presidencies of Lázaro Cárdenas and Luis*

Echeverría, edited by Amelia M. Kiddle and María L. O. Muñoz, 1–14. Tucson: University of Arizona Press, 2010.

———. *Populism in Twentieth Century Mexico: The Presidencies of Lázaro Cárdenas and Luis Echeverría*. Tucson: University of Arizona Press, 2010.

Klaiber, Jeffrey. *The Church, Dictatorships, and Democracy in Latin America*. Eugene, OR: Wipf and Stock Publishers, 2009.

Knight, Alan. "Cardenismo: Juggernaut or Jalopy?" *Journal of Latin American Studies* 26 (1994): 73–107.

———. "Racism, Revolution, and Indigenismo." In *The Idea of Race in Latin America*, edited by Richard Graham, 71–113. Austin: University of Texas Press, 1990.

———. "Revolutionary Anticlericalism." In *Faith and Impiety in Revolutionary Mexico*, edited by Matthew Butler, 21–56. New York: Palgrave Macmillan, 2007.

———. "The Weight of the State in Modern Mexico." In *Studies in the Formation of the Nation-State in Latin America*, edited by James Dunkerley, 212–53. London: ILAS, 2002.

Larumbe, Gloria. "Así era Oaxaca." In *De Papeles Mudos a Melodías Sonaras: La Música en la Catedral de Oaxaca*. Oaxaca City: Lito-Grapo, 1998.

Leal, Alicia. "La visita de Lázaro Cárdenas." In *Cuando Cárdenas Visitó Nuestro Pueblo*. México City: Instituto Lingüístico del Verano, 1980.

Leal, Otis. *Mary: A Tribute to God's Work in One of His Servants*. Garden Grove, CA: Otis Leal, 1997.

———. "Problems in Zapotec Translation." *Bible Translator* 2 (1951): 164–66.

———. "That Each May Hear in His Own Tongue: The Task of Translating the Bible Is Not Always Easy." *Presbyterian Guardian* (December 1947): 340.

Leal, Otis, and Mary Leal. "Noun Possession in Villa Alta Zapotec." *International Journal of American Linguistics* 20 (1954): 215–16.

Lee, Joseph. *The Bible and the Gun: Christianity in South China, 1860–1900*. New York: Routledge, 2003.

Lehmann, Hartmut. "Friends and Foes: The Formation and Consolidation of the Protestant Ethic Thesis." In *The Protestant Ethic Turns 100: Essays on the Centenary of the Weber Thesis*, edited by William H. Swatos Jr. and Lutz Kaelber, 1–22. New York: Routledge, 2005.

Lenti, Joseph U. *Redeeming the Revolution: The State and Organized Labor in Post-Tlatelolco Mexico*. Lincoln: University of Nebraska Press, 2017.

Levine, Daniel, ed. *Religion and Political Conflict in Latin America*. Chapel Hill: University of North Carolina Press, 1986.

Lewis, Laura A. *Hall of Mirrors: Power, Witchcraft and Caste in Colonial Mexico*. Durham, NC: Duke University Press, 2003.

Lewis, Stephen E. "Mexico's National Indigenist Institute and the Negotiation of Applied Anthropology in Highland Chiapas, 1951–1954." *Ethnohistory* 55, no. 4 (Fall 2008): 609–32.

Lindhardt, Mark, ed. *New Ways of Being Pentecostal in Latin America*. Lanham, MD: Lexington Books, 2016.

Lipp, Frank J. *The Mixe of Oaxaca: Religion, Ritual, and Healing*. Austin: University of Texas Press, 1991.

Loewe, Ronald. *Maya or Mestizo? Nationalism, Modernity and its Discontents*. Toronto: University of Toronto Press, 2011.

Lona Reyes, Arturo. "Violence against the Indians in Oaxaca." *Estudios Indígenas* 3, no. 4 (December 1978): 32–34.

López Trujillo, Alfonso. "Declaration of Los Andes." In *Religion in Latin America: A Documentary History*, edited by Lee M. Penyak and Walter J. Petry, 314–16. Maryknoll, NY: Orbis Books, 2006.

MacNabb, Valerie Ann, and Martha W. Rees. "Liberation or Theology? Ecclesial Base Communities in Oaxaca, Mexico." *Journal of Church and State* 25 (Autumn 1993): 723–49.

Mallon, Florencia. *Courage Tastes of Blood: The Mapuche Community of Nicolás Ailío and the Chilean State, 1906–2001*. Durham, NC: Duke University Press, 2005.

Mantecón, Verónica Vázquez. "Lázaro Cárdenas en la memoria colectiva." *Política y cultura* 31 (2009): 183–209.

Marroquín, Enrique. *El Botín Sagrado: La Dinámica Religiosa en Oaxaca*. Oaxaca City: UABJO, 1992.

———. *El Conflicto Religioso: Oaxaca, 1976–1992*. México City: Universidad Nacional Autónoma de México, 2007.

Martin, David. *Tongues of Fire: The Explosion of Protestantism in Latin America*. Oxford: Blackwell Press, 1993.

Martínez Cruz, Juventino, and Edwin Farris, eds. *Cuando Cárdenas Visitó Nuestro Pueblo*. México City: Instituto Lingüístico de Verano, 1980.

Martínez Novo, Carmen. *Who Defines Indigenous?* New Brunswick, NJ: Rutgers University Press, 2006.

Marx, Karl. *The Communist Manifesto*. New York: W. W. Norton & Company, 1988.

Matovina, Timothy. *Latino Catholicism: Transformation in America's Largest Church*. Princeton, NJ: Princeton University Press, 2011.

McAdam, Doug, John D. McCarthy, and Mayer N. Zald, eds. *Comparative Perspectives on Social Movements: Political Opportunities, Mobilizing Structures, and Cultural Framings*. New York: Cambridge University Press, 1996.

McIntosh, John. "Activities of the Summer Institute of Linguistics for the Year 1953." *Boletín Indigenista* 14, no. 2 (1954): 1–7.

Meyer, Jean. *El conflicto religioso en Oaxaca, 1926–1938*. Oaxaca City: UABJO, 2006.

———. *The Cristero Rebellion: The Mexican People between Church and State, 1926–1929*. New York: Cambridge University Press, 2008.

———. "Religious Conflict and Catholic Resistance in 1930s Oaxaca." In *Faith and Impiety in Revolutionary Mexico*, edited by Matthew Butler, 185–201. New York: Palgrave Macmillan, 2007.

Middlebrook, Kevin J. *The Paradox of Revolution: Labor, the State and Authoritarianism in Mexico*. Baltimore: Johns Hopkins University Press, 1995.

Miller, Walter S. *Cuentos Mixes*. México City: INI, 1956.

———. "El tonalamatl mixe y los hongos sagrados." In *Summa Antropológica*, edited by Antonio Pompa and Pompa, 317–28. México City: Instituto Nacional de Antropología e Historia, 1966.

Moksnes, Heidi. *Maya Exodus: Indigenous Struggle for Citizenship in Chiapas*. Norman: University of Oklahoma Press, 2012.

Mondragón, Carlos. *Like Leaven in the Dough: Protestant Social Thought in Latin America, 1920–1950*. Madison, NJ: Fairleigh Dickinson Press, 2010.

Montes García, Olga. "Las dinámicas de los conflictos religiosos en Oaxaca, 1975–1992." *Sociología* 14, no. 41 (September–December 1999): 157–79.

———. "Los conflictos religiosos en Oaxaca: una aproximación a su estudio." In *Persecución Religiosa en Oaxaca? Los Nuevos Movimientos Religiosos*, edited by Enrique Marroquín, 28–35. México City: Instituto Oaxaqueño de las Culturas, Instituto de Investigaciones Sociológicas de la UABJO, 1995.

Mountz, Alison, and Richard Wright. "Daily Life in the Transnational Migrant Community of San Agustín Yatareni and Poughkeepsie, New York." *Diaspora* 5, no. 3 (Winter 1996): 403–28.

Muñoz, María L. O. "Populism, Indigenismo, and Indigenous Mobilization." In *Populism in Twentieth Century Mexico*, edited by Amelia M. Kiddle and María L. O. Muñoz, 122–34. Tucson: University of Arizona Press, 2010.

———. *Stand Up and Fight: Participatory Indigenismo, Populism, and Mobilization in Mexico, 1970–1984*. Tucson: University of Arizona Press, 2016.

Nader, Laura. *Harmony Ideology: Justice and Control in a Zapotec Mountain Town*. Stanford, CA: Stanford University Press, 1991.

Nagengast, Carole, and Michael Kearney. "Mixtec Ethnicity: Social Identity, Political Consciousness and Political Activism." *Latin American Research Review* 25, no. 2 (1990): 61–91.

Nahmad Sittón, Salomón. "Oaxaca y el CIESAS: Una experiencia hacia una nueva antropología." *América Indígena* 50, no. 2–3 (April–September 1996): 11–32.

Nash, June. "The Fiesta of the Word: The Zapatista Uprising and Radical Democracy in Mexico." *American Anthropologist* 99, no. 2 (June 1997): 261–74.

———. "Protestantism in an Indian Village in the Western Highlands of Guatemala." *Alpha Kappa Deltan: A Sociological Journal* (Winter 1960): 49–53.

Newcomer, Daniel. *Reconciling Modernity: Urban State Formation in 1940s León, Mexico*. Lincoln: University of Nebraska Press, 2004.

Nolasco, Margarita. "Educación Indígena, una experiencia en Oaxaca." In *México Indígena INI: 30 Años Después*. México City: Instituto Nacional Indigenista, 1978.

Norget, Kristin. "Progressive Theology and Popular Religiosity in Oaxaca, Mexico." *Ethnology* 36, no. 1 (Winter 1997): 67–83.

———. "Progressive Theology and Popular Religiosity in Oaxaca, Mexico." In *Latin American Religion in Motion*, edited by Christian Smith and Joshua Prokopy, 88–107. New York: Routledge Press, 1999.

Oak, Sung-Deuk. *The Making of Korean Christianity: Protestant Encounters with Korean Religions, 1876–1915*. Waco, TX: Baylor University Press, 2013.

Occhipinti, Laurie A. *Making a Difference in a Globalized World: Short-Term Missions That Work*. Lanham, MD: Rowman and Littlefield Press, 2014.

Ochoa Zazueta, Jesús Ángel. "El Instituto Lingüístico de Verano." *Cuadernos de Trabajo Estudios* 11 (1975): 78–81.

O'Connor, Mary I. *Mixtec Evangelicals: Globalization, Migration, and Religious Change in a Oaxacan Indigenous Group*. Boulder: University Press of Colorado, 2016.

Olcott, Jocelyn. "The Politics of Opportunity: Mexican Populism under Lázaro Cárdenas and Luis Echeverría." In *Gender and Populism in Latin America: Passionate Politics*, edited by Karen Kampwirth, 25–46. University Park: Pennsylvania State University Press, 2010.

———. *Revolutionary Women in Postrevolutionary Mexico*. Durham, NC: Duke University Press, 2005.

O'Neill, Kevin Lewis. *City of God: Christian Citizenship in Postwar Guatemala*. Berkeley: University of California Press, 2010.

———. *Secure the Soul: Christian Piety and Gang Prevention in Guatemala*. Oakland: University of California Press, 2015.

Orozco, Monica. "Not to Be Called Christian: Protestant Perceptions of Catholicism in Nineteenth Century Latin America." In *Religion and Society in Latin America: Interpretive Essays from Conquest to Present*, edited by Lee M. Penyak, 175–90. Maryknoll, NY: Orbis Books, 2009.

Overmyer-Velázquez, Mark, ed. *Beyond la Frontera: The History of Mexico-U. S. Migration*. New York: Oxford University Press, 2011.

———. *Visions of the Emerald City*. Durham, NC: Duke University Press, 2006.

Overmyer-Velázquez, Rebecca. *Folkloric Poverty: Neoliberal Multiculturalism in Mexico*. College Station: Pennsylvania State University Press, 2010.

Pallares, Amalia. *Peasant Struggles to Indigenous Resistance: The Ecuadorian Andes in the Late Twentieth Century*. Norman: University of Oklahoma Press, 2002.

Parmenter, Ross. *Lawrence in Oaxaca*. Layton, UT: Peregrine Smith Books, 1984.

Patterson, Frank W. *A Century of Baptist Work in Mexico*. El Paso, TX: Baptist Spanish Publishing House, 1979.

Paul, Doris A. *The Navajo Code Talkers*. Pittsburgh: Dorrance Books, 2003.

Paul VI. *Evangelii Nuntiandi*. Vatican website. December 8, 1975, http.//w2.vatican.va/content/paul-vi/en/apost_exhortations/documents/hf_p-vi_exh_19751208_evangelii-nuntiandi.html.

Perea, Francisco. *El Papa en México: Presencia y mensaje de Juan Pablo II*. México City: Editorial Diana, 1979.

Pérez, Gloria, and Scott S. Robinson. *La misión detras de la misión.* México City. Centro de Estudios Económicos y Sociales del Tercer Mundo, 1983.

Petersen, Douglas. "The Azusa Street Mission and Latin American Pentecostalism." *International Bulletin of Missionary Research* 30, no. 2 (April 2006): 66–67.

Peterson, Anna L., and Manuel A. Vásquez. "The New Evangelization in Latin American Perspective." *Cross Currents* 48, no. 3 (Fall 1998): 311–29.

Pew Research Center. *Religion in Latin America: Widespread Change in a Historically Catholic Region.* November 13, 2014. http://www.pewforum.org/2014/11/13/religion-in-latin-america/.

——. *The Shifting Religious Identity of Latinos in the United States.* May 17, 2014. http://www.pewforum.org/2014/05/07/the-shifting-religious-identity-of-latinos-in-the-united-states/.

Pike, Eunice. "Texts on Mazatec Food Witchcraft." *Tlalocan* 7 (1949): 287–94.

——. "William Cameron Townsend." In *Vigésimo-quinto Aniversario del Instituto Lingüístico de Verano,* edited by Benjamin F. Elson and Juan Comas, 3–8. México City: La Tipográfica Indena Cuernavaca, 1961.

Pontifical Council for the Family. "Reflection by Cardinal Alfonso López Trujillo on the 25th Anniversary of the Puebla Conference." Vatican website. http.//www.vatican.va/roman_curia/pontifical_councils/family/documents/rc_pc_family_doc_20040212_trujillo-puebla_en.html.

Pool, Stafford. *The Guadalupan Controversies in Mexico.* Stanford, CA: Stanford University Press, 2006.

Poole, Deborah. "An Image of 'Our Indian': Type Photographs and Racial Sentiments in Oaxaca, 1920–1940." *Hispanic American Historical Review* 84, no. 1 (February 2004): 37–82.

Purnell, Jennie. *Popular Movements and State Formation in Revolutionary Mexico: The Agraristas and Cristeros of Michoacán.* Durham, NC: Duke University Press, 1999.

Quinones, Sam. *True Tales from Another Mexico: The Lynch Mob, the Popsicle Kings, Chalino, and the Bronx.* Albuquerque: University of New Mexico Press, 2001.

Ramírez, Daniel. *Migrating Faith: Pentecostalism in the United States and Mexico in the Twentieth Century.* Chapel Hill: University of North Carolina Press, 2015.

Rankin, Melinda. *Twenty Years among the Mexicans: A Narrative of Missionary Labor.* Cincinnati: Central Book Concern, 1881.

Ratzinger, Joseph. "Instruction on Certain Aspects of the Theology of Liberation," 1984. Vatican website. http.//www.vatican.va/roman_curia/congregations/cfaith/documents/rc_con_cfaith_doc_19840806_theology-liberation_en.html.

Reuque Paillalef, Rosa Isolde, and Florencia Mallon. *When a Flower Was Reborn: The Life and Times of a Mapuche Feminist.* Durham, NC: Duke University Press, 2002.

Ricard, Robert. *The Spiritual Conquest of Mexico.* Berkeley: University of California Press, 1974.

Rivera Farfán, Carolina. *Diversidad religiosa y conflicto en Chiapas: Intereses, utopías y realidades*. México City: Universidad Nacional Autónoma de México, 2005.

Rivera-Salgado, Gaspar. "Transnational Political Strategies: The Case of Mexican Indigenous Migrants." In *Immigration Research for a New Century: Multidisciplinary Perspectives*, edited by Nancy Foner, 134–56. New York: Russel Sage Foundation, 2000.

———. "Welcome to Oaxacalifornia." *Cultural Survival Quarterly* 23, no. 1 (Spring 1999): 59–61.

Robeck, Cecil. *The Azusa Street Mission and Revival*. Nashville, TN: Thomas Nelson, 2006.

Rourke, Thomas R. *The Roots of Pope Francis's Social and Political Thought: From Argentina to the Vatican*. Lanham, MD: Rowman and Littlefield, 2016.

Rubin, Jeffrey. *Decentering the Regime: Ethnicity, Radicalism and Democracy in Juchitán, Mexico*. Durham, NC: Duke University Press, 1997.

Rudd, Margaret. *A Practical Mystic: A. B. Rudd*. Annandale, VA: Charles Baptie Studios, 1987.

Ruiz Guerra, Rubén. *New People: Methodism and Modernization in Mexico, 1873 to 1930*, translated by Daniel R. Miller. Grand Rapids, MI: Calvin College for Christian Scholarship, 2013.

Ruíz-Navarro, Patricia. "New Guadalupanos: Mexican Immigrants, a Grassroots Organization, and a Pilgrimage to New York." In *Gender, Religion, and Migration: Pathways of Integration*, edited by Bonifacio Glaenda Tibe and Vivienne S. M. Angeles. Lanham, MD: Lexington Books, 2010.

Saldaña, Ángel. *De sectas a sectas: una aproximación al estudio de un fenómeno apasionante*. Oaxaca City: UABJO, 1987.

Sámano Rentería, Miguel Ángel. "El Indigenismo institucionalizado en México (1936–2000): un análisis." In *La construcción del Estado nacional: democracia, justicia, paz y Estado de derecho*, edited by José Emilio Rolando Ordoñez Cifuentes, 141–55. México City: Instituto de Investigaciones Jurídicas, UNAM, 2004.

Sánchez, Héctor. "A New Era in the Department of Indian Affairs." *Boletín Indigenista* 3 (1948).

Schmitt, Karl. "American Protestant Missionaries and the Díaz Regime in Mexico: 1876–1911." *Journal of Church and State* 25, no. 2 (Spring 1983): 253–77.

Schwaller, John F. *The History of the Catholic Church in Latin America: From Conquest to Revolution and Beyond*. New York: NYU Press, 2011.

Scott, James C. "Prestige as the Public Discourse of Domination." *Cultural Critique* 12 (Spring 1989): 145–66.

Scott, Lindy. *Salt of the Earth: A Socio-Political History of Mexico City Evangelical Protestants, 1964–1991*. México City: Editorial Kyrios, 1991.

Secretario de Desarrollo Urbano y Ecología. *Oaxaca. monumentos del centro histórico, patrimonio cultural de la humaniad*. México City: Secretaría de Desarrollo Urbano y Ecológica, 1987.

Sheppard, Randal. *A Persistent Revolution: History, Nationalism, and Politics in Mexico since 1968.* Albuquerque: University of New Mexico Press, 2016.

Sherman, Amy. *The Soul of Development.* New York: Oxford University Press, 1997.

Sierra, Justo. *Juárez, su obra y su tiempo.* México City: Universidad Nacional Autónoma de México, 2006.

Sigmund, Paul E. *Liberation Theology at the Crossroads.* New York: Oxford University Press, 1990.

Silletta, Alfredo. *Las Sectas Invaden La Argentina.* Buenos Aires: Editorial Contrapunto, 1986.

Simon, Joel. "Crisis in el Campo." In *Endangered Mexico: An Environment on the Edge*, 35–59. San Francisco: Sierra Club Books, 1997.

Siverts, Henning. "Ethnic Stability and Boundary Dynamics in Southern Mexico." In *Ethnic Groups and Boundaries: The Social Organization of Culture Difference*, edited by Fredrik Barth, 101–16. Long Grove, IL: Waveland Press, 1998.

Slocum, Marianna, and Sam Holmes, eds. "Airman's Halo." In *Who Brought the Word*, edited by Marianna Slocum and Sam Homes, 38–41. Santa Ana, CA: Wycliffe Bible Translators, 1963.

———. *Who Brought the Word.* Santa Ana, CA: Wycliffe Bible Translators, 1963.

Smith, Benjamin T. "Anticlericalism, Politics, and Freemasonry in Mexico, 1920–1940." *The Americas* 65, no. 4 (April 2009): 559–88.

———. *Pistoleros and Popular Movements: The Politics of State Formation in Postrevolutionary Oaxaca.* Lincoln: University of Nebraska Press, 2009.

Smith, Christian. *The Emergence of Liberation Theology.* Chicago: University of Chicago Press, 1991.

———. Introduction to *Latin American Religion in Motion*, edited by Christian Smith and Joshua Prokopy, 1–15. New York: Routledge, 1999.

Smith, Paul W., and Dorothy L. Smith. *One More Mountain to Climb.* Fairfax, VA: Xulon Press, 2002.

Snow, David A., ed. *The Blackwell Companion to Social Movements.* Malden, MA: Wiley-Blackwell, 2007.

Speed, Shannon, and Jane F. Collier. "Limiting Indigenous Autonomy in Chiapas, Mexico: The Government's Use of Human Rights." *Human Rights Quarterly* 22, no. 4 (2000): 877–905.

Stahler-Sholk, Richard. "Resisting Neoliberal Homogenization: The Zapatista Autonomy Movement." *Latin American Perspectives* 34, no. 2 (March 2007): 48–63.

Starr, Frederick. *In Indian Mexico: A Narrative of Travel and Labor.* Chicago: Forbes & Company, 1908.

Steigenga, Timothy J. "The Politics of Pentecostalized Religion: Conversion as Pentecostalization in Guatemala." In *Conversion of a Continent: Contemporary Religious Change in Latin America*, 256–79. New Brunswick, NJ: Rutgers University Press, 2007.

Steigenga, Timothy J., and Edward L. Cleary. *Conversion of a Continent:*

Contemporary Religious Change in Latin America. New Brunswick, NJ: Rutgers University Press, 2007.

Stephen, Lynn. "The Creation and Re-Creation of Ethnicity: Lessons from the Zapotec and Mixtec of Oaxaca." *Latin American Perspectives* 23, no. 2 (Spring 1996): 17–37.

———. *Transborder Lives: Indigenous Oaxacans in Mexico, California, and Oregon*. Durham, NC: Duke University Press, 2007.

———. *We Are the Face of Oaxaca: Testimony and Social Movements*. Durham, NC: Duke University Press, 2013.

———. *¡Zapata Lives! Histories and Cultural Politics in Southern Mexico*. Berkeley: University of California Press, 2002.

———. *Zapotec Women: Gender, Class, and Ethnicity in Globalized Oaxaca*. Durham, NC: Duke University Press, 2005.

Steven, Hugh, ed. *Doorway to the World: The Mexico Years. The Memoirs of W. Cameron Townsend, 1934–1947*. Wheaton, IL: Harold Shaw Publishers, 2000.

———. *A Thousand Trails: Personal Journal of William Cameron Townsend, 1917–1919*. White Rock, British Columbia: Credo Publishing, 1984.

Stolen, Kristi Anne. *Guatemalans in the Aftermath of Violence: The Refugees' Return*. Philadelphia: University of Pennsylvania Press, 2007.

Stoll, David. *Fishers of Men or Founders of Empire?: The Wycliffe Bible Translators in Latin America*. London: Zed Press, 1982.

———. *Is Latin America Turning Protestant? The Politics of Evangelical Growth*. Berkeley: University of California Press, 1990.

———. Review of James W. Dow and Alan R. Sandstrom, eds., *Holy Saints and Fiery Preachers: The Anthropology of Protestantism in Mexico and Central America*. In *The Journal of the Royal Anthropological Institute* 9, no. 3 (September 2003): 595–96.

———. "The Summer Institute of Linguistics and Indigenous Movements." *Latin American Perspectives* 9, no. 2 (1982): 84–99.

Svelmoe, William Lawrence. *A New Vision for Missions: William Cameron Townsend, the Wycliffe Bible Translators, and the Culture of Early Evangelical Faith Missions, 1896–1945*. Tuscaloosa: University of Alabama Press, 2008.

Teichman, Judith. *Policy-making in Mexico: From Boom to Crisis*. Boston: Allen & Unwin, 1988.

Terraciano, Kevin. *The Mixtecs of Colonial Oaxaca: Ñudzahui History, Sixteenth through Eighteenth Centuries*. Stanford, CA: Stanford University Press, 2001.

Townsend, Camilla. "Burying the White Gods: New Perspectives on the Conquest of Mexico." *American Historical Review* 108, no. 3 (June 2003): 659–87.

Townsend, William C. *Lázaro Cárdenas: Mexican Democrat*. Waxhaw, NC: Summer Institute of Linguistics, 1979.

———. "Tribes, Tongues and Translators." In *Who Brought the Word*, edited by Marianna Slocum and Sam Holmes, 7–8. Santa Ana, CA: Wycliffe Bible Translators, 1963.

———. *The Truth about Mexico's Oil: As Observed by W. Cameron Townsend*. México City: Ocampo Hermanos, 1940.
Treviño Osuna, Alejandro. *Historia de los trabajos Bautistas en México*. El Paso, TX: Casa Bautista de Publicaciones, 1939.
United Nations. *The Universal Declaration of Human Rights, 1948–1998*. New York: United Nations Dept. of Public Information, 1998.
Valencia, Eliecer. *Guatemalan Refugees in Mexico, 1980–1984*. New York: Americas Watch Committee, 1984.
Van De Donk, William, ed. *Cyberprotest: New Media, Citizens, and Social Movements*. New York: Routledge, 2004.
VanWey, Leah K., Catherine M. Tucker, and Eileen Diaz McConnell. "Community Organization, Migration and Remittances in Oaxaca." *Latin American Research Review* 40, no. 1 (February 2005): 83–107.
Varese, Stefano. "Memories of Solidarity: Anthropology and the Indigenous Movements in Latin America." *Cultural Survival Quarterly* 21, no. 3 (Fall 1997): 23–26.
Vaughan, Mary Kay. *Cultural Politics in Revolution: Teachers, Peasants, and Schools in Mexico, 1930–1940*. Tucson: University of Arizona Press, 1997.
Vázquez, Apolonio. *Los que sembraron con lágrimas: Apuntes históricos del presbiterianismo en México*. México City: El Faro, 1985.
Velásquez, María Cristina. "Migrant Communities, Gender, and Political Power in Oaxaca." In *Indigenous Mexican Migrants in the United States*, edited by Jonathan Fox and Gaspar Rivera-Salgado, 483–94. La Jolla, CA: Center for US-Mexican Studies, 2004.
Wallis, Ethel, and Mary Bennett. *Two Thousand Tongues to Go: The Adventures of the Wycliffe Bible Translators throughout the World Today*. London: Hodder and Stoughton, 1966.
Warman, Arturo, Margarita Nolasco, Guillermo Bonfil, Mercedes Olivera, and Enrique Valencia. *De eso que llaman antropología mexicana*. México City: Editorial Nuestro Tiempo, 1970.
Warren, Kay B. *Indigenous Movements and Their Critics: Pan-Maya Activism in Guatemala*. Princeton, NJ: Princeton University Press, 1998.
———. "Indigenous Movements as a Challenge to the Unified Social Movement Paradigm for Guatemala." In *Cultures of Politics, Politics of Cultures*, edited by Sonia E. Alvarez, Evelina Dagnino, and Arturo Escobar, 165–95. Boulder, CO: Westview Press, 1998.
Weber, Max. *The Protestant Ethic and the Spirit of Capitalism*. London: Penguin, 2002.
Wheeler, W. Reginald. *Modern Missions in Mexico*. Philadelphia: Westminster Press, 1925.
Whitt, Joseph A., Jr. "The Mexican Peso Crisis." *Economic Review* 81, no. 1 (1996): 1–20.

Wilson, Bryan R. *The Social Dimensions of Sectarianism: Sects and New Religious Movements in Contemporary Society*. Oxford: Oxford University Press, 1990.

Wortham, Erica. *Indigenous Media in Mexico: Culture, Community, and the State*. Durham, NC: Duke University Press, 2013.

Wright, N. Pelham. "Gift of Tongues." *Américas* 10 (April 1958): 18–20.

Wright-Rios, Edward. *Revolutions in Mexican Catholicism: Reform and Revelation in Oaxaca, 1887–1934*. Durham, NC: Duke University Press, 2009.

Yannakakis, Yanna. *The Art of Being In-Between: Native Intermediaries, Indian Identity, and Local Rule in Colonial Oaxaca*. Durham, NC: Duke University Press, 2008.

Yashar, Deborah J. *Contesting Citizenship in Latin America: The Rise of Indigenous Movements and the Postliberal Challenge*. Cambridge: Cambridge University Press, 2005.

Yohn, Susan M. *A Contest of Faiths: Missionary Women and Pluralism in the American Southwest*. Ithaca, NY: Cornell University Press, 1995.

Young, Daniel James. "The Cincinnati Plan and the National Presbyterian Church of Mexico: A Brief Study of Relations between American Mission Boards and Mexican Protestant Churches during the Mexican Revolution." Master's Thesis, University of Texas, El Paso, 2006.

Zafra, Gloria. "Problemática agraria en Oaxaca." In *Sociedad y Política en Oaxaca: 15 estudios de caso 1980*, edited by Raúl Benitez Zenteno, 331–49. Oaxaca City: UBJAO, 1982.

Zanetta, Cecilia. *The Influence of the World Bank on National Housing and Urban Policies: The Case of Mexico and Argentina during the 1990s*. Burlington, VT: Ashgate, 2004.

Index

Page numbers in italic text indicate illustrations.

Aaby, Peter, 100
Abrams, Lynn, 63
Acción Católica (Catholic Action), 57, 78
agrarianism, 53, 57, 145–46, 165
agricultural crisis, 159, 161, 232n7, 233n9
agricultural jobs, 84
Aguila award, Townsend granted, 115–16, 222n158
Aguirre Beltrán, Gonzalo, 98
Alcalá, Juan, 105
alcohol/alcoholism, 42–44, 49, 61, 103, 111–12, 150–51, 195n44
Alemán Valdés, Miguel, 69, 96
Allende, Ignacio, 77
alma (soul), 50
Alsop, John, 112
Altamirano, Waldo, 72–73
alternative Christians, 13, 154, 166, 182, 192n16
American Bible Society, 17–18, 19, 29
"American colony," 30
Anderson, Benedict, 11
Ángeles, Damián, 56–57

anticlericalism, 53; Catholicism after period of, 209n8; international relations, participatory indigenism, and, 135–45
anti-imperialism, 116–17
Aponte González, Valente, 173
APPO. *See* Popular Assembly of the Peoples of Oaxaca
Arévalo, Moisés, 52
Asamblea Popular de los Pueblos de Oaxaca. *See* Popular Assembly of the Peoples of Oaxaca
asamblea (public meeting), 6, 73; and women, 105
assimilation, modernization and, 7
authoritarianism, 152, 189
autonomy, 2–3, 86; indigenous and, 127, 137, 184; local and, 108; sovereignty and, 100, 105–6
Aves, Henry D., 30
Ávila Camacho, Manuel, 69, 96, 209n8

Báez, Victoriano D., 29, 34
Bautista Aguilar, Manuel, 164–65

Bautista Cruz, Serafín, 178–79
Bautista Fabián, José E., 180
Benedict XVI (Pope), 133
Bible, translation of, 95, 100–101, 148–49
bilingual advocate (*promotor bilingüe*), 105
bilingual education, 99, 114, 116–17, 125, 127
Blancarte, Roberto J., 157
blood sports, 29
Boff, Leonardo, 133–35
Bonfil Batalla, Guillermo, 98, 117
Borocio, Eva, 49
Bowen, Kurt, 99
bracero program, 84, 213n62, 232n5
brainwashing, by Pentecostal pastors, 174
Brena Torres, Rodolfo, 74–76, 81, 82
burning: of haystacks by Catholics, 82; of homes by Catholics, 84–85; of saints' images by Protestants, 61
Butler, Inez M., 108–10
Butler, John Wesley, 34

caciques (landowners), 141, 149
Calles Law, 35, 54–55
Calles, Plutarco Elías, 7, 54
Camp Wycliffe linguistics workshop, 92
Canales Valverde, Tristan, 74
Cananea mining strike, 29–30
capitalism, 33, 100, 165
Cardenal, Ernesto, 133
Cárdenas, Amalia, 115
Cárdenas, Lázaro, 7, 9, 56–59, 60, 115, 145–46; role of, 193n27; Townsend relationship with, 93–94; Yosondúa visited by, 104–5
cargo system (obligation), 6, 49, 111, 186, 193n18, 233n17, 237n79
Carrasco Altamirano, Diódoro, 185
Carrasco, Bartolomé, Archbishop of Oaxaca, 140–41, 145, 152, 154

Carter, David W., 22
Carter, James Earl, 135–36, 157
cartoons, political, 122–23, 136, 141, 142–44
Caso, Alfonso, 98
Castellanos Morales, Juan B., 174–76
Castillo, Pablo, 81
Castro, Fidel, 135
Catholic Action (Acción Católica), 57, 78
Catholic Charismatic Renewal (CCR), 190
Catholic Church: concerns of, 132; interior of Tlacochahuaya, 45; loss of followers for, 155–57; mayordomos outside of Tlacochahuaya, 45; monetary donations involving, 179–81; persecution by, 82; privileges of, 71; Protestantism competition with, 33, 153, 195n46, 202n4; resentment over power of, 141; social justice commitment of, 158
Catholicism, 3, 32, 192n15; after anticlericalism period, 209n8; challenges to, 154–57; colonialism and, 69; criticism of, 77, 211n37; enculturated, 195n42; folk, 42–43, 49, 102; Mason criticism of, 56; perceptions of, 47; Protestantism as threat to, 145; rekindling excitement around, 156; syncretic, 3, 140–41, 161, 169, 188
Catholics: arguments from, 76; contesting community space narratives of, 78–79; haystacks burned by, 82; homes burned by, 84; peace between Protestants and, 83; population of, in Mexico, 4; socioeconomic levels of, 195n37; splintering of, 153
Cavazos, Andrés R., 48
CCR. *See* Catholic Charismatic Renewal

CEAS. *See* National College of Ethnologists and Social Anthropologists
CELAM. *See* Second General Conference of Latin American Bishops
Central Intelligence Agency (CIA), 101, 113–14, 221n136, 221n138
Children's Literacy Army, 202n8
Choápam, Santiago, 1
Christian Citizenship, 15; and Guatemala, 148, 229n70
church permits, 69
CIA. *See* Central Intelligence Agency
citizens (*ciudadanos*), 11; *ciudadano de bien*, 15; community citizenship, 160, 186; and migration, 161; and tequio, 168; and usos y costumbres, 181
Clark, Francis, 19
Clark, Harriet, 19
clientalism, 228n62
CNBM. *See* National Baptist Convention of Mexico
Coalition of Workers, Peasants, and Students of the Isthmus (Coalición Obrera Campesina Estudiantil del Istmo) (COCEI), 124, 189–90, 224n179, 227n47, 228n62
COC. *See* Confederación Oaxaqueña de Campesinos
COCEI. *See* Coalition of Workers, Peasants, and Students of the Isthmus
Coheto Martínez, Cándido, 106, 117, 137–38
Colegio de Etnólogos y Antropólogos Sociales. *See* National College of Ethnologists and Social Anthropologists
collective identity, 3, 61, 169
collective rights, 1–2, 68; individual and, in indigenous communities, 86; individual rights, religious freedom and, 189

collective work. *See* tequio
colonialism, 14, 66; Catholicism and, 69; internal, 116; neocolonialism, 34, 87, 99; resistance to, 77; tradition and, 42
comal (griddle), 24
Comité Nacional Evangélico de Defensa. *See* National Evangelical Defense Committee
communally owned lands. *See* ejidal land distribution
communism, 151
communitarian privileges: migration and, 163; women's rights and, 239n21
community solidarity, 83; community space, 78
CONEDEF. *See* National Evangelical Defense Committee
Confederación Oaxaqueña de Campesinos (COC), 55
Confraternity of Evangelical Christian Pastors of Oaxaca (Confraternidad de Pastores Cristianos Evangélicos del Estado de Oaxaca) (COPACEO), 153
Consejo Episcopal Latinoamericano. *See* Second General Conference of Latin American Bishops
Conservative party, 18
constitutional law: friction between customary and, 68, 77, 160, 188; religious conflict and, 86–87; understanding of, 79
Constitution, Mexican (1917), 7, 34, 53–54, 191n6; accusations of violation of, 78; Article 24 of, 8, 68, 70–71, 77, 80, 83, 86, 170, 212n47; Article 27 of, 60, 184, 191n6; Articles of, 193n20; customary law in, 165; religious freedom rights in, 77; stipulations in, 80

Contreras, Epifanio, 74
Convención Nacional Bautista de México. *See* National Baptist Convention of Mexico
conversion, Protestant, 29, 60, 103, 148, 195nn44–46, 234n25; in Cuicatlán, 76; as disruptive, 188; impact of, 2–3; indigenous identity strengthened by, 104, 129; of indigenous people, 11–12; individualism and, 208n112; migration, social organization and, 162–63; problems created by, 61; stemming from health care access, 205n59; as undermining culture and nationalism, 117
Conzatti, Cassiano, 26
COPACEO. *See* Confraternity of Evangelical Christian Pastors of Oaxaca
corn, 24, 58–59, 161, 208n107
corn mill (*molino de nixtamal*), 58; and rural women, 59
corporatism, 10
Cortés, Hernán, 117, 140, 142–43
Coyula, Mexico: intervention demanded in, 79; religious intolerance in, 78, 87
creyentes (believers), 53
Cristero rebellion, 54, 62, 66, 136, 184
Cristiada era (1926–1929), 10, 35
crucifixes, 20–21, 187
Cruz García, Elvira, 56, 58–60, 62, 64, 65
Cruz Orozco, Efraín, 1–2, 166
Cué Monteagudo, Gabino, 189–90
Cuicatlán, Mexico, 67, 210n27; law enforcement by justice of, 82; protests in, 73; religious conflict in, 71–72
cultural ethnocide, 118
Cultural Missions program, 39
culture: conversion undermining nationalism and, 117; enculturated Catholicism, 195n42; identifying with different, 111; language and, 188; mestizos on Zapotec, 38; multiculturalism, 90, 184–85, 189; traditions and, in indigenous communities, 103–4, 167
curanderas (healers), 50
customary law, 2–3, 238n98; in Constitution, 165; disruption to, 208n113; friction between constitutional and, 68, 77, 160, 188; strength of, 172

DAAI. *See* Departamento Autónomo de Asuntos Indígenas
dancing, 61, 111–12
Daniels, Josephus, 94
DAR. *See* Department of Religious Affairs
Declaration of Barbados, 98–99, 137, 217nn64–66, 227n29
defanaticization, 7, 39, 202n9
democracy, neo-Pentecostalism and, 191n3
Departamento Autónomo de Asuntos Indígenas (DAAI), 93
Department of Religious Affairs (Departamento de Asuntos Religiosos) (DAR), 160, 168, 172, 178, 186
Díaz, Porfirio, 18, 29
dictatorship (*dictablanda*), 9
dignity, indigenous people rights to, 149
dissenters, 163
dominant oppressors, 99
Dormady, Jason, 192n7
dough (*masa*), 24, 58
dysentery, 109

earthquake: Mexico City, 1985, 124, 228n62; Oaxaca, 2017, 190

Echeverría Álvarez, Luis, 90, 105, 137, 145–46, 165, 217n61, 232n7
ecumenicism, 132, 149–50
education, 17, 19; bilingual, 99, 114, 116–17, 125, 127; civic, 54; critique of manuals for, 118; goals for, 39; modernization, migration and, 181–82, 188
education programs, 70
Ejército Guerrillero de los Pobres (Guerilla Army of the Poor), 147–48
Ejército Zapatista de Liberación Nacional. *See* Zapatista National Liberation Army
ejidal land distribution (communally owned lands), 2–3, 146, 149, 165
El Divino Pastor National Presbyterian Church, 72, 77
enculturated Catholicism, 195n42
energy crisis, US, 135, 226n26
Espina, Conrado, 170
espionage, 101
Estrada Zurita, Zarafin, 123
ethnic identity, 10; constructed through migration, 12; popular worship and, 2
ethnocide, 137–38
ethnolinguistic identities, 128
Ethnologue, 126
evangelical defense movements, 77, 86
evangelization, 19, 24–28; in indigenous communities, 39, 90; new campaigns for, 155; opportunities for, 35; relationships shaped by, 97; sites for, 67; technology and, 79
evil eye (*mal de ojo*), 50
expansionism, 22
EZLN. *See* Zapatista National Liberation Army

fanaticism, 25, 47–48, 66, 71, 170–71
Farris, Edwin, 101–8

Farris, Kathryn, 101–4, 107–8
fiesta system (patron saints fiestas), 61, 111, 150–51, 163, 196n55, 208n112, 234n21, 235n52
First Baptist Church of Monterrey (Primera Iglesia Bautista de Monterrey), 19
First National Congress of Indigenous Peoples (1975), 105, 124
Flores, Aarón Joaquín, 156
foreign relations, nationalism, liberation theology, indigenous rights and, 132
Francis (Pope), 158
free-market system, 17
Freire, Paulo, 133

Galeano, Eduardo, 91
Gamio, Manuel, 98
García, Amada T. de, 48
García Cruz, Miguel, 85
García Gatica, Tadeo, 84–85
García, Jonás, 44, 202n7
García, Leopoldo A., 34
García Santiago, Eduardo, 124–25
García Toledo, Anastasio, 54, 57
gender roles, 49–50, 195n41. *See also* women
Gillingham, Paul, 9
Gillow, Eulogio, 32, 201n94
globalization, 165
griddle (*comal*), 24
Guatemala, civil war in, 147–48
Guerilla Army of the Poor (Ejército Guerrillero de los Pobres), 147–48
Guerrero, Luis, 162
Gutiérrez, Gustavo, 132–35
Guzmán, Martín Luis, 203n32, 210n18

hacendados (large landholders), 54
Hale, Sara, 40
Hall, Clarence, 95

Hamer, Lloyd, 31
Hamer, W. R., 31
Hartch, Todd, 222n158
healing ceremonies, 50
health care, 13, 39, 109; access to, 112, 205n59; literacy, religious freedom and, 62; traditional remedies in, 51; Western, 50
Hernández, Amos, 112–13
Hernández, Esteban, 139
Hernández Jiménez, Feliciano, 81–82
Hernández Juárez, Salomón, 57, 65
Hernández López, Bartolo, 83–86
Hernández Underwood, Carlos, 166, 168
historical memory, 59–63
History of Oaxaca (Báez), 29
Hobsbawm, Eric, 11
Hollenbach, Barbara, 113–14
Hollenbach, Bruce, 113–14
Holy Week (*semana santa*), 31
Hoogshagen, Hilda, 103
Hoogshagen, Searle, 103, 218n81
House of the Voice of the Rain (Ve'e Tu'un Savi), 126
Hvalkof, Søren, 100

identity, 60; collective, 3, 6, 61, 169; contrasting notions of, 38; ethnolinguistic, 128; nationalism, tradition, memory and, 66; transnational, 162. See also ethnic identity; indigenous identities
idolatry, 42
Iglesia Nacional Presbiteriana "San Pablo," 75
imagined communities, 11, 183, 188
imperialism, American, 10, 18, 22, 78, 86–87, 91, 119, 147, 196n50
INAH. See Institute of Anthropology and History
Independence Movement, 44
Independent Evangelical Pentecostal Church Movement (Movimiento Iglesia Evangélica Pentecostés Independiente) (MIEPI), 173
Indian Problem, the, 94, 96, 100
indigenism (*indigenismo*), 7–9, 99; commitment to, 93; national, 137; original architects of, 120; racism and, 215n22; regional interpretations of, 41. See also participatory indigenism
indigenous communities, 2; assertiveness of, 181; bracero program and, 232n5; churches symbolism in, 187; citizenship questioned by, 146; culture and traditions in, 103–4, 167; development in, 97, 120; divisions in, 150; evangelization in, 39, 90; individual and collective rights in, 86; INI outreach to, 118–19; modernization of, 93; in Oaxaca, 3; policy change for, 90; in remote zones, 156; SIL work in, 96–98
indigenous heritage, celebrating of, 138–39
indigenous identities, 2, 64, 137, 162, 191n4; conceptualizations of, 91, 125; constructing of, 14; framing social movements by, 239n12; nationalism, martyrdom and, 38; politicization of, 191n3; through religious change, 182; as strengthened by conversion, 104, 129; used to frame protests for working conditions, 196n53
indigenous people, 191n4; as childlike, 117–18; civilizations of, 97; conversion of, 11–12; exploitation of, 33; incorporation of, 3; liberation of, 137; marginalization of, 96; relocation of, 90; rights to dignity, 149; uprising of, 185; Vatican policy and, 140

indigenous rights, 2, 3; language revitalization and, 124–27; nationalism, foreign relations, liberation theology and, 132; in national press, 157; to self-determination, 99; violations of, 100, 145
individualism, 61, 208n112
individual rights, 1–2; collective and, in indigenous communities, 86; collective rights, religious freedom and, 189; fighting for, 77; to new religion, 83
industrialization, 96
INI. *See* National Indigenist Institute
Institute of Anthropology and History (Instituto Nacional de Antropología e Historia) (INAH), 62, 93
institutional church, 133
Institutional Revolutionary Party (Partido Revolucionario Institucional) (PRI), 8–9, 98, 149–50, 159, 185; compromise by, 189–90; focus on participatory indigenism, 132; LDM and, 192n7; opposition to, 228n62
Instituto Lingüístico de Verano. *See* Summer Institute of Linguistics
Instituto Nacional Indigenista. *See* National Indigenist Institute
Interdenominational Christian Church, 78
international relations, anticlericalism, participatory indigenism and, 135–45
Internet, 114

JAARS. *See* Jungle Aviation and Radio Services
Jamieson, Alan, 119
Jehovah's Witnesses, 5–6, 13, 192n16, 196n57, 234n27, 235n40; as agents of sociopolitical change, 160; blame toward, 155; contributions from, 175; core beliefs of, 167, 171–72; as expelled, 159; opposition to, 147, 168–71; religious violence toward, 169–70
Jiménez Crispin, Saúl, 169–71
Jiménez, Francisco, 84
Jiménez, Mariano, 22
Jiménez Ruiz, Eliseo, 139, 164, 184
John Paul II (Pope), 14–15, 54, 129, 152; background of, 133–34; expectations for, 137–38; gifts for, 142; liberation theology view of, 225n12; money spent on visit of, 144; social justice and, 145; travel to Mexico, 131, 137–45, 155, 157–58, 184
Juan Diego II, 33, 158, 232n127
Juárez, Benito, 1–2, 17, 35; call for separation of church and state, 139; death of, 18; national holiday for, 120; SIL compared with, 112–13
Juárez García, Samuel, 38, 40–46, 52–56, 187, 203n15; death of, 57–60, 66; legacy of, 62
Jungle Aviation and Radio Services (JAARS), 94, 110

Knight, Alan, 8

landowners (*caciques*), 141, 149
language revitalization movements, 91
languages: culture and, 188; motives for learning, 218n83; preservation of native, 123, 124–27; prioritizing of, 132; religion, customs and, 77; skills, 90; standardization of, 127; tonal, 100–101, 108–9. *See also* Spanish language
large landholders (*hacendados*), 54
Laviada, Iñigo, 113
Law of the Rights of Indigenous Peoples, 185

LDM. *See* Luz del Mundo
Leal, Mary, 108–9
Leal, Otis, 108–9
Legters, L. L., 92
Lerdo Law, 22, 198n19
Ley de la Reforma (1857), 17
Liberal party, 18
liberation theology, 225n12; history of, 135–36; nationalism, foreign relations, indigenous rights and, 132; Pacífico Sur Bishops and, 145; political context shifting messages of, 157; promoting of, 145; radical tenets of, 140; reactions to, 133; regional impact of, 134; spread of, 155
Light of the World. *See* Luz del Mundo
Lind, John, 119
literacy, 39; campaigns for, 94, 96; classes for, 76, 109; health care, religious freedom and, 62; lack of, taken advantage of, 155; spreading of, 97
Lona Reyes, Arturo, 146
López de Trujillo, Alfonso, 134–35
López, Flaviano Nicolás, 105–6, 110
López Llaguno, Telésforo, 109–12, 128
López Mateos, Adolfo, 69
López Portillo, José, 135–38, 146, 226n26
López, Severo I., 28–29
lucha (struggle), 15
Luis Palau festival (2008), 183–84, 238n2
Luz del Mundo (Light of the World) (LDM), 10, 156, 192n7

Madero Clubs, 29
de la Madrid Hurtado, Miguel, 120–23, 176
mal de ojo (evil eye), 50
malinchistas (sellouts), 116–17, 143
Manzano, Eliseo, 55–56
marginalization: of indigenous people, 96; resistance to, 141
Martin, David, 188, 194n32

Martínez Álvarez, Jesus, 168
Martínez, Carlos, 60–61
Martínez, Fortunata, 78, 79–80
Martínez León, Guillermo, 71, 79–80, 211n40, 212n47
Martinez Peña, Manuel, 20
martyrdom: indigenous identity, nationalism and, 38; memory and, 57–59; patriotism and, 63; for religious freedom, 59
martyrs, 13, 19–20, 27, 37
Marx, Karl, 99
Marxism, 133–34, 157
masa (dough), 24, 58
Masons, 56, 201n85
mayordomías (sponsorships), 12, 233n20
Mayrén Peláez, Wilfrido (Padre Ubi), 153, 230n94
McCabe, C. C., 27
McIntosh, John, 96
memory, 13; as gendered, 64; historical, 59–63; martyrdom and, 57–59; nationalism, tradition, identities and, 66; use of, as source, 202n6
Mendoza García, Gerardo, 177–81
Mendoza, Pablo Fabián, 175
mescal, 43–44, 61
mestizaje, 98
mestizos, 24, 32–33, 38–39, 48–51
metates (stone slabs), 24, 58
Methodist Mission Society, 26
Mexican-American War (1846–1848), 18, 22
Mexican Revolution (1910), 3–4, 8–9, 34, 37, 165, 209n2; accomplishments of, 59; ideology development surrounding, 195n46
Mielke, Elaine, 115
MIEPI. *See* Independent Evangelical Pentecostal Church Movement
migration, 145, 196n53, 233n20; conversion, social organization and, 162–63; ethnic identity constructed

through, 12; modernization, education and, 181–82, 188; religious freedom and, 163–64; rising rate of, 160–62
Miller, Walter S., 113, 166, 218n78, 235n35
mining industry, 29–30, 201n78, 205n67
Ministry of Public Education (Secretaría de Educación Pública) (SEP), 60, 76, 87, 92, 104–8, 202n8; bilingual textbooks production and, 94; partnership with SIL, 114–19; pressures on, 99
Ministry of the Interior, Mexican, 74, 86
minority religious rights, 15, 68; Protestantism and, 69–70
modernity, transition to, 97–98
modernization, 1, 18, 59, 145, 209n2; assimilation and, 7; goals for, 39; of indigenous communities, 93; migration, education and, 181–82, 188; programs for, 94; through social and educational programs, 70
molino de nixtamal (corn mill), 58, 207n103
de Montes, Esther Gutiérrez, 47–48
Morales, Ignacio, 41, 55–56
Morales, Sergio, 103
Mormons, 5–6, 13, 147, 166, 192n16, 196n57, 234n27
Morrow, Dwight, 54
Mott, John R., 91
Movimiento Iglesia Evangélica Pentecostés Independiente. *See* Independent Evangelical Pentecostal Church Movement
multiculturalism, 90, 184–85, 189
Murat Hinojosa, Alejandro, 190
music, 81, 102

NAFTA. *See* North American Free Trade Agreement

Nahmad Sittón, Salomón, 98–99, 114–16, 118–19, 221nn137–38
National Baptist Convention of Mexico (Convención Nacional Bautista de México) (CNBM), 38, 202n3, 208n105; financial pledge from, 40; pioneer mission of, 46
National College of Ethnologists and Social Anthropologists (Colegio de Etnólogos y Antropólogos Sociales) (CEAS), 116
National Evangelical Defense Committee (Comité Nacional Evangélico de Defensa) (CONEDEF), 14, 69–71, 177–78; communicative alerts from, 79; poster advertising, 72
National Indigenist Institute (Instituto Nacional Indigenista) (INI), 87, 90, 105–8, 197n59, 209n5; the Indian Problem outlined for, 96; outreach to indigenous communities, 118–19; pressures on, 99; severing ties with SIL, 115
nationalism, 15, 35, 39, 53, 116; challenging notions of, 157; conversion undermining culture and, 117; at forefront of foreign policy, 135; indigenous identity, martyrdom and, 38; indigenous rights, foreign relations, liberation theology and, 132; patriotism and, 38; postrevolutionary themes of, 19; Protestantism as threatening to, 76; questioning of, 98, 137; tradition, memory, identities and, 66. *See also* state formation
National Parents Association (Unión Nacional de Padres de Familia), 120, 121
natural resources, 3; control over, 105; exploitation of, 91; respect for, 98
neocolonialism, 34, 87, 99

neoimperialism, 129
neoliberalism, 9, 134
neo-Pentecostalism, democracy and, 191n3
networking movements, 68
Nolasco, Margarita, 99, 117
Nonnatus, Raymond, 32
North American Free Trade Agreement (NAFTA), 149, 184, 228n61
Núñez y Zárate, José Othón, 54–55

Oaxacalifornia, 162, 182, 233n11, 238n100
Oaxacan Evangelical Society, 20–22
Oaxaca, regions of, 5. *See also specific topics*
Obispos de la Región Pacífico Sur. *See* Southern Pacific Regional Episcopacy
obligations. *See* cargo system
Obregón, Álvaro, 54
Ochoa Zazueta, Jesús Ángel, 116
O'Connor, Mary I., 195n37
oil, 94, 135–36, 226n26
Ojeda, Isidoro Santiago, 103–4, 107–8, 129
Open Veins of Latin America (Galeano), 91
Orozco, Pascual, Jr., 202n7
Ortega López, Timoteo, 79
Ortiz Arana, José, 121
Ortiz, José, 79–80
Ortiz Marcos, Nicolás, 173
Osorio, Ismael, 106

Pacheco Armas, Ricardo, 74
Pacífico Sur pastoral region, 14, 135, 141, 145–54
paganism, 42, 89
participatory indigenism, 90–91, 98, 105, 124, 132, 214n7; anticlericalism, international relations and, 135–45; meaning of, 193n24;
mobilization through, 219n100; PRI focus on, 132
Partido de la Revolución Democrática. *See* Party of the Democratic Revolution
Partido Revolucionario Institucional. *See* Institutional Revolutionary Party
Party of the Democratic Revolution (Partido de la Revolución Democrática) (PRD), 115, 159
pastoral policies, revising of, 155
Patiño, Julio, 82
patriotism, 195n46; conceptualizations of, 77; martyrdom and, 63; nationalism and, 38
Paul VI (Pope), 133
PCA. *See* Presbyterian Church in America
Pentecostalism, 5–6, 15, 153–57, 166, 190, 194n32; brainwashing by pastors of, 174; commitment to, 177; emergence of, 172–73, 236n68; neo-Pentecostalism, 191n3; religious violence toward, 178–79; restrictions imposed for, 175; socioeconomic levels of, 195n37; sociopolitical change and, 160; tequio and, 174–78; as toxic, 176
Pérez García, Eliseo, 116
Pérez Gasca, Alfonso, 67, 70–71, 73–74, 78–79
Pérez Peña, Rubén, 77
Pérez, Simón, 112–13
Pike, Kenneth, 97, 100, 104, 218n78
Pimentel, Emilio, 29
Pius IX (Pope), 32
Plan de Cincinnati, 52–53
Poland's Solidarity movement, 151–52
Polish United Workers' Party, 152
Popular Assembly of the Peoples of Oaxaca (Asamblea Popular de los

Pueblos de Oaxaca) (APPO), 152–53
popular church, 133
Porfiriato era, 18, 31
pottery shards (*tepalcates*), 106
Poughkeepsie, New York, 163
poverty, 91, 99–100, 132, 141
PRD. *See* Party of the Democratic Revolution
Presbyterian Church in America (PCA), 101
PRI. *See* Institutional Revolutionary Party
Primera Iglesia Bautista de Monterrey (First Baptist Church of Monterrey), 19
promotor bilingüe (bilingual advocate), 105
propaganda, 81, 83, 166
proselytism, 93, 155
Protestant-Catholic conflict (1953), 69
Protestantism: as attack on tradition, 8; beginnings of, in Porfiriato era, 18; Catholic Church competition with, 33, 153, 195n46, 202n4; explosion of, 194n32; growth of, 55, 156–58; in Guatemala, 147–48; as incompatible with customs and rituals, 111; opposition to, 2, 159; popularity of, 162; as religious choice for indigenous peoples, 78; as revitalizing respect for tradition, 103; social hierarchies broken down by, 128; state violence and, 53–57; strength of, 183; terms for, 4–5, 192n14; as threatening to nationalism, 76; as threat to Catholicism, 145; traditions changed from, 114; as transcending territorial boundaries, 87; values reflected by, 188–89
Protestant organizations: denunciations of, 196n51; founding of, 209n5; government relationship with, 206n82; intervention of, 68. *See also specific types*
Protestants, 12–13; abuses committed against, 71; accusations toward, 219n108; criticisms on waste from, 200n62; negotiating new beliefs, 187; peace between Catholics and, 83
protests: in Cuicatlán, 73; against SIL, 121–23; by students, 98, 141; in Tlatelolco, 9
public meeting (*asamblea*), 6, 73, 105. *See also* usos y costumbres

Quetzalcoatl legend, 140, 142
Quinones, Sam, 162–63
Quiroga Dorantes, Daniel, 155

racism, indigenism and, 215n22
radio, 114
railroads, 18, 23–24, 31, 205n67
Ramírez, Cándido, 70
Ramírez de Aguilar, Ramón, 55
Ramírez Gijon, Ausencio, 165
Ramírez, Ignacio, 119
Ramírez, Rafael, 93
Ramírez Ríos, Jenaro, 164
Ramírez Ruiz, Donato, 48
Ramos Ramírez, Agapito, 70–71, 73–74
Rankin, Melinda, 20, 62, 198n13, 206n72
Reagan, Ronald, 136, 147
religion: hiding behind, 84; individual rights to new, 83; as invisible weapon, 82; language, customs and, 77; state formation, 6–15; traditions balanced with, 111
religious change: indigenous identity through, 182; as rapid, 166
religious competition, 132

religious conflicts, 2, 33–34, 235n52; earliest of, 81; as fatal, 85; government authority in, 160; negotiations surrounding, 3; notions of tradition dominating, 159; in Oaxaca, 10–11, 54; as violent, 55; as volatile, 186. *See also* Protestant-Catholic conflict
religious freedom, 73, 138; collective and individual rights and, 189; commitment to, 54; federal laws on, 68; global perspective of, 79; implementing of, 86; lack of, 68; literacy, health care and, 62; martyrdom for, 59; migration and, 163–64; right to, 77; upholding of, 80
Religious Freedom Act (1860), 17, 20, 197n1
religious intolerance, 38, 69–70, 176, 209n8, 209n10; in Coyula, 78, 87; mediating of, 160
religious persecution, 71, 87
relocation, of indigenous people, 90
remittances, 162–63
repression: allegations of, 79; liberation from poverty and, 132, 149
respectable masculinity, 64, 208n110
Reyes Gómez, Juan Carlos, 125–26
Rickards, Adela Durán, 31
Rickards, Constantine, Jr., 31, 35
Rickards, Edward, 32, 35
Ríos Montt, Efraín, 147–48, 153
rituals, 43, 61, 102–3, 151; abstaining from, 87; disruption to, 208n113; Protestantism not compatible with, 111; as threatening social structures, 162
Rivera, Arturo, 67, 73
Romanism, 41
Roosevelt, Franklin, 94
Rudd, A. B., 39, 43–44, 203n15, 204n38

Ruiz Cortines, Adolfo, 69, 84, 209n8, 209n10
Ruiz Guerra, Rubén, 25
Ruiz Ortiz, Ulises, 152–53, 183–84
Ruiz, Samuel, 148–49, 231n115
Russell, Charles T., 156

Sáenz, Moisés, 92–93, 202n7
Salazar, Santiago, 117
Salinas, Carlos, 136, 149, 184
Sámano de López Mateos, Eva, 69–70, 75
San Andrés Peace Accords (1996), 184
San Baltazar Yatzachi, 108–12, 128
Sánchez, Enrique, 74
Sánchez, Héctor, 96, 99–100
Sánchez Hernández, Marcelino, 153–54
Sánchez, Muñiz, Felipe, 78–79
San Juan Juquila Mixes, 166–72
San Juan Tabaá, Mexico, 172–81
Santa María Texcatitlán, 81, 82, 87
Sapir, Edward, 92
Satan, 41, 121–22
Saucedo, José, 141, 150
schools, 34; building of, 25, 192n8; Cristiada rebellion taught in, 62; introduction of, 114; primers in, 117–18; Smith, L., starting, 67; textbooks for, 210n18
Second General Conference of Latin American Bishops (Consejo Episcopal Latinoamericano) (CELAM), 132, 134–35
Second Vatican Council, 132, 150
Secretaría de Educación Pública. *See* Ministry of Public Education
sectarianism, 150
self-defense, community, 3
self-determination, 99, 118, 124, 137, 184
sellouts (*malinchistas*), 116–17, 143
semana santa (Holy Week), 31
SEP. *See* Ministry of Public Education

Serrano Rivas, Antonio, 81, 82
Seventh-day Adventists, 80–82, 87, 192n16, 234n27
SIL. *See* Summer Institute of Linguistics
Siverts, Henning, 124
Smelting, Magdalena, 31
Smith, Benjamin, 9
Smith, Dorothy, 97
Smith, Lucius C., 22–28, 34, 67, 187, 200n54
Smith, Paul, 97
sobriety, 39
socialism, 135
social justice, 134, 152, 155; Catholic Church commitment to, 158; John Paul and, 145
social media, 12, 213n74
social movements: framing of, by indigenous identities, 239n12; mobilization of, 80
social organization, migration, conversion and, 162–63
Solana Morales, Fernando, 114, 120
soul (*alma*), 50
Southern Pacific Regional Episcopacy (Obispos de la Región Pacífico Sur), 14, 145–54
Spanish language: fluency in, 7; training in, 4, 50
splintering, of Catholics, 153
sponsorships (*mayordomías*), 12, 233n20
Starr, Fredrick, 26
State formation, 6–12, 15, 185–87, 189; friction between constitutional law and customary law, 68, 77, 167; negotiating with indigenous communities, 80; revolutionary state, 98
Stavenhagen, Rodolfo, 117
Stephen, Lynn, 10
Stoll, David, 10, 216n41
stone slabs (*metates*), 24, 58

strike, Oaxacan teachers (2006), 152
struggle (*lucha*), 15
Summer Institute of Linguistics (Instituto Lingüístico de Verano) (SIL), 7, 14, 24, 127–29; CIA connection to, 113–14, 221n136, 221n138; condemnation of, 100, 116; criticism of, 113; depicted as Satan, 120–22; exodus of, 119; founding of, 209n5; funding for, 95; headquarters of, 90, 110; indigenous communities work of, 96–98; INI severing ties with, 115; intellectual climate of 1970s and, 98–100; language facilities of, 121; letterhead for, 94–95; linguistic prowess of, 97; missionaries for, 100; name of, 215n26; partnership with SEP, 114–19; presence in, 91; protests against, 121–23; in San Baltazar Yatzachi, 108–12; suspicions surrounding motives of, 218n83; tequio criticism, 116, 176; workshops by, 92–93; in Yosondúa, 102–8
symbolism, 60, 187

Taylor, William, 200n54
technology, 79, 80, 128
telegraph line, telegrams, 80, 87, 212n48
television (TV), 114
Templo de la Compañía Church and Convent, 21, 198n19
tepalcates (pottery shards), 106
tequio (collective work), 6, 49, 81–82, 84, 85, 159; conflicts with, 116, 163–67, 176; description of, 193n18; migration and, 161, 163, 176; Pentecostalism and, 174–78
Thompson, James, 17
Tiburcio Espina, Félix, 167–69, 188
Tlacochahuaya, Mexico, 13, 38–45, 50–51, 55, 57, 61–63

Toledo, Narciso, 70
tonal languages, 100–101, 108–9
tourism, 139, 163
Tovar Hernández, Rául, 97
Townsend, William Cameron, 90–95, 114–16, 119, 215n26, 222n158
traditions: colonialism and, 42; culture and, in indigenous communities, 103–4, 167; defending of, 86; fighting to retain, 80; nationalism, memory, identities and, 66; notions of, dominating religious conflict, 159; as oral, 58; Protestantism as attack on, 8; Protestantism as revitalizing respect for, 103; Protestantism changing, 114; religion balanced with, 111; respect for, 98; vulnerability and, 47
translation, of Bible, 95, 100–101, 148–49
transnational identity, 162
Treviño Osuna, Alejandro, 19, 40
TV. *See* television

Ubico, Jorge, 92
Unión Nacional de Padres de Familia. *See* National Parents Association
Unión Nacional Femenil Bautista. *See* Women's National Baptist Union
Universal Declaration of Human Rights, 79, 211n43
urbanization, 96
Uriegas, Ernesto, 48
Urirre, Ramón, 178
usos y costumbres system (ways and customs), 2, 15, 49, 150, 161, 181, 186, 189, 197nn62–63. *See also* customary law

vaccination crusades, 96
Valdez, Josué, 40
Valencia Arriaga, Manuel Donato, 72

Van Slyke, Lawrence, 1, 7, 52, 108, 220n112
Vásquez Barceló, Victor, 170
Vásquez Colmenares, Pedro, 120, 164, 167, 173
Vásquez, Flor, 117
Vaughan, Mary Kay, 60
Ve'e Tu'un Savi (House of the Voice of the Rain), 126
Velasco, Saúl, 74
Villalobos, Mario, 113
violence, religious, 37–38, 55, 60, 71, 151, 181; blind eye to, 80; in communities, 84; example of, 78; toward Jehovah's Witnesses, 169–70; toward Pentecostals, 178–79
violence, state: combating, 151; condemning of, 146–47; criticism of, 193n28; Protestantism and, 53–57
Virgin Mary, 18, 25, 32–33, 43
Virgin of Guadalupe, 33, 43, 66, 157–58
Virgin of Juquila, 43, 62
Virgin of Soledad, 32–33
vulnerability, traditions and, 47

War of La Reforma, Mexican (1858–1861), 13, 20, 71
Warren, Kay B., 127
Watergate, 114
Watson, William, 30–31
ways and customs system. *See* customary law; usos y costumbres system
WBT. *See* Wycliffe Bible Translators
Weber's Protestant ethic thesis, 87
Wesley, John, 23–24
Westrup, John, 19
Westrup, Thomas, 19
Wheeler, W. Reginald, 37
witchcraft, 109, 220n119
women: Acción Católica, 78; "American colony," 24; exclusion of, 185–86; integration of, 207n103; and

mescal, 44; practices condemned by, 205n60; role of, 47, 201n80; and SIL, 113, 118; support for, 110; violence against Protestants, 58, 169; voting rights of, 239n21
Women's National Baptist Union (Unión Nacional Femenil Bautista), 40, 47–51, 64
worship, 2; ceasing of, 83; holidays surrounding, 33; lack of official permission to, 81; lack of permission for, 83; laws for, 74; petitioning for places of, 77; right to free, 77
Wright, N. Pelham, 95, 97
Wycliffe Bible Translators (WBT), 95
Wycliffe Jungle Camp, 100

Yashar, Deborah, 3, 191n3
YMCA. *See* Young Men's Christian Association
Yosondúa, Mexico, 83–86, 102–8, 117, 127
Young Men's Christian Association (YMCA), 35

Zapata, Emiliano, 60, 149
Zapatista National Liberation Army (Ejército Zapatista de Liberación Nacional) (EZLN), 149
Zapatista Revolution (1994), 3, 60, 135, 197n63